D0352890

**RED SQUARE AND
KITAY GOROD**
See pp98–113
Street Finder maps 3, 4, 7, 8

RED SQUARE AND
KITAY GOROD

KREMLIN
See pp52–67
Street Finder maps 2, 3, 6, 7

KREMLIN

Москва

Moskva

Водоотводный

Канал

Канал

Яуза

ZAMOSKVORECHE
See pp114–125
Street Finder maps 6, 7

ZAMOSKVORECHE

EYEWITNESS TRAVEL

MOSCOW

Main contributors: CHRISTOPHER AND MELANIE RICE

DK

LONDON, NEW YORK,
MELBOURNE, MUNICH AND DELHI
www.dk.com

PROJECT EDITOR Marcus Hardy
ART EDITOR Marisa Renzullo
EDITORS Catherine Day, Jane Oliver, Lynda Warrington
DESIGNERS Gillian Andrews, Carolyn Hewitson,
Paul Jackson, Elly King, Nicola Rodway
VISUALIZER Joy Fitzsimmons
MAP CO-ORDINATORS Emily Green, David Pugh

MAIN CONTRIBUTORS
Christopher Rice, Melanie Rice

MAPS
Maria Donnelly (Colourmap Scanning Ltd)

PHOTOGRAPHER
Demetrio Carrasco

ILLUSTRATORS
Stephen Conlin, Richard Draper, Stephen Gyapay,
Claire Littlejohn, Chris Orr & Associates

Reproduced by Colourscan, Singapore
Printed and bound by South China Printing Co. Ltd., China

First published in Great Britain in 1998
by Dorling Kindersley Limited
80 Strand, London WC2R 0RL

Reprinted with revisions 2000, 2001, 2004, 2007, 2010

Copyright 1998, 2010 © Dorling Kindersley Limited, London
A Penguin Company

ISBN 978-1-40535-036-5

FLOORS ARE REFERRED TO THROUGHOUT IN ACCORDANCE WITH EUROPEAN
USAGE; IE THE "FIRST FLOOR" IS THE FLOOR ABOVE GROUND LEVEL.

Front cover main image: Domes of the Church of St George

We're trying to be cleaner and greener:

- we recycle waste and switch things off
- we use paper from responsibly managed forests whenever possible
- we ask our printers to actively reduce water and energy consumption
- we check out our suppliers' working conditions – they never use child labour

Find out more about our values and
best practices at www.dk.com

**The information in this
DK Eyewitness Travel Guide is checked regularly.**
Every effort has been made to ensure that this book is as up-to-date
as possible at the time of going to press. Some details, however,
such as telephone numbers, opening hours, prices, gallery hanging
arrangements and travel information are liable to change. The
publishers cannot accept responsibility for any consequences arising
from the use of this book, nor for any material on third party
websites, and cannot guarantee that any website address in this
book will be a suitable source of travel information. We value the
views and suggestions of our readers very highly. Please write to:
Publisher, DK Eyewitness Travel Guides, Dorling Kindersley,
80 Strand, London WC2R 0RL, Great Britain.

◁ **The Kremlin at night, in all its splendour**

CONTENTS

HOW TO USE
THIS GUIDE **6**

Socialist-Realist sculpture of Soviet
farm workers at the All-Russian
Exhibition Centre *(see p145)*

INTRODUCING
MOSCOW

FOUR GREAT DAYS IN
MOSCOW **10**

PUTTING MOSCOW
ON THE MAP **12**

THE HISTORY OF
MOSCOW **16**

MOSCOW THROUGH
THE YEAR **32**

MOSCOW AT A GLANCE
36

The Tsar Bell *(see p57)*, created
for Tsarina Anna, in the Kremlin

MOSCOW
AREA BY AREA

THE KREMLIN
52

ARBATSKAYA **68**

TVERSKAYA **84**

RED SQUARE
AND KITAY GOROD
98

ZAMOSKVORECHE
114

FURTHER AFIELD **126**

TWO GUIDED
WALKS 146

BEYOND MOSCOW
152

Magnificent iconostasis at the Danilovskiy Monastery *(see pp136–7)*

SURVIVAL GUIDE

PRACTICAL
INFORMATION
206

GETTING TO
MOSCOW
216

GETTING AROUND
MOSCOW
220

MOSCOW
STREET FINDER
228

GENERAL INDEX
246

ACKNOWLEDGMENTS
258

PHRASE BOOK
AND TRANSLITERATION
260

The Tretyakov Gallery *(see pp118–21)*, housing Russian fine art

TRAVELLERS'
NEEDS

WHERE TO STAY
168

RESTAURANTS, CAFÉS
AND BARS **178**

SHOPS AND MARKETS
192

ENTERTAINMENT IN
MOSCOW
198

St Basil's Cathedral
(see pp108–9)

HOW TO USE THIS GUIDE

This guide will help you to get the most from your visit to Moscow. It provides expert recommendations together with detailed practical information. *Introducing Moscow* maps the city and sets it in its geographical, historical and cultural context, and the quick-reference timeline on the history pages gives the dates of Russia's rulers and significant events. *Moscow at a Glance* is an overview of the city's main attractions. *Moscow Area by Area*

Neo-Classical statue, Kuskovo, *(see pp142–3)*

starts on page 50 and describes all the important sights, using maps, photographs and illustrations. The sights are arranged in three groups: those in Moscow's central districts, those a little further afield, and finally those beyond Moscow which require one- or two-day excursions. Hotel, restaurant and entertainment recommendations can be found in *Travellers' Needs*, while the *Survival Guide* includes tips on everything from transport and telephones to personal safety.

FINDING YOUR WAY AROUND THE SIGHTSEEING SECTION

Each of the seven sightseeing areas is colour-coded for easy reference. Every chapter opens with an introduction to the area it covers, describing its history and character. For central districts, this is followed by

a Street-by-Street map illustrating a particularly interesting part of the area; for sights further away, by a regional map. A simple numbering system relates sights to the maps. Important sights are covered by several pages.

1 Introduction to the Area
For easy reference, the sights are numbered and plotted on an area map, with metro stations shown where helpful. The key sights (great buildings, museums and open-air sights) are listed by category.

A locator map shows where you are in relation to other areas of the city centre.

Colour-coded thumb tabs mark each area.

Locator map

The area shaded in pink is shown in greater detail on the Street-by-Street map.

2 Street-by-Street Map
This gives a bird's eye view of interesting and important parts of each sightseeing area, with accurate drawings of all the buildings within them. The numbering of the sights ties in with the preceding area map and with the fuller descriptions on the pages that follow.

Suggested walking route

A list of star sights recommends the places that no visitor should miss.

MOSCOW AREA MAP

The coloured areas shown on this map *(see pp14–15)* are the five main sightseeing areas into which central Moscow has been divided for this guide. Each is covered in a full chapter in the *Moscow Area by Area* section *(pp50–125)*. The areas are also highlighted on other maps throughout the book. In *Moscow at a Glance (pp36–49)*, for example, they help you locate the most important sights that no visitor should miss. The maps' coloured borders match the coloured thumb tabs at the top corner of each page.

Numbers refer to each sight's position on the area map and its place in the chapter.

Practical information lists all the information you need to visit every sight, including a map reference to the *Street Finder* maps *(pp220–37)*

3 Detailed information on each sight

All the important sights are described individually. They are listed to follow the numbering on the area map at the start of the section. The key to the symbols summarizing practical information is on the back flap.

A visitors' checklist provides the practical information you will need to plan your visit.

Illustrated maps show in detail the layout of extensive sights.

4 Moscow's Major Sights

These are given more extensive coverage, sometimes two or more full pages. Historic buildings are dissected to reveal their interiors; museums and galleries have colour-coded floorplans to help you find important exhibits.

Stars indicate the best features or works of art.

Story boxes provide details on famous people or historical events.

INTRODUCING MOSCOW

FOUR GREAT DAYS IN MOSCOW 10–11

PUTTING MOSCOW ON THE MAP 12–15

THE HISTORY OF MOSCOW 16–31

MOSCOW THROUGH THE YEAR 32–35

MOSCOW AT A GLANCE 36–49

FOUR GREAT DAYS IN MOSCOW

The Russian capital, having endured wars, revolutions and drastic social change, is today a place where the past and present combine to captivate and charm. From the multi-coloured onion domes of churches to the graves of Soviet heroes, reminders of the city's past are on almost every corner. Galleries like

Badge with Soviet symbols

the Tretyakov are treasure troves of art, while the State Armoury contains treasure pure and simple, from Fabergé eggs to diamonds galore. A city of around 10 million, Moscow may seem daunting at first, but these itineraries will help you find your way around it all. The price guide includes the cost of food and admission fees.

MOSCOW'S PAST

- First stop Red Square
- Heroes and villains
- Colourful domes of
  St Basil's Cathedral
- Inside the Kremlin

TWO ADULTS allow at least $150

Morning
A whistle-stop tour through Russian history begins with a stroll across **Red Square** *(see p106)*, a vast expanse that accommodated huge military parades during the Soviet era. From here, head into **Lenin's Mausoleum** *(see p107)* to pay your respects to the leader of Russia's historic 1917 revolution. Afterwards, follow the path to the Kremlin Walls, to see the graves of other well-known Soviets including the ruthless dictator Joseph Stalin, and Yuriy Gagarin, the first man to orbit the planet. From the Kremlin Walls, make your way to **St Basil's Cathedral** *(see pp108–9)*, one of Russia's enduring symbols. According to legend, Ivan the Terrible had the

cathedral's architect blinded to ensure that he would never again create anything to rival its beauty.

Afternoon
Feeling peckish? Make your way to Kamergerskiy pereulok, just off **Tverskaya ulitsa** *(see p89)*. This pleasant, traffic-free zone is in one of the city's main shopping districts and has a good choice of restaurants and cafés offering flavours from all over the world.

Afterwards, you can visit the **Kremlin** itself *(see pp53–67)*. Long the seat of power in Russia, the complex of cathedrals and palaces was not open to the public until the death of Stalin in 1955. Tickets are sold for separate sights, but be sure not to miss the collection of royal treasures at the **State Armoury** *(see pp64–5)* or icons and gilded frescoes at the **Cathedral of the Assumption** *(see pp58–9)*. Make time, too, for **Ivan the Great's Bell Tower** *(see p57)*. The 200-tonne behemoth of a bell outside the tower is the largest in the world.

Art works by local street artists for sale on Old Arbat (Ulitsa Arbat)

ART & ARCHITECTURE

- Treasures of Tretyakov
- Lunch in the park
- Exploring Old Arbat

TWO ADULTS allow at least $160

Morning
Start the day with a visit to the world-class **Tretyakov Gallery** *(see pp118–21)*. The priceless collection of Russian art includes the 15th-century *Trinity* icon by

Historic Red Square, with the distinctive onion domes of St Basil's Cathedral in the distance

Riverboat on the Moskva river, passing by the Kremlin

Andrey Rublev and *The Appearance of Christ to the People*, a colossal work that took artist Aleksandr Ivanov 20 years to paint. The gift shop is a good place to stock up on souvenirs.

For a bite to eat, take a wander through leafy **Alexander Gardens** *(see p67)*, which has a good choice of cafés including pizzerias and an English-style pub.

Afternoon
Suitably refreshed, head for **Old Arbat** *(see pp70–71)*. Once the favoured haunt of writers, artists and poets, this lively pedestrianized area is a good place to seek out mementoes of the Soviet era, such as flags, statuettes and old bits of Red Army kit, from the many stalls and shops that line the streets. There are also a few shops specializing in traditional icons.

The area has some fine examples of Russian architecture including the 19th-century **Pushkin House-Museum** *(see p73)*, which gives visitors a good idea of what life in Moscow was like when this literary giant lived here. Afterwards, take a detour down Krivoarbatskiy pereulok to peek at **Melnikov House** *(see p72)*, a cylindrical building designed in the 1920s by Konstantin Melnikov, one of Russia's greatest Constructivist architects. For a late dinner, try **Restaurant Rus** *(see p184)*, on Old Arbat, for pancakes, caviar and perhaps a glass or two of vodka.

A FAMILY DAY

- **A gentle river cruise**
- **Exploring Gorky Park**
- **The magical circus**

FAMILY OF 4 allow at least $130

Morning
In summer there is nothing more pleasant than taking a **Moscow River Cruise** *(see p221)*. Winding through the heart of the city, the double-decker river boats pass several of the major sights including the Kremlin and the Cathedral of Christ the Redeemer. Jump ship at **Gorky Park** *(see p129)*, where the many attractions include fairground rides, ice skating (in winter), boating lakes and the Buran Shuttle, a flight simulator that offers the chance for would-be cosmonauts to hurtle into orbit. Safely back on terra firma, the park is a good picnic spot.

Afternoon
Later, head off to the **Old Circus** *(see p198)* for a breathtaking display by world-renowned acrobats and trapeze artists. The antics of the circus's performing bears and tigers are not to everyone's taste, however. The colourful marionettes of the **Moscow Puppet Theatre** *(see p191)* are a worthwhile alternative.

HISTORY & FRESH AIR

- **A fortified convent**
- **Famous graves**
- **A trip to the country**

TWO ADULTS allow at least $80

Morning
Hop on the metro for **Novodevichiy Convent** *(see pp130–31)*, where you can soak up some of the 16th-century atmosphere of this fortified religious complex. Novodevichiy's nearby cemetery reads like a *Who's Who* of Russian history and contains the graves of literary luminary Anton Chekhov and political heavyweight Nikita Khrushchev.

Afternoon
Afterwards, take the metro to **Kolomenskoe** *(see pp138–9)*, a country estate much loved by the tsars that is now a museum of architecture. Enjoy a lunch of traditional Russian food in one of the small wooden buildings. Highlights include the 16th-century Church of the Ascension and a log cabin built for Peter the Great. The park is also a wonderul place for a walk along the Moskva river, especially in winter when it often freezes over.

16th-century Cathedral of the Virgin of Smolensk, Novodevichiy Convent

Putting Moscow on the Map

The Russian Federation (usually simply known as Russia) stretches from the Baltic to the Pacific. With an area of 17 million sq km (6.6 million sq miles), it was the largest of the USSR's 15 republics and is now the world's largest country, almost twice the size of the US. Moscow, the capital with 9 million inhabitants, lies at the heart of European Russia. St Petersburg is Russia's second largest city. Russia is a member of the CIS – a commonwealth of most of the former Soviet republics.

KEY

- Motorway
- Major road
- Minor road
- Railway
- International boundary

0 kilometres   180

0 miles   180

MOSCOW AND ENVIRONS

Yahroma · Kirzhach · Solnechnogorsk · Lobnya · Istra · Sheremetyevo · Noginsk · Elektrostal · Ruza · Zhukovskiy · Vnukovo · Podolsk · Domodedovo · Naro-Fominsk · Vereya · Chekhov · Kolomna

A107 · M8 · A108 · A103 · M7 · A108 · M9 · A107 · Moskve (Moskva) · M1 E30 · A107 · M2 · M5 · Moskva (Moskva) · M3 · A101 · M4 M6

Moscow and Environs
Concentric ring roads surround Moscow. Most of the city lies inside the MKAD motorway.

Pechora · Pechora · Mezen · Ukhta · Pechora · Pinega · Vycheyda · Kotlas · Kirov · RUSSIAN · Ufa · Magnitogorsk · Ural · Oka · Ryazan · Tolyatti · Samara · Orenburg · Orsk · Turgay · M5 · Saratov · Chelkar · KAZAKSTAN · ronezh · M5 · Volgograd · Volga · Don · Donets · Astrakhan · Rostov-na-Donu · Mariupol · a of ov · Krasnodar · CASPIAN SEA · TURKMENISTAN

An infrared satellite image of Moscow

PUTTING RUSSIA ON THE MAP

Arctic Ocean · RUSSIAN FEDERATION · Bering Sea · NORWAY · SWEDEN · FINLAND · ESTONIA · LATVIA · LITHUANIA · POLAND · BELARUS · UNITED KINGDOM · REP OF IRELAND · GERMANY · CZECH · UKRAINE · FRANCE · HUNGARY · ROMANIA · SPAIN · ITALY · BULGARIA · GEORGIA · UZBEKISTAN · KAZAKSTAN · MONGOLIA · Pacific Ocean · PORTUGAL · GREECE · TURKEY · TURK MENISTAN · KYRGYZSTAN · TAJIKISTAN · N KOREA · MOROCCO · TUNISIA · SYRIA · IRAQ · IRAN · AFGHAN ISTAN · CHINA · S KOREA · JAPAN · ALGERIA · LIBYA · EGYPT · SAUDI ARABIA · PAKISTAN · NEPAL · INDIA · BERMA

Central Moscow

Most of Moscow's sights are situated in the city centre, within the area bounded by the Garden Ring and the Boulevard Ring. In this book the centre has been divided into five sightseeing areas, while two further sections cover the outskirts and day trips into the countryside. Each of the central areas has a distinctive character, with the sights in each one lying within easy walking distance of one another. All of these sights are also well served by public transport.

Hotel National
Located in the heart of Tverskaya, close to the Bolshoy Theatre (see pp90–91), the National (see p89) is an eclectic mixture of Style Moderne and Classical style.

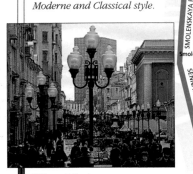

Ulitsa Arbat
Running the length of what was a suburb in 15th-century Moscow, ulitsa Arbat (see pp70–71) is today a crowded, pedestrianized street, lined with shops and restaurants.

The Kremlin
The heart of the city, the Kremlin (see pp52–67) has dominated Russian life for over 800 years. Its buildings are from the 15th–20th centuries.

| 0 metres | 400 |
| 0 yards | 400 |

KEY

◼	Major sight
◼	Place of interest
M	Metro station
⛴	River boat pier
🚓	Police station
✝	Orthodox church
✝	Non-Orthodox church
✡	Synagogue
C	Mosque
⊠	Post office

Tretyakov Gallery
Across the river from Moscow's other main sights, the Tretyakov Gallery (see pp118–21) houses a vast collection of Russian art.

St Basil's Cathedral
Located in Red Square (see p106), west of the historic district of Kitay Gorod, St Basil's (see pp108–9) is probably Russia's most enduring image.

THE HISTORY OF MOSCOW

F*rom her 12th-century origins as an obscure defensive outpost, Moscow came to govern one sixth of the earth's surface and cast her shadow even further. The story of her rise is laced with glory and setbacks, including the two centuries when St Petersburg was the capital of Russia and Moscow lived the life of a dignified dowager.*

THE FIRST SETTLERS

The forested area around Moscow was sparsely populated, but the fertile lands of southern Russia and the Ukraine had long supported trade routes between the Orient and Europe. It was here that the Slavs, the ancestors of the Russian people, first settled. They came from Eastern Europe in the 6th century, and established isolated villages along the major rivers. In the 8th century they came into contact with the Varangians (Vikings), who navigated these waterways to trade amber, furs and fair-skinned slaves.

Bloodthirsty and fearless, this lacquer box shows Mongol warriors riding into battle

KIEVAN RUS

Endemic in-fighting between the Slavic tribes was quelled when Rurik, a Varangian chief, assumed power in the region. Rurik settled in Novgorod, but his successor Oleg took Kiev and made it his capital. In 988 Grand Prince Vladimir I, a descendant of Rurik, was baptised into Orthodox Christianity *(see p137)* and married the sister of the

Vladimir's conversion in the *Baptism of Russia* by Vasnetsov

Byzantine emperor. Vladimir's conversion deeply affected the future of Russia, which remained an Orthodox country right into the 20th century.

THE MONGOL INVASION

By the 12th century, Kiev's supremacy had already been challenged by the powerful Russian principalities to the north, including Rostov-Suzdal *(see p161)*, of which the wooden kremlin at Moscow formed part. As a result, when the fierce horse-borne Mongols invaded in 1237, the disunited Russians fell easy victims to the well-organized troops of Batu Khan. For the next 240 years the Russian principalities paid an exorbitant yearly tribute to the khans, though they were left to govern themselves.

TIMELINE

c. 800 Varangians arrive in the region to trade and find local tribes in conflict	*Rurik, Varangian chief* **988** Grand Prince Vladimir I converts to Christianity	**1147** Moscow first documented, as the site of a small fortress	**1156** Prince Yuriy Dolgorukiy builds Moscow's first wooden kremlin	**1240** Mongols control most of Rus after the sack of Kiev
800	**900**	**1000**	**1100**	**1200**
862 Rurik takes Novgorod and establishes a Varangian stronghold	**882** Rurik's successor Oleg takes Kiev and makes it capital **863** Missionaries Cyril and Methodius invent the Cyrillic alphabet, based on the Greek one; literacy grows with the spread of Christianity	**1108** The town of Vladimir *(see p161)* is founded	**1223** First Mongol raid **1236–42** Prince Aleksandr Nevskiy of Novgorod defeats first the invading Swedes and then the Teutonic Knights	

◁ **The symbol of Moscow, St George and the Dragon, on a 15th-century icon housed in the Tretyakov Gallery**

THE RISE OF MOSCOW

In the 14th century, the Mongols chose Moscow's power-hungry Grand Prince Ivan I, "Kalita" or "Moneybags" (1325–40), to collect tribute from all their conquered principalities, giving the city supremacy over its neighbours. Ivan had already shown his obsequiousness by crushing a revolt against the Mongols led by his neighbour, the Grand Prince of Tver. Yet the Mongols were sealing their own fate, for, as Moscow flourished under their benevolence, she ultimately became a real threat to their power.

Map of 16th-century Moscow, showing neat rows of wooden houses and several churches behind the city's first stone walls

Within 50 years an army of soldiers from several Russian principalities, led by Moscow's Grand Prince Dmitriy Donskoy (1359–89), inflicted their first defeat on the Mongols, and the idea of a Russian nation was born.

It was not until the reign of Ivan III, "the Great" (1462–1505), when Moscow ruled a kingdom which stretched as far as the Arctic Ocean and the Urals, that the Mongols were finally vanquished. Ivan married the niece of the last emperor of Byzantium, who had fled Constantinople when it had fallen to the Ottomans in 1453. This increased Moscow's prestige further, and particularly her claim to being the last defender of true Orthodoxy. Ivan also sought to assert Moscow's status through a grand building programme. He started the tradition of importing foreign architects, including the Italians (see p44) who built the present Kremlin walls.

Ivan the Terrible (1533–84)

IVAN THE TERRIBLE

It was Ivan the Great's grandson, Ivan IV, "the Terrible" (1533–84), who transformed himself from Grand Prince of Moscow to "Tsar of All the Russias". During his reign Russia expanded beyond the Urals into Siberia and strong trading links were established with England. Moscow's walls were strengthened for, even as late as 1571, the Crimean Mongols continued to venture sporadic attacks on the Russian capital.

Yet, powerful though he was, Ivan suffered dreadful paranoia. After the death of his beloved wife Anastasia, he became convinced that she had been poisoned by the boyars (see p20) and set up Russia's first police state. A sinister force of black-hooded agents called the oprichniki murdered whole villages to stamp out the tsar's supposed enemies. Ivan also imposed restrictions on the aristocracy and peasantry alike, establishing those

TIMELINE

1328 Ivan I becomes Grand Prince of Vladimir	**c.1345** St Sergius founds the Trinity Monastery of St Sergius (see pp162–5)	**1380** Dmitriy Donskoy defeats the Mongols at the pivotal Battle of Kulikovo (see p161)	**1453** Constantinople, previously Moscow's Orthodox ally, falls to the Ottomans	**1470s** The Cathedral of the Assumption is built
1300		**1350**	**1400**	**1450**
1300 Metropolitan See is transferred from Kiev to Vladimir	**1328** Metropolitan See is transferred from Vladimir to Moscow **1325–40** Ivan I rules Moscow and strengthens its position	**1367** Dmitriy Donskoy rebuilds Kremlin walls in limestone *Rebuilding of the Kremlin walls*		**1462–1505** Reign of Ivan III **1476** Ivan III stops paying tribute to Mongols

autocratic traditions that were to prove the country's downfall. Ivan's more immediate legacy was his contribution to the end of the Varangian dynasty, the murder of his only competent son, also named Ivan, in a paranoid rage.

THE TIME OF TROUBLES

This ushered in a period known as the Time of Troubles. For fourteen years, Ivan's retarded son Fyodor (1584–98) ruled under the guidance of Boris Godunov, a former and much-hated *oprichnik*. When Fyodor died childless, Godunov installed himself in the Kremlin, but he soon become target of a pretender to the throne. The pretender claimed to be Ivan the Terrible's dead youngest son Dimitry, sought support from Poland and marched on Moscow with an army of 4,000 in 1604. With the death of Boris Godunov in 1605 he was installed on the throne. The pretender was soon to enrage the Moscow boyars, who killed him, and replaced him with Vasiliy Shuiskiy, a boyar of some distinction. Faced with a second "False Dmitry" marching on Moscow in 1607, Shuiskiy appealed to Sweden for help only to provoke a new Polish intervention. The Poles reached Moscow in 1610 and Shuiskiy was then deposed by the boyars. In the north, the Swedes used the internal instability of Russia to capture Novgorod. Only in these desperate circumstances did the Russians finally unite to expel the occupying Poles, under the leadership of Minin and Prince Pozharskiy *(see p108)*. The siege of the Kremlin thus ended in 1612.

Boris Godunov (1598–1605)

THE FIRST ROMANOVS

Determined to put an end to this period of anarchy, Moscow's leading citizens came together to nominate the 16-year old Mikhail Romanov, great-nephew of Ivan's first wife Anastasia, as hereditary tsar, thus initiating the 300-year rule of the Romanovs. Under Mikhail (1613–45), who ruled with his father Filaret, the patriarch of Moscow, Russia recovered from her exhausting upheavals. His greatest legacy, however, was his heir Alexis (1645–76). An intelligent and pious man, Alexis tried to modernize the state. He oversaw the first codification of Russian law and encouraged an influx of foreign technicians, against the will of the Church. During the reign of Alexis the Church saw difficult times due to the schism between the reformers, led by Patriarch Nikon *(see p57)*, and the conservative Old Believers. Nikon, however, grew too important for his own good which resulted in Alexis asserting the power of the State over the Church.

Ambassadors of the Council of the Realm entreating young Mikhail Romanov to accept the tsar's crown in 1613

1485 Ivan III commissions Italian architects to rebuild the Kremlin walls	**1533–84** Reign of Ivan IV	**1561** Building of St Basil's Cathedral is completed	**1589** Moscow attains status of Patriarchate	**1613** Mikhail is elected first tsar of the Romanov dynasty	**1653–67** Religious schism between Patriarch Nikon and the Old Believers
1500		**1550**		**1600**	**1650**
1478 Ivan III revokes Novgorod's charter of independence	**1547** Ivan IV takes title "Tsar" **1552** Victory over Mongols as Ivan IV takes town of Kazan	**1570** Ivan IV orders massacre of Novgorod	**1571** Mongols raid Moscow **1598–1605** Reign of Boris Godunov	**1610** Moscow falls to the Poles but they are driven out two years later	**1654–67** Second war with Poland *Patriarch Nikon*

Medieval Moscow

Moscow developed in 400 years from an isolated wooden fortress (kremlin), built in 1156, into a thriving capital city, "shining like Jerusalem from without, but like Bethlehem inside". Its circle of outer walls enclosed a series of smaller districts centred on the Kremlin, whose wooden stockade was replaced with white limestone in 1367 to protect the city from Mongol raids, and by massive brick walls in 1495. It boasted a clutch of stone cathedrals, befitting its role as the "Third Rome" after the fall of Constantinople in 1453. Next to the Kremlin lay Red Square, where public spectacles ranged from executions to fairs. The rest of the city housed boyars, merchants, servants, hawkers and artisans.

EXTENT OF THE CITY

☐ *13th century* ☐ *1590*

The public sauna *(banya)* was always sited near water, isolated where possible from the dense crush of wooden housing.

Andrey Rublev (c.1370–1430)
Moscow's finest icon painter, Andrey Rublev is seen here painting a fresco at the Monastery of the Saviour and Andronicus (see p140). Icons (see p61) were used for the religious education of the people.

A Silver Kovsh
Originally made in wood, this ceremonial drinking vessel, known as a kovsh, *began to be crafted in metal in the 14th century. Elaborately decorated* kovshi *were often given by the tsar to favoured subjects. These treasured artifacts would be displayed as a symbol of wealth when not in use.*

THE WALLED CITY
Vasnetsov's *(see p144)* painting of the Kremlin in the 15th century shows the warren of wooden houses which surrounded the palaces and churches. Among them were the renowned Kremlin workshops.

Boyars and Merchants
Though richly dressed, boyars (noblemen) in medieval Russia were largely illiterate and often crude in their habits. Their material needs were looked after by merchants who traded in furs from the north and silk from Turkey.

Foreigners in Moscow

From the 16th century, foreign diplomats and traders began to visit the isolated and xenophobic Russia. The adventurer Richard Chancellor, who attempted to find the northwest passage to the Orient but ended up in Russia, managed to negotiate a trading treaty with Ivan the Terrible.

Wooden houses could be bought prefabricated from a market outside the city walls. They quickly replaced houses that were lost in Moscow's frequent fires.

Limestone walls, erected by Dmitriy Donskoy *(see p161)*

Cathedral of the Assumption

Small trading vessels thronged the banks of the Moskva river, unloading goods for the growing city. Russia's rivers were her trading routes and were far more efficient than travel by land.

WHERE TO SEE MEDIEVAL MOSCOW

The Kremlin's medieval buildings include its Cathedrals of the Assumption *(see pp58–9)*, the Archangel *(p60)* and the Annunciation *(p60)*. The State Armoury *(pp64–5)*, also in the Kremlin, displays medieval artifacts and armour while the daily life of the nobility is recreated in the Palace of the Romanov Boyars *(pp102–3)*. St Basil's Cathedral *(pp108–9)* also dates from this time.

The dining room *in the Palace of the Romanov Boyars.*

Building a Cathedral

During the reign of Ivan I (1325–40), when the first stone Cathedral of the Assumption was built, Metropolitan Peter moved to Moscow to be head of the Orthodox Church. This manuscript illustration shows him blessing the new cathedral.

Ivan the Terrible

Though Ivan IV's reign (1533–84) did much to benefit Russia, he certainly deserved his epithet. Among the many souls on his conscience was his only worthy son and heir, Ivan, killed in a fit of rage which the tsar regretted for the rest of his life.

PETER THE GREAT

The extraordinary reign of Alexis's son Peter I, "the Great", really put Russia back on her feet. Brought up in an atmosphere of reform, Peter was determined to make Russia a modern European state. In 1697, he became the first tsar ever to go abroad, with the particular aim of studying shipbuilding and other European technologies. On his return, he began immediately to build a

Vasiliy Surikov's portrayal of Peter the Great watching Streltsy Guards being led to their deaths in 1698, as punishment for their earlier rebellion

Russian navy, reformed the army and insisted on Western-style clothing for his courtiers. At Poltava in 1709, Peter dramatically defeated the Swedes, who had been a threat to Russia for a century, and stunned Europe into taking note of an emerging power.

Peter's effect on Moscow was double-edged. At the age of ten he had seen relatives murdered in the Kremlin during the Streltsy Rebellion. This revolt had sprung from rivalry between his mother's family, the Naryshkins, and that of his father's first wife, the Miloslavskiys, over the succession. In the end Peter was made co-tsar with his half-brother Ivan, but developed a pathological distrust of Moscow. He took a long-awaited and grim revenge on the Streltsys 16 years

Tsar Peter the Great
(1682–1725)

later, when he executed over a thousand of them. He also began to build a new city on the boggy banks of the Neva to the north and ordered the imperial family and government to move.
In 1712 he declared the cold, damp St Petersburg capital of Russia. For the next 200 years Moscow was Russia's second city.

Tsarina Elizabeth
(1741–62)

THE PETTICOAT PERIOD

After Peter the Great's death in 1725, Russia was ruled by women for most of the 18th century: Catherine I, Anna, Elizabeth and Catherine II. Though they were all crowned in the Cathedral of the Assumption (see pp58–9), most preferred to live in Europeanized St Petersburg. However, Elizabeth, Peter's boisterous, fun-loving daughter, insisted on living in Moscow periodically. During Peter's reign constructions in stone outside St Petersburg had been banned, but under Elizabeth a flurry of new buildings appeared in Moscow, especially since some of Russia's leading families preferred to live there.

TIMELINE

1696 Ivan dies. Peter I is sole ruler	**1698** The Streltsys are crushed	**1721** Peter I replaces patriarchiate with less-powerful church synod		**1773–4** Pugachev Rebellion
	1700–21 Great Northern War against Sweden	**1730–40** Reign of Anna	**1741–62** Reign of Elizabeth	**1768–74** First Russo-Turkish War

1700	1725		1750

1682 The Streltsy Rebellion; Peter I is co-tsar with half-brother Ivan V and his half-sister Sophia as regent	**1709** Great Russian victory at the Battle of Poltava	**1712** Capital is transferred to St Petersburg **1727–30** Reign of Peter II. Moscow is capital for two years	**1725–7** Reign of Catherine I	*Tsarina Anna*	**1762** Peter III is killed His wife seizes the throne as Catherine II **1755** Mikhail Lomonosov founds Moscow University

Elizabeth founded Russia's first university in Moscow *(see p94)*, under the guidance of Russia's 18th-century Renaissance man, the poet, scientist and academic Mikhail Lomonosov. But Moscow was still protected from the Westernization affecting the capital and thus retained a more purely Russian soul and identity.

CATHERINE THE GREAT

In 1762 Catherine II, "the Great", a German princess, usurped the throne of her feeble husband Peter III with the help of her lover Grigoriy Orlov, a guards officer. Under her energetic, intelligent leadership, the country saw another vast expansion in its prestige and made territorial gains

Catherine the Great (1762–96)

at the expense of Turkey and its old adversary Poland. Catherine purchased great collections of European art and books (including Voltaire's library) and in 1767 published her *Nakaz* (Imperial Instruction) upon which a reform of Russia's legal system was to be based. Unsurprisingly, this modern European monarch regarded Moscow as inward-looking and backward and spent little time there.

19TH-CENTURY MOSCOW

Napoleon's invasion in 1812 and the heroic part played in his defeat by Moscow *(see pp24–5)* appeared to reinvigorate the city. Aleksandr Herzen *(see p71)* claimed that "Moscow was again made the 'capital' of the Russian people by Napoleon", and, indeed, the destruction of two thirds of the city by fire resulted in a bold new archi-

tectural plan. The Napoleonic Wars also marked a turning point in Russian political history, as soldiers returned from Europe bringing with them the seeds of liberal ideas. Far from the court of Nicholas I, the Iron Tsar, Moscow became a fertile environment for underground debate among early revolutionaries such as Herzen and the Decembrists. Yet most of Moscow society was trapped in a comfortable and conservative cocoon, financed by the system of serfdom. With the Emancipation of the Serfs in 1861, however, the economic strength of most nobles was radically curtailed. The freed serfs who were too poor to buy their own land, flocked to the factories of mercantile and industrial entrepreneurs. In Moscow, at the old heart of the empire, these entrepreneurs came to usurp the position of the aristocrats, making vast fortunes from trade, textiles, railways, banking and publishing, and financing a renaissance in the Russian arts on the proceeds.

The Bolshoy Theatre, favoured by Moscow's aristocracy, along with balls and lavish suppers, for an evening's entertainment

1787–92 Second Russo-Turkish War	1805–7 War with France; Russia is defeated at battles of Austerlitz, Friedland	*Tsar Nicholas I*	1835 First modern law code comes into effect	1851 The Nicholas Railway between Moscow and St Petersburg is opened	1853–6 Crimean War
	1800		**1825**		**1850**
1796 Death of Catherine II. Paul I accedes	1807 Treaty of Tilsit		1855 Nicholas I dies. Alexander II succeeds		
1801 Paul I is assassinated. Alexander I becomes tsar and begins a programme of reforms	1812 Napoleon invades Moscow but has to retreat	1816–19 Emancipation of serfs in Baltic provinces	1825 Nicholas I becomes tsar. The Decembrist Rebellion is crushed in St Petersburg	1861 Emancipation of all serfs	1865–9 Tolstoy publishes *War and Peace*

War and Peace

Russia's glorious rise to the ranks of a world power accelerated in the period between 1800 and 1830. Even though she suffered severe defeats against France, including the Battle of Austerlitz (1805), and signed the Treaty of Tilsit in 1807. The uneasy peace ended in 1812, with the invasion of Napoleon's Grande Armée. But Russia turned disaster into victory and in 1814–15, Tsar Alexander I sat down to decide Europe's future at the Congress of Vienna. The war marked an important cultural shift in Russia as liberal Western European political ideas first filtered into the country, although their time had not yet come.

EXTENT OF THE CITY

▨ *1812, before the fire*

☐ *Areas razed by the fire*

Alexander I (1801–25)
The handsome young tsar was initially infected by the ideals of enlightened government, but became increasingly influenced by his reactionary advisers.

The Kremlin was damaged more by the looting of the French than by the fire outside.

Napoleon stayed in the tsar's apartments for a few days before retreating to safety outside the city.

MOSCOW BURNING

After Field Marshal Mikhail Kutuzov's retreat at Borodino, the French army was able to enter Moscow. But Muscovites set light to their city and fled. In just four days, two thirds of the city burnt down, leaving the army without shelter or provisions. Combined with Alexander I's refusal to negotiate while Napoleon remained on Russian territory, this resulted in the French emperor's defeat.

The French soldiers soon fell to undisciplined drinking and looting.

Battle of Borodino, September 1812
The Battle of Borodino (see p158) lasted 15 hours, causing the death of 70,000 men, half of them French. Yet Napoleon declared the battle a victory and advanced on Moscow.

Retreat of Napoleon's Grande Armée
Facing the winter without supplies, the army began its retreat in October. Only 30,000 out of 600,000 men made it back.

Empire Style
Many things, from chairs to plates, were designed in the popular Empire style (see p45). This cup and saucer with a Classical motif were made at the Popov factory near Moscow in 1810.

WHERE TO SEE NEO-CLASSICAL MOSCOW

Pediment, Kuskovo Palace

Early examples of Neo-Classicism can be seen at the palaces of Ostankino *(see p144)* and Kuskovo *(pp142–3)*, at Pashkov House *(p75)* and at Moscow Old University *(p94)*. The fire of 1812 allowed vast areas to be developed to an Empire-style city plan. Bolshaya Nikitskaya ulitsa *(p93)*, ulitsa Prechistenka *(p74)* and Theatre Square *(p88)* are lined with fine buildings from this time.

Moscow University
It was after the Napoleonic Wars that the University of Moscow, founded in 1755, gained a reputation as a hotbed of liberalism. However, political discussions still had to be conducted at secret salons.

Alexander Pushkin
The great Romantic poet Alexander Pushkin (see p73) captured the spirit of the time. Pushkin and his wife Natalya were often invited to court balls, such as the one shown here. This enabled Nicholas I to keep an eye on the liberal poet as well as on his enchanting wife.

New fires were started deliberately throughout the city, on the orders of the tsarist governor.

The river proved no barrier to the fire, whipped up by a fierce wind.

The Millstone of Serfdom
In the shadow of the nobility's easy life, and to a great extent enabling it, were millions of serfs toiling in slavery on large estates. This painting shows a serf owner settling his debts by selling a girl to a new master.

THE END OF AN EMPIRE

Though the 1890s saw rapid advances in industrialization, Russia experienced a disastrous slump at the turn of the 20th century. Nicholas II's diversionary war with Japan backfired, causing economic unrest, adding to the misery of the working classes and finally culminating in the 1905 Revolution. On 9th January 1905, a demonstration in St Petersburg carried a petition of grievances to the tsar and was met by bullets. News of this "Bloody Sunday" spread like wildfire and strikes broke out all over the country. To avert further disaster Nicholas had to promise basic civil rights, and an elected parliament which he, however, simply dissolved whenever it displeased him. This high-handed behaviour, along with the imperial family's friendship with the "holy man" Rasputin, further damaged the Romanovs' reputation.

The Bolshevik by Boris Kustodiev, painted in 1920

The outbreak of World War I brought a surge of patriotism which the inexperienced Nicholas sought to ride by taking personal command of the troops.

Tsar Nicholas II surrounded by his wife Alexandra, their four daughters and Tsarevich Alexis in 1913

By late 1916, however, Russia had lost 3,500,000 men, morale at the front was very low and supplies of food at home had become increasingly scarce.

REVOLUTION AND CIVIL WAR

In early 1917 strikes broke out in St Petersburg. People took to the streets, jails were stormed and the February Revolution began. The tsar was forced to abdicate and his family was placed under house arrest. Exiled revolutionaries flooded back into the country to set up workers' and soldiers' soviets. Elected by the workers as an alternative to an unelected provisional government they formed a powerful anti-war lobby. In October the leadership of the Bolsheviks, urged on by Lenin, decided on an armed uprising, under the rallying cries of "All power to the soviets!" and "Peace, bread and land". In the early hours of 26th October, they arrested the provisional government in St Petersburg's Winter Palace.

Within months the Bolsheviks had shown themselves as careless of democracy as the tsar, dismissing the constituent assembly and setting up their own secret police, the Cheka.

TIMELINE

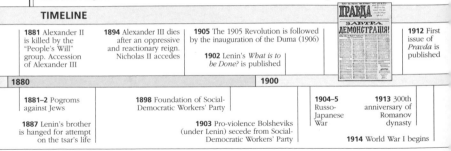

1881 Alexander II is killed by the "People's Will" group. Accession of Alexander III	**1894** Alexander III dies after an oppressive and reactionary reign. Nicholas II accedes	**1905** The 1905 Revolution is followed by the inauguration of the Duma (1906)	**1912** First issue of *Pravda* is published
		1902 Lenin's *What is to be Done?* is published	

1880   **1900**

1881–2 Pogroms against Jews	**1898** Foundation of Social-Democratic Workers' Party	**1904–5** Russo-Japanese War	**1913** 300th anniversary of Romanov dynasty
1887 Lenin's brother is hanged for attempt on the tsar's life	**1903** Pro-violence Bolsheviks (under Lenin) secede from Social-Democratic Workers' Party		**1914** World War I begins

In March 1918, however, they stayed true to their promise and took Russia out of World War I, instead plunging the soldiers straight into a vicious civil war. The capital was moved back to Moscow, and from here Lenin and his government directed their "Red" army against the diverse coalition of anti-revolutionary groups known as the "Whites". When White soldiers got closer to the exiled Romanovs in Yekaterinburg in July 1918, the royal family was brutally butchered by its captors. But the Whites were a disparate force, and by November 1920 Soviet Russia was rid of them, only to face two years of appalling famine.

Cathedral of the Redeemer, torn down on the orders of Stalin as part of his new city plan (see pp74–5)

A 1937 propaganda poster showing Joseph Stalin

THE STALIN YEARS

In the five years after Lenin's death in 1924, Joseph Stalin used his position as General Secretary of the Communist Party to remove rivals such as Leon Trotsky and establish his dictatorship.

The terror began in the countryside, with the collectivization of agriculture which forced the peasantry to give up their land, machinery and livestock to collective farms in return for a salary. During this time, and in the ensuing famine of 1931–2, up to 10 million people are thought to have died.

The first major purge of intellectuals took place in urban areas in 1928–9. Then, in December 1934, Sergey Kirov, the local party leader in Leningrad, was assassinated on the secret orders of Stalin, although the murder was blamed on an underground anti-Stalinist cell. This was the catalyst for five years of purges, by the end of which over a million people had been executed and some 15 million arrested and sent to labour camps, where they often died.

In his purge of the Red Army in 1937–8, Stalin dismissed or executed three quarters of his officers. When the Germans invaded in 1941 they were able to advance rapidly, subjecting Leningrad to a horrendous siege of nearly 900 days. But Moscow was never taken since Hitler, like Napoleon before him, underestimated both the harshness of the Russian winter and his enemies' willingness to fight.

After the German defeat, the Russian people, who had lost over 20 million souls in the war, were subjected to a renewed internal terror by Stalin, which lasted until his death in 1953.

"Let us defend our beloved Moscow", 1941 propaganda poster

1917 The Russian revolution (see pp28–9)

1918 Civil War starts. Capital moves to Moscow

1932 Socialist Realism becomes the officially approved style in art

1934 Leningrad Party Secretary Sergey Kirov is murdered; purges begin

1947 The term "Cold War" is coined

1920

1940

1924 Lenin dies

1922 Stalin becomes General Secretary

1921 Lenin bans all opposition. NEP (New Economic Policy) is introduced

1941 Hitler attacks Soviet Union, reaches outskirts of Moscow. Siege of Leningrad

1939 Nazi-Soviet pact

Sergey Kirov

The Russian Revolution

The Russian Revolution, which began in St Petersburg and made Moscow once more a capital city, was pivotal to the history of the 20th century. By late 1916, with Russia facing defeat in World War I and starvation at home, even ministers and generals were doubting the tsar's ability to rule. In 1917 there were two uprisings, the February Revolution which began with massive strikes and led to the abdication of Nicholas II, and the October Revolution which overturned the provisional government and swept the Communists to power. They emerged victoriously from the Civil War that followed, to attempt to build a new society.

EXTENT OF THE CITY

■ *1917* □ *Today*

Many soldiers deserting from the front were happy to put on the new Red Army uniform instead.

Middle class people as well as the poor took part in the Revolution.

The Ex-Tsar

Nicholas II, seen here clearing snow during his house arrest outside St Petersburg, was later taken with his family to Yekaterinburg in the Urals. There, in 1918, they were shot and their bodies thrown down a mine shaft.

REDS OUTSIDE THE KREMLIN

In October, the fight for control of the Kremlin was intense in comparison to the one in St Petersburg. The Bolshevik seizure was reversed after three days, and it took the revolutionaries another six days to overcome loyalist troops in the fortress and elsewhere in the city.

Women took part in demonstrations and strikes.

Comrade Lenin

A charismatic speaker, depicted here by Viktor Ivanov, the exiled Lenin returned in April to lead the Revolution. By late 1917 his Bolshevik party had gained power.

Revolutionary Plate

Ceramics with revolutionary themes, mixed with touches of Russian folklore, were produced to commemorate special events. This plate marks the founding of the Third International Communist group in 1919.

Propaganda

One hallmark of the Soviet regime was its powerful propaganda. Many talented artists were employed to design posters, which spread the Socialist message through striking graphics. During the Civil War (1918–20), posters such as this one extolled the "pacifist army of workers" to support War Communism.

Leon Trotsky

The intellectual Trotsky played a leading military role in the Revolution. In 1928, during the power struggle after Lenin's death, he was exiled by Stalin. He was murdered in Mexico, in 1940, by a Stalinist agent.

Banner proclaiming freedom to the world

Avant-Garde Art

Even before 1917, Russia's artists had been in a state of revolution, producing the world's first truly abstract paintings. A fine example of avant-garde art is Supremus No. 56, painted in 1916 by Kazimir Malevich.

Old and young were swept away by the revolutionary fervour.

New Values

Traditions were radically altered by the Revolution; instead of church weddings, couples exchanged vows under the red flag. Loudly trumpeted sexual equality meant that women had to work twice as hard – at home and in the factories.

TIMELINE

February Revolution in St Petersburg	**March** The tsar is persuaded to abdicate. Provisional government is led by Prince Lvov	**October** Bolsheviks storm Winter Palace in St Petersburg, after signal from *Aurora*, and oust provisional government	**March** Bolsheviks sign Brest Litovsk peace treaty with Germany, taking Russia out of World War I. Capital is moved to Moscow

1917	1918

July Kerenskiy becomes prime minister of provisional government	**1918 January** Trotsky becomes Commissar of War	**July** Start of Civil War. Tsar and family murdered in prison at Yekaterinburg
Battleship Aurora	**December** Lenin forms the Cheka (secret police)	

The Washington Dove of Peace (1953), a Russian caricature from the days of the Cold War

BEHIND THE IRON CURTAIN

Three years after Stalin's death his successor, Nikita Khrushchev, denounced his crimes at the 20th Party Congress and the period known as "The Thaw" began. Thousands of political prisoners were released and books critical of Stalin were published. In foreign affairs, things were not so liberal. Soviet tanks invaded Hungary in 1956 and in 1962 Khrushchev's decision to base nuclear missiles on Cuba brought the world to the brink of nuclear war.

When Leonid Brezhnev took over in 1964, the intellectual climate froze once more. The first ten years of his office were a time of relative plenty, but beneath the surface there was a vast black market and growing corruption. The party apparatchiks, who benefitted from the corruption, had no interest in rocking the boat. When Brezhnev died in 1982, the Politburo was determined to prevent the accession of a younger generation. He was succeeded by the 68-year-old Andropov, followed by the 72-year-old Chernenko.

GLASNOST AND PERESTROIKA

It was only in 1985, when the new leader, 53-year-old Mikhail Gorbachev, announced his policies of perestroika (restructuring) and *glasnost* (openness), that the true bankruptcy of the old system became apparent. Yet he had no idea of the immense changes that they would bring in their wake. For the first time since 1917 the elections to the Congress of People's Deputies in 1989 contained an element of true choice, with rebels such as human-rights campaigner Andrey Sakharov and Boris Yeltsin winning seats. In the autumn and winter of that year the Warsaw Pact

Mikhail Gorbachev with George Bush

disintegrated as country after country in Eastern Europe declared its independence from the Soviet Union. Local elections within the Union in 1990 brought nationalist candidates to power in the republics and democrats in the most important Russian local councils.

FIRST IN SPACE

Under Khrushchev the Soviet Union achieved her greatest coup against the West, when she sent *Sputnik 1* into space in 1957. That same year the dog Laika was the first living creature in space, on *Sputnik 2*. She never came back but, four years later, Yuriy Gagarin made history as the first man in space, returning as a hero. The Soviets lost the race to put a man on the moon, but the space programme was a powerful propaganda tool, backing the claims of politicians that Russia would soon catch up with and overtake the West.

Sputnik 2 and the space dog Laika, 1957

TIMELINE

1950–53 Korean War	**1961** Building of Berlin Wall. Yuriy Gagarin is first man in space	**1964** Brezhnev takes over the role of General Secretary after Krushchev	**1968** Soviet troops enter Czechoslovakia to suppress "Prague Spring"	**1980** Moscow Olympics are boycotted by the West
	1953 Stalin dies			**1979** USSR invades Afghanistan

1950	1960	1970	1980

| **1955** Warsaw Pact | **1957** *Sputnik 1* is launched | **1962** Cuban missile crisis | **1969** Strategic Arms Limitation Talks (SALT) with USA | *Leonid Brezhnev* |
| **1956** Stalin denounced at 20th Party Congress. Hungarian uprising crushed | | **1961** Stalin's body is removed from the Kremlin Mausoleum | | **1982** Brezhnev die and is replace by Andropo |

Communist hero fallen from grace after the 1991 coup

In 1991 the Baltic Republics and Russia herself seceded from the Soviet Union. With his massive victory in the election for President of the Russian Republic, Yeltsin gained the mandate he needed to deal the death blow to the Soviet Union. It came after the military coup against Gorbachev in August 1991, when Yeltsin's stand against the tanks in Moscow made him a hero. After Gorbachev's return from house arrest in the Crimea, Yeltsin forced him to outlaw the Communist Party. By the end of the year the Soviet Union was no more as all the republics declared their independence.

Moscow 850-years poster

to soak up their desire to party. Much of the city was renovated in 1997 in honour of Moscow's 850th anniversary. The Cathedral of Christ the Redeemer *(see p74)*, demolished by Stalin in 1931, was rebuilt as part of the restoration programme. This was also a sign of the renewed importance of the Orthodox Church, which was forced underground during the Soviet era. Churches are now filled once again for weddings, baptisms and religious holidays. The crime rate has fallen from its dizzying high in 1995, as the city's criminal groups, or *mafiya*, have resolved their territorial battles. President Putin's second term in office saw Russia grow rich on oil dollars, and living standards rose drastically, especially in the capital. However, the global financial crisis in 2009 hit the country hard and Moscow and other cities across the Russian Federation are experiencing rising unemployment.

MOSCOW TODAY

The 1990s have had a profound effect on the drab old Moscow of Soviet times. With Russia's vast natural resources attracting a rush of inward investment, Moscow saw the lion's share of that money passing through its hands. A wealthy elite, the "New Russians", suddenly had a vastly improved standard of living and, for instance, car ownership in the city quadrupled in 1991–7. No amount of nightclubs seemed able

A church wedding, popular once more since religion has gained new importance among the young

1984 Chernenko replaces Andropov

1989 USSR leaves Afghanistan

1994 Reconstruction programme in city initiated

2000 Vladimir Putin becomes President of Russia

Vladimir Putin

2008 Putin becomes Prime Minister while Dmitry Medvedev takes office as President

1990

2000

2010

1986 Chernobyl nuclear disaster

1985 Gorbachev is elected General Secretary of Communist Party

1991 Yeltsin is elected president of Russia. August coup fails; the USSR is dissolved in December

Boris Yeltsin with the Russian flag

2004 Chechen separatists seize school in Beslan; more than 300 left dead after special forces storm the building

MOSCOW THROUGH THE YEAR

Muscovites are ready to celebrate at any time and take their public holidays seriously. Flowers play a particularly important role, from mimosa for International Women's Day to lilac as a symbol that summer is on its way. All the official holidays, as well as some local festivals such as City Day, are marked with concerts and night-time fireworks all over the city. Music,

Lilac, a sign that summer is coming

whether classical, folk or contemporary, is the central theme of a large number of festivals, bringing in talent from all over the world. For really big celebrations top Russian and international singers perform for crowds of thousands in Red Square. Even without an official holiday, people love to get out and about, whether skiing in winter, picnicking in spring or summer, or gathering mushrooms in autumn.

Performers wearing papier-mâché costumes at The Rite of Spring

SPRING

When flocks of rooks appear in the city, usually in late March, and the violets and snowdrops bloom, spring is reckoned to have arrived.

To warm themselves up after the months of cold, locals celebrate *maslennitsa*, the feast of blini-making before Lent. Willow branches with catkins are gathered as a symbol of the approaching Palm Sunday and on Forgiveness Sunday, just before Lent, people ask forgiveness of those they may have offended in the past year.

Easter service, Trinity Monastery of St Sergius *(see pp162–5)*

Wealthy Muscovites usually make a first visit to their *dacha* at this time to put the garden in order and to plant their own fruits and vegetables.

MARCH

Maslenitsa end Feb–early Mar. A festival involving events such as concerts and carnivals held at venues throughout the city.
International Women's Day *(Mezhdunarodnyy den zhenshchin)*, 8 Mar. Men buy flowers for their womenfolk and congratulate them on the holiday with the words *"s prazdnikom"*. Theatres hold special performances.
St Patrick's Day, first Sunday after 16 March. Moscow's Irish community organize a few local marches and concerts.
Easter Sunday *(Paskha)*, March–early May, following the Orthodox calendar. Churches are filled with chanting and candles. After the greeting *Khristos voskres* (Christ is risen) and the reply *Voistine voskres* (He is truly risen), people kiss one another three times.

APRIL

April Fool's Day *(Den durakov)*, 1 Apr. Russians play tricks with particular glee.
Cosmonauts' Day *(Den kosmonavtiki)*, 12 Apr. Space exploration was one of the glories of the Soviet Union and is celebrated with fireworks.
Alternative Festival, end Apr–May. Annual modern music festival in Gorky Park.
Moscow Forum, end Apr–May. Annual festival of classical and modern music held at various city venues.

War veterans on parade in Red Square on Victory Day

MAY

Labour Day *(Den truda)*, 1 May. In the Soviet era, huge military parades filled Red Square. Now much more low-key, with impromptu concerts.
Victory Day *(Den pobedy)*, 9 May. War veterans fill Red Square and Tverskaya ulitsa in memory of the 1945 Nazi surrender. A military parade is held in Red Square.
Border Troopers' Day *(Den pogranichnika)*, 28 May. Retired Border Troopers gather at the Bolshoy Theatre and in Gorky Park to get drunk, sing and watch fireworks.

AVERAGE DAILY HOURS OF SUNSHINE

| Jan | Feb | Mar | Apr | May | Jun | Jul | Aug | Sep | Oct | Nov | Dec |

Sunshine Chart
Moscow is often thought of as a cold and snowy city. However, it has more hours of sunshine in the summer months than many cities in northern Europe. May, June and July are the sunniest months. The short, cold days of winter provide a stark contrast, with an average of only around one hour of sunshine a day.

SUMMER

Life in Moscow is much less hectic in July and August as most enterprises close down for their summer breaks and many Muscovites move out of the city, either to their *dacha* or to spend holidays abroad. Although most of the theatres also close or go on tour for these two months, there is still plenty going on in and around the city for the visitor to enjoy. Some of the large estates and stately homes outside Moscow, such as Kuskovo *(see pp142–3)* and Ostankino Palace *(see pp144–5)*, hold outdoor concerts at this time of year. Gorky Park offers a number of options on a fine summer day – from bungee jumping or hiring a rowing boat or pedalo to enjoying a picnic. Outdoor cafés and bars are a favourite with Muscovites remaining in the city and there is even an outdoor casino at the Marilyn Entertainment Complex, at Krasina ulitsa 14.

Women in national costume for Peter the Great's birthday

JUNE

Trinity Sunday *(Troitsa)*, late May–late June. Believers and atheists alike go to tidy the graves of their loved ones and drink a toast to their souls.
Tchaikovsky International Competition, June, held every four years (next in 2006). One of the world's most prestigious musical awards *(see p200)*. Concerts are held throughout the city.
Day of Russia *(Den Rossii)*, 12 Jun. One of the country's newest holidays marks the day Russia became independent of the Soviet Union in 1991.
Peter the Great's Birthday *(Den rozhdeniya Petra Pervovo)*, first Sunday after 9 Jun. Costumed celebrations at Kuskovo *(see pp142–3)*.
International Music Assemblies Festival, mid-June. Russian music through eight centuries performed at concert halls and art galleries.

JULY

US Independence Day, 4 July. A big celebration takes place, enjoyed by Moscow's huge American community and pro-Western Muscovites at the Kuskovo estate.
Navy Day *(Den voenno-morskovo flota)*, first Sunday after 22 July. Spectacular fireworks are accompanied by costumed celebrations across the city. Since Moscow is not a port city, celebrations are not on as lavish a scale as those held in St Petersburg.
Moscow International Film Festival, held every two years (in odd-numbered years) in July or August *(see p201)*. A glamorous event attended by both celebrities and the general public, and featuring the latest releases from all over the world.

AUGUST

Summer Music Festival, throughout Aug. Evening recitals of classical music featuring distinguished graduates of the Moscow Conservatory.
Moscow Annual Airshow, end of Aug, in the town of Zhukovskiy, south-east of Moscow. A chance to see famous Russian aeroplanes.
Russian Cinema Day, 27 Aug. Showings of favourite, mostly Russian, films on television and in cinemas all over the city.

Relaxing on a summer's day at an outdoor café in Arbat

AVERAGE MONTHLY PRECIPITATION

mm / Inches

Jan Feb Mar Apr May Jun Jul Aug Sep Oct Nov Dec

Precipitation Chart
In the winter months, precipitation falls mainly as snow, most of which settles until the spring, reaching a depth of 35 cm (14 in). In summer, even hot days are often interrupted by brief, but heavy, rain showers.

■ Rainfall (from axis)
□ Snowfall (from axis)

AUTUMN

City life begins to pick up as people return from the country and prepare their children for school. In the last weeks of August, Moscow is filled with posters noting the advent of the school year and shops are packed with parents buying new school clothes and books. Theatres open again in September, with premieres of plays and operas.

The crisp autumn weather is perfect for mushroom gathering. Muscovites often head out early in the morning to the forests around the city to hunt for white (the favourite) and brown mushrooms, orange-cap bolens, chanterelles and oyster mushrooms. However, dangerously poisonous as well as edible mushrooms abound and gathering them is best left to the experts.

Chanterelle mushrooms

Other popular autumnal pastimes include horse riding at the Hippodrome *(see p202)* and taking a boat trip along the Moskva river.

SEPTEMBER

New Academic Year *(Novyy uchebnyy god),* 1 Sep. The first day back at school. Those going for the first time often take flowers with them.

City Day *(Den goroda),* first Sunday in Sep. Celebrations are held all over the city to mark the founding of Moscow in 1147 *(see p17).* More low-key than it once was as this is also the anniversary of the Beslan massacre in 2004.

OCTOBER

Talents of Russia *(Talanty Rossii),* 1–10 Oct. Festival of classical music, with musicians from all over the country.

Children with flowers for teachers at the start of the new school year

Punk Festival, early Oct. Russian bands play in Gorky Park and at other venues.

NOVEMBER

Students of the Moscow ballet schools give the first of their annual winter performances at various venues. This is the worst month to visit as Moscow is dirty and slushy.
Day of National Unity *(Den Narodnogo Edinstva),* 4 Nov. Holiday to replace the Day of Reconciliation (previously called the Day of the Great October Revolution).

Open-air folk dancing at Moscow's City Day celebrations

PUBLIC HOLIDAYS
New Year's Holiday
(1–5 Jan)
Russian Orthodox Christmas (7 Jan)
International Women's Day (8 Mar)
Easter Sunday (Mar/Apr/May)
Labour Day (1 May)
Victory Day (9 May)
Day of Russia (12 Jun)
Day of National Unity (4 Nov)

AVERAGE MONTHLY TEMPERATURE

C° F°

30 — 86
20 — 68
10 — 50
0 — 32
-10 — 14
-20 — -4

Jan Feb Mar Apr May Jun Jul Aug Sep Oct Nov Dec

Temperature Chart
The chart shows the average minimum and maximum temperatures for each month. Winter temperatures well below freezing may seem daunting, and do limit the length of time it is possible to stay out, but the cold is dry and can be exhilarating and there is very little wind.

WINTER

As the ice thickens and the snow deepens, people head outdoors. Gorky *(see p129)*, Sokolniki and Luzhniki parks become the venues for ice-skating and skiing. The hardened locals, the so-called "walruses", break the ice at Serebryaniy Bor on the western outskirts of Moscow to take a dip early every morning.

In the midst of winter sports come New Year and Christmas. New Year is the big holiday, while Christmas is celebrated on 7 January, in accordance with the Orthodox calendar. Many people also still celebrate Old New Year which falls a week later on 14 January.

One great pleasure of this season is the Christmas ballet, *The Nutcracker*, performed at the Bolshoy Theatre *(see pp90–91)* largely by children.

DECEMBER

New Year's Eve *(Novyy god)*, 31 Dec. Still the biggest holiday of the year, New Year's Eve is celebrated with the local *shampanskoe* (sparkling wine). This is primarily a family occasion: at circuses and balls, actors dress up as the traditional bringers of presents, the Snow Maiden and Grandfather Frost. More recently, people have begun gathering in Red Square to see in the New Year.

Svyatoslav Richter December Nights *(Dekabrskie vechera imeni Svyatoslava Rikhtera)*, throughout Dec. Classical music dedicated to the Russian pianist at the Pushkin Museum of Fine Arts *(see pp78–81)*.

Russian Winter *(Russkaya zima)*, end Dec–mid Jan. Classical music festival.

JANUARY

Russian Orthodox Christmas *(Rozhdestvo)*, 7 Jan. Christmas is celebrated in a quieter fashion than Easter, with a traditional visit to an evening service on Christmas eve, when bells ring out through the frosty air from all over Moscow. Children's celebrations are held at various venues, including the Great Kremlin Palace *(see p63)*. The parties are called *Yolka* (Christmas tree).

Christmas Premier Festival, end Dec–mid Jan. Annual classical music festival.

Christmas in Moscow, first two weeks in Jan. Festival of medieval and classical music.

Ice Sculpture Festival in Gorky Park. This festival lasts for several months, but it is never possible to tell exactly

Fisherman fishing through a hole in the ice

Street entertainer

when it will start. It depends entirely on the weather and some years can start as early as December. During the festival Gorky Park is taken over by numerous ice sculptures, usually of fairy-tale characters, which remain in the park until the thaw.

Tatyana's Day *(Tatyanin den)*, 25 Jan. St Tatyana's feast day is largely a holiday for students rather than a religious holiday, since the decree founding Moscow University *(see p94)* was signed on this day in 1755.

FEBRUARY

International Festival of the Orthodox Church, throughout Feb. The music and cultural heritage of the Orthodox Church is celebrated in various city venues.

Valentine's Day *(Den svyatovo Valentina)*, 14 Feb. A recent addition to Moscow's calendar, although it is not as popular as it is in the West.

Defenders of the Motherland Day *(Den zashchitnikov rodiny)*, 23 Feb. Low-key male version of Women's Day. Elderly veterans, and men generally, receive presents.

An ice sculpture of an octopus, part of the festival in Gorky Park

MOSCOW AT A GLANCE

More than 100 places of interest are described in the *Area by Area* section of this book. These range from the historic treasures of State and Church, enclosed within the Kremlin walls, to galleries housing incomparable religious icons among spectacular collections of Russian and Western art. The city's liveliest streets and most beautiful parks, which offer different attractions in winter and summer, are also included. To help make the most of a visit, the next 12 pages offer a guide to the very best that Moscow has to offer. Museums and architecture each have their own section, and there is a special feature on Moscow's grandiose metro stations. The sights mentioned here are cross referenced to their own full entries for ease of use. Below is a selection of the top sights that no visitor should miss.

MOSCOW TOP TEN ATTRACTIONS

Bolshoy Theatre
See pp90–91.

St Basil's Cathedral
See pp108–9.

Tretyakov Gallery
See pp118–21.

Kolomenskoe
See pp138–9.

KREMLIN SIGHTS

State Armoury
See pp64–5.

Red Square
See p106.

Lenin Mausoleum
See p107.

Cathedral of the Assumption
See pp58–9.

Pushkin Museum of Fine Arts
See pp78–81.

Kuskovo
See pp142–3.

◁ The Ivan the Great Bell Tower, with the huge Tsar Bell in front of it and the Assumption Belfry to the right

Moscow's Best: Metro Stations

Not many of the world's underground railways can claim to be tourist attractions and artistic monuments in their own right. The Moscow metro is an exception. Its station platforms and concourses resemble miniature palaces with chandeliers, sculptures and lavish mosaics. Moreover, this is one of the busiest and most efficient metro networks in the world. Some of the finest stations are shown here and further information can be found on pp40–41. Practical details about using the metro are given on pp222–3.

Belorusskaya

Named after the nearby Belorusskiy railway station, Belorusskaya has a central hall with mosaics of rural scenes and a tiled floor based on a traditional pattern from a Belorussian rug.

Mayakovskaya

A bust of poet Vladimir Mayakovsky stands in this station, which is named in his honour. Recesses in the ceiling contain a series of mosaics depicting planes and sporting scenes.

Tverskaya

Arbatskaya

Kievskaya

Large, ostentatious mosaics decorate the walls of this station. They include idealized scenes representing Russia's friendship with the Ukraine and pictures of Soviet agriculture.

Kropotkinskaya

Clean lines and simple colours distinguish this elegant station, designed by Aleksey Dushkin in the 1930s. It is named after the anarchist, Prince Pyotr Kropotkin.

Park Kultury

Niches in the walls of this station's central hall hold white, marble bas-relief medallions. These show people involved in various recreational activities such as ice-skating, reading, playing chess and dancing.

Teatralnaya
The differing cultures of the republics of the former Soviet Union provide the theme for this station. The ceiling panels depict some of their national costumes.

Komsomolskaya
This is the main entrance to Komsomolskaya station, named in honour of the Communist Youth League (Komsomol) which helped to construct the metro.

Red Square and Kitay Gorod

| 0 metres | 600 |
| 0 yards | 600 |

Kremlin

Zamoskvoreche

Ploshchad Revolyutsii
The main hall of this station contains lifesize bronze statues of ordinary citizens, such as a farmer, who helped to build the Soviet State.

Novokuznetskaya
A bas-relief frieze runs along the central hall of this station, which was constructed in 1943. The frieze shows a variety of Russian military heroes, such as World War II soldiers.

Exploring the Moscow Metro

Bas-relief at Park Kultury

When the idea of an underground railway was first proposed for Moscow in 1902 the idea was rejected by one local newspaper as "a staggeringly impudent encroachment on everything Russian people hold dear in the city of Moscow". By the 1930s, however, the need for better transportation had become urgent as the population of the city more than doubled to meet the demands of rapid industrialization. Two prominent young Communists, Nikita Khrushchev and Lazar Kaganovich, were entrusted with building a metro that would serve as a showcase for socialism and the achievements of workers and peasants.

METRO STATISTICS

The Moscow metro is still expanding, but there are already 165 stations and approximately 265 km (155 miles) of track. Over 9,300 trains operate every day, travelling at speeds of up to 90 km/h (56 mph). The Moscow metro carries 8-9 million passengers per day, more than the London and New York systems combined. During peak periods trains arrive at stations every 1–2 minutes.

Members of the Communist Youth League helping to build the metro

BUILDING THE METRO

Construction work on the metro began in December 1931, during the period of Stalin's first Five Year Plan of 1928–33. The Communist Party decreed that "the whole country will build the metro", so workers – both men and women – were drafted in from all over the Soviet Union. They were assisted by soldiers of the Red Army and by over 13,000 members of the Communist Youth League (Komsomol).

The latter worked as volunteers in their free time and their massive contribution was commemorated by naming **Komsomolskaya** after them. The materials, too, came from different parts of the country: rails from the steelworks of Kuznetsk, marble from the Urals and Caucasus and granite from Karelia and the Ukraine.

Work was completed on the first 11.6-km (7.2-mile) section of track, linking Sokolniki with **Park Kultury**, in February 1935 and the first 13 stations were opened in May. Many of

those who had worked on the project were subsequently rewarded with medals, including the much-coveted Order of Lenin. Construction work continued rapidly and by 1939 there were 22 stations serving over one million passengers.

METRO DECORATION

Some of the Soviet Union's finest artists were employed to decorate the metro. Working within the confines of Socialist Realism *(see p135)*, many dealt with themes such as the Revolution, national defence and the Soviet way of life.

The earliest metro stations are generally regarded as the most architecturally successful. **Mayakovskaya**, designed by Aleksey Dushkin in 1938, won the Grand Prix at the New York World's Fair. Its spacious halls are supported by columns of stainless steel and marble. **Kropotkinskaya** (1935) and **Ploshchad Revolyutsii** (1938) are also by Dushkin. The main hall of the latter has a series of

marble-lined arches. On either side of each stands a life-sized bronze figure cast by sculptor Matvey Manizer. Red Guards, workers, sailors, sportsmen and women, a Young Pioneer and a mother and child are among the "everyday heroes" who made the Revolution possible or helped to build the subsequent Soviet State. Several stations, including **Komsomolskaya**, consist of two or more linked sections on different metro lines. One of Komsomolskaya's two sections, on the Kirovo-Frunzenskaya line, was built in 1935. Its decor is relatively restrained, with rose-coloured marble pillars and majolica panels by Yevgeniy Lanseray showing heroic metro workers. The other station, on the circle line, was completed 17 years later and is much more ostentatious, with florid stucco mouldings and glittering chandeliers. Designed by leading architect Aleksey Shchusev it was also a prizewinner at the New York

The simple, yet stylish, Mayakovskaya, designed by Aleksey Dushkin

World's Fair. The gold mosaics showing military parades and figures from Russian history are the work of artist Pavel Korin.

Martial themes predominated during and after World War II. At **Novokuznetskaya** (1943), for example, architects Vladimir Gelfreikh and Igor Rozhin commissioned a bas-relief frieze from Nikolay Tomskiy showing Russian military heroes as diverse as Minin and Pozharskiy *(see p108)* and Field Marshal Kutuzov *(see p158)*.

Many of the stations built in the 1940s and 1950s extol the virtues of the Soviet regime. Ceramic panels at **Teatralnaya** (1940) celebrate the arts of the former Soviet Republics, while mosaics at **Belorusskaya** (1952) and **Kievskaya** (1937 and 1954) show healthy, contented peasants celebrating agricultural abundance. These ignore the terrible famine that resulted from Stalin's forced collectivization policy of the early 1930s.

In the Soviet mind, athletic prowess was the natural preparation for heroic achievement. Sport and recreation are the twin themes of the bas-reliefs by artist Sergey Rabinovich at **Park Kultury** (1935 and 1949).

Revolutionary figures at Belorusskaya

Even the station exteriors above ground were designed to work as propaganda. Seen from above, the entrance to **Arbatskaya** (1935) is in the shape of the Soviet red star.

Although financial constraints now impose limits, artistic leeway has still been possible in the design of some of the newer stations such as **Chekhovskaya** (1987), and **Park Pobedy**, the world's deepest metro station, completed in 2003.

Part of Komsomolskaya, designed by architect Aleksey Shchusev

THE METRO AND WAR

The early metro lines were laid deep underground so that they could be used as bomb shelters in times of war. By November 1941 German troops had reached the outskirts of Moscow and the Soviet Union was fighting for survival. **Mayakovskaya**, completed just three years earlier, became the headquarters of the Anti-Aircraft Defence Forces. It was in the station's spacious central hall that Stalin addressed generals and party activists the evening before the Red Army marched off to the front.

Kirovskaya (now known as **Chistye Prudy**) was the headquarters of the General Staff throughout World War II. It was here that Stalin and his advisors planned the first offensives against the Nazis. Consequently, the metro system became an important symbol of resistance to the Nazi invasion. In fact, its propaganda value was deemed so great that the designs for the mosaics at **Novokuznetskaya** were evacuated from St Petersburg when their creator, Viktor Frolov, died there during the prolonged siege of 1941–4.

METRO MUSEUM

The history and workings of the Moscow metro are fully explained in this interesting museum, located above the main hall of Sportivnaya in Sparrow Hills *(see p129)*. Some rather dated photomontages show the construction of the track and stations. There are numerous displays including models of trains and escalators, a reconstruction of a driver's cabin and the first ticket, sold in 1935.

🏛 **Moscow Metro Museum**
Sportivnaya metro. *Tel (495) 622 7309.* ⬜ 9am–3:30pm Tue–Fri, 11am–5:30pm Mon. 🎫 *(groups only except Thu 9am–4pm).*

WHERE TO SEE THE METRO

Arbatskaya **Map** 6 E1
Belorusskaya **Map** 1 C2
Chekhovskaya **Map** 2 F4
Chistye Prudy **Map** 3 C4
Kievskaya **Map** 5 B2
Komsomolskaya **Map** 4 D2
Kropotkinskaya **Map** 6 E2
Mayakovskaya **Map** 2 E3
Novokuznetskaya **Map** 7 B3
Park Kultury **Map** 6 D4 & 6 E3
Ploshchad Revolyutsii **Map** 3 A5
Teatralnaya **Map** 3 A5

The entrance to Arbatskaya, in the shape of the Soviet red star

Moscow's Best: Architecture

Visitors to Moscow are often pleasantly surprised by the
wealth and variety of architecture the city has to
offer. As well as magnificent palaces and cathedrals, such
as those in the Kremlin, there are also smaller churches
and chapels, homely boyars' residences, imposing Neo-
Classical mansions and some beautiful municipal buildings.
A stark contrast to this older architecture is provided by
early 20th-century Constructivist buildings and Communist
landmarks such as Stalinist-Gothic skyscrapers. For
further information about architecture see pp44–5.

Moscow Old University
*The colonnade of pillars
along the front of this
building and its ochre and
white colouring are typ-
ical Neo-Classical features.*

Gorky House-Museum
*Stunning stained-glass windows grace the
Gorky House-Museum, a Style-Moderne
masterpiece built by Fyodor Shekhtel in 1900.*

Tverskaya

Arbatskaya

Krem

Cathedral of the Assumption
*A miraculous fusion of
Renaissance and Early-Russian
styles, this superb
cathedral was built in
1475–9 to a design
by Italian architect
Aristotele Fioravanti.*

Foreign Ministry
*This is one of seven
skyscrapers designed in
a hybrid style often
referred to as Stalinist
Gothic. The Foreign
Ministry building was
finished in 1952 shortly
before Stalin's death.*

Pashkov House
*The Neo-Classical Pashkov
House, which has been
restored, has a colonnaded
porch with relief sculptures.*

Polytechnical Museum
The central part of the Polytechnical Museum, built in 1877, is the work of Ippolit Monighetti. It is an outstanding example of Russian Revival, a style that draws heavily on the architecture of Russia's past.

St Basil's Cathedral
Pointed roofs over the entrance steps and tiers of arched gables typify the stunning architectural diversity of this cathedral, built in 1555–61 for Ivan the Terrible.

Red Square and Kitay Gorod

Old English Court
Presented to an English trade delegation in 1556, this 16th-century, whitewashed, stone house has a wooden roof and few windows.

Zamoskvoreche

| 0 metres | 600 |
| 0 yards | 600 |

Church of the Resurrection in Kadashi
This Moscow-Baroque church has tiers of ornate limestone carvings in place of the kokoshniki gables normally seen on Early-Russian churches. The church's onion domes are a traditional feature, but they are an unusual jade green colour.

Exploring Moscow's Architecture

Part of a floral fresco in St Basil's Cathedral

Russian architecture has always been innovative. The medieval Novgorod, Yaroslavl and Pskov schools of architecture developed several of the distinctive features found on Moscow's churches. These included the onion dome, rounded *zakomary* gables and *kokoshniki* gables, which are semi-circular or shaped like the cross-section of an onion. In later centuries Moscow's architects became increasingly influential, developing new styles, such as Constructivism, and giving a Russian flavour to others.

The Baroque Gate Church of the Intercession at Novodevichiy

Study in the Palace of the Romanov Boyars

In the 15th and 16th centuries the tsars employed a succession of Italian architects to construct prestigious buildings in the Kremlin. They combined the Early-Russian style with Italian Renaissance features to create magnificent buildings such as the **Cathedral of the Assumption** *(see pp58–9)*.

Another 16th-century innovation was the spire-like tent roof, used, for example, on **St Basil's Cathedral** *(see pp108–9)*. In the mid-17th century Patriarch Nikon banned its use, insisting that plans for new churches must be based on ancient Byzantine designs.

The majority of Moscow's early secular buildings have not survived. The few exceptions include the ornate 16th-century **Palace of the Romanov Boyars** *(see pp102–3)* and the charming early 16th-century Old English Court *(see p102)*.

EARLY RUSSIAN

Moscow's earliest buildings were constructed entirely from wood. From around the 14th century, stone and brick began to be used for important buildings, but wood continued to be the main building material until the great fire of 1812 *(see p24)* when much of the city was burnt to the ground.

The majority of Moscow's oldest surviving buildings are churches. One of the earliest is the Cathedral of the Saviour in the **Monastery of the Saviour and Andronicus** *(see p140)*.

BAROQUE

The Bridge Tower (1670s) at **Izmaylovo Park** *(see p141)* is an early example of Moscow Baroque. Its filigree limestone trimmings and pilaster decoration, set against a background of red brick, are typical of the style. The gate churches in the **Novodevichiy Convent** *(see pp130–31)*, the buildings of the **Krutitskoe Mission** *(see p140)* and the spectacular **Church of the Resurrection in Kadashi** *(see p122)*, with its limestone ornamentation carved to resemble lace, are also fine examples of this style of architecture.

A number of Baroque buildings, including the **Church of the Intercession in Fili** *(see p128)*, were built with money from the wealthy and powerful Naryshkin family. This has led to Moscow Baroque also being known as Naryshkin Baroque.

NEO-CLASSICAL

The Accession of Catherine the Great in 1762 heralded a new direction for Russian architecture. She favoured the Neo-Classical style, which drew on the architecture of ancient Greece and Rome. This style has been used to great effect in the **Pashkov House** *(see p75)*, thought to have been designed by Vasiliy Bazhenov in 1784 (sadly, the building is now covered by hoarding).

Bazhenov's assistant, the prolific Matvey Kazakov, demonstrated the flexibility of Neo-Classicism in his designs for a wide range of buildings,

---

THE NEW PATRIOTISM

The reconstruction of the city's pre-Revolutionary buildings, including the **Kazan Cathedral** *(see p105)* and the **Cathedral of Christ the Redeemer** *(see p74)*, is evidence of a growing nostalgia for Russia's past, and a renewed interest in the nation's architectural heritage. The revival of the Orthodox Church, in particular, has led to the restoration of hundreds of churches across Moscow.

The Cathedral of Christ the Redeemer, rebuilt in 1994–7

including churches, hospitals, the **Moscow Old University** *(see p94)* and the **House of Unions** *(see pp88–9)*. He is best known for the **Senate** *(see pp66–7)* in the Kremlin.

The huge fire that followed Napoleon's brief occupation of the city in 1812 led to a whole-sale reconstruction. Moscow's nobility built new homes along **ulitsa Prechistenka** *(see p74)* in the newly fashionable Empire style. Leading architects of this more decorative style included Afanasiy Grigorev and Osip Bove, who designed **Theatre Square** *(see p88)*.

The House of Friendship, a wonderful example of Eclecticism

A Neo-Classical bas-relief in the House of Unions, built in the 1780s

HISTORICISM AND STYLE MODERNE

Historicism replaced Neo-Classicism in the mid-19th century. It arose from a desire to create a national style by re-viving architectural styles from the past. The **Great Kremlin Palace** *(see p63)* and **State Armoury** *(see pp64–5)*, both designed by Konstantin Ton around 1840, are typical. They combine various styles includ-ing Renaissance, Classical and Baroque. Ton also designed the extravagant Byzantine-style

The Style-Moderne Gorky House-Museum

Cathedral of Christ the Redeemer *(see p74)*, finished in 1883 and rebuilt in 1994–7.

Eclecticism combined past and present architectural styles from all over the world to create fantastical buildings such as the **House of Friendship** *(see p95)*, which was designed by Vladimir Mazyrin in 1898.

Traditional wooden archi-tecture and folk art were rich sources of inspiration for the architects that formulated the Russian-Revival style. The flam-boyant **Historical Museum** *(see p106)* and **Polytechnical Museum** *(see p110)* are fine examples of the genre. However, the finest, and most functional, is **GUM** *(see p107)* design-ed by Aleksandr Pomerantsev.

Style Moderne was a radical new architectural style akin to Art Nouveau. One of the earliest examples is the **Hotel Metropol** *(see p88)*, de-signed in 1899 by Englishman William Walcot. The greatest advocate of Style Moderne was Fyodor Shekhtel. The mansion he built for Stepan Ryabushinskiy is now the **Gorky House-Museum** *(see p95)*. It is highly unconven-tional and uses mosaic friezes, glazed brick and stained glass to stunning effect.

Mosaic of irises from the frieze around the Gorky House-Museum

ARCHITECTURE AFTER THE REVOLUTION

Constructivism was a novel attempt to combine form and function, and was the most popular style to emerge in the decade after the Revolution. The offices of the newspaper **Izvestiya**, on Pushkin Square *(see p97)*, were designed by Grigoriy Barkhin in 1927. His use of glass and reinforced concrete to create geometrical designs is typical of the Constructivist style. Another lead-ing Constructivist was Konstantin Melnikov. The unique **Melnikov House** *(see p72)*, which consists of two interlocking cylinders, is the home that he built for himself in 1927. In the 1930s Stalin formulated a grand plan to rebuild large areas of the city. He favoured a new monumental style and Constructivism went out of vogue. The monumental style is exemplified by Aleksey Shchusev's grandiose "proletar-ian" apartments at the lower end of Tverskaya ulitsa and culminates in Stalinist Gothic. This term is used to describe the seven matching skyscrapers erected at key points in the city in the 1940s and 1950s. The **Foreign Ministry** build-ing *(see p70)*, designed by architects Mikhail Minkus and Vladimir Gelfreikh, is typical of this style, which is often called "wedding-cake" architecture.

Moscow's Best: Museums

Moscow has more than 80 museums offering a fascinating insight into the history and culture of the people of Russia. Some, such as the Tretyakov Gallery and State Armoury, have collections including works by world-famous artists and craftsmen, while others house exhibits of local or specialist interest. Among the most evocative are those commemorating the lives of artists, writers and musicians. The rooms where they lived and worked have been lovingly preserved. For further information on museums see pp48–9.

State Armoury

This elaborate 17th-century enamel work is exhibited in the State Armoury, along with a dazzling array of gold and silverware, jewellery and royal regalia. The current Armoury building was constructed in 1844 on the orders of Tsar Nicholas I.

Shalyapin House-Museum

Portraits of the opera star Fyodor Shalyapin on display in his former home include formal paintings, images of him on stage and drawings by his children.

Tverskaya

Arbatskaya

Pushkin Museum of Fine Arts

As well as a fine collection of Byzantine and Western European art from the 8th to the 18th centuries, this gallery houses artifacts from ancient Egypt, Greece and Rome, including this Egyptian funeral mask.

| 0 metres | 600 |
| 0 yards | 600 |

Tolstoy House-Museum

For over 20 years this traditionl house was the winter home of Leo Tolstoy, author of the epic novel War and Peace. *It is now an evocative museum which recaptures the daily lives of the writer and his family.*

Lenin Mausoleum
The red and black pyramid of the Lenin Mausoleum was erected in 1930 to a design by architect Aleksey Shchusev. It contains the embalmed body of Vladimir Lenin, the first Soviet leader.

Mayakovsky Museum
This thought-provoking museum commemorates the revolutionary poet, playwright and artist Vladimir Mayakovsky. The abstract exhibits in this room symbolize his childhood in Georgia.

Palace of the Romanov Boyars
The restored interiors and luxurious clothes and possessions in this house effectively evoke the daily lives of the Moscow aristocracy in the 16th and 17th centuries. The house was constructed for boyar Nikita Romanov.

Red Square and
Kitay Gorod

mlin

Zamoskvoreche

FURTHER AFIELD

| 0 kilometres | 4 |
| 0 miles | 2 |

Kuskovo was the rural estate of the aristocratic Sheremetev family in the 18th-century.

Kolomenskoe was a favourite country residence for Tsar Alexis Mikhailovich. An open-air museum of architecture now forms part of the estate.

Tretyakov Gallery
Valentin Serov's Girl with Peaches *(1887) in the Tretyakov Gallery is part of the largest collection of Russian art in the world.*

Exploring Moscow's Museums

Wherever visitors' interests lie, whether it be in painting and the fine arts, science, the Revolution, the history of the Russian theatre or the lives of the nobility, there will be something in Moscow's museums to appeal to them. As well as the many museums in the city, there are a number of country estates in the area around Moscow. Several of these, including Kuskovo and Kolomenskoe, are easily accessible by metro and make good half-day or day excursions *(see p227)*. However, it is worth bearing in mind that a number of museums are currently undergoing much-needed renovation and, in some cases, ideological reassessment.

Nijinsky's ballet shoe, Bakhrushin Theatre Museum

The elegant drawing room of the Lermontov House-Museum

Young Acrobat on a Ball, Picasso, in the Gallery of European and American Art

PAINTING AND DECORATIVE ARTS

The world's most important collection of Russian art is on display in the recently renovated **Tretyakov Gallery** *(see pp118–21)*. The gallery owns over 100,000 works, but only a fraction of them are on show at any one time. They include amongst others, paintings by most of the group of artists called the Wanderers *(peredvizhniki)*. The gallery's extensive collection of post-Revolution (20th-Century) art is now housed in the **New Tretyakov Gallery** *(see p135)*. The **Tropinin Museum** *(see pp124–5)* has a fine collection of works by the 19th-century portrait artist Vasiliy Tropinin and his contemporaries.

The **Museum of Private Collections** *(see p75)* is a new gallery, housed in a 19th-century building. It exhibits previously unseen drawings, watercolours, sketches and paintings, mainly by Russian artists of the 19th and 20th centuries.

On the same street, the **Pushkin Museum of Fine Arts** *(see p78–81)* and **The Gallery of European and American Art of the 19th–20th Centuries** *(see p75)*, are two of Moscow's finest art galleries. The former displays old masters such as Botticelli, Rubens and Rembrandt, while the latter boasts a superb collection of Impressionist and post-Impressionist paintings.

A superb collection of decorative and applied art spanning the last seven centuries or so is housed in the **State Armoury** *(see pp64–5)* in the Kremlin. There are rooms devoted to arms and armour, jewellery, gold and silverware, religious vestments and imperial regalia.

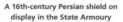
A 16th-century Persian shield on display in the State Armoury

HOUSE-MUSEUMS

The houses and flats where many important Russian cultural figures lived have been preserved as museums. The sturdy, timber-framed **Tolstoy House-Museum** *(see p134)* contains many personal possessions that belonged to Leo Tolstoy. The novelist and his family spent many winters in the house. Among their regular visitors was the playwright Anton Chekhov. The house where this writer began his career in the 1880s is also open to the public as the **Chekhov House-Museum** *(see p96)*. Across the road from Chekhov's house is the **Shalyapin House-Museum** *(see p83)* where the great opera singer, Fyodor Shalyapin, lived. Visitors can enjoy the beautifully furnished rooms while listening to old recordings of his singing.

The **Stanislavskiy House-Museum** *(see p93)* is the former home of Konstantin Stanislavskiy, theatrical director and the co-founder of the Moscow Arts Theatre *(see p92)*. It contains costumes, props and other memorabilia.

Along with a few items once owned by Alexander Pushkin, the **Pushkin House-Museum** *(see p73)* contains an interesting display of pictures that show what Moscow was like in 1831, when the poet lived here. The **Bely House-Museum** *(see p73)*, in the building next door, was once the home of the Symbolist poet, Andrei Bely. Nearby is the **Skryabin House-Museum** *(see p72)*, the last home of composer Aleksandr Skryabin.

The tower blocks of Novyy Arbat dwarf the **Lermontov House-Museum** *(see pp82–3)*, the simple timber house where Pushkin's contemporary, the poet Mikhail Lermontov, was brought up by his grandmother in the early 1830s.

The extraordinary life of Vladimir Mayakovsky is brilliantly realized in the displays in the **Mayakovsky Museum** *(see p111)*. This flat, near the former KGB building *(see p112)*, is where the Futurist poet lived from 1919–30.

The artist Viktor Vasnetsov designed his own home. In his studio, now the **Vasnetsov House-Museum** *(see p144)*, visitors can see his enormous canvases based on folk tales.

The **Tchaikovsky House-Museum** *(see p159)* at Klin still contains furnishings used by composer Pyotr Tchaikovsky, including the desk where he finished his *Sixth Symphony*.

COUNTRY ESTATES

Several palaces and estates on the outskirts of Moscow are open to the public. **Ostankino Palace** *(see pp144–5)*, built in the 18th century for the fabulously wealthy Sheremetev family, is famous for its exquisite theatre, where serf actors and musicians once took the stage. **Kuskovo** *(see pp142–3)* was also built for the Sheremetevs. In the palace's beautiful gardens is a ceramics museum.

Clay sledge in the History of Moscow Museum

A number of superb 16th- and 17th-century buildings still stand at the former royal estate of **Kolomenskoe** *(see pp138–9)*. Also on the estate is a fascinating museum of wooden architecture.

Picturesque, Gothic-style ruins are all that remain of the palace at **Tsaritsyno** *(see p137)*. This ambitious project, commissioned by Catherine the Great, was never finished.

Works of art by 19th- and 20th-century Russian artists are on show at the **Abramtsevo Estate-Museum** *(see p160)*, formerly an artists' colony.

Sweet wrappers, boxes and scales in the Museum of Modern History

HISTORY MUSEUMS

A number of museums and other sites in and around the city provide fascinating glimpses into Moscow's past.

The **History of Moscow Museum** *(see p111)* traces the city's history, with earliest exhibits including archaeological finds from around the Kremlin. There is speculation that the museum may be moved.

The life of the boyars *(see p20)* in Moscow in the early 17th century is recreated in the **Palace of the Romanov Boyars** *(see pp102–3)*.

Visitors interested in Napoleon's winter invasion of Russia in 1812 *(see pp23–4)* will want to make the day trip to **Borodino** *(see p158)*. This was the scene of one of the bloodiest encounters of the campaign. There are over 30 monuments around the battlefield and a museum nearby tells the story of the battle. They may also like to visit the **Borodino Panorama Museum** *(see p129)* on Kutuzovskiy prospekt. This circular pavilion contains an enormous painting of the famous battle.

The monumental scale of the **Lenin Mausoleum** *(see p107)*, containing Lenin's embalmed body, gives an insight into the importance of the role played by Lenin *(see pp27–8)* in 20th-century Russian history.

Displays at the **Museum of Modern History** *(see p97)* cover Russian history from 1900 until the collapse of the Soviet Union in 1991. Sweet wrappers depicting Marx and Lenin and home-made grenades are among the exhibits.

The **Museum of the Great Patriotic War** *(see p129)* has dioramas of major battles from World War II, shown largely from a Soviet viewpoint.

SPECIALIST MUSEUMS

Among the city's handful of specialist museums is the **Polytechnical Museum** *(see p110)*, which charts important developments in science and technology in Russia.

The **Bakhrushin Theatre Museum** *(see p125)* houses an exciting collection of theatre memorabilia, including ballet shoes worn by Nijinsky, while the **Shchusev Museum of Architecture** *(see p150)* gives a history of Russian architecture.

A model of a reactor from a nuclear power station, one of the displays at the Polytechnical Museum

Grand buildings on the bustling ulitsa Arbat, in the late-afternoon sunlight ▷

MOSCOW
AREA BY AREA

THE KREMLIN 52–67

ARBATSKAYA 68–83

TVERSKAYA 84–97

RED SQUARE AND KITAY GOROD 98–113

ZAMOSKVORECHE 114–125

FURTHER AFIELD 126–145

THE KREMLIN

Citadel of the Tsars, headquarters of the Soviet Union and now the residence of the Russian president, for centuries the Kremlin has been a symbol of the power of the State. In 1156, Prince Yuriy Dolgorukiy chose the confluence of the Moskva and Neglinnaya rivers as the site for the first wooden Kremlin (*kreml* means "fortress"). Late in the 15th century, Tsar Ivan III (*see p18*) invited several leading Italian architects to build a sumptuous new complex. They designed the Cathedral of the Assumption and the Faceted Palace, among other buildings, in a fascinating fusion of Early-Russian and imported Renaissance styles (*see p44*).

The Tsar's Cannon in the Kremlin

The Kremlin did not escape the architectural vandalism of the 1930s, when it was closed and several of its churches and palaces were destroyed on Stalin's orders (*see p75*). Only in 1955, two years after his death, was the Kremlin partially reopened to the public.

SIGHTS AT A GLANCE

Churches and Cathedrals
Cathedral of the Annunciation ❼
Cathedral of the Archangel ❻
Cathedral of the Assumption pp58–9 ❺
Church of the Deposition of the Robe ❾

Historic Buildings and Monuments
Arsenal ⓰
Faceted Palace ❽
Great Kremlin Palace ⓫
Ivan the Great Bell Tower ❹
State Kremlin Palace ❷
Presidential Administration ⓮
Saviour's Tower ⓭
Senate ⓯
Terem Palace ❿
Trinity Tower ❶

Museums
Patriarch's Palace ❸
State Armoury p64–5 ⓬

Gardens
Alexander Gardens ⓱

GETTING THERE
Biblioteka imeni Lenina and Borovitskaya metro stations are just outside the walls of the Kremlin, within easy walking distance of the main sights. Trolleybus routes 1, 2, 12, and 33 and buses 6 and K are also useful.

KEY

Street-by-Street map pp54–5

Ⓜ Metro station

0 metres 200
0 yards 200

◁ **The Cathedral of the Annunciation, crowned by golden onion domes, on the Kremlin's main square**

Street by Street: The Kremlin

The Kremlin is home to the Russian president and the seat
of his administration. As a result less than half of it is
accessible to the public, but highlights including the State
Armoury, the Patriarch's Palace and the churches in Cathedral
Square are open to visitors. Christians have worshipped on
this site for more than eight centuries, but their early stone
churches were demolished in the 1470s to make way for
the present magnificent ensemble of cathedrals. In imperial
times, these were the setting for great state occasions such
as coronations, baptisms and burials.

Ticket office

Trinity Tower
*Napoleon marched in triumph
through this gate when he entered
the Kremlin in 1812 (see pp23–5).
He left defeated a month later* **1**

State Kremlin Palace
*Originally built in 1961
for Communist Party
congresses, the palace is
now used for a range
of cultural events* **2**

Terem Palace
*A chequered roof and
11 golden cupolas
topped by crosses are
all that is visible of
this hidden jewel
of the Kremlin* **10**

Great Kremlin Palace
*The palace contains several
vast ceremonial halls. The
sumptuous stucco work of St
George's Hall provides a
magnificent backdrop for
state receptions. Its marble
walls are inscribed with the
names of military heroes* **11**

0 metres	50
0 yards	50

★ State Armoury
*The State Armoury was designed by
Konstantin Ton to complement the Great
Kremlin Palace. Constructed in 1844–51,
this building is now a museum. It houses
the stunning imperial collections of
decorative and applied art and the
priceless State Diamond Fund* **12**

**Borovitskaya
Tower**, and
entrance if
visiting State
Armoury only.

STAR SIGHTS

★ State Armoury

★ Cathedral of
   the Assumption

KEY

– – – Suggested route

Church of the Deposition of the Robe

This graceful church was the domestic church of the metropolitans and patriarchs ❾

The Tsar Cannon, cast in 1586, weighs a massive 40 tonnes.

Church of the Twelve Apostles *(see p56)*

LOCATOR MAP
See Street Finder, maps 6 & 7

VISITORS' CHECKLIST

Map 7 A1 & A2. *Tel* (495) 695 3776. Ⓜ *Biblioteka imeni Lenina, Borovitskaya.* 🚍 6, K. 🚋 1, 2, 12, 33. ◯ 10am–5pm Fri–Wed. ✎ *Tickets (including separate tickets for the State Armoury) are sold at the Kremlin entrance and separately at some sights.* ♿ *complex, but not buildings.* ✍ *English (book in advance on (495) 697 4115).* ▣ **www. kremlin.museum.ru**

Ivan the Great Bell Tower

When the third storey was added to this beautiful octagonal bell tower in 1600, it became the tallest building in Russia ❹

Tsar Bell *(see p57)*

Patriarch's Palace

This imposing palace, rebuilt for Patriarch Nikon in 1652–6, now houses the Museum of 17th-Century Life and Applied Art ❸

Cathedral of the Archangel

The tomb of Tsarevich Dmitry, the younger son of Ivan the Terrible, is one of many found in this cathedral ❻

Cathedral Square

Faceted Palace

Two Italian architects, Marco Ruffo and Pietro Solario, constructed this striking Renaissance palace between 1485 and 1491 ❽

Cathedral of the Annunciation

Frescoes cover the walls and ceiling of this cathedral. In the dome above the iconostasis is a painting of Christ Pantocrator, above tiers of pictures of angels, prophets and patriarchs ❼

★ Cathedral of the Assumption

This 12th-century painting of St George the Warrior is one of the oldest surviving Russian icons. It forms part of the iconostasis in the cathedral's richly decorated interior ❺

Trinity Tower, with the modern Palace of Congresses on the right

Trinity Tower ❶
Троицкая башня
Troitskaya bashnya

The Kremlin. **Map** 7 A1.

This tower takes its name from the Trinity Monastery of St Sergius *(see pp162–5)*, which once had a mission nearby. The tower's Trinity Gate used to be the entrance for patriarchs and the tsars' wives and daughters. Today it is one of only two that admit visitors. The other is in the Borovitskaya Tower *(see p66)* to the southwest.

At 76 m (249 ft) high, the seven-storey Trinity Tower is the Kremlin's tallest. It was built in 1495–9 and in 1516 was linked by a bridge over the Neglinnaya river to the Kutafya Tower. The river now

runs underground and the Kutafya Tower is the sole survivor of the circle of towers that were originally built to defend the Kremlin walls.

In September 1812 Napoleon triumphantly marched his army into the Kremlin through the Trinity Gate – they left only a month later when the Russians set fire to the city *(see pp24–5)*.

State Kremlin Palace ❷
Госуддрственныи Кремлёвский дворец
Gosudarstvennyy Kremlevskiy dvorets

The Kremlin. **Map** 7 A1.
🔾 *for performances only.*

Commissioned by Russian premier Nikita Khrushchev in 1959 to host Communist Party conferences, the Palace of Congresses is the Kremlin's only modern building. It was completed in 1961 by a team of architects led by Mikhail Posokhin. Roughly 120 m (395 ft) long, the palace was sunk 15 m (49ft) into the ground so as not to dwarf the surrounding buildings.

Tsarevich Alexis' school book

Until 1991 the 6,000-seat auditorium was the venue for political meetings. Now it is used by the Kremlin Ballet Company *(see p200)* and for staging operas and rock concerts.

Patriarch's Palace ❸
Патриарший дворец
Patriarshiy dvorets

The Kremlin. **Map** 7 A1.
🔾 *10am–5pm Fri–Wed.* 🈸

The metropolitans of the Russian Orthodox Church lived on the site of the current Patriarch's Palace for many years. In the 16th century, the patriarchate was created, and the patriarch took over from the metropolitans as the most senior figure in the Russian Church. As a result the bishops of Krutitsy became metropolitans *(see p140)* while the patriarch lived in the Kremlin.

When Nikon became the patriarch in 1652, he felt that the existing residence and the small Church of the Deposition of the Robe *(see pp62–3)* were not grand enough for him. He had the residence extended and renovated to create the Patriarch's Palace, with its integral Church of the Twelve Apostles. Completed in 1656, the work was carried out by a team of master builders led by Ivan Semenov and Aleksey Korolkov.

The palace is now the Museum of 17th-Century Life and Applied Art. Recently renovated, it comprises a new exhibition hall and more than 1,000 exhibits drawn from the State Armoury collection *(see pp64–5)* and from churches and monasteries that were destroyed by Stalin in the 1930s *(see p75)*.

Entry to the museum is up a short flight of stairs. The first room houses an exhibition on the history of the palace. In the Gala Antechamber is a dazzling array of 17th-century patriarchs' robes. Some of Nikon's own vestments are on display, including a chasuble *(sakkos)*, a set of beautifully carved staffs and a cowl made from damask and satin, and embroidered with gold thread.

Two rooms in the museum have been refurbished in the style of a 17th-century boyar's apartment. In one of them is

Refurbished residence of a boyar in the Patriarch's Palace

a display of old, hand-written books, including Tsarevich Alexis' primer. Each page features one letter of the alphabet and a selection of objects beginning with that letter.

The impressive Chamber of the Cross, to the left of the stairs, has an area of 280 sq m (3,013 sq ft). When this ceremonial hall was built, it was the largest room in Russia without columns supporting its roof. Its ceiling is painted with a delicate tracery of flowers. The room was later used for producing consecrated oil called *miro*, and the silver vats and ornate stove used still stand in the room.

Nikon's rejection of new architectural forms, such as tent roofs, dictated a traditional design for the Church of the Twelve Apostles. Located to the right of the stairs, it houses some brilliant icons, including works by master iconographers such as Semen Ushakov. The iconostasis dates from around 1700. It was brought to the church from the Kremlin Convent of the Ascension prior to its demolition in 1929.

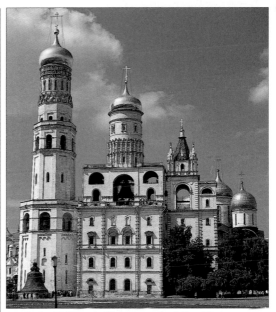

Ivan the Great Bell Tower, with the Assumption Belfry and annexe

PATRIARCH NIKON

A zealous reformer of the Russian Orthodox Church, Patriarch Nikon was so intent on returning it to its Byzantine roots that he caused his adversaries, the Old Believers, to split from the rest of the Church. Nikon also advocated the supremacy of Church over State, angering Tsar Alexis *(see p19)*. His autocratic style made him unpopular and he retreated to a monastery outside the city. He was deposed in 1667.

Ivan the Great Bell Tower ❹

Колокольня Ивана Великого
Kolokolnya Ivana Velikovo

The Kremlin. **Map 7 A1.**

This elegant bell tower (currently under restoration) was built in 1505–8 to a design by Marco Bon Friazin. It takes its name from the Church of St Ivan Climacus, which stood on the site in the 14th century. The bell tower is called "the Great" because of its height. In 1600 it became the tallest building in Moscow when Tsar Boris Godunov added a third story to extend it to 81m (266 ft).

The four-storey Assumption Belfry, with its single gilded dome, was built beside the bell tower by Petrok Maliy in 1532–43. It holds 21 bells, the largest of which, the 64-tonne Assumption Bell, traditionally tolled three times when the tsar died. A small museum on the first floor houses changing displays

about the Kremlin. The tent-roofed annexe next to the belfry was commissioned by Patriarch Filaret in 1642.

Outside the bell tower is the enormous Tsar Bell. The largest in the world, it weighs over 200 tonnes. When it fell from the bell tower and shattered in a fire in 1701, the fragments were used in a second bell ordered by Tsarina Anna. This still lay in its casting pit when the Kremlin caught fire again in 1737. Cold water was poured over the hot bell and a large piece (displayed beside the bell) broke off.

The Tsar Bell, the largest in the world, with the 11.5-tonne section that broke off

Cathedral of the Assumption ❺
Успенский собор
Uspenskiy sobor

From the early 14th century, the Cathedral of the Assumption
was the most important church in Moscow. It was here that
princes were crowned and the metropolitans and patriarchs of the
Orthodox Church were buried. In the 1470s Ivan the Great *(see p18)*
decided to build a more imposing cathedral, to reflect the growing
might of the nation during his reign. When the first version collapsed
possibly in an earthquake, Ivan summoned the Italian architect
Aristotele Fioravanti to
Moscow. He designed a
light and spacious
masterpiece in the spirit
of the Renaissance.

**The golden
domes** stand on
towers inset
with windows
which allow
light to flood
into the interior
of the cathedral.

**Orthodox
cross**

**Scenes from the Life
of Metropolitan Peter**
*Attributed to the great
artist Dionysius* (see
p61)*, this 15th-century
icon is located on the
cathedral's south wall. It
depicts different events in
the life of this religious
and political leader.*

★ **Frescoes**
*In 1642–4, a team of artists headed by
Sidor Pospeev and Ivan and Boris
Paisein painted these frescoes. The walls
of the cathedral were first gilded to give
the look of an illuminated manuscript.*

**Metropolitans' and patriarchs'
tombs** line the walls of the nave
and the crypt. Almost all of the
leaders of the Russian Orthodox
Church are buried in the cathedral.

**The Tsarina's
Throne** (17th–
19th centuries)
is gilded and has
a double–headed
eagle crest.

**The
Tabernacle**
contains holy relics including the remains
of Patriarch Hermogen, who starved to death
in 1612 during the Polish invasion *(see p19)*.

**Western door
and main
entrance**

STAR FEATURES

★ Frescoes

★ Iconostasis

★ Iconostasis
The haunting 14th-century Icon of the Saviour Not Made With Hands is one of several icons forming part of the cathedral's iconostasis The iconostasis itself dates from 1652.

VISITORS' CHECKLIST

Kremlin. **Map** 7 A1. M *Alexandrovskiy sad, Biblioteka imeni Lenina, Borovitskaya.* 6, K. 1, 2, 12, 16, 33. 10am–5pm Fri–Wed. religious holidays. www.kremlin.museum.ru

Frescoes in the central dome

The pillars that stand in the centre of the cathedral are painted with over 100 figures of canonized martyrs and warriors.

Royal Gate

South Portal
This splendid arched portal, decorated with 17th-century frescoes, was the entrance used for royal processions Brought to Moscow from Suzdal in 1401 the door's reverse side is engraved with scenes from the Bible,

THE MONOMAKH THRONE

The royal seat of Ivan the Terrible *(see p18)* is decorated with carvings relating the exploits of Prince Vladimir Monomakh *(see p161)*. The panels depict his military campaigns and one shows him receiving the crown from the Byzantine emperor Constantine Monomachus. This legend was used to confer legitimacy on the idea that the Russian monarchs were the heirs to Byzantium.

Inscribed legend of Prince Vladimir

Panels depicting scenes from Vladimir's life

Monomakh Throne

The Harvest Chandelier contains silver recovered from the French after their occupation of the city in 1812 *(see pp23–5).*

The Patriarch's Seat was carved from white stone in 1653 for use by the head of the Russian Orthodox Church.

Cathedral of the Archangel ❻

Архангельский собор
Arkhangelskiy sobor

The Kremlin. **Map** 7 A2. 🖼

This was the last of the great cathedrals in the Kremlin to be built. It was commissioned by Ivan III in 1505, shortly before his death. Designed by a Venetian architect, Aleviz Novyy, it is a skilful combination of Early-Russian and Italian Renaissance architecture. The most striking of the Italian features is the scallop shell motif underneath the *zakomary* gables *(see p44)*.

This site was the burial place for Moscow's princes and tsars from 1340, first in an earlier cathedral and then in the current building. The tombs of the tsars, white stone sarcophagi with bronze covers inscribed in Old Slavonic, are in the nave. The tomb of Tsarevich Dmitry, the youngest son of Ivan the Terrible *(see p18)*, has a carved, painted canopy above it. The tsars were no longer buried here after the capital city was moved to St Petersburg in 1712. Peter II, who died of smallpox in Moscow in 1730, was the only later ruler to be buried here.

The walls, pillars and domes of the cathedral are covered with superb frescoes painted in 1652–66 by a team of artists led by Semen Ushakov, the head of the icon workshop in the State Armoury *(see pp64–5)*. There are over 60 full-length idealized portraits of Russian rulers, as well as some striking images of the Archangel Michael, traditionally the protector of the rulers of early Moscow.

The fresco in the cathedral's central cupola depicts the threefold nature of God. The Father holds the Son on his lap and the Holy Spirit, in the form of a white dove, hovers between them.

The four-tiered iconostasis was constructed in 1680–81. However, the Icon of the Archangel Michael on the lowest tier dates from the 14th century.

The glorious Cathedral of the Annunciation

Cathedral of the Annunciation ❼

Благовещенский собор
Blagoveshchenskiy sobor

The Kremlin. **Map** 7 A2. 🔵 for renovations. 🖼

Unlike the other Kremlin cathedrals, which were created by Italians, this cathedral is a wholly Russian affair. Commissioned by Ivan III in 1484 as a royal chapel, it stands beside the Faceted Palace *(see p62)*, which is all that remains of a large palace built for Ivan III around the same time. The cathedral, built by architects from Pskov *(see p44)*, originally had three domes and open galleries on all sides but, after a fire in 1547, the corner chapels were added and the galleries were enclosed. On the south façade is the Groznenskiy Porch, added by Ivan the Terrible when he contravened church law by marrying for the fourth time in 1572. Barred from attending religious services, he could only watch through a grille in the porch.

The whole of the interior of the cathedral, including the galleries, is painted with frescoes. The artwork around the iconostasis was painted in 1508 by the monk Feodosius, the son of the icon painter Dionysius who worked on the Cathedral of the Assumption *(see pp58–9)*. The warm colours of the frescoes create an atmosphere of intimacy (this was the tsars' family church). At the same time the vertical thrust of the pillars draws the eye upwards to the cupola and its awe-inspiring painting of Christ Pantocrator (Christ as ruler of the universe).

Three of the greatest masters of icon painting in Russia contributed to the iconostasis, widely considered the finest in Russia. Theophanes the Greek painted the images of Christ, the Virgin and the Archangel Gabriel in the Deesis Tier, while the Icon of the Archangel Michael on this tier is attributed to Andrey Rublev. Several of the icons in the Festival Tier, including *The Annunciation* and *The Nativity* were also painted by Rublev. Most of the other icons in this tier, including the *The Last Supper* and *The Crucifixion* are the work of Prokhor Gorodetskiy.

The fresco in the central cupola of the Cathedral of the Archangel

The Art of Icon Painting in Russia

The Russian Orthodox church uses icons for both worship and teaching and there are strict rules for creating each image. Icons were thought to be imbued with power from the saint they depicted and were invoked for protection during wars. Because content was more important than style, old revered icons were often repainted. The first icons were brought to Russia from

Festival Tier icon

Byzantium. Kiev was Russia's main icon painting centre until the Mongols conquered it in 1240. Influential schools then sprang up in Novgorod and the Vladimir-Suzdal area. The Moscow school was founded in the late 14th century and its greatest period was during the 15th century, when renowned icon-painters such as Andrey Rublev and Dionysius were at work.

The Virgin of Vladimir, *from 12th-century Byzantium, is highly venerated and has had a profound influence on Russian iconography.*

Theophanes the Greek *(c.1340–1405) is thought to have painted this icon of the Assumption (ascent into heaven) of the Virgin Mary. Originally from Byzantium, Theophanes became famous first in Novgorod and then in Moscow. The figures in his icons are renowned for their delicate features and individual expressions.*

ICONOSTASIS

Separating the sanctuary from the main part of the church, the iconostasis also symbolizes the boundary between the spiritual and temporal worlds. The icons are arranged in tiers (usually four, five or six), each with its own subject matter and significance.

The Festival Tier depicts important feast days and holidays in the Russian Orthodox calendar.

Christ Enthroned is always shown at the centre of the Deesis Tier, and is normally flanked by the Virgin Mary and John the Baptist.

An additional tier between the Local and Deesis Tiers often depicts the months of the year

The top tier of the iconostasis depicts patriarchs and prophets of the Old Testament.

The Deesis Tier is the most important in the iconostasis and depicts saints, apostles and archangels.

The Royal Gate, at the centre of the Local Tier, is usually decorated with panels showing the four apostles and the Annunciation – when Mary learns she is to bear the Son of God. The gate represents the entrance from the temporal to the spiritual world.

Andrey Rublev *became a monk at the Trinity Monastery of St Sergius (see pp162–5). Later he moved to a monastery in Moscow. Rublev painted this icon of the Archangel Michael in about 1410. The benevolent appearance of the archangel is typical of Rublev's figures.*

The Local Tier contains icons of saints with a strong link to the church, such as the church's namesake or saints after whom patrons of the church were named.

The enormous vaulted main hall of the Faceted Palace, which was lavishly repainted in the 1880s

Faceted Palace ❽

Грановитая палата
Granovitaya palata

The Kremlin. **Map** *7 A2.* ⬤ *to public.*

In the 19th century, the Faceted Palace, along with the Terem Palace, was incorporated into the Great Kremlin Palace. Named after its distinctive stonework façade, the Faceted Palace is all that is left of a larger 15th-century royal palace. It was commissioned by Ivan III *(see p18)* in 1485 and finished six years later. The Faceted Palace is the work of two Italian architects, Marco Ruffo and Pietro Solario.

The first floor of the Faceted Palace consists of the main hall and adjoining Sacred Vestibule. Both are decorated with rich frescoes and gilded carvings. The splendid vaulted main hall has an area of about 500 sq m (5,380 sq ft). It was the throne room and banqueting hall of the tsars and is now used for holding receptions.

On the palace's southern façade is the Red Staircase. The tsars passed down this staircase on their way to the Cathedral of the Assumption for their coronations. The last such procession was at the coronation of Nicholas II in 1896.

In the Streltsy Rebellion of 1682 *(see p22)* several of Peter the Great's relatives were hurled down the Red Staircase onto the pikes of the Streltsy guard.

Demolished by Stalin in the 1930s, the staircase was rebuilt in 1994 at great expense.

Church of the Deposition of the Robe ❾

Церковь Ризположения
Tserkov Rizopolozheniya

The Kremlin. **Map** *7 A1.* 🖼

Crowned by a single golden dome, this beautiful, but simply designed, church was built as the domestic church of the metropolitans in 1484-6. It was designed by architects from Pskov *(see p44)*

The church is named after a Byzantine feast day, which celebrates the arrival, in the city of Constantinople, of a robe supposed to have belonged to the Virgin Mary. The robe is believed to have saved the city from invasion several times.

The exterior of the church has distinctive ogee arches, which are shaped like the cross-section of an onion and feature on many Russian churches from this

The southern façade of the Faceted Palace, with the Red Staircase

period. They are a favourite device of the Pskov school of architecture. Inside the church, the walls and slender columns are covered with 17th-century frescoes by artists including Ivan Borisov, Sidor Pospeev and Semen Abramov. Many depict scenes from the life of the Virgin. Others depict Christ, the prophets, royalty and the Moscow metropolitans.

The impressive iconostasis was created by Nazariy Istomin in 1627. To the left of the royal gate is a splendid image of the Trinity and to its right is the patronal Icon of the Deposition of the Virgin's Robe.

The small, single-domed Church of the Deposition of the Robe

Terem Palace ⑩
Теремной дворец
Teremnoy dvorets

The Kremlin. **Map** *7* A2. 🔲 *to public.*

Commissioned by Tsar Mikhail Romanov *(see p19)*, the Terem Palace was built next to the Faceted Palace in 1635-7. It was constructed by a team of stonemasons led by Bazhen Ogurtsov. The palace takes its name from the *terem*, a pavilion-like structure with a red and white chequered roof on top of the main building. The interior has small, low-vaulted, simply furnished rooms.

The Tsar had five sumptuous rooms situated on the third floor of the palace. The ante-room, where boyars *(see p20)* and foreign dignitaries waited to be received, leads into the council chamber, where the tsar held meetings with boyars.

The ornately decorated anteroom in the Terem Palace

Beyond this are the throne room, the tsar's bedchamber and a small prayer room.

Most of the splendid Terem Palace is not visible from the areas of the Kremlin to which the public have access. The eleven richly decorated onion domes of the four palace churches, at one end of the palace, are all that can be seen.

Great Kremlin Palace ⑪
Большой Кремлёвский дворец|
Bolshoy Kremlevskiy dvorets

The Kremlin. **Map** *7* A2. 🔲 *to public.*

The impressive 125-m (410-ft) façade of this yellow and white palace is best admired from the Kremlin embankment, outside the Kremlin walls. The Great Kremlin Palace was built to replace the 18th-century

Kremlin Palace that previously stood on the site but had become dilapidated. In 1837 Tsar Nicholas I commissioned the Great Kremlin Palace as the Moscow residence of the royal family, where they stayed when visiting from St Petersburg, then the capital. Designed by a team of architects led by Konstantin Ton *(see p45)*, it took 12 years to build. Ton's design integrated the Terem and Faceted Palaces with the new palace, creating a single complex. He also rebuilt the State Armoury *(see pp64–5)*.

On the palace's ground floor are the luxurious private rooms of the royal family. The state chambers, on the first floor, include several vast ceremonial halls. The imposing St George's Hall has white walls engraved in gold with the names of those awarded the Order of St George, one of Russia's highest military decorations.

Despite spending massive amounts on the interior, the tsar rarely used the palace. In the 1930s two of the halls were joined to form a huge meeting room for the Supreme Soviet. Now the palace's halls are used to receive foreign dignitaries.

The Great Kremlin Palace viewed from the Kremlin embankment

State Armoury ⑫

Оружейная палата

Oruzheynaya palata

The collection of the State Armoury represents the wealth accumulated by Russian princes and tsars over many centuries. The first written mention of a state armoury occurs in 1508, but there were forges in the Kremlin producing weapons and armour as early as the 13th century. Later, gold- and silversmiths, workshops producing icons and embroidery, and the Office of the Royal Stables all moved into the Kremlin. The original armoury was demolished in 1960 to make way for the State Kremlin Palace *(see p56)*. The current State Armoury was built as a museum on the orders of Nicholas I. It was designed by Konstantin Ton *(see p45)* in 1844 and was completed in 1851.

★ Fabergé Eggs

This egg, also a musical box, was made in 1904 in the St Petersburg workshops of the famous House of Fabergé. The egg forms part of a stylized model of the Kremlin.

Arms and armour made in the Kremlin workshops are on show here, along with items from Western Europe and Persia.

4

3

Carriages and Sledges

This magnificent collection includes the beautiful gilded summer carriage shown here. It was presented to Catherine the Great (see p23) by Count Orlov. The oldest carriage displayed was a gift from King James I of England to Boris Godunov.

5

First Floor

9

THE STATE DIAMOND FUND

This dazzling exhibition of diamonds, crowns, jewellery and state regalia includes the famous Orlov Diamond. Taken from an Indian temple, it was one of many presents given to Catherine the Great by her lover Count Grigoriy Orlov. The tsarina had it mounted at the top of her sceptre. Also on show are Catherine's imperial crown, inset with almost 5,000 gems, and the Shah Diamond, which was given to Tsar Nicholas I by Shah Mirza.

Ground floor

Ambassadors' gifts, presented by visiting emissaries from the Netherlands, Poland, England and Scandinavia are displayed here.

The Orlov Diamond on the sceptre of Catherine the Great

Main entrance from the Kremlin grounds

★ Crown of Monomakh

Emperor Constantine Monomachus was said to have given this 13th- or 14th-century gold crown to Vladimir Monomakh (see p59). Decorated with sable and gems, it was used at royal coronations until 1682.

VISITORS' CHECKLIST

The Kremlin. **Map** 7 A2. *Tel* (495) 921 4720. Ⓜ Alexandrovskiy sad, Biblioteka imeni Lenina, Borovitskaya. ⬜ admittance at 10am, 12pm, 2:30pm and 4:30pm Fri–Wed. 🎫 📷 🎦 English (book in advance: 202 4256). 🚻 **State Diamond Fund** *Tel* 629 2036. ⬜ 10am–1pm, 2pm–5pm Fri–Wed. 🎫 🎦 English. 🚻

Stairs to first floor

Stairs to ground floor

Precious fabrics

1

6

7

State Diamond Fund entrance

★ Catherine the Great's Coronation Dress

Among the richly decorated clothes from the royal court is an ornate brocade gown embroidered with double-headed eagles in gold thread. It was made in 1762 for Catherine the Great's coronation.

GALLERY GUIDE

Tickets for the State Armoury are sold at the Kremlin's main ticket office near Trinity Tower. If visiting in conjunction with other sights in the Kremlin, continue through the Trinity Tower. If only visiting the State Armoury, entry is via the Borovitskaya Tower. The State Diamond Fund, a separate museum, is also housed in this building.

Harnesses and other equipment, originally produced for the Office of the Royal Stables, are on show here.

Diamond Throne
Made in Persia in 1659, this throne was presented to Tsar Alexis (see p19) by an Armenian trading company. It is encrusted with 900 diamonds and turquoises and is the most valuable throne in the collection.

STAR EXHIBITS

- ★ Fabergé Eggs
- ★ Crown of Monomakh
- ★ Catherine the Great's Coronation Dress

KEY

⬜	Russian gold and silver
⬜	Arms and armour
⬜	Works by European craftsmen
⬜	Russian dress and fabrics
⬜	Carriages and harnesses
⬜	State regalia
⬜	Non-exhibition space

Saviour's Tower ⑬
Спасская башня
Spasskaya bashnya

The Kremlin. **Map** 7 B1.

Rising majestically above Red Square to a height of 70 m (230 ft), Saviour's Tower is named after an icon of Christ installed over its gate in 1648. The gate is no longer open to the public, but it used to be the Kremlin's main entrance.

Saviour's Tower, once the main entrance to the Kremlin

Every person using Saviour's Gate, even the tsar, had to indicate respect for the icon by taking his hat off. The icon was removed after the Revolution.

Saviour's Tower was built in two stages. The lower part was designed by Italian architect Pietro Solario in 1491. Bazhen Ogurtsov and Englishman Christopher Galloway added the upper part and tent roof in 1625. Originally the chimes of the clock played the *Preobrazhenskyy March* and *Kol' Slaven Nash Gospod' v Sione*. Now they play the Russian National Anthem.

Presidential Administration ⑭
Администрация Президента
Administraya Presidenta

The Kremlin. **Map** 7 A1. ⬤ *to public.*

Two important religious institutions, the Monastery of the Miracles and the Convent of the Ascension, used to stand here. They were demolished in 1929 to make way for the Presidential Administration. The building was originally used as a training school for Red Army officers, and later as the headquarters of the Presidium of the Supreme Soviet, an executive arm of the Soviet parliament. Today it is home to part of the Russian presidential administration.

The Presidential Administration

Senate ⑮
Сенат
Senat

The Kremlin. **Map** 7 A1. ⬤ *to public.*

Completed in 1790, this Neo-Classical building was constructed to house several of the Senate's departments. Designed by Matvey Kazakov (*see pp44–5*), who regarded it as his best work, it is triangular, with a central, domed rotunda, from which the Russian flag flies.

KREMLIN TOWERS

There are 19 towers in the walls of the Kremlin, with a bridge leading from the Trinity Tower to a 20th, the Kutafya Tower. In 1935 the double-headed imperial eagles were removed from the five tallest towers and replaced two years later with stars made of red glass, each weighing between 1 and 1.5 tonnes.

Borovitskaya Tower

Annunciation Tower

Armoury Tower

Commandant's Tower

Trinity Tower (*see p56*)

Middle Arsenal Tower (hidden)

Corner Arsenal Tower

Nicholas' Tower is the tower through which Minin and Pozharskiy (*see p108*) stormed the Kremlin.

Senate Tower

Water Tower

The Secret Tower has an underground passage leading to the river. It was used to obtain water during sieges.

First Nameless Tower

Second Nameless Tower

Peter's Tower

Constantine and Helena Tower

Beklemishevskaya Tower

Saviour's Tower

Tsar's Tower

Tocsin Tower

0 metres 100
0 yards 100

The domed rotunda of the yellow and white Senate, behind the Senate Tower and the Lenin Mausoleum

From 1918 to 1991, the Senate housed the Soviet government. Lenin had his office here and his family lived in a flat on the top floor. During World War II the Red Army Supreme Command, headed by Stalin, was based in the building.

Today the Senate is the official seat of the president of the Russian Federation.

Corner Arsenal Tower with the Arsenal and Nicholas' Tower

Arsenal **16**

Арсенал
Arsenal

The Kremlin. **Map** 7 A1. ● to public.

Peter the Great ordered the Arsenal to be built in 1701, but various setbacks, including a fire in 1711, delayed its completion until 1736. In 1812 the building was partly blown up by Napoleon's army *(see pp23–5)*. Architects Aleksandr

Bakarev, Ivan Tamanskiy, Ivan Mironovskiy and Evgraf Tyurin were commissioned to design a new Arsenal. Their attractive yellow and white Neo-Classical building was finished in 1828.

The Arsenal was constructed as a storehouse for weapons, ammunition and other military supplies. Around 750 cannons, including some that were captured from Napoleon's retreating troops, are lined up outside. Now the command post of the Kremlin guard, the interior and much of the exterior of the Arsenal are strictly out of bounds to visitors.

Alexander Gardens **17**

Александровский сад
Aleksandrovskiy sad

The Kremlin. **Map** 7 A1.

Designed by architect Osip Bove *(see p45)* in 1821, these gardens are named after Tsar Alexander I, who presided over the restoration of the city, including the Kremlin, after the Napoleonic Wars. Before the gardens were built, the Neglinnaya river, part of the Kremlin moat, was channelled underground. The only visible reminder of its presence is the stone bridge linking the Kutafya and Trinity towers.

In front of the Middle Arsenal Tower in the northern half of the gardens is an obelisk erected in 1913 to mark 300 years of the Romanov dynasty. The

imperial eagle was taken down after the Revolution and the inscription was replaced by the names of revolutionary thinkers, such as Karl Marx and Friedrich Engels.

The Tomb of the Unknown Soldier, a short distance away, was unveiled in 1967. Its eternal flame was lit with a torch lit from the flame at the Field of Mars in St Petersburg. It burns for all the Russians who died in World War II. The body of a soldier is buried beneath the monument, which bears an inscription, "Your name is unknown, your deeds immortal".

In 1996, a huge shopping complex was constructed beneath Manezhnaya ploshchad, the large square to the north of Alexander Gardens.

Path through Alexander Gardens, with the Trinity Tower behind

ARBATSKAYA

The name "Arbat" is thought to derive from a Mongol word meaning suburb, and was first applied in the 15th century to the entire area west of the Kremlin, then inhabited by the tsar's artisans and equerries. Though still commemorated in street names, the artisans moved elsewhere in the late 18th century. The aristocracy moved in and were followed by Moscow's professionals,

Fayoum portrait, Pushkin Museum

intellectuals and artists, attracted by the area's rambling backstreets, dilapidated cottages and overgrown courtyards. In the Old Arbat, with its pedestrianized main street, there are historic churches, timber houses and early 19th-century mansions around pereulok Sivtsev Vrazhek. Yet, not far away are the kiosks, cafés and huge Soviet-era apartment blocks and shops of the New Arbat.

SIGHTS AT A GLANCE

Museums and Galleries
Bely House-Museum **5**
Gallery of European and American Art of the 19th–20th Centuries **8**
Lermontov House-Museum **13**
Museum of Private Collections **10**
Pushkin House-Museum **4**
Pushkin Museum of Fine Arts pp78–81 **9**
Shalyapin House-Museum **14**
Skryabin House-Museum **1**

Cathedrals
Cathedral of Christ the Redeemer **7**

Historic Buildings
Melnikov House **3**
Pashkov House **11**

Streets and Squares
Arbat Square **12**
Spasopeskovskiy Pereulok **2**
Ulitsa Prechistenka **6**

KEY

Street-by-Street map *pp70–71*

M Metro station

GETTING THERE

This area is served by several metro stations: Arbatskaya, Biblioteka imeni Lenina, Borovitskaya, Kropotkinskaya and Smolenskaya. It is also easily accessible by trolleybus (1, 2, 5, 10, 15, 16, 31, 33, 39, 79, & B) and there are several buses that run through the district (6, 64, 132 & K).

0 metres 400
0 yards 400

◁ Busy ulitsa Arbat, the heart of the Old Arbat, overlooked by the monumental Stalinist Foreign Affairs Ministry

Street-by-Street: Old Arbat

At the heart of the Old Arbat is the pedestrianized ulitsa Arbat. It is lined with antique shops, boutiques, book stalls, pavement cafés and a variety of restaurants, from pizzerias and hamburger joints to lively examples of the traditional Russian pub (*traktir*). In the 19th century, the Old Arbat was the haunt of artists, musicians, poets, writers and intellectuals. Some of their homes have been preserved and opened as museums, and are among the district's many houses of that era that have been lovingly restored and painted in pastel shades of blue, green and ochre. Today, pavement artists, buskers and street poets give it a renewed bohemian atmosphere.

Spaso House
is a grand Neo-Classical mansion. It has been the residence of the US ambassador since 1933.

This small garden
contains a statue of the poet Alexander Pushkin.

Novyy Arbat ↑

★ Pushkin House-Museum
The poet Alexander Pushkin lived here just after his marriage in 1831. The interior of the house has been carefully renovated ❹

Ulitsa Arbat
By the time of the Soviet era, ulitsa Arbat had lost most of its 19th-century character. It was pedestrianized in 1985, however, and its lively shops, restaurants and cafés are now popular with Muscovites and visitors to the city alike.

Smolenskaya

Bely House-Museum
Andrei Bely, best known for two works, a novel, Petersburg, and his memoirs, lived in this flat for the first 26 years of his life. It is now a museum and the exhibits on display include this photo of Bely with his wife and the fascinating illustration, Line of Life *(see p73)* ❺

Georgian Centre

The Foreign Ministry
is one of Moscow's seven Stalinist-Gothic skyscrapers *(see p45)*.

Spasopeskovskiy Pereulok

On one side of this peaceful lane is the 18th-century Church of the Saviour on the Sands, with its white bell tower. It overlooks a secluded square and garden, a reminder that the Arbat was at that time a genteel suburb **2**

LOCATOR MAP
See Street Finder, map 6

The Vakhtangova Theatre was established here in 1921 by Yevgeniy Vakhtangov, one of Moscow's leading theatre directors. The current theatre building dates from 1947.

BOLSHOY NIKOLOPESKOVSKIY PEREULOK

Arbat Square

ULITSA ARBAT

KALOSHIN PEREULOK

★ Skryabin House-Museum

This comfortable apartment has been preserved as it was in 1912–15 when experimental composer Aleksandr Skryabin lived here. The furniture in the rooms is Style Moderne and the lighting is dim, since Skryabin disliked direct light **1**

Pushkin Museum of Fine Arts

The Herzen House-Museum was the home of the radical writer Aleksandr Herzen for three years from 1843.

| 0 metres | 100 |
| 0 yards | 100 |

STAR SIGHTS

★ Pushkin House-Museum

★ Skryabin House-Museum

KEY

- - - Suggested route

These pre-Revolution apartments, designed for wealthy Muscovites, are decorated with fanciful turrets and sculptures of knights.

Melnikov House

This unusual cylindrical house is now dwarfed by the apartments on ulitsa Arbat. It was built in the 1920s by Constructivist architect Konstantin Melnikov, who lived here until his death in 1974 **3**

Skryabin House-Museum ❶
Дом-музей АН Скрябина
Dom-muzey AN Skryabina

Bolshoy Nikolopeskovskiy pereulok 11. **Map** 6 D1. **Tel** *(499) 241 1901.* Ⓜ *Smolenskaya, Arbatskaya.* ◯ *noon–6pm Wed & Fri–Sun, 10am–5pm Thu.* 🎫 🎥 *English (book in advance).*

The flat where the pianist and composer Aleksandr Skryabin (1872–1915) died, at the age of 43, has been preserved as it was when he lived there. Skryabin studied at the Moscow Conservatory *(see p94)*, where he established an international reputation as a concert pianist. He was also a highly original composer and musical theorist, best known for his orchestral works such as *Prometheus* and *A Poem of Ecstasy*. Skryabin's music had a great influence on the young Igor Stravinsky (1882–1971), and leading composer Sergei Rachmaninov (1873–1943) was a regular visitor to his flat.

Although Skryabin spent much of his time abroad giving concerts, he was an aesthete and paid considerable attention to furnishing and decorating his fashionable apartment. The lofty rooms house his pianos, autographed manuscripts and Style-Moderne furniture. However, the most original item on

A room in Aleksandr Skryabin's apartment, with one of his pianos

The Classical-style Spaso House on Spasopeskovskaya ploshchad

show is a device for projecting flickering light. Regular concerts are held in the rooms on the ground floor.

Spasopeskovskiy Pereulok ❷
Спасопесковский переулок
Spasopeskovskiy pereulok

Map 6 D1. Ⓜ *Smolenskaya.*

The charms of the Old Arbat have been preserved in this secluded lane and the peaceful adjoining square, Spasopeskovskaya ploshchad. In 1878, Vasiliy Polenov painted *A Moscow Courtyard*, depicting Spasopeskovskaya ploshchad as a bucolic haven in the midst of the city. Today the square still provides a respite from the hustle and bustle prevailing elsewhere.

At the centre of Polenov's picture, now in the Tretyakov Gallery *(see pp118–21)*, is the white bell tower of the Church of the Saviour on the Sands (Tserkov Spas na Peskakh) from which the lane gets its name. This 18th-century church still dominates the square. In front of it is a small garden dedicated to the poet Alexander Pushkin.

The handsome Classical-style mansion standing on the far side of the square was built in 1913 as a private residence. Known as Spaso House, it has been the home of the US ambassador since 1933.

Melnikov House ❸
Дом Мельникова
Dom Melnikova

Krivoarbatskiy pereulok 10. **Map** 6 D1. Ⓜ *Smolenskaya.* ◯ *to public.*

This unique house, almost hidden by office blocks, was designed by Konstantin Melnikov (1890–1974), one of Russia's greatest Constructivist architects *(see p45)*, in 1927.

Made from brick overlaid with white stucco, the house consists of two interlocking cylinders. These are studded with rows of hexagonal

Viktor Melnikov's studio in the Melnikov House

windows, creating a curious honeycomb effect. A spiral staircase rises through the space where the cylinders overlap, linking the light, airy living spaces.

Melnikov's house was built for his family, but it was also to have been a prototype for future housing developments. However, his career was blighted when Stalin encouraged architects to adopt a new monumental style *(see p45)*. Although he had won the Gold Medal at the Paris World's Fair in 1925, Melnikov's work was ridiculed or ignored. However, he did remain in his house for the rest of his life, one of the very few residents of central Moscow allowed to live in a privately built dwelling.

Melnikov's son, Viktor Melnikov, had a studio in the house until his death in 2006.

ALEXANDER PUSHKIN

Born in 1799 into Russia's aristocracy, Alexander Pushkin is
Russia's most famous poet. He
had established a reputation as
both a poet and a rebel by the
time he was 20. In 1820, he
was sent into exile because the
Tsarist government did not
approve of his liberal verse,
but eventually was set free.

Pushkin's early work consisted
of narrative poems such as *The
Robber Brothers* (1821), and his
most famous work is *Eugene Onegin* (1823–30), a novel in
verse. From 1830 Pushkin wrote mostly prose. He developed
a unique style in pieces such as *The Queen of Spades* (1834)
and is credited with giving Russian literature its own identity.

Pushkin
House-Museum ❹

Музей-квартира АС
Пушкина
Muzey-kvartira AS Pushkina

Ulitsa Arbat 53. **Map** 6 D2. **Tel** (499)
241 9293. **M** *Smolenskaya.* ▢
10am–6pm Wed–Sun. 🖼 📷 📹
English (book in advance).

Alexander Pushkin rented this
elegant, blue and white Empire-
style flat for the first three
months of his marriage to
society beauty Natalya
Goncharova. They were married
in the Church of the Great
Ascension on Bolshaya
Nikitskaya ulitsa *(see p93)* in
February 1831, when she was
18 years old. Pushkin wrote to
his friend Pyotr Pletnev: "I am
married – and happy. My only
wish is that nothing in my life
should change; I couldn't
possibly expect anything better."

However, by May 1831
Pushkin had tired of
life in Moscow, and
the couple moved to
St Petersburg, where
sadly a tragic fate
awaited him. Gossip
began to circulate
there that Pushkin's
brother-in-law, a
French officer called
d'Anthès, was making
advances to Natalya.
Upon receiving letters
informing him that he
was now the "Grand
Master to the Order of
Cuckolds", Pushkin
challenged d'Anthès

to a duel. Mortally wounded in
the contest, Pushkin died two
days later.

The fascinating exhibition
located in the
museum's ground
floor rooms gives
an idea of what the
city would have
been like in the
period when
Pushkin was grow-
ing up, before the
great fire of 1812.
Among the prints,
lithographs and
watercolours are
some unusual wax
figures of a serf
orchestra that
belonged to the
Goncharova family.

Pushkin and Natalya lived on
the first floor. There are
disappointingly few personal
possessions here, although the
poet's writing bureau and some
family portraits are displayed.
The atmosphere resembles a

**A portrait of Pushkin's
wife, Natalya Goncharova**

shrine more than a museum.
Pushkin holds a special place
in Russians' hearts and they
treat his work and memory
with reverence.

Bely House-
Museum ❺

Музей-квартира Андрея
Белого
Muzey-kvartira Andreya Belovo

Ulitsa Arbat 55. **Map** 6 D2. **Tel** (199)
241 7702. **M** *Smolenskaya.* ▢
10am–6pm Wed–Sun. 🖼 📷 📹

In the adjoining building to
the Pushkin House-Museum
is the childhood home of the
symbolist writer Andrei Bely.
Bely was born Boris Bugaev
in 1880, but later adopted the
name by which he is known
as a writer. He grew up here
before becoming a
student at Moscow
University *(see
p94)*, where he
began to write
verse. He is best
known, however,
for *Petersburg*, a
novel completed
in 1916, and for
his memoirs.

Only two rooms
of the Bugaev fam-
ily apartment have
been preserved.
A photographic
exhibition on the
writer's life and
work is housed in one room.
The most interesting item in
the museum is the *Line of
Life*, an illustration by Bely to
show how his mood swings
combined with cultural influ-
ences to direct his work.

The *Line of Life* illustration drawn by the symbolist writer Andrei Bely

Stone eagles among the ornate decoration on No. 20 ulitsa Prechistenka

Ulitsa Prechistenka ❻

Улица Пречистенка
Ulitsa Prechistenka

Map 6 D3–E2. Ⓜ *Kropotkinskaya.*

Moscow's Aristocracy first settled in this street in the late 18th century and their elegant mansions still line it today. In Soviet times it was known as Kropotkinskaya ulitsa, after Prince Pyotr Kropotkin, a famous anarchist *(see p23)*.

The Empire-style house at No.12 ulitsa Prechistenka is now the Pushkin Literary Museum (not to be confused with the Pushkin House-Museum, *see p73*). The house was originally designed for the Khrushchev family (no connection with Nikita Khrushchev) by Afanasiy Grigorev *(see p45)*, one of the leading exponents of this style in Moscow. The building has a wooden frame, skilfully hidden by Classical columns and ornate stucco decoration.

Across the street another great writer is honoured at No. 11 in the Tolstoy Literary Museum. In contrast to the Tolstoy House-Museum *(see p134)*, it concentrates on the man's work rather than his life. The building however, has no connection with Tolstoy; it was built in 1822, also to a design by Afanasiy Grigorev, for the noble Lopukhin family. On display are many letters, manuscripts and family portraits.
At No. 20 is an elegant two-

storey mansion decorated with eagles, urns, heraldic symbols and scallop shells. Until 1861 it was home to General Aleksey Yermolov, a commander-in-chief in the Russian army. After the Revolution, the American dancer Isadora Duncan and the poet Sergey Yesenin lived here during their brief, tempestuous marriage.

The two spoke no common language, and Yesenin stated his feelings by writing the Russian for "I love you" in lipstick on the bedroom mirror.

Lion at No. 16 ulitsa Prechistenka

The most distinguished house is at No. 19. Rebuilt after the 1812 fire *(see p24)* for the Dolgorukov family, it has an ochre and white façade. Adjoining it, at No. 21, is another early 19th-century mansion, now the Academy of Arts, where exhibitions are sometimes put on.

Cathedral of Christ the Redeemer ❼

Храм Христа Спасителя
Khram Khrista Spasitelya

Ulitsa Volkhonka 15. **Map** 6 F2.
Ⓜ *Kropotkinskaya.*

Rebuilding this cathedral, blown up on Stalin's orders in 1931, was the most ambitious of the construction projects undertaken by the enterprising mayor of Moscow, Yuriy Luzhkov. The basic structure of the new cathedral

was built between 1994–97. For much of the intervening time, the site was occupied by an outdoor swimming pool, but this was eventually filled in.

The project courted controversy from the start, both on grounds of taste and cost. In 1995 a presidential decree declared that not a kopek of public money should be spent on it – funds were to be raised through donations from the public, the Russian Church and foreign donors among the big multinational companies operating in Russia. However, in practice, the better part of the total bill of over US$200 million came from the state budget, which raised objections at a time when Muscovites were suffering extreme poverty.

The original cathedral was built to commemorate the miraculous deliverance of Moscow from Napoleon's Grande Armée *(see pp23–4)*. Begun in 1839, but not completed until 1883, it was designed by Konstantin Ton *(see p45)*. The cathedral was the tallest building in Moscow at that time, the gilded dome rising to a height of 103 m (338 ft) and dominating the skyline for miles around. It could accommodate more than 10,000 worshippers.

Boris Yeltsin lay in state here after his death in 2007, and in 1998, a small museum and a church on the ground floor opened to the public. There are spectacular views of the city from the dome.

Cathedral of Christ the Redeemer, rebuilt in the 1990s at huge cost

Paul Cézanne's *Mont Ste Victoire*, painted in 1905

Gallery of 19th- and 20th-Century European and American Art ❽

Музей Галерея искусства стран Европы и Америки XIX–XX веков
Galeryeya Iskusstva Stran Evropi I Ameriki X1X–XX Vekov

Ulitsa Volkhonka 14. **Map** 6 F2. **Tel** *(495) 697 1546.* ☐ *10am–7pm Tue–Sun (last admission 6pm).* Ⓜ *Kropotkinskaya.* 🖼 📷

Opened in 2006, this museum consists of Impressionist and post-Impressionist paintings that were previously displayed in the Pushkin Museum of Fine Arts next door. Some of the paintings are also from the St Petersburg's Hermitage, where a large number were kept in storerooms for many years.

Many were displayed in a Soviet-era museum of Western art that was opened in 1918 under orders from Lenin. The museum was closed by Stalin in 1948, however, as he considered the works "bourgeois propaganda".

The first of the gallery's three floors displays mainly European oil paintings from the first half of the 19th century, with works by artists such as Alexandre-Gabriel Decamps.

The real masterpieces are on the remaining two floors, however. Here, there are a number of paintings by Vincent Van Gogh, including *The Red Vineyard at Arles* (1888) and *Prisoners Exercising* (1890), as well as Pierre Auguste Renoir's *Nude* (1876) and *Bathing on the Seine* (1879). The same floor also holds Paul Cézanne's *Mont Ste Victoire* (1905) and a series of paintings by Paul Gauguin, including a fine selection from the artist's Polynesian period.

The third floor is just as impressive, and contains a number of works by Henri Matisse, including *Goldfish* (1911–12), and Pablo Picasso's *Girl Standing on a Ball* (1905). Russia is also represented, with paintings by Wassily Kandinsky, including *Improvisation No. 20a* (1911).

Pushkin Museum of Fine Arts ❾

See pp78–81.

Museum of Private Collections ❿

Музей личных коллекций
Muzey lichnykh kollektsiy

Ulitsa Volkhonka 14. **Map** 6 F2. **Tel** *(495) 203 1546.* ☐ *noon–6pm Wed–Sun.* Ⓜ *Kropotkinskaya.* 🖼 📷

Before the revolution the Knyazhiy Dvor hotel, whose guests included Maxim Gorky and artist Ilya Repin, occupied this building.

The museum opened in 1994 and is based on private collections. The largest is that of Ilya Zilberstein, which includes a vast range of work by prominent Russian artists such as Ivan Shishkin, Ilya Repin and Konstantin Somov. There are also works by Aleksandr Rodchenko, and rooms devoted to periodic specialist exhibitions.

The Museum of Private Collections, housed in a former hotel

STALIN'S PLAN FOR A PALACE OF SOVIETS

The original Cathedral of Christ the Redeemer was to have been replaced by a Palace of Soviets – a soaring tower, 315m (1,034 ft) high, topped by a 100-m (328-ft) statue of Lenin. It was designed as the highlight of Stalin's reconstruction of Moscow, much of the rest of which was realized: broad boulevards, skyscrapers and the metro system *(see pp38–41)* are now familiar features of the city. The result was also, however, the destruction of many supposedly unnecessary buildings, especially churches and monasteries, even inside the Kremlin. The scheme for the Palace of Soviets was eventually abandoned and the cathedral was rebuilt in the 1990s.

Artist's impression of Stalin's proposed awe-inspiring Palace of Soviets

---

Pushkin Museum of Fine Arts ❾

Музей изобразительных искусств имени АС Пушкина
Muzey izobrazitelnykh iskusstv imeni AS Pushkina

Founded in 1898, the Pushkin Museum houses a fine collection of works from antiquity to the early 19th century. Following the collapse of the Soviet Union *(see pp30–31)*, the curators admitted that they had countless works of art hidden away. Some of these are now on show, including Schliemann's "Treasures of Troy" excavations, which were taken from the Museum of Ancient History in Berlin by Soviet military authorities in 1945. The building was designed by Roman Klein. It was first built to house plaster casts of classical sculptures for Moscow University art students to use for research.

Room 23 houses mostly 18th–19th-century French paintings.

Museum Building
The design of the building borrows from Ancient Greece, Italy, France and Germany to create a suitably impressive facade and interior.

Stairs to ground floor

First floor

Room 3 houses Schliemann's "Treasures of Troy".

GALLERY GUIDE

The ticket office is in the entrance hall. The displays are spread over two floors, but although the museum halls are numbered, the layout is not strictly chronological. The ground floor houses all of the works from ancient civilizations as well as Byzantine art and Italian, Dutch and Flemish art from the 13th to the 17th centuries. Spanish, Italian and French art from the 17th to the early 19th centuries is upstairs. The cloakroom and toilets are in the basement.

STAR PAINTINGS

★ Annunciation by Botticelli

★ Fayoum Portrait

★ Bacchanlia by Peter Paul Rubens

★ **Annunciation**
Painted around 1490 by Italian artist Sandro Botticelli, this work was originally part of a large altar-piece. It shows the angel Gabriel telling the Virgin Mary she is to bear the Son of God.

KEY

- ☐ Collection of plaster casts
- ☐ Art of ancient civilizations
- ☐ Italian art: 13th–16th centuries
- ☐ German, Dutch and Flemish art: 15th–17th centuries
- ☐ Spanish and Italian art: 17th–18th centuries
- ☐ French art: 17th–early 19th centuries
- ☐ Temporary exhibition space

Betrothal of the Venetian Doge to the Adriatic Sea
Venetian landscape painter, Canaletto, was known for his bold use of colour, exemplfied in this scene of the Grand Canal (1729–30).

VISITORS' CHECKLIST

Ulitsa Volkhonka 12.
Map 6 F2. **Tel** (495) 697 9578.
Ⓜ *Kropotkinskaya.* 🚌 1,2,16,
33. ◯ 10am–7pm Tue–Sun
(until 9pm Thu). 📷 ⬜ 🏪
📽 English.
www.museum.ru/gmii

Room 10 is dedicated to Rembrandt and his School and includes drawings, etchings and six paintings by the great master.

Ahasuerus, Haman and Esther
In this biblical scene by Rembrandt (1660), the Persian king, Ahasuerus, is flanked by his Jewish wife and his minister, Haman. Esther, lit by a single ray of light, accuses Haman of plotting to destroy the Jews.

Stairs to first floor

★ Bacchanalia
Based on the myth of the god of nature, vegetation and viniculture, Dionysus-Bacchus, this splendidly exuberant, sensual painting (c.1615) did not leave the possession of its artist, Peter Paul Rubens, his entire life.

Tickets and information

Entrance

★ Fayoum Portrait
Painted in the 1st century AD, this is one of a collection of portraits discovered at a burial ground at the Fayoum oasis in Egypt in the 1870s. They were painted while the subjects were still alive to be used as death masks

Ground floor

Exploring the Pushkin Museum of Fine Arts

Religious icon (c.14th–15th century)

In addition to the collection of plaster casts, the accumulated treasures of original work in the Pushkin Museum of Fine Arts reflect the tastes of many private collectors, whose holdings were given as gifts to the museum. The largest of these belonged to the Egyptologist Vladimir Golenishchev who assembled some 6,000 items during his travels in Egypt. The museum also contains many important pieces of European art from the 13th to the early 19th centuries, including work by Rembrandt, Rubens, Van Dyck, Botticelli, Poussin and Canaletto, among many others.

was a major artistic centre in the 14th century and Simone Martini was a leading master of the Sienese school. His naturalistic images of St Augustine and Mary Magdalene, painted in the 1320s, are among the exhibits.

There are also a number of later religious pieces on show, including a triptych by Pietro di Giovanni Lianori. Two outstanding old masters painted in the 1490s are also displayed here: the superb *Annunciation*, painted by Sandro Botticelli, and the *Madonna and Child* by Pietro Perugino.

Greek marble sarcophagus, dating from around AD 210

COLLECTION OF PLASTER CASTS

The huge collection of plaster casts fills ten rooms and offers a fine backdrop to the original works. Room 14, The Greek Courtyard, is devoted to Greek architecture and sculpture from the 4th and 5th centuries and includes a scale model of the Acropolis and Parthenon.

Room 15 reproduces the inner courtyard of the 14th-century palazzo de Podesta in Florence. On the first floor the collection continues with the art of ancient Greece and Rome, and Renaissance sculpture from Italy, the Netherlands and Germany. Room 29 is devoted entirely to the work of Michelangelo.

ART OF ANCIENT CIVILIZATIONS

The museum's archaeological exhibits come from as far afield as ancient Mesopotamia, Hindustan and the Mayan Empire. The display includes the renowned and remarkably vivid tomb portraits from Fayoum and two exquisite

ebony figurines of the high priest Amen-Hotep and his wife, the priestess Re-nai.

Another highlight is the fabulous Treasure of Troy display, with gold artifacts excavated from the legendary city in the 1870s. There is also an assortment of items from ancient Greece and Rome.

BYZANTINE ART AND ITALIAN ART: 13TH–16TH CENTUIRES

Room 7 contains a small, but memorable collection of Byzantine icons, including miniature folding icons and ivory carvings from the 10th century. There is also some later work, such as the splendidly luminous *Twelve Apostles* painted by Constantinopolitan masters in the early 14th century.

Italian Medieval and Renaissance art is also represented here. There is a series of altar panels painted in the Byzantine tradition by Italian artists. Siena

GERMAN, DUTCH AND FLEMISH ART: 15TH–17TH CENTURIES

The museum is particularly well endowed with German, Dutch and Flemish Renaissance art. Room 8 includes Pieter Breughel the Younger's *Winter Landscape with Bird Trap* (1620s) – a copy of a similar painting by his father, Breughel the Elder – and a strong collection by the Saxon court painter, Lucas Cranach the Elder. His *Virgin and Child* (c.1520), painted on wood, places the Virgin and Child in the context of a typical German landscape.

Rooms 9 and 11 are equally rich with masters. They include Anthony Van Dyck's accomplished portraits of the

A section of the *Virgin and Child*, painted by Lucas Cranach the Elder in about 1525

wealthy burgher, Adriaen Stevens, and his wife, Maria Boschaert, both painted in 1629, and some evocative landscapes by Jan Van Goyen and Jacob van Ruysdael. Also on show are still lifes by Frans Snyders, some delightful genre scenes by Jan Steen, Pieter de Hooch and Gabriel Metsu and several works by Peter Paul Rubens, including *Apotheosis of the Infanta Isabella* (1634) and, in place of honour, the characteristically flamboyant *Bacchanalia* (c.1615).

Six of Rembrandt's masterly canvases, along with some of his drawings and etchings, are displayed in Room 10 of the gallery. The paintings include the biblical *Ahasuerus, Haman and Esther* (1660), *Christ Driving the Money-Changers from the Temple* (1626) and the theatrical *The Incredulity of Thomas* (1634). However, it is perhaps the later *Portrait of an Old Woman* (1654), actually of the artist's mother, that demonstrates the great skill of the artist. Here, the shadowed, stooping figure seems almost weighed down by memories.

SPANISH AND ITALIAN ART: 17TH–18TH CENTURIES

Room 18 of the gallery has a modest collection of Spanish paintings from the 17th century and only the most important are on display. Of note are the lifelike religious figures by Fransciso de Zurbarán, such as *The Infant Christ* (1635–1640) painted late in his life. However it is another Spanish master, Bartholomé Esteban Murillo, known for the warmth and emotion caught in his religious scenes and portraits, who is probably the best known. Works include *Girl Selling Fruit* and *Archangel Raphael and Bishop Domonte* (1680).

Of the Italian works on display here, the influence of Caravaggio is felt, particularly in *Christ is Crowned with Thorns* (c. 1610) by the relatively unknown artist Tommaso Salini, and the great artist's pupil Domenico Fetti

and his follower Bernardo Strozzi. The latter's *Old Coquette* (after 1630) shows a grey-haired woman sitting in front of a mirror, while her maids giggle in the background. It is a grotesque yet poignant depiction of the cruelty of time. Another trend of the era was the academic style of the Bologna school. Guido Reni's work is exemplary. In *Adoration of the Shepherds* (c.1640) the careful composition and light colouring made his style very popular at the time.

In the 18th century, it was the Venetian school that dominated Italian painting. In Room 17 the colourful *Betrothal of the Venetian Doge to the Adriatic Sea* (1729–30) by Canaletto is on display. The artist is widely considered the master of the style of urban landscape known as *veduta*.

Guido Reni's *Adoration of the Shepherds* (c.1640)

Hercules and Omphale, painted in the 1730s by François Boucher

FRENCH ART: 17TH–EARLY 19TH CENTURIES

The Pushkin Museum is justly famous for its collection of French art, which includes paintings of classical and epic subjects by a variety of artists. 17th-century pieces are held in Room 21 and include a good collection by one of the greatest French painters of the period, Nicolas Poussin. He

was an exponent of High Renaissance styles, preferring balance and order in his work. The early piece *Victory of Joshua over the Amorites* (c.1625) shows an almost austere pictorial manner. Later work includes his poetic *Rinaldo and Armida* (early 1630s) and landscapes such as *Landscape with Hercules and Cacus* (1656). In the same room is the earliest known work by eminent Versailles painter and art theorist, Charles Lebrun. His *Crucifixion* (1637), painted when the artist was still a teenager, shows the influence of Rubens. Also on display is his portrait of the playwright Molière, painted much later.

Room 22 moves to the 18th century and the art of the French Rococo period. A leading exponent of the style, François Boucher, is well represented here. An early piece, and typical of the ornamental Rococo style, is *Hercules and Omphale* (1730s), which depicts the myth of Hercules, who was sold as a slave to Queen Omphale.

Finally, French art from the second half of the 18th century to the early 19th century is housed in Room 23. At this time, landscape became a popular genre and there are some fine examples by celebrated artists of the day Claude-Joseph Vernet and Hubert Robert. Sculpture is also on display here. Jean-Antoine Houdon's bronzes of Enlightenment thinker Voltaire brought him much fame.

The wide expanse of Arbat Square, located between the Old and New Arbat

Pashkov House ⑩

Дом Пашкова

Dom Pashkova

Ulitsa Znamenka 6. **Map** 6 F1.
Ⓒ *to public.* Ⓜ *Borovitskaya,
Biblioteka imeni Lenina.*

This magnificent mansion
was once the finest private
house in Moscow and enjoys
a wonderful hilltop location
overlooking the Kremlin. It
was built in the Neo-Classical
style in 1784–8 for the fabulously wealthy Captain Pyotr
Pashkov. Pashkov encouraged
his architect, who is thought
to have been Vasiliy Bazhenov
(see p44), to surpass himself
with the grandeur of the
design. The mansion's height
was achieved by placing it on
an enormous stone base and
the building is surmounted by
a beautifully proportioned
rotunda. Surprisingly the most
impressive façade is to the
rear of the building, which
originally led to a garden.
   In 1839, a relative of
Captain Pashkov sold the
house to the
Moscow
Institute for

The imposing Pashkov House overlooking the
Kremlin

Nobles, which occupied the
premises until 1861. It was
then taken over by the
Rumyantsev Museum, which
moved to the capital from St
Petersburg at that time. The
museum brought with it an art
collection and a library of more
than one million volumes.
   The building has been
completely renovated, and can
now be rented out for private
events – for $100,000 a week!

Arbat Square ⑫

Арбатская площадь

Arbatskaya ploshchad

Map 6 E1. Ⓜ *Arbatskaya.*

A chaotic mass of kiosks,
traffic and underpasses,
Arbat Square is the link
between the vividly contrasting areas of Old and New
Arbat. Beneath the square,
the underpasses contain a
society of their own. Expect
to come across an impromptu
rock concert, kittens and
puppies for sale and, in late
summer, children selling
bulbous, hand-picked mushrooms (though buying these
may not be advisable).
   On the corner of
ulitsa Arbat is the
yellow wedge-
shaped Praga res-
taurant *(see p184)*,
dating from before the
Revolution, but
reconstructed in
1954. Despite still
retaining the ele-
gance of its dining
halls, it became a
fairly uninspiring
snack-bar during
the later Soviet era.
However, it has
now been entirely

refurbished to re-emerge as a
very elegant establishment
serving high-quality cuisine in
a variety of national styles.
   The small white building at
the other end of the underpass
dates from 1909, but it was
redesigned three years later
by Fyodor Shekhtel *(see p45)*
for the pioneering Russian
film studio boss, Aleksandr
Khanzhonkov. Now known as
the Arts Cinema *(see p201)*, it
was one of the first cinemas
to open in Moscow.

Lermontov House-Museum ⑬

Дом-музей МЮ Лермонтова

Dom-muzey MYu Lermontova

Ulitsa Malaya Molchanovka 2.
Map 6 D1. **Tel** (495) 691 5298. Ⓜ
Arbatskaya. ☐ *2pm–6pm Wed, Fri,
11am–5pm Thu & Sat.* 📷

A portrait of the poet and novelist
Lermontov (1814–41) as a child

Tucked away behind the
tower blocks of the New
Arbat is the modest timber
house that was once home to
Mikhail Lermontov. The great
Romantic poet and novelist
lived here with his grandmother, Yelizaveta Arseneva,
from 1829–32 while he was a
student at Moscow University.
While here, he wrote an early
draft of his narrative poem
The Demon (1839).
   Lermontov was more interested in writing poetry than in
his studies and left university
without graduating. He then
became a guardsman. How-
ever, he was exiled to the
Caucasus for a year because
of the bitter criticisms of the
authorities expressed in his

Lermontov's tranquil study in the Lermontov House-Museum

poem *Death of a Poet* (1837). This poem about the death of Pushkin *(see p73)* marked a turning point in Lermontov's writing and is generally agreed to be the first of his mature works. His most famous composition, the novel *A Hero of our Time*, was written in 1840. Lermontov died the next year, aged only 26. Like Pushkin, he was killed in a duel.

There are only five rooms in the museum, but each bears testament both to Lermontov's dazzling intellectual gifts and also to his zest for life. The study on the mezzanine was his favourite room. Here he would play the guitar, piano and violin, and even compose music.

The drawing room, which still contains many of its original furnishings, was often the site of lively dancing, singing and masquerades.

Many of Lermontov's manuscripts are on display downstairs, together with drawings and watercolours, some by Lermontov himself.

Shalyapin House-Museum 🄮
Дом-музей Ф.И. Шаляпина
Dom-muzey FI Shalyapina

Novinskiy bulvar 25. **Map** 1 C5.
Tel *(499) 255 6399.* Ⓜ *Smolenskaya, Barrikadnaya.* ⏰ *10am–5pm Tue & Sat, 11:30am–7pm Wed & Thu, 10am–3pm Sun.*

A stone bust and inscription outside a yellow Empire-style mansion record that one of the greatest opera singers of the 20th century once lived here. The renowned Russian bass, Fyodor Shalyapin, occupied this large house from 1910 until he emigrated from Soviet Russia in 1922.

Born in Kazan in 1873, Shalyapin began his career in great poverty, working as a stevedore on the Volga before his unique vocal talent was discovered. He made his international debut at La Scala, Milan, in 1901, and went on to sing a variety of the great operatic bass roles, including *Don Quixote, Ivan the Terrible* and *Boris Godunov*.

Shalyapin died in Paris in 1938, but his remains have since been returned to Russia and were reburied in the Novodevichiy Cemetery *(see p131)* alongside other famous Russians.

This is one of Moscow's newer house-museums and one of the best. Amusing drawings of Shalyapin by his children and a china doll bought in France decorate the green-upholstered sitting room. The mementos in the blue study, meanwhile, include portraits of the singer in his various operatic roles.

The carved chair in front of the dining room stove was a gift from writer Maxim Gorky *(see p95)*, while the paintings on the walls are by the artist Konstantin Korovin.

The heavily labelled trunks stored in the box room are a reminder that Shalyapin was also in great demand at opera houses abroad. Other items on display in the house include the singer's make-up table and one of his wigs. In the concert room visitors can listen to recordings of Shalyapin at work. After singing for his guests, Shalyapin would often take them next door for a game of billiards. Shalyapin was not a very good loser and, depending on his mood, his wife would only invite friends with grace enough to let him win.

Stone bust of opera singer Shalyapin

Pictures drawn by Shalyapin's children, on display in the sitting room

TVERSKAYA

At heart a commercial district, Tverskaya centres on the road of the same name, which originally led to St Petersburg and was the processional route used by the tsars. Now Moscow's premier shopping street, Tverskaya ulitsa underwent a major redevelopment in the 1930s during the huge reconstruction of Moscow ordered by Stalin (see p75). At that time many buildings were torn down so

Shell detail on the House of Friendship

that the street could be widened and massive new apartment blocks were erected for workers. These looming grey buildings make the street a showcase of the monumental style of architecture (see p45) favoured by Stalin. The area's surprisingly tranquil backstreets have been home to many famous artists, writers and actors, and, despite Stalin's best efforts, still have some interesting pre-Revolutionary houses.

SIGHTS AT A GLANCE

Museums
Bulgakov Flat-Museum **19**
Chekhov House-Museum **16**
Gorky House-Museum **15**
Museum of Modern History **20**
Stanislavskiy House-Museum **9**

Historic Buildings
Hotel Metropol **1**
Hotel National **5**
House of Friendship **14**
House of Unions **4**
Manège **13**
Morozov Mansion **17**
Moscow Conservatory **11**
Moscow Old University **12**

Monasteries
Upper Monastery of St Peter **22**

Streets and Squares
Bolshaya Nikitskaya Ulitsa **10**
Bryusov Pereulok **8**
Patriarch's Pond **18**
Pushkin Square **21**
Theatre Square **2**
Tverskaya Ulitsa **6**

Theatres
Bolshoy Theatre pp90–91 **3**
Moscow Arts Theatre **7**

0 metres 400
0 yards 400

KEY

▨	Street-by-Street map pp86–7
Ⓜ	Metro station

GETTING THERE

Trolleybuses converge on this area from every direction: the 1, 2, 3, 5, 10, 12, 15, 31, 33 and Б are useful routes. The 6 and K buses run to a number of sights in the district. Metro stations in the area include Okhotnyy Ryad, Teatralnaya, Chekhovskaya, Tverskaya, Pushkinskaya, Mayakovskaya and Biblioteka imeni Lenina.

◁ **The exquisitely ornate interior of the 19th-century Yeliseev's Food Hall (see p89) on Tverskaya ulitsa**

Street-by-Street: Around Theatre Square

Moscow's Theatreland is centred, quite appropriately, around Theatre Square. Dominating the square is one of the most famous opera and ballet stages in the world, the Bolshoy Theatre. The Malyy (Small) Theatre is on the east side of the square, while the Russian Academic Youth Theatre is on the west. Further to the west is the city's main shopping street, Tverskaya ulitsa, and two more theatres, the Yermolova Theatre and the Moscow Arts Theatre. There are also several excellent restaurants and bars in this lively neighbourhood.

Yuriy Dolgorukiy, Moscow's founder (*see p17*), is depicted in this statue. It was unveiled in 1954, seven years after the city's 800th anniversary.

Pushkin Square

Bryusov Pereulok
A granite archway leads from Tverskaya ulitsa to this quiet lane, once home to director Vsevolod Meyerhold. The 17th-century Church of the Resurrection is visible further down the lane ❽

TVERSKAYA PLOSHCHAD

STOLESHNIKOV PEREULOK

BOLSHAYA DMITROVKA

KAMERGERSKIY PEREULOK

TVERSKAYA ULITSA

Tverskaya Ulitsa
Most of the imposing Stalinist blocks on Moscow's main shopping street date from the 1930s, but a few older buildings survive ❻

Bolshaya Nikitskaya ulitsa

Central Telegraph Office

Yermolova Theatre

Lower Chamber of the Russian Parliament

Moscow Arts Theatre
This famous theatre will always be associated with the dramatist Anton Chekhov (see p92). Several of his plays, including The Cherry Orchard, *were premiered here* ❼

Okhotnyy Ryad

Hotel National
The National is a mix of Style Moderne and Classical style. Now restored, its decor is as impressive as it was before the Revolution, when it was Moscow's finest hotel ❺

STAR SIGHTS

★ Bolshoy Theatre

★ House of Unions

★ Bolshoy Theatre

Two earlier theatres on this site, including the first Bolshoy, were destroyed in fires. The current building was completed by Albert Kavos in 1856 ❸

Petrovskiy Passage is a fashionable shopping arcade *(see p194).*

The Malyy Theatre is one of the oldest in Moscow. A statue of the great 19th-century playwright Aleksandr Ostrovskiy stands in front of it *(see p200).*

Bolshoy Small Stage *(see p90)*

Russian Academic Youth Theatre *(see p199)*

Teatralnaya

LOCATOR MAP

See Street Finder, maps 2 & 3

| 0 metres | 150 |
| 0 yards | 150 |

KEY

— — — Suggested route

Hotel Metropol

Built in 1899–1905 by Englishman William Walcot, the Metropol (see p174) is one of Moscow's grandest hotels. This painted, glazed ceiling is the outstanding feature of the main dining room ❶

PLOSHCHAD REVOLYUTSII

The Moskva Hotel *(see p170)* is being rebuilt.

Red Square

★ House of Unions

In the 1780s, architect Matvey Kazakov converted this Neo-Classical mansion into a noble-men's club. The trade unions took it over in the Soviet era ❹

Theatre Square

Laid out in its present form in the 1820s, part of Theatre Square served as a military parade ground from 1839–1911. Playbills around the city advertise performances in the theatres on the square ❷

The statue of Aleksandr Ostrovskiy in front of the Malyy Theatre

Hotel Metropol ❶
Гостиница Метрополь
Gostinitsa Metropol

Teatralnyy prospekt 1/4. **Map** 3 A5.
Tel *(499) 501 7800.* Ⓜ *Teatralnaya.*
See **Where to Stay** *p174.*

The Hotel Metropol, built
by William Walcot and Lev
Kekushev in 1899–1905, is a
fine example of Style-Moderne
architecture *(see p45).* The exterior walls sport a number
of ceramic panels, including
Mikhail Vrubel's large work at
the top of the façade. Called
The Daydreaming Princess, it is
based on scenes from the play
La Princesse Lointaine, written
in 1895 by Edmond Rostand,
author of *Cyrano de Bergerac.*
The building also has ornate
wrought-iron balconies and a
superb painted glass roof in
its Metropol Zal restaurant.
Over the years the Metropol
has welcomed guests as varied
and famous as Irish dramatist
George Bernard Shaw and
American pop star
Michael Jackson.

Theatre Square ❷
Театральная площадь
Teatralnaya ploshchad

Map 3 A5. Ⓜ *Teatralnaya, Ploshchad
Revolyutsii, Okhotnyy Ryad.*

This Elegant Square is named
after the theatres on three
of its sides. Originally this area
was marshy ground, regularly
flooded by the Neglinnaya
river. In the 1820s it was paved
over and the square was laid
out to a design by Osip Bove
(see p45). In 1839–1911 a
military parade ground occupied part of the square. Today,
Theatre Square is dominated
by the Bolshoy Theatre.
On the square's east
side is a converted private
mansion that houses the
Malyy (Small) Theatre
(see p200). The Malyy is
particularly associated
with playwright Aleksandr
Ostrovskiy (1823–86),
whose satirical plays were
performed here. A sombre
statue of him by Nikolay
Andreev was erected in
the forecourt in 1929.
The Russian Academic
Youth Theatre *(see p199),*
with its elaborate Neo-
Classical porch, stands on
the square's west side.Origi-
nally designed by Osip Bove
(see p45), it was almost entirely
rebuilt by Boris Freidenberg in
1882. The theatre has occupied
this building since 1936.
To the northwest of Theatre
Square is the Operetta Theatre
(see p200). In the 1890s the
private opera company
of the wealthy

industrialist and arts patron
Savva Mamontov (1842–1914)
performed here. The careers of
opera singer Fyodor Shalyapin
(see p83), composer Sergei
Rachmaninov and artist Vasiliy
Polenov, who designed sets
and costumes, all began here
with Mamontov's company.
In the centre of the square is
a granite statue of Karl Marx.
Sculpted in 1961 by Leonid
Kerbel, it bears the words
"Workers of the world unite!"

Bolshoy Theatre ❸

See pp90–91.

**The well-proportioned Hall of Columns in
the elegant, 18th-century House of Unions**

House of Unions ❹
Дом Союзов
Dom Soyuzov

Bolshaya Dmitrovka ulitsa 1.
Map 3 A5. ⬜ *for performances
only.* Ⓜ *Teatralnaya, Okhotnyy Ryad.*

This green and white Neo-
Classical mansion was originally
built in the first half of the 18th
century. In the early 1780s, it
was bought by a group of
Moscow nobles who
commissioned architect Matvey
Kazakov *(see pp44–5)* to turn it
into a noblemen's club. Kazakov
added a number of rooms to the
existing building including the
magnificent ballroom, known as
the Hall of Columns. It was here,
in 1856, that Tsar Alexander II
addressed an audience of the
Russian nobility on the need to
emancipate the serfs.
After the Revolution, trade
unions took over the building,
hence its current name. In 1924
the hall was opened to the
public for more than a million

The façade of the Hotel Metropol, designed by William Walcot

people to file past Lenin's open coffin. Many of his closest colleagues, members of the guard of honour on that occasion, were later tried here during the show trials of 1936–8 *(see p27)*. Stalin, who was behind these travesties of justice, also lay in state here in 1953.

Nowadays the House of Unions is used for concerts and public meetings.

Hotel National ❺
Гостиница Националь
Gostinitsa Natsional

Mokhovaya ulitsa 15/1. **Map** 2 F5. **Tel** *(495) 258 7000.* **M** *Okhotnyy Ryad.* **&** **✦** See **Where to Stay** *p174.*

Designed in 1903 by architect Aleksandr Ivanov, the Hotel National is an eclectic mixture of Style-Moderne and Classical-style architecture *(see pp44–5)*. The façade is decorated with sculpted nymphs and ornate stone tracery, but is topped by a mosaic from the Soviet era. This features factory chimneys belching smoke, oil derricks, electricity pylons, railway engines and tractors.

The National's most famous guest was Lenin, who stayed in room 107 at the hotel for a week, in March 1918, before he moved to the Kremlin.

Tverskaya ulitsa, one of Moscow's most popular shopping streets

The National was completely refurbished in the early 1990s and its Style-Moderne interiors have been faithfully restored to their original splendour.

Tverskaya ulitsa ❻
Тверская улица
Tverskaya ulitsa

Map 2 F5, F4, E3. **M** *Okhotnyy Ryad, Tverskaya, Pushkinskaya.*

Tverskaya Ulitsa was the grandest thoroughfare in Moscow in the 19th century, when it was famous for its restaurants, theatres, hotels and purveyors of French fashions. Stalin's reconstruction of the city in the 1930s resulted in Tverskaya ulitsa being widened by 42 m (138 ft) and its name being changed to ulitsa Gorkovo to commemorate the writer Maxim Gorky. Many buildings were torn down to make way for huge apartment blocks to house party bureaucrats, such as those at Nos. 9–11. Other buildings were rebuilt further back to stand on the new, wider road. Now called Tverskaya ulitsa again, the street carries a huge volume of traffic. However, it is still one of the city's most popular places to eat out and shop.

At No.7 is the Central Telegraph Office,

a severe grey building with an illuminated globe outside. It was designed by Ilya Rerberg in 1927. Through the arch on the other side of the road is a green-tiled building with floral friezes and tent-roofed turrets. Built in 1905, this was the Moscow mission of the Savvinskiy Monastery. It is now luxury flats and offices.

Further up the street is the soulless Tverskaya square, dominated by an equestrian statue of Moscow's founder, Prince Yuriy Dolgorukiy *(see p86)*. On the west side of the square looms the red and white city hall. Designed in 1782 by Matvey Kazakov *(see pp44–5)*, it was the residence of the governor-general before the Revolution and later became the Moscow City Soviet or town hall. In 1944–6 extra storeys were added, more than doubling its height.

Beyond Tverskaya square, at No. 14, is Moscow's most famous delicatessen. Now known by its pre-Revolutionary name, Yeliseev's Food Hall *(see p194)*, in Soviet times it was called Gastronom No.1. In the 1820s this mansion was the home of Princess Zinaida Volkonskaya, whose soirées were attended by great figures of the day, including Alexander Pushkin *(see p73)*. In 1898 Grigoriy Yeliseev bought the building, and had it lavishly redecorated with stained-glass windows, crystal chandeliers, carved pillars, polished wood counters and large mirrors. It now stocks a wide range of imported and Russian delicacies.

Lobby of the Hotel National, with Style-Moderne windows and Classical statues

Bolshoy Theatre ❸

Большой театр
Bolshoy teatr

Home to one of the oldest, and probably the most famous, ballet companies in the world, the Bolshoy Theatre is also one of Moscow's major landmarks. The first Bolshoy Theatre opened in 1780 and presented masquerades, comedies and comic operas. It burnt down in 1805, but its successor was completed in 1825 to a design by Osip Bove (see p45) and Andrey Mikhaylov. This building too was destroyed by fire, in 1853, but the essentials of its highly praised design were retained in Albert Kavos' reconstruction of 1856. The theatre is closed for renovation until 2011. Performances are being staged at the Bolshoy Small Stage opposite.

★ Royal Box
Situated at the centre of the gallery, the royal box, hung with crimson velvet, is one of over 120 boxes. The imperial crown on its pediment was removed in the Soviet era but has now been restored.

Neo-Classical Pediment
The relief on the Neo-Classical pediment was an addition by Albert Kavos during his reconstruction of the theatre. It depicts a pair of angels bearing aloft the lyre of Apollo, the Greek god of music and light.

★ Apollo in the Chariot of the Sun
This eye-catching sculpture by Pyotr Klodt, part of the original 1825 building, was retained by Albert Kavos. It depicts Apollo driving the chariot on which he carried the sun across the sky.

Entrance

Vestibule
Patrons entering the theatre find themselves in this grand, black and white tiled vestibule. Magnificent staircases, lined with white marble, lead up from either side of the vestibule to the spacious main foyer.

Eight-columned portico

Beethoven Hall
This ornately decorated room was formerly known as the Imperial Foyer. It is now used for occasional chamber concerts and lectures. The stuccoed decoration on the ceiling includes approximately 3,000 rosettes and the walls are adorned with delicately embroidered panels of crimson silk.

Main stage

The backstage area provides jobs for over 700 workers, including craftsmen and women making ballet shoes, costumes and stage props.

Apollo and the Muses
The ten painted panels decorating the auditorium's ceiling are by Pyotr Titov. They depict Apollo dancing with the nine muses of Greek myth, each of which is connected with a different branch of the arts or sciences.

STAR FEATURES

★ Apollo in the Chariot of the Sun

★ Royal Box

Artists' dressing room

The auditorium has six tiers and a seating capacity of 2,500. When Kavos rebuilt it he modified its shape to improve its acoustics.

The main foyer extends around the whole of the front of the building on the first floor. Its vaulted ceiling is decorated with paintings and elaborate stucco work.

THE BOLSHOY BALLET IN THE SOVIET ERA

In the 1920s and 1930s new ballets conforming to Revolutionary ideals were created for the Bolshoy, but the company's heyday was in the 1950s and 1960s. Ballets such as *Spartacus* were produced and the dancers toured abroad for the first time to widespread acclaim. Yet a number of dancers also defected to the West in this period, in protest at the company's harsh management and a lack of artistic freedom.

A production of *Spartacus* (1954), by Aram Khachaturian, at the Bolshoy

Arch at the entrance to Bryusov pereulok, a street where artists and musicians lived in the 1920s

Moscow Arts Theatre ❼

МХАТ имени АП Чехова
MKhAT imeni AP Chekhova

Kamergerskiy pereulok 3. **Map** 2 F5.
Tel *(495) 629 8760/6748.* Ⓜ *Teatralnaya, Okhotnyy Ryad.* ◯ *performances only. See* **Entertainment** *p200.*

The first ever performance at the Moscow Arts Theatre (MKhAT) took place in 1898. The theatre was founded by a group of young enthusiasts, led by the directors Konstantin Stanislavskiy and Vladimir Nemirovich-Danchenko. The MKhAT company had an early success with their pro-

The Moscow Arts Theatre entrance with *The Wave* **bas-relief above**

duction of Anton Chekhov's play *The Seagull* in the theatre's first year. When the play had been performed three years earlier in St Petersburg, it had been a disastrous flop but, performed using Stanislavskiy's new Method acting, it was extremely well received.

In 1902 architect Fyodor Shekhtel *(see p45)* completely reconstructed the interior of the theatre, adding innovations such as a central lighting box and a revolving stage. The auditorium had very little decoration, so that audiences were forced to concentrate on the performance.

The theatre continued to flourish after the Revolution, but its repertoire was restricted by state censorship. Most of the plays produced were written by Maxim Gorky, whose work was in favour with the government. The frustrations and compromises of the period were brilliantly satirized in the 1930s by Mikhail Bulgakov (who also worked as an assistant director in the theatre) in his novel *Teatralnyy Roman.* These problems continued and in the 1980s part of the company moved to the Gorky Arts Theatre on Tverskoy bulvar.

Today a variety of productions are staged at the Moscow Arts Theatre, including many of Anton Chekhov's plays.

Stylized seagull on the exterior of the Moscow Arts Theatre

Bryusov Pereulok ❽

Брюсов переулок
Bryusov pereulok

Map 2 F5. Ⓜ *Okhotnyy Ryad, Arbatskaya.*

A Granite Arch on Tverskaya ulitsa marks the entrance to this quiet side street. It is named after the Bruces, a Scots family who were involved with the Russian court.

In the 1920s new apartments here were assigned to the staff of the Moscow state theatres. No. 17 was the home of two actors from the Moscow Arts Theatre, Vasiliy Kachalov and Ivan Moskvin.

No. 12 was home to the avant-garde director Vsevolod Meyerhold, who directed premieres of Vladimir Mayakovsky's satires. He lived here from 1928 until his arrest in 1939 at the height of Stalin's Great Purge *(see p27).*

The Composers' Union was at Nos. 8–10. It was here that composers Sergey Prokofiev and Dmitriy Shostakovich were forced to read an apology for works that deviated from Socialist Realism *(see p135).*

About halfway along Bryusov pereulok is the 17th-century single-domed Church of the Resurrection. This was one of the few churches to remain open during the Soviet era.

Stanislavskiy House-Museum ❾

Дом-музей КС Станиславского
Dom-muzey KS Stanislavskovo

Leontevskiy pereulok 6. **Map** 2 E5.
Tel (495) 629 2855. Ⓜ *Arbatskaya,
Tverskaya.* ⬜ *11am–5pm Thu,
Sat–Sun, noon–7pm Wed, Fri.*
⬤ *public holidays.* 🖼 📷 ✅

This 18th-century mansion
was the home of the great
director and actor Konstantin
Stanislavskiy. He lived on the
first floor from 1920 until he
died in 1938, at the age of 75.
    Stanislavskiy found himself
disillusioned with the conservative ethos of the old Moscow
Theatre School, and created
an outlet for his innovative
ideas by founding the Moscow
Arts Theatre (MKhAT) in 1898.
After moving into this flat, he
converted his ballroom into a
makeshift theatre where he
rehearsed his experimental
Opera Dramatic Group. Later,
when he was too ill to go out,
he also held rehearsals here
for the MKhAT company.
    Stanislavskiy's living room
and study, the dining room and
the bedroom of his wife, Maria
Lilina, are all open. Also on
display are an early Edison
phonograph and a vase that
was a gift from the dancer
Isadora Duncan. Downstairs
are props and costumes from
Stanislavskiy's productions.

Bolshaya Nikitskaya Ulitsa ❿

Большая Никитская улица
Bolshaya Nikitskaya ulitsa

Map 2 F5, E5. Ⓜ *Arbatskaya,
Okhotnyy Ryad, Biblioteka imeni Lenina.*

This historic street, once the
main road to Novgorod, is
named after the Nikitskiy Convent which was founded in
the 16th century, but pulled
down by Stalin in the 1930s.
    Prominent aristocratic famil-
ies such as the Menshikovs
and Orlovs built their palaces
here in the 18th century. The
finest is the former residence
of Prince Sergey Menshikov,
which can be reached via
Gazetniy pereulok. The pale

STANISLAVSKIY AND CHEKHOV

**Konstantin Stanislavskiy in the
play Uncle Vanya by Chekhov**

Konstantin Stanislavskiy's successful production of Anton
Chekhov's *The Seagull* took
the theatre world by storm.
Stanislavskiy's secret was his
new school of Method acting,
in which performers explored
their characters' inner motives.
Stanislavskiy and Chekhov
collaborated on the premieres
of other Chekhov plays and
the success of the productions
was such that their names
have been linked ever since.

---

blue façade was reconstructed
following the great fire of 1812
(see pp24–5). The Neo-Classical
rear façade, which survived the
fire, dates from around 1775.
    Just opposite the Moscow
Conservatory *(see p94),* is the
attractive white Church of the
Little Ascension.
Built around the
end of the 16th
century, it was
restored in 1739
following a fire.
Behind it is the
Gothic tower of St
Andrew's Anglican
Church. It was
built for Moscow's
English community
in 1882 by British
architect Richard
Freeman.
    The heavily ornamented red-
brick building at Nos. 19–20
was once called the Paradise
Theatre. It was renamed the
Mayakovsky Theatre after the
poet Vladimir Mayakovsky
(see p111). His plays *Bath
House* and *The Bed Bug* were
premiered here in 1928 and

**Stone relief on Church
of the Great Ascension**

1929, directed by avant-garde
director Vsevolod Meyerhold.
One of the greatest innovators
of his era, Meyerhold was
executed by the State in 1940,
largely because his work did
not agree with the canons of
Socialist Realism *(see p135).*
    About halfway
along the road is
Nikitskie Vorota
ploshchad, named
after the medieval
gate that used to
stand here. On the
square is a modern
white building with
a sign in the shape
of a large globe
hanging beneath
its porch. This is
the ITAR-TASS
news agency, the mouthpiece
of the Communist Party in the
Soviet era and now Russia's
main news agency.
    Opposite is the Church of
the Great Ascension. Begun
in 1798, it was rebuilt after the
1812 fire. Alexander Pushkin
(see p73) married Natalya
Goncharova here in 1831.

Sign in the shape of a globe hanging outside the ITAR-TASS news agency

The Bolshoy Zal (Great Hall) in the Moscow Conservatory

Moscow Conservatory ⑪
Московская консерватория
Moskovskaya Konservatoriya

Bolshaya Nikitskaya ulitsa 13. **Map** 2 F5. **Tel** (495) 629 9401. Ⓜ *Arbatskaya, Pushkinskaya.* ☐ *performances only.* **www**.mosconsv.ru

The largest music school in Russia was founded in 1866 by Nikolay Rubinstein, the brother of composer and pianist Anton Rubinstein.

One of the Conservatory's teachers was the young Pyotr Tchaikovsky, who taught here until 1878. On the forecourt is his statue, wielding a baton despite the fact that Tchaikovsky detested conducting. The work of Vera Mukhina, it dates from 1954. The pattern on the forecourt railings is made up of the opening notes from some of Tchaikovsky's works.

Portraits of famous composers adorn the walls of the light, airy Bolshoy Zal (Great Hall). Used for concerts since 1898, it is also the setting for the prestigious Tchaikovsky International Competition *(see p200)*. The Conservatory has a small museum that is open during perfomances.

The Conservatory has always been an important training ground for young Russian composers and performers. Among its best-known alumni are pianist-composers Sergei Rachmaninov and Aleksandr Skryabin *(see p72)*. Dmitriy Shostakovich, the great Soviet composer, lived nearby, at the Composers' Union on Bryusov pereulok *(see p92)*. He taught

at the Conservatory from 1942 until he fell from favour and was sacked six years later for "professional incompetence" during Stalin's Purges *(see p27)*.

Moscow Old University ⑫
Московский университет
Moskovskiy Universitet

Mokhovaya ulitsa 9. **Map** 2 F5. Ⓜ *Okhotnyy Ryad, Biblioteka imeni Lenina.*

Founded by the scholar Mikhail Lomonosov in 1755, this is the oldest university in Russia. It moved into this imposing building (now called the Old University) in 1793. Designed by Matvey Kazakov *(see pp44–5)*, it was extensively rebuilt by Domenico Gilardi after the 1812 fire *(see pp24–5)* and is a fine example of Neo-Classical architecture *(see pp44–5)*. Outside are statues of radical writers Nikolay Ogarev and Aleksandr

Herzen. In 1836 the university acquired a building on the far side of Bolshaya Nikitskaya ulitsa. In front of the New University is a statue of Mikhail Lomonosov. Nearby is the chapel of St Tatyana, whose feast day is celebrated by the students.

Manège ⑬
Манеж
Manezh

Manezhnaya ploshchad 1. **Map** 6 F1. **Tel** (495) 926 2828. Ⓜ *Biblioteka imeni Lenina, Okhotnyy Ryad.* ☐ *exhibitions only.* 🖼 ▢

The Manège was originally built in 1817 as a military parade ground to a design by General Augustin de Béthencourt. The 45-m- (148-ft-) wide roof had no supporting columns, leaving an uninterrupted floor space large enough for an infantry regiment to practise in.

In 1823–5 Osip Bove *(see p45)* added a colonnade and decorative frieze to the exterior.

The Manège became the Central Exhibition Hall in 1957 and it was at an exhibition here in 1962 that Nikita Khrushchev *(see p30)* famously condemned abstract art. The brunt of the attack was borne by the sculptor Ernst Neizvestniy but, curiously, in his will Khrushchev chose Neizvestniy to design his tombstone *(see p131)*. Fire partly destroyed the building in 2004 but it was swiftly rebuilt. Today the Manège is still mostly used to house exhibitions.

Statue of Mikhail Lomonosov

The Manège, designed by Augustin de Béthencourt in 1817

The extravagant interior of the 19th-century House of Friendship

House of Friendship ⑭

Дом дружбы

Dom Druzhby

Vozdvizhenka ulitsa 16. **Map** 6 E1. *Tel* (495) 290 2069. Ⓜ *Arbatskaya, Biblioteka imeni Lenina.* ◯ *performances only.*

This incredible mansion has towers encrusted with stone shells and topped by lacelike stonework. Vladimir Mazyrin designed it at the end of the 19th century for the playboy Arseny Morozov, a member of the wealthy Morozov family *(see p96)*. The interior is just as showy; rooms include a hunting hall filled with carved animal heads. The only way to see inside is to attend a concert or lecture held here. In Soviet times the mansion was used by the Union of Friendship Societies, hence its name.

Gorky House-Museum ⑮

Дом-музей АМ Горького

Dom-muzey AM Gorkovo

Malaya Nikitskaya ulitsa 6/2. **Map** 2 E5. *Tel* (495) 690 0535. Ⓜ *Pushkinskaya.* ◯ *11am–5:30pm Wed–Sun* ◯ *last Thu of the month.* ◯ ◯ *English.*

A frieze of irises against a background of blue and purple clouds runs round the top of the yellow glazed-brick walls

of this extraordinary mansion. Fyodor Shekhtel designed this masterpiece of Style-Moderne architecture *(see p45)* in 1900. The house belonged to arts patron and millionaire banker Stepan Ryabushinskiy until he left Russia with his family after the Revolution. In 1931 Stalin presented the mansion as a gift to the famous socialist writer Maxim Gorky.

The interior of the house is spectacular, featuring ceilings with elaborate mouldings, stained-glass windows and carved door frames. However, the *pièce de résistance* is the flowing staircase of polished Estonian limestone, which ends in a lamp resembling a jellyfish.

By the time Gorky moved to this house, his career as a novelist and playwright was in decline. While living here, he wrote only one play, *Yegor Bulychev and Others* (1932), and part of a novel, *The Life of Klim Samgin* (unfinished at his

death). However his fame and his earlier support for the Bolshevik Party made him a useful propaganda tool for the Soviet government. He served this function by being president of the Union of Writers, which explains why the rooms are full of photos of the author in the company of aspiring dramatists, Young Pioneers and ambitious Communist officials.

On display are Gorky's hat, overcoat and walking stick, his remarkable collection of oriental carvings and many of his letters and books, including some first editions.

Shortly after Gorky died in 1936, Genrikh Yagoda, the former head of the NKVD (secret police), was accused of murdering him. Although the charge was probably fabricated, Yagoda was found guilty in one of the last of the notorious show trials *(see p27)*. Rumours persist that Gorky was killed on Stalin's orders.

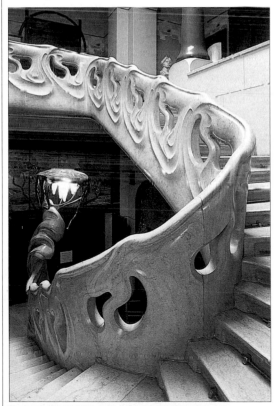

The spectacular Style-Moderne staircase in the Gorky House-Museum

Chekhov House-Museum ⑯

Дом-музей АП Чехова
Dom-muzey AP Chekhova

Sadovaya-Kudrinskaya ulitsa 6.
Map 2 D5. **Tel** *(495) 691 6154.*
Ⓜ *Barrikadnaya.* ◯ *2pm–6pm
Wed–Fri, 11am–4pm Thu, Sat–Sun.*
▨ ⊘ ▣ *(book in advance).*

Anton Chekhov (1860–1904)
lived in this two-storey
house in 1886–90. It was later
refurbished in consultation
with the author's widow, act-
ress Olga Knipper-Chekhova,
and opened as a museum in
1954. However, it is only partially successful in recreating
a period feeling and contains
few of Chekhov's possessions.
   Chekhov was a qualified
doctor and was practising
medicine when he lived here,
as the brass plate by the front
door testifies. He shared the
house with his parents, his
brother, Mikhail, and his sister,
Mariya. As the family's main
breadwinner, Chekhov could
only write in his spare time,
but it was here that he created
his first major play, *Ivanov*. He
also wrote many short stories
and several one-act plays here.
   Exhibits in the study, which
doubled as a consulting room,
include Chekhov's doctor's
bag, manuscripts and pictures,
including some of him with
Leo Tolstoy *(see p134).*
   Upstairs are a richly decorated living room and Mariya's
room, which, in some ways,
is the most attractive in the
house. Its furnishings include
a sewing machine, ornaments
and embroidered tablecloths.
   There is also an exhibition
about Chekhov's later career as
a playwright *(see p93)*, which
includes adverts for his plays
and first editions of his works.

The Gothic-style Morozov Mansion, designed by Fyodor Shekhtel

Picture of Chekhov (on the left) talking with
Leo Tolstoy, in the Chekhov House-Museum

Morozov Mansion ⑰

Дом ЗГ Морозовой
Dom ZG Morozovoy

Ulitsa Spiridonovka 17. **Map** 2 D4.
Ⓜ *Mayakovskaya.* ◉ *to public.*

Fyodor Shekhtel *(see p45)*
built this house for his patron, Savva Morozov, in 1893–8.
Savva Morozov was a wealthy
textiles manufacturer and arts
patron, a member of one of the
city's richest merchant families.
   The mansion was built in
the Gothic style to resemble a
baronial castle, with turrets,
gargoyles and arched windows.
Some of the stained-glass windows were designed by the
Symbolist artist Mikhail Vrubel.

Patriarch's Pond ⑱

Патриаршие пруды
Patriarshie prudy

Map 2 D4. Ⓜ *Mayakovskaya.*

Just a few minutes' walk from
the busy Garden Ring is a
secluded, tree-lined square
with the large Patriarch's
Pond at its heart. The pond is
named after the patriarch who
formerly owned the land.
   Near the children's
playground is a bronze
statue of the 19th-
century playwright and
writer of popular fables
Ivan Krylov. Sculptures
of the creatures from
his stories are dotted
among the trees.
   Patriarch's Pond is
probably best known
as the setting for the
opening scene in
Mikhail Bulgakov's
novel *The Master and*

Margarita, in which the
Devil appears in Moscow
and causes havoc. Bulgakov
lived nearby for three years
during the 1920s.

Graffiti at Bulgakov's flat by
enthusiasts of his work

Bulgakov Flat-Museum ⑲

Булгакова дом-музей
Bulgakova dom-muzey

Bolshaya Sadovaya ulitsa 10, flat 52.
Map 2 D3. **Tel** *(495) 970 0619.* Ⓜ
Mayakovskaya. ◯ *1–11pm Sun–
Thu, 1pm–1am Fri–Sat.* ▤

This museum is dedicated
to Mikhail Bulgakov (1891–
1940), the Russian author
whose best-known work,
The Master and Margarita, was
not published until long after
his death. During his lifetime,
many of his satirical plays were
banned. Bulgakov became so
frustrated that he wrote to
Stalin asking to be exiled.
Instead, he was given a job at
the Moscow Arts Theatre *(see
p92)*. The museum displays
many of Bulgakov's
possessions, but he actually
lived two doors down the road.

Maxim gun used in the Civil War, in the Museum of Modern History

Museum of Modern History ⑳

Музей современной истории
Muzey sovremennoy istorii

Tverskaya ulitsa 21, **Map** 2 E4. **Tel** (495) 699 6724. **M** *Pushkinskaya, Tverskaya.* ◯ *10am–6pm Tue–Sun.* 🖼 ∅ 🌐 *English.* ☐ www.sovr.ru

A pair of stone lions guards this elegant red mansion, built in the late 18th century. The wings and Empire-style façade *(see p45)* were added some decades later. In 1831 the mansion became a gentlemen's club, known as the English Club, and until the Revolution, the Muscovite aristocracy drank and gambled here.

Ironically, this building, with all its aristocratic associations, became the Museum of the Revolution. However, since the Soviet Union broke up in 1991, the collections display a more objective view of 20th-century Russian history; the name of the museum has also been changed to reflect this shift.

Laid out chronologically, the exhibits cover 1900–91. They include home-made grenades, a Maxim gun on a converted carriage (used in the Civil War), sweet wrappers depicting Marx and Lenin and former premier Nikita Khrushchev's hat and camera from his 1959 trip to the United States. The collection of so-called propaganda porcelain and a display of gifts presented to Soviet rulers are also interesting.

Pushkin Square ㉑

Пушкинская площадь
Pushkinskaya ploshchad

Map 2 F4. **M** *Pushkinskaya, Tverskaya, Chekhovskaya.*

The bronze statue of poet Alexander Pushkin was unveiled in the presence of two other Russian literary giants, Fyodor Dostoevsky and Ivan Turgenev, in 1880. The statue, located on the south side of Pushkin Square, was sculpted by Alexander Opekushin.

Pushkin has long epitomized the spirit of freedom in Russia and the statue occasionally became a rallying point for demonstrations in the 1960s and 1970s, which sometimes ended in clashes between the KGB and demonstrators.

Before the Revolution Pushkin Square was called Strastnaya ploshchad (Passion Square) after the 17th-century Convent of the Passion which used to stand here. The convent was demolished in 1935 to make way for the monstrous Rossiya cinema *(see p201)*.

The statue of poet Alexander Pushkin, on Pushkin Square

Just beyond the cinema, on Malaya Dmitrovka ulitsa, is the Church of the Nativity of the Virgin in Putinki. Built in 1649–52, this attractive church has clustered tent roofs, tiered *kokoshniki* gables *(see p44)* and blue onion domes.

On the northeast corner of the square stand the offices of the newspaper *Izvestiya*. Once an official mouthpiece of the Soviet government, *Izvestiya* is now one of Russia's independent daily newspapers.

Upper Monastery of St Peter ㉒

Высоко-Петровский монастырь
Vysoko-Petrovskiy monastyr

Ulitsa Petrovka 28. **Map** 3 A3. **Tel** (495) 923 7580. **M** *Pushkinskaya, Chekhovskaya.* ◯ *9:30am–6pm daily.* 🖼

This monastery was founded in the reign of Ivan I *(see p18)*. It was rebuilt in the late 17th century with sponsorship from the Naryshkin family, relatives of Peter the Great. Its six churches include the Church of the Metropolitan Peter after which the monastery is named. This single-domed church was built in 1514–17 to a design by Aleviz Novyy. The Church of the Icon of the Virgin of Bogolyubovo commemorates three of Peter the Great's uncles killed in the 1682 Streltsy Rebellion *(see p22)*. The Refectory Church of St Sergius has five cupolas and scallop shell decoration. The monastery complex also includes a green domed bell tower and the monks' cells.

Iconostasis in the Baroque bell tower of the Upper Monastery of St Peter

RED SQUARE AND KITAY GOROD

Moscow's first suburb, Kitay Gorod, was settled as early as the 12th century by tradesmen and artisans employed by the tsar. The word *kitay* is thought to refer to the wattle used to build the ramparts around the suburb. Red Square was created as a market square beside the Kremlin *(see pp52–67)* in the late 15th century. Behind it, trading rows were set up, each line of wooden cabins

Icon of St George, Resurrection Gate

specializing in a particular item, such as icons, pans or hats. In the 16th century, a number of boyars *(see p20)*, including Russia's future rulers, the Romanovs, built their estates nearby, while the presence of merchants from Novgorod and as far away as England was actively encouraged. Later, in the 19th century, Kitay Gorod became Moscow's financial district, home to the Stock Exchange and major banks.

SIGHTS AT A GLANCE

Cathedrals, Churches, Convents and Monasteries

Church of the Trinity in Nikitniki **4**
Convent of the Nativity of the Virgin **22**
Kazan Cathedral **8**
Monastery of the Epiphany **6**
St Basil's Cathedral pp108–9 **13**

Streets and Squares

Chistoprudnyy Bulvar **19**
Ivanovskaya Hill **14**
Lubyanka Square **18**
Nikolskaya Ulitsa **7**
Red Square **10**
Ulitsa Ilinka **5**
Ulitsa Varvarka **1**

Historic Buildings

GUM **12**
Menshikov's Tower **20**
Old English Court **2**
Perlov Tea House **21**
Resurrection Gate **9**
Sandunovskiy Baths **23**

Museums and Galleries

History of Moscow Museum **16**
Lenin Mausoleum **11**
Mayakovsky Museum **17**
Palace of the Romanov Boyars **3**
Polytechnical Museum **15**

0 metres 400
0 yards 400

KEY

▢ Street-by-Street map pp100–101

Ⓜ Metro station

▤ River boat pier

GETTING THERE

This area is well served by trolleybuses (2, 8, 9, 16, 25, 33, 45, 48, & 63), buses (25 & 158) and trams (3, 39 & A). The metro runs to Ploshchad Revolyutsii, Kitay Gorod, Lubyanka, Kuznetskiy Most or Turgenevskaya.

◁ The Russian-Revival façade of the Historical Museum at the northern end of Red Square

Street-by-Street: Kitay Gorod

Commerce and religion go hand-in-hand in this ancient part of the city. The heart of Moscow's financial district is Birzhevaya ploshchad, and the surrounding area has been home to traders for centuries. Among the banks and offices are an increasing number of up-market stores, especially lining Nikolskaya ulitsa, and the area now rivals Russia's best-known shopping arcade, GUM (see p107). At one time there were more than 40 churches and monasteries dotted about these narrow streets. Only around a dozen have survived and most of these are now undergoing painstaking restoration.

Monastery of the Epiphany
Founded in 1296, this is the second oldest monastery in Moscow. Its cathedral, built between 1693–6, is a fine example of florid Moscow Baroque 6

Russian Supreme Court

Ploshchad Revolyutsii

Red Square

Nikolskaya Ulitsa
Well-heeled shoppers now head to this street's boutiques and jewellery shops. Among its more colourful sights is the Gothic-style Synodal Printing House, which dates from the 19th century 7

The Old Merchants' Chambers (Staryy Gostinyy Dvor), from the 18th–19th centuries, houses a shopping arcade.

STAR SIGHTS

★ Church of the Trinity in Nikitniki

★ Palace of the Romanov Boyars

KEY

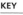 — — — Suggested route

Ulitsa Ilinka
Halfway along ulitsa Ilinka is Birzhevaya ploshchad, where the former Stock Exchange is located. Constructed in 1873–5 by Aleksandr Kaminskiy, this attractive, pink, Classical-style building is now the home of the Russian Chamber of Industry and Commerce 5

Church of St Barbara

Ulitsa Varvarka
Several historic churches line this ancient route out of Moscow. Among them is the Church of St Maxim the Blessed, which was paid for by Novgorod merchants trading in Kitay Gorod and consecrated in 1698 **1**

LOCATOR MAP
See Street Finder, maps 3 & 7

★ **Church of the Trinity in Nikitniki**
Commissioned by the wealthy merchant Grigoriy Nikitnikov and completed in 1635, the church is famous both for its exuberant architecture and for its vivid frescoes. It is closed for renovations until mid to late 2010 **4**

This house belonged to Simon Ushakov, a leading 17th-century icon and fresco painter. He worked on the nearby Church of the Trinity in Nikitniki.

★ **Palace of the Romanov Boyars**
This palace was originally lived in by powerful Muscovite boyar (see p20) Nikita Romanov. It is now a fascinating museum which evokes the life of noble families in the 16th and 17th centuries **3**

Kitay Gorod metro

Church of St George

Monastery of the Sign

Old English Court
Restored to its 17th-century appearance, this merchants' residence was given to visiting English traders by Ivan the Terrible in the hope of securing arms and other goods from them **2**

0 metres	100
0 yards	100

Ulitsa Varvarka ❶

Улица Варварка
Ulitsa Varvarka

Map 7 B1–C1. Ⓜ *Kitay Gorod.*

The heart of the former merchants' quarter of Zaryade, ulitsa Varvarka is one of Moscow's oldest streets. It is named after the original Church of St Barbara (Varvara) the Martyr. This earlier building was demolished in 1796 to make way for a new pink and white Neo-Classical church of the same name, designed by Rodion Kazakov.

A little further along is the single-domed Church of St Maxim the Blessed. Built by traders from Novgorod to house the bones of St Maxim, it was consecrated in 1698. Between the two churches stands the Old English Court.

Across the road are the Old Merchants' Chambers (Staryy gostinyy dvor), which are fronted by a row of Corinthian columns. Italian architect Giacomo Quarenghi drew up plans for this market in 1790, and the work was supervised by Moscow architects Semen Karin and Ivan Selekhov. There are shops here and perform-ances and exhibitions are held in the covered yard. Be-yond the Church of St Maxim are the 17th-century Monastery of the Sign and the Palace of the Romanov Boyars.

At the end of ulitsa Varvarka is the Church of St George, built in 1657–8 by merchants from Pskov, a town known

The five domes of the Church of St George on ulitsa Varvarka

for its architects *(see p44)*. To the right, on Kitaygorodskiy proezd, is one of the few sections of the old city walls to survive. At the end of this street, beside the Moskva river, is the mid-16th-century Church of the Conception of St Anna.

Old English Court ❷

Старый английский двор
Staryy angliyskiy dvor

Ulitsa Varvarka 4a. **Map** 7 B1. *Tel* (495) 298 3952. ⬜ *10am–6pm Tue, Thu, Sat– Sun, 11am–7pm Wed, Fri.* Ⓜ *Ploshchad Revolyutsii, Kitay Gorod.* 🖼 📷 ▶ *English.*

In 1553, while searching the northern coast of Russia for a passage to the east, the English merchant adventurer Richard Chancellor *(see p21)* was shipwrecked. He was taken to Moscow and received by Ivan the Terrible, whose desire to trade with England

later led him to propose marriage to Queen Elizabeth I. On returning to Russia in 1556, Chancellor and his trading mission were given this large property in Zaryade. It was to serve as a storage and trading house and as accommodation for English merchants.

In the mid-17th century, the estate passed into Russian hands and by the 1900s it had been extensively altered. After the Revolution *(see pp26–9)*, the house was restored. It later reopened as a museum dur-ing the official visit of Queen Elizabeth II to Russia in 1994.

Inside, an exhibition high-lights the history of the Old English Court and its role in developing Anglo-Russian relations. Winding stone stair-cases lead down to the cellars and the official chamber used for negotiations and functions. The English merchants fitted the Russian stove in this chamber with an open hearth to remind themselves of home.

Spartan interior of the official chamber in the Old English Court

Palace of the Romanov Boyars ❸

Музей-палаты в Зарядье
Muzey-palaty v Zaryade

Ulitsa Varvarka 10. **Map** 7 B1. *Tel* (495) 298 3706. ⬜ *10am–5pm Sun. Pre-booked groups only: 10am–5pm Thu–Sat, Mon, 11am–6pm Wed.* Ⓜ *Kitay Gorod.* 🖼 📷 ▶ *English.*

Only the upper storeys of this palace can be seen from ulitsa Varvarka. This is largely because the palace is built on a steep slope leading away from the street down towards the Moskva river.

The palace was originally built by the boyar *(see p20)* Nikita Romanov in the 16th century. It was home to the Romanovs until 1613 when

A view along ulitsa Varkarva, with the Old English Court straight ahead

Mikhail Romanov (see p19) became tsar and the family moved to the Kremlin. The palace has been protected as a museum since 1859.

The main entrance is reached via a courtyard; a double-headed eagle, the Romanov family crest, adorns the arch-way leading to the courtyard.

The ground and first floors of the palace probably date from the 17th century. In the painted hall, personal effects of the early Romanovs are displayed, including gold dishes, ancient title deeds, ledgers inlaid with precious gems and the robes of Nikita's eldest son, Patriarch Fyodor Filaret. The rooms have been refurbished in the lavish style of the period, with walls covered in gilt-embossed leather or painted in rich reds, greens and golds.

In the 16th and 17th centuries even the richest families had to tolerate rather cramped and dim conditions. The portals in the palace are so low that a man of average height has to stoop, and little light is let in by the windows as they are made of mica, a translucent mineral, rather than glass.

In the mid 19th century the light and airy, wooden upper storey was added to the building. The main hall on this level has a beautifully carved wooden ceiling. An anteroom has a display of embroidery.

The vaulted cellars are the least interesting rooms of the museum and contain an odd mix of baskets, trunks and kitchen equipment.

Gilded iconostasis in the Church of the Trinity in Nikitniki

Ornate dining room in the Palace of the Romanov Boyars

Church of the Trinity in Nikitniki ❹

Церковь Троицы в Никитниках
Tserkov Troitsy v Nikitnikakh

Nikitnikov pereulok 3. **Map** 7 C1.
Ⓜ *Kitay Gorod.* ⬤ *to public.*

Like the churches on ulitsa Varvarka, this marvellous church is dwarfed by monstrous post-war buildings that were formerly Communist Party offices. When it was founded in 1635 by the wealthy merchant, Grigoriy Nikitnikov, the church would have dominated the local skyline. It is at present closed while it is being restored.

Carvings on the porch of the Church of the Trinity in Nikitniki

The church has five green domes, a profusion of decoration and painted tiles, and tiers of *kokoshniki* gables (see p44). The equally elaborate tent-roofed bell tower, which is linked to the main building by an enclosed gallery, was added shortly after the church was finished.

The Church of the Trinity is famous for its frescoes, which were finished in 1656, shortly after Nikitnikov died from the plague. They portray scenes from the Gospels, such as *The Parable of the Rich Man*, in direct, emotional terms.

Among the artists who made an important contribution to the church's decoration was the great fresco and icon painter Semen Ushakov. He painted a number of the frescoes and several of the panels in the splendid gilded iconostasis. Among his works is the *Annunciation of the Virgin*, which can be seen to the left of the Royal Gate (see p61) on the iconostasis. Members of the Nikitnikov family are commemorated in the frescoes in the corner Chapel of St Nikita the Martyr.

Semen Ushakov was a parishioner and his house is around the corner from the church on Ipatevskiy pereulok. It is an unremarkable 17th-century, red-brick building.

Striking 19th-century commercial buildings lining ulitsa Ilinka

Ulitsa Ilinka ⑤

Улица Ильинка
Ulitsa Ilinka

Map 7 B1. Ⓜ *Kitay Gorod.*

In the 19th century this narrow but majestic street was the commercial heart of Kitay Gorod, and home to numerous banks and trading offices. Their richly decorated façades were intended to impress and are still the chief pleasure of a stroll along the street. Today, ulitsa Ilinka is once more the location of a number of commercial and financial institutions, including the Ministry of Finance.

The name Ilinka refers to the former Ilinskiy Monastery, of which no traces now remain. The monastery once stood where the 17th-century Church of St Elijah can now be seen, at No. 3. Further along, at No. 6, on the corner of Birzhevaya ploshchad, is a peach-coloured building with a Neo-Classical portico, which at present houses the Russian Chamber of Industry and Commerce. Originally these were the premises of Moscow's Stock Exchange, which was re-built by Aleksandr Kamenskiy in 1873–5, having first opened in 1836. At that time many of Moscow's merchants still wore long patriarchal beards and the traditional kaftan, and were used to dealing with one another in the street. They at first refused to enter the new Stock Exchange and, in the end, were corralled into the building by the police.

Across the street from this building is the former Trinity Sergius Hostel, which was the city mission of the Trinity Monastery of St Sergius *(see pp162–5)*. Now part of the Russian Supreme Court, it was built by Pavel Skomoroshenko in 1876 and is a restrained example of the Russian-Revival style *(see p45)*.

A building which formerly served as offices for the Soviet government stands at the corner of ulitsa Ilinka and Bolshoy Cherkasskiy pereulok. Uncompromisingly plain, with glazed tiles and rows of narrowly spaced windows, it was designed by Vladimir Mayat in the 1920s.

Monastery of the Epiphany ⑥

Богоявленский монастырь
Bogoyavlenskiy monastery

Bogoyavlenskiy pereulok 2, stroenie 4. **Map** 3 A5. **Tel** *(495) 298 3771.* Ⓜ *Ploshchad Revolyutsii.* ⭕ *8am–8pm daily.* ⬛

Founded by Prince Daniil, father of Grand Prince Ivan I *(see p18)* in 1296, the Monastery of the Epiphany is Moscow's second oldest monastery, after the Danilovskiy Monastery *(see pp136–7)*. It was built at what was at that time the edge of the city, beyond the merchants' quarters.

The oldest building to survive is the cathedral. This is an addition to the original medieval complex and dates from 1693–6. The building is distinguished by its massive but refined tower, a masterpiece of Moscow Baroque *(see p44)*. Among the other surviving features are a bishop's palace, a few 18th-century monastic cells and some trading rows.

Nikolskaya Ulitsa ⑦

Никольская улица
Nikolskaya ulitsa

Map 3 A5. Ⓜ *Lubyanka, Ploshchad Revolyutsii.*

By the end of the 12th century, this street, which is named after the Kremlin's Nicholas' Tower *(see p66)*, had been settled by merchants and traders. Trading stalls and shops remained a feature of the street until the Revolution. Following a dowdy period under communism, Nikolskaya ulitsa has recently moved up-market with the arrival of several expensive clothing stores and jewellers.

Through the courtyard at No. 7 is a gateway leading into the Zaikonospasskiy Monastery, which was founded in the 15th century or earlier. The name means Saviour Beyond the Icons and recalls the time when there was a brisk trade in icons here. The monastery church, with its dilapidated red brick tower and spire, dates from the 17th century. It is now open again for worship. From 1687–1814 the monastery also housed Moscow's first institute of higher education, referred

Gothic-style façade of the Synodal Printing House, Nikolskaya ulitsa

Kazan Cathedral, a faithful 1990s reconstruction of the original cathedral

Kazan Cathedral ❽

Казанский собор
Kazanskiy sobor

Nikolskaya ulitsa 3. **Map** 3 A5. *Tel* (495) 298 0131. Ⓜ *Okhotnyy Ryad.*

This diminutive cathedral is a replica of an original demolished in 1936. Its predecessor was consecrated in 1637 and housed the Icon of the Kazan Virgin. The icon was revered because it had accompanied Prince Dmitriy Pozharskiy during his victorious campaign against the invading Poles 25 years earlier *(see p108)*.

Detailed plans and photographs, preserved by architect Pyotr Baranovskiy, assisted reconstruction of the cathedral in 1990–93 *(see p44)*. It was reconsecrated by Patriarch Aleksey II in the presence of President Boris Yeltsin and the mayor of Moscow, Yuriy Luzhkov. The Icon of the Kazan Virgin in the cathedral is a copy, the original having been stolen in 1904.

Resurrection Gate ❾

Воскресенские ворота
Voskresenskie vorota

Krasnaya ploshchad.
Map 3 A5. Ⓜ *Okhotnyy Ryad.*
Ploshchad Revolyutsii.

Rebuilt in 1995 *(see p44)*, this gateway, with its twin red towers topped by green tent spires, is an exact copy of the original completed on this site in 1680. The first gateway was demolished in 1931. Note the mosaic icons on the gate, one of which depicts Moscow's patron saint, St George, slaying the dragon.

Within the gateway is the equally colourful Chapel of the Iverian Virgin, originally built in the late 18th century to house an icon. Whenever the tsar came to Moscow, he would visit this shrine before entering the Kremlin *(see pp52–67)*. Visitors should try to see the gate at night, when it is impressively lit up.

to laboriously as the Slavic Greek Latin Academy. Among its famous pupils was the famous polymath and future founder of Moscow University, Mikhail Lomonosov *(see p94)*.

At No. 15 are the fanciful Gothic style spires of the Synodal Printing House. The pale blue building, with a lion and unicorn sculpted over its central window, contrasting with an incongruous hammer and sickle above, dates from 1810–14. The courtyard is enhanced by a colourful chequered roof and walls of blue and white tiles. In the chambers previously on this site Ivan Fyodorov produced Russia's first printed book, *The Acts of the Apostles*, in 1564.

Next door, in the courtyard of No. 17, is the Slavyanskiy Bazaar restaurant, which opened in 1870. Among its former patrons is Anton Chekhov *(see p96)*. This restaurant is also where the theatre directors Konstantin Stanislavskiy and Vladimir Nemirovich-Danchenko began a meeting which concluded with the founding of the Moscow Arts Theatre *(see p92)*. Following a fire in 1994, the restaurant was closed for repairs, but it has now been reopened.

On the opposite side of the road is a building that used to house the Chizhevskoe Inn, a combined inn and warehouse for traders passing through Kitay Gorod. In the courtyard behind it is the 17th-century Church of the Assumption.

Floodlit Resurrection Gate, inside which is the Chapel of the Iverian Virgin

The vast expanse of Red Square, with the Historical Museum at the far end

Red Square ⑩
Красная площадь
Krasnaya ploshchad

Map 7 B1. Ⓜ *Ploshchad Revolyutsii, Okhotnyy Ryad.* **Historical Museum** *Tel* (495) 692 4019. ◯ *11am–6pm Mon, Wed–Sat, 11am–8pm Sun.* 🎟 ♿ 🛍 🖋 🖼

Towards the end of the 15th century, Ivan III *(see p18)* gave orders for houses in front of the Kremlin to be cleared to make way for this square. It originally served as a market called the *torg*, but the wooden stalls burned down so often that the area later became popularly known as Fire Square. The current name dates from the 17th century and is derived from the Russian word *krasnyy*, which originally meant "beautiful" but later came to denote "red". The association between the colour red and Communism is purely coincidental.

Red Square, which is approximately 500m (1,600ft) in length, was also the setting for public announcements and executions. At its southern end, in front of St Basil's Cathedral *(see pp108–9)*, there is a small circular dais. Called Lobnoe Mesto, this is the platform from which the tsars and patriarchs would address the people. In 1606 the first "False Dmitry" *(see p19)*, a usurper of the throne, was killed by a hostile crowd. His body was finally left at Lobnoe Mesto.

Six years later, a second pretender to the throne, who like the first "False Dmitry" was backed by Poland, took

power. He was expelled from the Kremlin by an army led by the Russian heroes Dmitriy Pozharskiy and Kuzma Minin, who proclaimed Russia's deliverance from Lobnoe Mesto. In 1818, a statue was erected in their honour *(see p108)*. This now stands in front of St Basil's.

Red Square has also long been a stage for pageants and processions. Before the Revolution *(see pp26–9)*, the patriarch would ride an ass through Saviour's Gate *(see p66)* to St Basil's each Palm Sunday to commemorate Christ's entry into Jerusalem.

Religious processions were abolished in the Communist era. Military parades took their place and were staged each year on May Day and on the anniversary of the Revolution. Rows of grim-faced Soviet leaders observed them from

Lobnoe Mesto, the platform from which the tsar spoke

outside the Lenin Mausoleum. They, in turn, would be keenly studied by professional kremlinologists in the West trying to work out the current pecking order.

Today the square is used for a variety of cultural events, concerts, firework displays and other public occasions.

The red-brick building facing St Basil's Cathedral was constructed by Vladimir Sherwood in 1883 in the Russian-Revival style *(see p45)*. It houses the Historical Museum. The museum boasts over four million exhibits covering the rise and expansion of the Russian state.

In front of the museum's façade on Manezhnaya ploshchad is a statue by Vyacheslav Klykov of one of the heroes of World War II *(see p27)*, Marshal Georgiy Zhukov. This statue of him was unveiled in 1995 to mark the 50th anniversary of the end of World War II.

Aleksey Shchusev's Lenin Mausoleum, with the Kremlin Wall behind

---

RED SQUARE

RESURRECTION GATE
HISTORICAL MUSEUM
KAZAN CATHEDRAL
RED SQUARE
GUM
KREMLIN WALL
LENIN MAUSOLEUM
LOBNOE MESTO
SAVIOUR'S GATE
ST BASIL'S CATHEDRAL

Lenin Mausoleum ⑪
Мавзолей ВИ Ленина
Mavzoley VI Lenina

Krasnaya ploshchad. **Map** 7 A1. **Tel**
(495) 923 5527. Ⓜ Ploshchad Revolyutsii, Okhotnyy Ryad. ☐ 10am–
1pm Tue–Thu, Sat–Sun. ⬛ Strictly no
cameras, even if it is in your bag.

Following Lenin's death in 1924,
and against his wishes, it was
decided to preserve the former
Soviet leader's body for
posterity. The body was
embalmed and placed in a
temporary wooden mausoleum
in Red Square. Once it became
clear that the embalming
process had worked, Aleksey
Shchusev *(see p45)* designed
the current mausoleum of a
pyramid of cubes cut from red
granite and black labradorite.

Paying one's respects to
Lenin's remains was once akin
to a religious experience, and
queues used to trail all over
Red Square. In 1993, however,
the goose-stepping guard of
honour was replaced by a
lone militiaman and now the
mausoleum attracts mostly
tourists. There are rumours
that Lenin will soon be
moved elsewhere or buried.

Behind the mausoleum at the
foot of the Kremlin Wall are the
graves of other famous
communists. They include
Lenin's successors, Joseph
Stalin (at one time laid alongside Lenin in the Mausoleum),
Leonid Brezhnev and Yuriy
Andropov. Lenin's wife and
sister are also buried here,
as are the first man in space,
Yuriy Gagarin, writer Maxim
Gorky and American John
Reed. The latter was honoured
as the author of *Ten Days that
Shook the World*, an account of
the October Revolution.

The glass-roofed interior of Russia's largest department store, GUM

GUM ⑫
ГУМ
GUM

Krasnaya ploshchad 3. **Map** 7 B1.
Tel (495) 921 5763. Ⓜ Ploshchad
Revolyutsii, Okhotnyy Ryad. ☐
10am-10pm daily. ♿ www.gum.ru

Before the Revolution, this
building was known as
the Upper Trading Rows after
the covered market that used to
stand on the site. In fact, lines of
stalls used to run all the way
from here to the Moskva river.
GUM has three separate arcades
which are still called "lines". The
store's name, Gosudarstvennyy
universalnyy magazin, dates
from its nationalization in 1921.

The building was designed
by Aleksandr Pomerantsev in
1889–93 in the then fashionable Russian-Revival style. Its
archways, wrought-iron railings and stuccoed galleries
inside are especially impressive when sunlight streams
through the glass roof.

There were once more than
1,000 shops here, selling goods
ranging from furs and silks to
humble candles. For a period,
however, during the rule of
Stalin *(see p27)*, GUM's shops
were requisitioned as offices.
Nowadays, Western firms like
Benetton, Estée Lauder and
Christian Dior dominate the
prestigious ground floor along
with a variety of Western-style
cafés and restaurants.

EMBALMING LENIN

"Do not raise monuments to him, or palaces to
his name, do not organize pompous ceremonies
in his memory." Such were the words of Lenin's
widow, Krupskaya. Despite this, Lenin's body was
embalmed by two professors and, after a delay to
see if the process had worked, put on display. A
laboratory is dedicated to preserving the body,
which needs regular applications of special fluids.
Rumours that parts or all of the body have been
replaced with wax substitutes are vigorously denied.

St Basil's Cathedral ⑬

Собор Василия Блаженного

Sobor Vasiliya Blazhennovo

Detail, Chapel of the Entry of Christ into Jerusalem

Commissioned by Ivan the Terrible *(see p18)* to celebrate the capture of the Mongol stronghold of Kazan in 1552, St Basil's Cathedral was completed in 1561. It is reputed to have been designed by the architect Postnik Yakovlev. According to legend, Ivan was so amazed at the beauty of his work that he had him blinded so that he would never be able to design anything as exquisite again. The church was officially called the Cathedral of the Intercession because the final siege of Kazan began on the Feast of the Intercession of the Virgin. However, it is usually known as St Basil's after the "holy fool" Basil the Blessed whose remains are interred within. The cathedral's design, which was inspired by traditional Russian timber architecture, is a riot of gables, tent roofs and twisting onion domes.

Bell tower

Chapel of the Trinity

★ Domes

Following a fire in 1583 the original helmet-shaped cupolas were replaced by ribbed or faceted onion domes. It is only since 1670 that the domes have been painted many colours; at one time St Basil's was white with golden domes.

Chapel of St Cyprian

This is one of eight main chapels commemorating the campaigns of Ivan the Terrible against the town of Kazan, to the east of Moscow. It is dedicated to St Cyprian, whose feast is on 2 October, the day after the last attack.

MININ AND POZHARSKIY

A bronze statue by Ivan Martos depicts two heroes from the Time of Troubles *(see p19)*, the butcher Kuzma Minin and Prince Dmitriy Pozharskiy. They raised a volunteer force to fight the invading Poles and, in 1612, led their army to victory when they drove the Poles out of the Kremlin. The statue was erected in 1818, in the triumphal afterglow of the Napoleonic Wars.

Originally placed in the centre of Red Square facing the Kremlin, it was moved to its present site in front of St Basil's during the Soviet era.

Monument to Minin and Prince Pozharskiy

The Chapel of St Basil, the ninth chapel to be added to the cathedral, was built in 1588 to house the remains of the "holy fool", Basil the Blessed.

Chapel of the Three Patriarchs

Entrance to the cathedral

Tent roof
on the
Central
Chapel

Chapel of
St Nicholas

Central Chapel
of the Intercession
*Light floods in through the
windows of the tent-roofed
central church, which soars
to a height of 61 m (200 ft).*

VISITORS' CHECKLIST

Krasnaya ploshchad 2. **Map** 7 B1.
Tel (495) 698 3304. ◯ *May–
Nov: 10am–6pm Wed–Mon (Dec–
Apr: 10am–5pm).* Ⓜ *Okhotnyy
Ryad, Ploshchad Revolyutsii.* ▭
25. ▭ *8.* 🅿 🇬🇧 *English.* ▭
religious hols. **www.shm.ru**

★ Main Iconostasis
*The Baroque-style
iconostasis in the
Central Chapel of the
Intercession dates
from the 19th
century. However,
some of the icons
contained in it were
painted much earlier.*

Chapel of
St Varlaam
of Khutynskiy

Tiered gables

STAR FEATURES

★ Domes

★ Gallery

★ Main Iconostasis

**The Chapel of the Entry
of Christ into Jerusalem**
was used as a ceremonial
entrance during the annual
Palm Sunday proces-
sion. On this day the
patriarch rode from
the Kremlin to St
Basil's Cathedral on a
horse dressed up to
look like a donkey.

★ Gallery
*Running around
the outside of the
Central Chapel, the gallery
connects it to the other eight
chapels. It was roofed over at
the end of the 17th century
and the walls and ceilings
were decorated with floral
tiles in the late 18th century.*

Chapel of
Bishop
Gregory

Ivanovskaya Hill ⑭

Ивановская горка
Ivanovskaya gorka

Map 3 C5. Ⓜ *Kitay Gorod.*

This hilly area takes its name from the Ivanovskiy Convent on the corner of ulitsa Zabelina and Malyy Ivanovskiy pereulok. The convent's rather neglected remains can be seen behind a twin-towered gateway and high encircling walls.

Yelena Glinska, mother of Ivan the Terrible *(see p18)*, founded the convent in 1533 as a gesture of thanks for the birth of her son. Later, however, it doubled as a prison for many years – its most famous inmate was Avgusta Tarakanova, the illegitimate daughter of Tsarina Elizabeth *(see p22)* and Count Aleksey Razumovskiy. She was educated abroad before being brought to Russia in 1785 and put into the convent under an assumed name. She spent the rest of her life here as a solitary nun, forbidden to receive any visitors except for the mother superior. She died in 1810.

Across the road is the Church of St Vladimir in the Old Gardens. It was built in 1514 by Italian architect Aleviz Novyy, but it was extensively altered at the end of the 17th century. Its name refers to the tsar's orchards, which used to occupy the slopes of the hill.

One of the pleasures of this area is exploring its unusually quiet backstreets. At the end of Malyy Ivanovskiy pereulok, which runs down from the Ivanovskiy Convent, is Podkolokolnyy pereulok (Lane Beneath the Bells). This street is dominated by the Church of St Nicholas the Wonder-worker, which dates from the mid-17th century and is recognizable by its outsized red bell tower. Perhaps the most impressive church in the area is SS Peter and Paul on Petropavlovskiy pereulok. It was built in 1700 and contains an icon of the Bogolyubovskaya Virgin, which used to hang in a chapel near the gate to the city at the end of ulitsa Varvarka *(see p102)*.

To the north, at No. 10 Kolpachiy pereulok is the 17th-century mansion that reputedly belonged to the Ukrainian chief Ivan Mazepa. He fled to Turkish-controlled Moldova in 1709, after betraying Peter the Great *(see p22)* to the Swedes and then being defeated by him. Tchaikovsky set the story to music in his opera, *Mazepa*. The name of another street, Kokhlovskiy pereulok, may also have a Ukrainian link; Ukrainians used to be known as *khokhly* because of the tufts of hair they grew at the back of their shaved heads; (*khokhly* means tufted in Russian).

The most notable building standing on ulitsa Maroseyka is the blue and white mansion at No. 17. This is now the Belarussian embassy.

Russian space programme exhibit at the Polytechnical Museum

Polytechnical Museum ⑮

Политехнический музей
Politekhnicheskiy muzey

Novaya ploshchad 3/4. **Map** 3 B5. **Tel** *(495) 923 0756.* ◯ *10am–6pm Wed–Mon.* ⬤ *last Thu of the month.* Ⓜ *Kitay Gorod.* 🎦 🚫 🎬 *English (book in advance).* **www**.polymus.ru

Designed by architect Ippolit Monighetti, the central section of this museum was built in 1877 and is a superb example of Russian-Revival architecture *(see p45)*. The north and south wings were added in 1896 and 1907 respectively.

The items on display were originally assembled for an exhibition staged in the Alexander Gardens *(see p67)* in 1872. This marked the 200th anniversary of the birth of Peter the Great, himself an enthusiastic amateur scientist.

The museum is a popular outing for schoolchildren. Its original collection has been expanded to trace the development of Russian science and technology during the 19th and 20th centuries. Exhibits range from early clocks and cameras to cars and space capsules. Every two hours there are demonstrations of devices such as robots, working models and sound equipment.

A typically quiet, gently sloping backstreet on Ivanovskaya Hill

History of Moscow Museum ⑯

Музей истории города Москвы

Muzey istorii goroda Moskvy

Novaya ploshchad 12. **Map** 3 B5.
Tel *(495) 924 8490.* 🕐 *10am–6pm Tue, Thu, Sat–Sun; 11am–7pm Wed, Fri.* Ⓜ *Lubyanka.* 📷 📹 📷
www.museum.ru/moscow

This museum was founded in 1896 and is housed in the 19th-century church of St John the Divine Under the Elm. There has been some speculation about finding larger premises, but this has yet to be decided upon.

Only a fraction of the one million items in the collection can be displayed at any time. These include Iron and Bronze Age artifacts, colossal timbers from a medieval log cabin, unearthed during the building of the State Kremlin Palace *(see p56)* in the Kremlin, and a growing treasure-trove of jewellery, toys and pottery. There are also priceless early maps, rare illuminated books, paintings, glass, ceramics and scale models of the Kremlin.

Wooden model of the Kremlin in the History of Moscow Museum

Mayakovsky Museum ⑰

Музей-квартира ВВ Маяковского

Muzey-kvartira VV Mayakovskovo

Lubyanskiy proezd 3/6. **Map** 3 B5.
Tel *(495) 921 9387.* 🕐 *10am–5pm Fri–Tue, 1–8pm Thu.* ⚫ *last Fri of the month.* Ⓜ *Lubyanka.* 📷 📹 📷

Vladimir Mayakovsky, poet, iconoclast, exhibitionist and consummate self-publicist, was above all a revolutionary. In his short but eventful life his poetry, plays, film scripts and

The striking Constructivist entrance to the Mayakovsky Museum

poster art gave a strident voice to the Revolution and its vision of modernity. The terse and uncompromising agitprop posters he designed with Aleksandr Rodchenko are a prominent feature of the museum.

By nature, Mayakovsky was both provocative and extraordinary,

Room designed to symbolize Mayakovsky's poetic origins

and this is brilliantly reflected in this apparently anarchic museum. Huge frameworks of metal bars, designed in the Constructivist style influential in the 1920s, lean at fantastic angles and provide a backdrop for the other exhibits. Mayakovsky's artworks and belongings are intermingled: chairs, old boots, typewriters, painted cannon balls, large posters and photomontages, cracked mirrors, sewing machines and manuscripts.

Mayakovsky actually lived in this block from 1919 until his death in 1930: a single room on the fourth floor has been furnished to look as it would have done when he moved in. While living in this house, Mayakovsky continued his long-running love affair with Lilya Brik, the wife of his friend Osip Brik. This was also the period in which he wrote his best known plays, the caustic satires *The Bed Bug* and *Bath House*.

The last part of the exhibition deals with Mayakovsky's suicide at the age of 37. On display are two death masks, one black and one white. After his death, Stalin *(see p27)* praised Mayakovsky as the most talented of Soviet poets and continued to use his work for propaganda purposes.

VLADIMIR MAYAKOVSKY

Born in Georgia in 1893, Mayakovsky was brought up in Moscow, where he became involved in the revolutionary movement at the tender age of 14. Earning his revolutionary honours by being arrested three times in the space of two years, he was also drawn to the avant-garde and in 1912 became a founder of the Futurist movement by contributing to its manifesto, *A Slap in the Face for Public Taste*. Mayakovsky wholeheartedly endorsed the Revolution *(see p26–9)*, becoming one of its most effective propagandists, but became increasingly disillusioned with the straitjacketed attitudes of Soviet society in the 1920s; this may have contributed to his suicide in 1930.

Lubyanka Square ⑱
Лубянская площадь
Lubyanskaya ploshchad

Map 3 B5. Ⓜ *Lubyanka.*

Synonymous with terror and the secret police, the name Lubyanka struck fear into the hearts of generations of Soviet citizens. In 1918, the Cheka (the forerunners of the KGB), led by the hated "Iron" Feliks Dzerzhinskiy, took over what had been the Rossiya Insurance Offices at the northern end of the square.

In the 1930s the building was extended and the enormous, underground Lubyanka Prison added, where the KGB interrogated, tortured, imprisoned and killed hundreds of thousands of people. By 1947 the incredible numbers of those accused in the course of Stalin's rule *(see p27)* led to the building of an additional wing, designed by Aleksey Shchusev *(see p45)*. Despite numerous changes of name (and protestations of changes in ethos), the Russian intelligence services still occupy the building.

Feliks Dzerzhinskiy (1877–1926)

A statue of Dzerzhinskiy used to stand in the centre of Lubyanka square. It was unceremoniously toppled in front of a cheering crowd, following the unsuccessful coup against President Gorbachev in 1991 *(see p31)*. The statue can now be seen in the Graveyard of Fallen Monuments *(see p135)*.

With a customary lack of irony, the Soviet authorities built Russia's largest toy store, Detskiy Mir, now closed *(see p193)*, directly opposite the KGB headquarters in 1957.

Chistoprudnyy Bulvar ⑲
Чистопрудный бульвар
Chistoprudnyy bulvar

Map 3 C4. Ⓜ *Chistye Prudy.*

This road is part of the historic Boulevard Ring, which was laid out along the line of the old Belyy Gorod (White City) wall after the great fire of 1812 *(see p24)*. There are several fine houses located along Chistoprudnyy bulvar. At No. 19a is the elegant, Classical-style portico of the Sovremennik Theatre, which was built as a cinema by Roman Klein in 1914. Just beyond is the mansion where Sergey Eisenstein, director of *October* and *Battleship Potemkin*, lived from 1920–34.

Chistoprudnyy bulvar is part of the area which used to be known as Myasnitskaya after the butchers *(myasniki)* who worked here in the 17th century. The *myasniki* are still commemorated in the name of Myasnitskaya ulitsa, which runs from Lubyanka Square to Chistoprudnyy bulvar.

Between the carriageways of Chistoprudnyy bulvar is a large pond. It was created as

Detail of the fine stone carvings on Menshikov's Tower

a place for the butchers to dump offal and other waste products but, by 1703, the stench and risk of disease were so bad that the pond was cleared and renamed Chistye prudy (Clean Pond).

The beautiful, pale blue mansion just round the corner, at No. 22 ulitsa Pokrovka, was built between 1766–72. Before the communist coup in October 1917, the building used to be one of the best male secondary schools in Moscow, dating from 1861.

Menshikov's Tower ⑳
Меншикова башня
Menshikova bashnya

Arkhangelskiy pereulok 15.
Map 3 C4. Ⓜ *Turgenevskaya, Chistye Prudy.* ♿ ⌀

This church was constructed on the orders of Prince Aleksandr Menshikov, Peter the Great's advisor and favourite. With Peter the Great's backing, Menshikov rose from the position of lowly pie-seller to be one of most powerful and wealthy men in Russia. It was typical of the flamboyant Menshikov that, when he commissioned the church from Ivan Zarudniy in 1701, he instructed the architect to make it just a little taller than the Ivan the Great Bell Tower *(see p57)*, until then the tallest structure in all of Russia.

Specialist stonemasons from Yaroslavl and Kostroma and a variety of Italian sculptors worked on the church, accounting for the beauty of the stone carvings and stuccoed festoons. The wooden spire was capped by a gilded angel and contained an expensive English clock, which chimed on the quarter-hour.

The infamous former headquarters of the KGB on Lubyanka Square

However, pious Muscovites remained unimpressed by the display of wealth and when the tower was destroyed by lightning in 1723 many saw in it the hand of God. The tower was rebuilt without the spire in 1773–80. The church was one of the few to remain open during the Soviet era and much of its interior decoration has survived.

Next to the tower is the small Church of St Fyodor Stratilit, which was heated in winter for the benefit of the parishioners. It was built in 1806, probably by Ivan Yegotov.

Perlov Tea House ㉑

Чай-кофе магазин

Chay-kofe magazin

Myasnitskaya ulitsa 19. **Map** 3 B4
Tel *(495) 925 4656.* ☐ *10am–6pm daily.* Ⓜ *Chistye Prudy, Turgenevskaya.*

This building was originally designed by Roman Klein in 1890 for the tea merchant Sergey Perlov. Five years later Perlov heard that the official representative of the Chinese emperor would be visiting Moscow. He hastily commissioned Karl Gippius to redesign the shop in the hope of receiving him. The façade is a fanciful vision of the Orient, including serpents, dragons and pagoda-style details. The oriental theme is followed up inside with lacquered columns and counters painted with

Shelves of tea behind the counter of the elegant Perlov Tea House

The waiting area inside the luxurious Sandunovskiy Baths

golden dragons. In the event the Chinese official mistakenly visited Perlov's nephew, who was also a tea merchant.

Convent of the Nativity of the Virgin ㉒

Рождественский монастырь

Rozhdestvenskiy monastyr

Ulitsa Rozhdestvenka 20. **Map** 3 A4.
Tel *(495) 921 3986.* ☐ *8am–7:30pm daily.* Ⓜ *Kuznetskiy Most.* ♿ ⃠

Converted to provide housing in Soviet times, this small cluster of buildings was neglected until 1991, when it was returned to the Russian Orthodox Church.

Founded in 1386 by Princess Maria Serpukhovskiy, daughter-in-law of Ivan I *(see p18),* the convent is one of a ring of fortified monasteries constructed around Moscow.

The beautifully proportioned cathedral, commissioned between 1501–5 by Tsar Ivan III *(see p18),* has tiers of *kokoshniki* gables *(see p44)* surmounted by a single cupola.

The small Church of St John of Zlatoust, with five domes, has also survived, along with a short section of the original brick ramparts. The yellow, tiered bell tower was designed by Nikolay Kozlovskiy in 1835.

The bell tower of the Convent of the Nativity of the Virgin

Sandunovskiy Baths ㉓

Сандуновские бани

Sandunovskie bani

Neglinnaya ulitsa 14, stroenie 4–7.
Map 3 A4. ***Tel*** *(495) 925 4631.* ☐
8am–10pm daily (last adm 8pm).
Ⓜ *Kuznetskiy Most.* ▨ ⃠
www.sanduny.ru

The original Sandunovskiy Baths were built for actor Sila Sandunov in 1808. In 1895 they were replaced by this building designed by Boris Freidenberg and with a decorative Beaux Arts façade.

The main entrance is through an ornate archway, decorated with sculptures of nymphs on horseback, emerging from the sea and using triton shells as trumpets.

However, it is the sumptuous interiors, decorated in a flamboyant mix of Baroque, Gothic and Moorish styles, that make the baths famous. The Alhambra Palace in Spain was one of the sources of inspiration for the ornate decoration. The baths can accommodate up to 2,000 customers a day. The best, most expensive, rooms are located on the first floor. Here patrons can still buy birch twigs to beat themselves with, an essential part of a Russian steam bath.

ZAMOSKVORECHE

First settled in the 13th century, Zamoskvoreche (literally "beyond the Moscow river") acted as an outpost against the Mongols. Its main road, Bolshaya Ordynka, was the route to the *Orda*, or Golden Horde, the Mongol headquarters on the Volga river. Later, under Ivan the Terrible, the Streltsy (royal guard) was stationed here. Artisans serving the court also moved in, living in areas according to their trades, each of which sponsored a church. These historic churches,

Icon at the Convent of SS Martha and Mary

now in varying states of repair, and the fact that the area was almost untouched by the replanning of the 1930s, give it a more old-fashioned atmosphere than the centre, which is dominated by massive Soviet architecture. In the 19th century wealthy merchants settled here, many of whom, such as Aleksey Bakhrushin and Pavel Tretyakov, were patrons of the arts. Based on its founder's acquisitions, the Tretyakov Gallery is the nation's most important collection of Russian art.

SIGHTS AT A GLANCE

Churches and Convents

Church of the Consolation of All Sorrows ❸
Church of the Resurrection in Kadashi ❷
Church of St Catherine ❻
Church of St Clement ❹
Church of St Nicholas in Pyzhy ❺
Convent of SS Martha and Mary ❼

Museums and Galleries

Bakhrushin Theatre Museum ❾
Tretyakov Gallery pp118–21 ❶

Tropinin Museum ❽

Streets

Sophia Embankment ❿

GETTING THERE

If using the metro, it is best to head for Tretyakovskaya, Novokuznetskaya or Paveletskaya metro stations. Trolleybuses, buses and trams all cross the Moskva River at various points to reach Zamoskvoreche. Trolleybus routes include the 1, 4, 8, 33 and 62, while buses 6, 25 and K and trams 3, 39 and A also serve the area.

KEY

Street-by-Street map
pp116–17

Ⓜ Metro station

0 metres 400
0 yards 400

◁ **The Vodootvodnyy canal in Zamoskvoreche, blanketed by snow in Moscow's freezing winter**

Street-by-Street: Around Pyatnitskaya Ulitsa

An old-fashioned atmosphere still prevails in
the area around Pyatnitskaya ulitsa. The
well-established streets are lined with attractive
19th-century churches and imposing Neo-Classical
mansions. The busiest part of the district is the
area around Tretyakovskaya metro. The market
stalls on the station forecourt spill over onto
Klimentovskiy pereulok, and nearby Pyatnitskaya
ulitsa is the main shopping street. A short walk to
the west is the stunning Tretyakov Gallery. To the
north, the area is bordered by the Vodootvodnyy
canal, which was built in 1783–6 to prevent the
regular spring flooding of the Moskva river.

Vodootvodnyy Canal

★ Church of the Resurrection in Kadashi
*With its tapering bell tower and
lavish limestone ornamentation
this magnificent church is a fine
example of the style known as
Moscow Baroque (see p44)* ②

★ Tretyakov Gallery
*The world's largest collection of
Russian art is housed here. Taken
down in the Soviet era, the statue
of Pavel Tretyakov (see p120) has
now been restored to its rightful
place in front of the gallery* ①

The Demidov House was
built in 1789–91 by a family
of well-known industrialists.

Church of the Consolation of All Sorrows
*Two of Moscow's best-known
architects contributed to this
much-loved church. Vasiliy
Bazhenov designed the bell
tower and Osip Bove (see
p45) the rotunda* ④

The Church of SS Michael and Fyodor, dating from the late 17th century, is named after two martyrs killed by Mongols when they refused to renounce Christianity.

Kremlin

Church of St John the Baptist has a distinctive green bell-tower and was built in the 18th century.

Cultural Centre of Pan Slavism

LOCATOR MAP
See Street Finder, map 7

Novokuznetskaya Metro Station, designed by Ivan Taranov and Natalia Bykova, was opened in 1943 at the height World War II, and the design of the interior is based on military subjects.

PYATNITSKAYA ULITSA

ULITSA BOLSHAYA ORDYNKA

Church of St Clement
Building began on this splendid Baroque church in 1720 and continued in phases over the next few decades: in 1756–8 a rectory and belfry were added. The church has four black, star-spangled domes and a central golden dome **5**

KLIMENTOVSKIY PEREULOK

Small shops on Klimentovskiy pereulok sell groceries, magazines, perfumes and other goods.

retyakovskaya

| 0 metres | 100 |
| 0 yards | 100 |

STAR SIGHTS

★ Tretyakov Gallery

★ Church of the Resurrection

The Dolgov House has an elaborately decorated Neo-Classical exterior. This fine town house was built in the 1770s for a wealthy merchant named Dolgov, possibly by his son-in-law, Vasiliy Bazhenov *(see p44).*

KEY

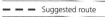

– – – Suggested route

Tretyakov Gallery ❶
Третьяковская галерея
Tretyakovskaya galereya

The Tretyakov Gallery was founded in 1856 by the wealthy merchant Pavel Tretyakov. He presented his private museum of Russian art to the city in 1892. His brother Sergey also donated a number of works and the gallery's collection has been expanding ever since. Today the Tretyakov has the largest collection of Russian art in the world. The building has a striking façade, designed by artist Viktor Vasnetsov, with a bas-relief of St George and the dragon at its centre. A new wing was added to the gallery in 1930. Many of the early 20th-century works from the collection have now been housed in the New Tretyakov Gallery *(see p135).*

Stairs down to ground floor

Portraits by Ivan Kramskoy *(see p120)*

First floor

The Appearance of Christ to the People is by the 19th-century Romantic artist, Aleksandr Ivanov *(see p120).*

The Rooks Have Come *(1871)*
This bleak winter scene by Aleksey Savrasov contains a message of hope: rooks are taken by Russians as a sign of the coming spring.

Portrait of Arseny Tropinin, the Artist's Son *(c.1818)*
This portrait was painted by the renowned artist Vasiliy Tropinin. He was a serf for 47 years before gaining his freedom and finding commercial success.

Stairs from basement

Portraits by Ilya Repin *(see p120)*

GALLERY GUIDE
The gallery has 62 rooms on two main floors. On entering the museum, visitors first descend to the basement ticket office, then head straight up to the first floor. Paintings are hung in chronological order in rooms 1–54: visitors take some stairs back down to the ground floor after viewing room 34. Russian jewellery is housed on the ground floor in room 55, while rooms 56–62 contain icons and jewellery.

★ **Demon Seated** *(1890) This is one of several paintings by Mikhail Vrubel, who adopted a new, strikingly modern style. They are inspired by Mikhail Lermontov's Symbolist poem,* The Demon *(see p82), with which Vrubel became obsessed.*

Religious Procession in Kursk Province
*(1880–3) Ilya Repin painted this to show the
different attitudes of those in the procession to the
icon being carried at
the head of it.*

**Ground
floor**

**The Morning of the
Execution of the
Streltsy** is by Vasiliy
Surikov, who
specialized in using
historical subjects to
illustrate contem-
porary social
issues.

28
39
38
41
37 36
42 40 35 61 60
62
55 54 53 52 51 50 59 57 58

★ **The Trinity** *(1420s)
This beautiful icon was
painted by Andrey Rublev
(see p61) for the Trinity
Monastery of St Sergius
(see pp162–5), where
he had been a novice
monk. He dedicated
it to the monastery's
founder, St Sergius of
Radonezh (see p165).*

Stairs from first floor

Stairs down to basement

Exit

Main entrance leading to basement for tickets, information,
toilets and cloakrooms

**Russian
jewellery**

Main Façade
*The gallery's façade
was designed in 1902
by Viktor Vasnetsov. An
example of the Russian-
Revival style (see p45),
it has a frieze inspired
by medieval manuscripts.*

STAR EXHIBITS

★ The Trinity
by Rublev

★ Demon Seated
by Vrubel

KEY

☐	18th and early 19th centuries
☐	Second half of the 19th century
☐	Late 19th and early 20th centuries
☐	Drawings and watercolours of the 18th–20th centuries
☐	Icons and jewellery
⬛	Non-exhibition space

Exploring the Tretyakov Gallery

Although the gallery's collection began with the paintings donated by Pavel Tretyakov, it continued to expand after the Revolution as numerous private collections were nationalized by the Soviet regime. There are currently more than 100,000 Russian works in the collection. Paintings from after the Revolution – mainly Socialist-Realist works – are now exhibited in the New Tretyakov Gallery (*see p135*), while the main gallery displays Russian art ranging from the icons of the medieval period to early 20th-century paintings.

Portrait of Ursula Mnichek
by Dmitriy Levitskiy

18TH AND EARLY 19TH CENTURIES

Painting in Russia was exclusively religious in character for over 600 years. However, a profound transformation occurred in the 18th century as secular art from Europe began to influence Russian artists. Portrait painting came into its own with technically accomplished canvases by artists such as Vladimir Borovikovskiy (1757–1825), Fyodor Rokotov (c.1736–1808) and Dmitriy Levitskiy (c.1735–1822), whose charming *Portrait of Ursula Mnichek* is among those in the gallery. The Romantic movement is represented in the collection by such pictures as Vasiliy Tropinin's refined but sentimental portrait of his son and Orest Kiprenskiy's famous *Portrait of the Poet Alexander Pushkin* (1827). Several of Aleksandr Ivanov's (1806–58) historical canvases are also displayed here, including his outstanding painting, *The Appearance of Christ to the People*. Begun in 1837, it took 20 years to finish.

SECOND HALF OF THE 19TH CENTURY

The art of this period was dominated by Realism. In 1870 a group of artists founded the Association of Travelling Art Exhibitions. Its members, who became known as the Wanderers *(peredvizhniki)*, began to produce "socially useful art" highlighting injustices and inequalities. One of the leaders of the movement was Vasiliy Perov (1834–82) whose satirical *Tea-drinking in Mytishchi* exposes hypocrisy among the clergy. Another Wanderer was Vasiliy Surikov, whose picture of *The Morning of the Execution of the Streltsy* (1881) instils new realism into a dramatic episode of Russian history. Ivan Kramskoy, the head of the group, aimed to portray the moral character of his subjects in paintings such as *Portrait of Pavel Tretyakov*.

Landscapes were popular subjects for the Wanderers and the gallery's many examples

PAVEL TRETYAKOV

Pavel Tretyakov began collecting Russian art in 1856 and was particularly interested in works by the Wanderers *(peredvizhniki)*. His collection grew and in 1892 he donated it to the city of Moscow. His home was opened as a gallery and, much extended, still houses the collection today. Pavel Tretyakov was director of the gallery for the last six years of his life.

Portrait of Pavel Tretyakov
(1876), by Ivan Kramskoy

include Vasiliy Polenov's *A Moscow Courtyard* (1878) and *The Rooks Have Come* (1871) by Aleksey Savrasov.

A number of works by Ilya Repin (1844–1930), the most versatile of the Wanderers, are on display. They include the enormous canvases *Religious Procession in Kursk Province; They Did Not Expect Him* and *Ivan the Terrible and his Son Ivan on 16 November, 1581*, and striking portraits of Repin's friends and contemporaries.

Ivan the Terrible and his Son Ivan on 16 November, 1581 **(1885), by Ilya Repin**

Above the Eternal Peace (1894), painted by Isaak Levitan

Vasiliy Vereschagin (1842–1904), whose paintings are on display in room 27, is another great amongst the Wanderers. He travelled widely in Asia and volunteered for the Russian army, garnering impressions he would later use in his massive, highly detailed paintings. One of Vereschagin's most famous works is *Apotheosis of War* (1871), depicting a pyramid of skulls and ironically dedicated to "all the great conquerors of the past, present and future". He was revolutionary in his approach to exhibitions, being the first artist in Russia to present his work in specially prepared environments, with darkened halls and black walls enhancing the mood of his paintings.

LATE 19TH AND EARLY 20TH CENTURIES

During the 1890s, the social ideals that inspired the Wanderers no longer appealed to a new generation of artists. Instead they rallied behind a call for "art for art's sake".

The innovative artist Mikhail Vrubel (1856–1910) was influenced by the poetry of the Russian Symbolists. Many of his dark, brooding works, such as *Demon Seated*, also reflect his troubled mental state.

French painting had a huge impact on this and subsequent generations of artists. This influence can be seen in the Impressionist work *Paris, Boulevard des Capucines*, painted in 1911 by Konstantin Korovin. The style of Valentin Serov's (1865–1911) early paintings was also close to Impressionism. His *Girl with Peaches (see p47)* is a charming portrait of the daughter of art patron Savva Mamontov.

In the decade leading up to World War I, Moscow was the centre of Russia's avant-garde movement, receptive to developments from abroad, such as Cubism and Futurism, as well as taking ideas from indigenous folk art, which inspired Primitivism. Primitivist works feature bold shapes and bright colours. *Staro Basmannaya – Board No. 1* by Vladimir Tatlin (1885–1953) and *Bathing Horses* by Natalya Goncharova (1881–1962) are among the gallery's works in this style.

The Transfiguration (c.1403), painted by a follower of Theophanes the Greek

DRAWINGS AND WATERCOLOURS

The gallery owns a substantial collection of sketches, lithographs and watercolours by artists from the 18th–20th centuries but, to avoid exhibits being damaged by exposure to light, only a small proportion are on show at any time.

Among the watercolours are a delightful equestrian portrait by Karl Bryullov (1799–1852) and some preparatory biblical sketches by Aleksandr Ivanov. Landscapes by Isaak Levitan (1861–1900) and Konstantin Korovin contrast with delicate pencil portraits by artists as diverse as Ilya Repin, Valentin Serov and Natalya Goncharova.

ICONS AND JEWELLERY

A fine collection of religious icons dating from the 12th–17th centuries is housed in the Tretyakov. Russian icon painting inherited the dark colours and immobile, otherworldly images of the saints from Byzantine art. One of the most revered icons, the 12th-century Virgin of Vladimir *(see p61)*, originated in Byzantium, but was brought to Moscow via Kiev and Vladimir.

However, Russian icon painters lightened their palettes, introducing shades such as yellow ochre, vermilion and white. A typical example is *The Transfiguration* (c.1403), painted by a follower of Theophanes the Greek *(see p61)*. It shows Christ standing over cowering sinners.

Andrey Rublev's stunning icon *The Trinity* dates from around 1420.

Alongside it are icons by other masters of the Moscow school *(see p61)*, including Dionysius (c.1440–c.1508).

Also on the ground floor is a room devoted to Russian jewellery from the 13th–20th centuries.

Church of the Resurrection in Kadashi ❷

Церковь Воскресения в Кадашах

Tserkov Voskreseniya v Kadashakh

2-oy Kadashevskiy pereulok 7. **Map** 7 B3. Ⓜ *Tretyakovskaya.* 🚇 *to public.*

This five-domed church is among the most striking examples of Moscow Baroque *(see p44)* and is thought to have been designed by Sergey Turchaninov, favourite architect of Patriarch Nikon *(see pp56–7)*. The small group of buildings around it also includes a refectory and tiered bell tower. It was paid for by a wealthy guild of weavers who had moved into the street by the 17th century. Before that an earlier church stood here, in what was at that time the district of Kadeshevo, hence the name that survives today.

The church was built around 1687, and the slender, tapering bell tower added in the 1690s.

Apart from the five green onion domes, visible from all over the neighbourhood, the most notable features are the tiers of lace-like limestone balustrades just below the drums supporting the domes. The church is now an art restoration workshop.

Church of the Consolation of All Sorrows ❸

Церковь Богоматери Всех Скорбящих Радость

Tserkov Bogomateri Vsekh Skorbyashchikh Radost

Ulitsa Bolshaya Ordynka 20. **Map** 7 B3. Ⓜ *Tretyakovskaya.*

Both the church of the Consolation of All Sorrows and the Neo-Classical yellow mansion opposite belonged to the Dolgovs, a wealthy merchant family. After completion of their house in the 1770s, they commissioned the church from Vasiliy Bazhenov *(see p44)*, a relation by marriage. He first built a new

The Empire-style Church of the Consolation of All Sorrows

belfry and refectory, which are among the few surviving buildings in Moscow by this talented architect, and then replaced the existing medieval church in 1783–91. It was finished by the Kumanins, another merchant family.

That church, however, was destroyed in the great fire of 1812 *(see p24)*. Another new one was designed by Osip Bove *(see p45)*, who was the architect in charge of Moscow's reconstruction after the fire. His Empire-style rotunda and dome, which still survive today, were finished in 1833.

The interior is unusual in an Orthodox church due to its lavish Empire-style colonnade, theatrical iconostasis and exuberant sculpted angels. On display in the church's left aisle, originally dedicated to the Transfiguration, is the Icon of Our Lady of Consolation of All Sorrows. It is said to have miraculously cured the ailing sister of Patriarch Joachim in the 17th century.

Church of St Clement ❹

Церковь Святого Климента

Tserkov Svyatovo Klimenta

Klimentovskiy pereulok 7. **Map** 7 B3. Ⓜ *Tretyakovskaya.* 🚇 *to public.*

This imposing, red-painted 18th-century church is now in a sadly decayed state. In 1756–8 the present refectory and belfry were built onto a church dating from the 1720s. This was pulled down in the 1760s when a new church was commissioned by the merchant Kuzma Matveev, a wealthy

The bell tower and domes of the Church of the Resurrection in Kadashi

The remarkably decorated, 17th-century Church of St Nicholas in Pyzhy

parishoner. The result is an outstanding example of late Moscow Baroque. The design is thought to have been conceived by the Italian architect Pietro Antonio Trezzini. The building of the church was completed by 1774.

The red and white façade is crowned by four black domes with golden stars surrounding a fifth, golden, cupola. Unfortunately, the church has

Baroque domes of the Church of St Clement, completed in 1774

been unsafe to enter for some years and it is unlikely that it will reopen in the near future.

Church of St Nicholas in Pyzhy ❻
Церковь Николая в Пыжах
Tserkov Nikolaya v Pyzhakh

Ulitsa Bolshaya Ordynka 27a/8.
Map 7 B3. **M** *Tretyakovskaya.*

Small crowns, as well as the traditional crosses, decorate the silver domes of this splendid church. It was constructed between 1670–72 in the area of the city once inhabited by the Streltsy, the royal guard, who provided the funds for it. Some of these men were later executed by Peter the Great for their role in the 1682 Streltsy Rebellion *(see p22)*. Funds were, in particular, generously lavished on the exterior decoration, which includes remarkable fretted cornices and finely chiselled window frames. The church's slender, tiered bell tower is

one of the finest in the city, whilst the iconostasis contains some original icons as well as copies of more famous ones.

Church of St Catherine ❻
Церковь Екатерины
Tserkov Yekateriny

Ulitsa Bolshaya Ordynka 60/2.
Map 7 B3. **M** *Tretyakovskaya.*

Originally a wooden church built by the cosmetic merchants' guild in the 16th century, Catherine the Great commissioned the architect Karl Blank to redesign and rebuild the church in the 1760s. It is dedicated to St Catherine of Alexandria who was beheaded in the 4th century on the orders of the Roman emperor Maximian for refusing to renounce her Christian faith.

The distinct architecture of the Church of St Catherine combines certain elements of Moscow baroque and rococo. Of interest are the ornate metal railings outside, which are superb and unique examples of 18th-century metalwork. Originally, they were located in the Kremlin between the Cathedral of the

The rotunda of the Church of St Catherine

Archangel Michael and the Patriarchal Palace.

In 1931 the church was closed, its bell-tower dismantled and almost all the icons (painted by Levitsky and Vasilevsky) were removed. Since the early 1990s, however, it has been undergoing a programme of restoration to return it to its former glory.

The Convent of SS Martha and Mary, founded in 1908 and designed by Aleksey Shchusev

Convent of SS Martha and Mary ❼

Марфо-Мариинская обитель
Marfo-Mariinskaya obitel

Ulitsa Bolshaya Ordynka 34. **Map** 7 B4. **Tel** *(495) 951 8446.* Ⓜ *Tretyakovskaya, Polyanka.* ◯ *10am–7pm.* ▨

A low archway leads from the street to this secluded compound, containing what appear at first glance to be medieval buildings. In fact they date from 1908–12 and were designed by Aleksey Shchusev *(see p45)*.

The convent was conceived to house a dispensary, a clinic, a small women's hospital and a school. It was run by the Order of the Sisters of Charity which was founded by the Grand Duchess Yelizaveta Fyodorovna, sister-in-law of Tsar Nicholas II. She had

turned to charitable work after her husband, Grand Prince Sergei (Tsar Nicholas II's uncle), was assassinated by a terrorist bomb in the troubled year of 1905 *(see p26)*. Yelizaveta also met a violent death: the day after the shooting of Tsar Nicholas II and his family in 1918, the Bolsheviks pushed her down a mine shaft with further members of the royal family.

When designing the Church of the Intercession, the convent's main building, Shchusev carried out considerable research into Russian religious architecture, particularly that of the Pskov and Novgorod schools *(see p44)*. Shchusev's ingenious design juxtaposed a highly traditional style with Style-Moderne features such as boldly pointed gables, limestone carvings of mythical creatures and Slavonic script on the outer walls.

The artist Mikhail Nesterov, a protegé of industrialist and art patron Savva Mamontov *(see p160)*, was commissioned to design and paint the frescoes in the interior of the church. He also designed the pale grey and white habits of the nuns.

After the Revolution the Order of the Sisters of Charity was suppressed and the church was used as a workshop for restoring icons for a number of years. The nuns have now returned to staff the clinic.

Tropinin Museum ❽

Музей ВА Тропинина
Muzey VA Tropinina

Shchetininskiy pereulok 10.
Map 7 B4. **Tel** *(495) 953 9750.* Ⓜ
Dobryninskaya, Polyanka. ◉ *for refurbishment; Opening expected in 2009.* ▨ ▨ ▨

A highly talented portrait artist, Vasiliy Tropinin executed a staggering 3,000 paintings in his life. As well as painting figures in high society, he is noted as one of the first Russian artists to depict working people. Works spanning his career are displayed in this attractive museum set in a blue and white Neo-Classical house. The furnishings and ornaments are from Tropinin's time and are mostly in Empire style.

The museum's collection is based on works gathered by Feliks Vishnevskiy (1902–78). Having been a supporter of the Revolution, he was able to collect during the Soviet period when paintings were relatively cheap. In addition to Tropinin's oil portraits, there are works by

***Girl in Ukrainian Dress* painted by Vasiliy Tropinin**

VASILIY TROPININ (1776–1857)

Though born a serf in Karpovo near Novgorod, Vasiliy Tropinin's prodigious talent was recognized at an early age. He was sent to the St Petersburg Academy of Arts in 1798, but was withdrawn by his master and brought back to work as an interior decorator, pastry-cook and footman on his estates. Tropinin and his wife gained their freedom in 1823 and moved to Moscow, where Tropinin became a professional portrait artist. Unlike many other painters of the time, he did not limit himself to painting members of the aristocracy. Instead, his portraits depicted a cross-section of society, from peasants to nobles.

Some of the Empire-style furnishings in the Tropinin Museum

some of his contemporaries, including Orest Kiprenskiy and Dmitriy Levitskiy. Like Tropinin, they were students at the St Petersburg Academy of Arts. The museum has been refurbished, reopening in 2009.

Bakhrushin Theatre Museum ❾

Театральный музей имени А. А. Бахрушина

Teatralnyy muzey imeni AA Bakhrushina

Ulitsa Bakhrushina 31/12. **Map** 7 C5. *Tel (495) 953 4470.* Ⓜ *Paveletskaya.* ⬜ *noon–7pm Wed–Mon (last ticket 6pm).* ⬛ *last Mon of the month.* 🎦 📷 ☎ *English (book in advance).*

Founded in 1894 by Aleksey Bakhrushin, a merchant and patron of the arts, this museum contains probably the most important collection of theatre memorabilia in

Russia. Spread over two floors, the exhibits range from sets and costumes to theatre tickets, programmes, advertisements and signed photographs.

The basement is filled with items relating to the career of the great opera singer Fyodor Shalyapin *(see p83).* One of the highlights is a richly brocaded costume he wore for the title role in Modest Mussorgsky's opera *Boris Godunov.*

A display on early Russian theatre includes puppets, models of theatres and sets, and paintings and engravings of theatrical entertainments.

Exhibits on 19th-century theatre include costumes and sets from the Ballets Russes. This famous company, formed by Sergey Diaghilev in 1909, revolutionized ballet. The sets include some designed by Michel Fokine, the company's inspired choreographer. A pair of ballet shoes belonging

to Vaslaw Nijinsky, one of the principal dancers, is also on show.

The room on 20th-century avant-garde theatre includes stage models created for outstanding directors Konstantin Stanislavskiy *(see p93)* and Vsevolod Meyerhold *(see p92).*

View of the Kremlin from the Sophia Embankment

Sophia Embankment ❿

Софийская набережная

Sofiyskaya naberezhnaya

Map 7 A2. Ⓜ *Kropotkinskaya, Borovitskaya, Novokuznetskaya.*

Situated opposite the Kremlin, on the southern bank of the Moskva river, the Sophia Embankment stretches from the Bolshoy Kamennyy most (Great Stone bridge) to the Bolshoy Moskvoretskiy most (Great Moscow river bridge).

The embankment was built up to its current height at the end of the 18th century and was greatly improved in 1836. It offers spectacular views over the Kremlin and the city.

Novgorodians settled on the river bank in the 14th century and built the original Church of St Sophia. The present church dates from the mid-17th century. Aleksandr Kaminskiy added the bell tower in 1862.

The mansion at No. 14 was designed by Vasiliy Zalesskiy in 1893 for a sugar baron and is now the British ambassador's residence. The interiors are by Fyodor Shekhtel *(see p45).*

Set design by Michel Fokine, on show in the Bakhrushin Theatre Museum

FURTHER AFIELD

Moscow's suburbs are generally rather bleak, but they conceal a surprising number of attractions, all accessible by metro. To the south of the centre lies a number of fortified monasteries, built to defend the city against the Mongols and the Poles. The most spectacular of them is Novodevichiy Convent, a serene 16th-century sanctuary with a glorious cathedral, but the Donskoy Monastery is also well worth a visit. The Danilovskiy Monastery, with its handsome cathedral, is the oldest in the city.

Cathedral fresco, Novodevichiy Convent

Visitors to Moscow are often surprised at the beauty and variety of its green spaces. Gorky, Izmaylovo and Victory parks are the perfect places in which to relax, while Sparrow Hills offers fantastic views. The city's best-kept secrets, however, are the grand estates away from the centre in what was formerly countryside There the Sheremetev family built two elegant Neo-Classical summer residences: Kuskovo and Ostankino. Both have beautifully preserved gardens and palaces full of fine paintings and period furnishings.

SIGHTS AT A GLANCE

Churches, Convents and Monasteries
Church of the Intercession in Fili **1**
Church of St John the Warrior **10**
Church of St Nicholas of the Weavers **8**
Danilovskiy Monastery **12**
Donskoy Monastery **11**
Krutitskoe Mission **15**
Monastery of the Saviour and Andronicus **17**
Novodevichiy Convent pp130–31 **6**

Palaces
Kuskovo pp142–3 **16**
Ostankino Palace **21**

Museums and Galleries
Kolomenskoe pp138–9 **13**
New Tretyakov Gallery **9**
Tolstoy House-Museum **7**
Vasnetsov House-Museum **20**

Historic buildings
Tsaritsyno **14**
White House **2**

Parks and Open Spaces
All-Russian Exhibition Centre (VVTs) **22**
Gorky Park **5**
Izmaylovo Park **18**
Komsomolskaya Ploshchad **19**
Sparrow Hills **4**
Victory Park **3**

KEY

▦	Central Moscow
▢	Greater Moscow
🚉	Railway station
═	Motorway
▬	Major road
═	Minor road
—	Railway

0 kilometres 5
0 miles 5

◁ **Ostankino's magnificent Italian Pavilion, designed by Moscow-based Italian architect Vincenzo Brenna**

Church of the Intercession in Fili ❶

Церковь Покрова в Филях
Tserkov Pokrova v Filyakh

Ulitsa Novozavodskaya 6. **Tel** *(499) 148 4552*. Ⓜ *Fili*. ◯ *11am–6pm Thu–Mon (May–Oct: upper church only)*. 🖼 📷

This stunning church was commissioned by an uncle of Peter the Great, Prince Lev Naryshkin, and is in the style known as Moscow, or Naryshkin, Baroque *(see p44)*. Built by an unknown architect, between 1690 and 1693 it is an extraordinary tiered structure of red brick, with lace-like ornamentation and pilasters of white stone.

Russian churches often comprise two buildings: a grand, unheated one for summer, and a smaller, simpler one that can be heated easily in winter.

Here, the winter church at ground level has changing displays of religious art. In front of it a double staircase rises to a terrace surrounding the upper summer church. This staircase would once have provided the setting for processions. Inside, there is an iconostasis, mainly the work of the 17th-century painter Karp Zolotarev, and a carved gilt pew used by Peter the Great.

The elegant Church of the Intercession in Fili, the city's best example of Moscow Baroque

Gilded crest on the clock tower of the White House

White House ❷

Белый дом
Belyy dom

Krasnopresnenskaya naberezhnaya 2. **Map** 1 B5. Ⓜ *Krasnopresnenskaya*. ⬤ *to public*.

A marble-clad building with a gilded clock tower, the White House is still a "must-see" for tourists interested in recent political history.

Once the seat of the Russian Federation's parliament, it first claimed the world's attention in August 1991 when it was the focus of resistance to the Communist hardliners' coup against Mikhail Gorbachev, the president of the Soviet Union. The rebels detained Gorbachev at his Black Sea villa, where he was holidaying at the time, so it was Boris Yeltsin, the president of the smaller Russian Federation, who led the opposition to the coup. The world watched as he passed through the lines of tanks surrounding the White House without anyone daring to arrest him. Then he climbed onto a tank to proclaim: "You can build a throne of bayonets, but you cannot sit on it for long".

The coup failed, and the victory of Yeltsin and his supporters was soon followed by the break-up of the Soviet Union and the end of Communist rule.

However, in September 1993, a reversal of roles occurred at the White House when Yeltsin became the besieger. Hundreds of deputies locked themselves into it in protest when Yeltsin summarily suspended parliament over its increasing opposition to his new draft constitution. The siege ended after two weeks when army tanks bombarded the deputies into submission.

The charred building was quickly repaired, but never regained its former significance; today the Russian parliament occupies a building on ulitsa Okhotnyy ryad *(see p86)*, and the presidential offices are in the Kremlin *(see pp52–67)*.

The Triumphal Arch, celebrating Napoleon's defeat in the 1812 war

Victory Park ❸

Парк победы
Park pobedy

Kutuzovskiy prospekt. Ⓜ *Kutuzovskaya*. **Museum of the Great Patriotic War Tel** *(499) 148 5550*. ◯ *10am–5pm Tue–Sun*. ⬤ *Last Thu of the month*. ♿ 📷 **Borodino Panorama Museum Tel** *(499) 148 1967*. ◯ *10am–6pm Sat–Thu*. 🖼 📷

Commemorating victory in the Great Patriotic War, the Russian name for World War II *(see p27)*, Victory Park was originally intended to have a vast monument to Mother Russia at its centre. After the end of Communist rule, plans were scaled down and the park was finally completed in 1995, in time for the 50th anniversary of the end of the war.

The park is formally laid out, with straight alleys dividing the sparsely-treed grass. The main,

The Stalinist-Gothic skyscraper of the Moscow State University

fountain-lined avenue leads from Kutuzovskiy prospekt to the central Nike Monument, a towering, 142-m (466-ft) obelisk designed by Zurab Tsereteli to honour the Greek goddess of victory.

Behind the monument is the domed, semi-circular Museum of the Great Patriotic War. The dioramas, models, maps and weapons on show give an informative picture of the war as experienced by the Russians.

Just to the side of the central avenue is the simple Church of St George the Victorious, built in 1995, probably the first to be built in Russia after the Revolution. Next to it is a monument to war victims.

East along Kutuzovskiy prospekt are two large scale memorials to the war of 1812 (see pp23–5). Moscow's final deliverance from the French is celebrated by the grand Triumphal Arch. It was designed by Osip Bove (see p45), with sculptures of Russian and Classical warriors by Ivan Vitali and Ivan Timofeev. Originally built on Tverskaya ulitsa in 1834, the arch was dismantled in the 1930s during street-widening. The sculptures were preserved and in 1968 the arch was rebuilt at its present site.

Further along the street, at No. 38, is the circular Borodino Panorama Museum, which contains a vast painting, 115-m (377-ft) long and 14-m (46-ft) high. It was created by Franz Roubaud in 1912 to mark the centenary of the battle between Russian forces and Napoleon's army at Borodino (see p138).

Sparrow Hills ❹
Воробьёвы горы
Vorobevy gory

Ⓜ *Universitet.*

The summit of this wooded ridge offers unsurpassed views across the city. There is an observation point on ulitsa Kosygina and newly-wed couples traditionally come here to have their photograph taken against the panorama. It is also a favourite pitch for a large number of souvenir sellers.

The hills are dominated by the Moscow State University (MGU) building commissioned by Stalin, designed by Lev Rudnev and completed in 1953. At 36 floors high it is the tallest of the seven Stalinist Gothic "wedding-cakes" (see p45).

The small, green-domed Church of the Trinity (1811) can also be seen close by, to the left of the observation platform. There are also a couple of long, but somewhat rickety, ski jumps on the hills.

On prospekt Vernadskovo, on the southeast edge of the hills, is the Palace of Youth and Creative Work, a studio complex built for

Plaque at the entrance to Gorky Park

the Communist youth organization. Also on this street are the silver-roofed New Moscow Circus (see p198) built in 1971, and the Nataliya Sats Children's Musical Theatre (see p199).

Gorky Park ❺
Парк культуры и отдыха имени М. Горького
Park Kultury i otdykha imeni M. Gorkovo

Krymskiy val 9. **Map** 6 E4. Ⓜ *Park Kultury, Oktyabrskaya.* **Tel** (495) 637 0707. ◷ *10am–10pm daily (pleasure park open May–Oct).*

Moscow's most famous park is named in honour of the writer Maxim Gorky and extends for more than 120 ha (297 acres) along the banks of the Moskva river. Opened in 1928 as the Park of Culture and Rest, it incorporates the Golitsyn Gardens, laid out by Matvey Kazakov (see p44) in the late 18th century, and a 19th-century pleasure park. During the Soviet era, loudspeakers were used to deliver speeches by Communist leaders across the park. Today the highlights include fairground rides, woodland walks, boating lakes, a 10,000-seat outdoor theatre and, in the winter months, an ice rink.

The park was immortalized in the opening scenes of Michael Apted's film *Gorky Park*. However, because of the tense political climate of 1983, the film was actually shot in Finland.

Outdoor ice-skating in Gorky Park, a popular activity in the winter months

Novodevichiy Convent ➏
Новодевичий монастырь
Novodevichiy monastyr

Probably the most beautiful of the semi-circle of fortified religious institutions to the south of Moscow is Novodevichiy Convent, founded by Basil III in 1524 to commemorate the capture of Smolensk from the Lithuanians. Only the Cathedral of the Virgin of Smolensk was built at this time. Most of the other buildings were added in the late 17th century by Peter the Great's half-sister, the Regent Sophia. After Peter deposed her and reclaimed his throne in 1689 *(see p22)*, he confined her here for the rest of her life. In 1812 Napoleon's troops tried to blow up the convent but, according to a popular story, it was saved by the nuns, who snuffed out the fuses.

The Church of the Assumption and adjoining refectory were built in the 1680s on the orders of the Regent Sophia.

Faceted Tower

Nuns' cells

Refectory

Setunskaya Tower

Gate Church of the Intercession
It is not known who designed this church, but it is believed to have been built in the second half of the 17th century.

The Palace of Irina Gudunova was home to the widow of Tsar Fyodor I.

Novodevichiy Cemetery

Church of St Ambrose

Maria's Chambers were used by the daughter of Tsar Alexis Mikhailovich, Maria.

STAR FEATURES

★ Cathedral of the Virgin of Smolensk

★ Bell Tower

★ Gate Church of the Transfiguration

★ **Cathedral of the Virgin of Smolensk**
The oldest building in the convent is the cathedral, built in 1524. The five-tier iconostasis, the rich frescoes and the onion domes all date from the 17th century.

Vorobeva Tower

Shoemaker's Tower

0 metres	25
0 yards	25

NOVODEVICHIY CEMETERY

Many famous Russians are buried in this cemetery. Among the leading cultural figures are playwright Anton Chekhov, writers Nikolai Gogol and Mikhail Bulgakov, composers Sergey Prokofiev, Aleksandr Skryabin *(see p72)* and Dmitriy Shostakovich and opera singer Fyodor Shalyapin *(see p83)*. The cemetery is also the final resting place for many military and political dignitaries, including Nikita Khrushchev *(see p30)* and Boris Yeltsin.

The tombstone of Nikita Khrushchev

VISITORS' CHECKLIST

Novodevichiy proezd 1. **Tel** (495) 246 8526. M Sportivnaya. 64, 132 (see p227). 5, 15. 10am–5pm Wed–Mon. some public hols. grounds only. English (book in advance). 8am, 5pm Mon–Sat, 7am & 10am Sun. **Cemetery** 10am–6pm daily.

Naprudnaya Tower

This guard house is where the Regent Sophia was imprisoned.

Entrance

Sportivnaya metro

Tsaritsa's Tower

★ Gate Church of the Transfiguration

A cornice of scallop-shell gables, topped by five gilded domes and crosses, crowns this grand Baroque church. It stands over the main gate to the convent and was completed in 1688.

St Nicholas' Tower

Tailor's Tower

Hospital

★ Bell Tower

Completed in 1690, this tower is one of the most exuberant examples of Baroque architecture in Moscow. The Church of St John the Divine occupies the second storey of the six-tiered, octagonal tower, which stands 72 m (236 ft) high.

Lopukhin Palace

This palace was built in 1687–9. After Peter the Great's death in 1725 his first wife, Yevdokiya Lopukhina, moved here from the Suzdal convent where she had been sent after Peter tired of her.

Magnificent towers and domed churches of Novodevichiy, viewed from the north ▷

Tolstoy House-Museum ❼

Музей-усадьба ЛН Толстого

Muzey-usadba LN Tolstovo

Ulitsa Lva Tolstovo 21. **Map** 6 D4.
Tel *(499) 766 9328.* **M** *Park Kultury.*
🕐 *10am–6pm daily (last tickets at
5pm).* 📷 🚫 ♿ *English (book in
advance).* **www**.tolstoymuseum.ru

The presence of one of
Russia's greatest novelists
can be felt in every corner of
this evocative, wooden house.
It was here that Leo Tolstoy
(1828–1910) spent the winters
between 1882 and 1901 with
his long-suffering wife, Sofya
Andreevna, and the nine
surviving of their 13 children.
The summers were spent on
the Tolstoy ancestral estate at
Yasnaya Polyana *(see p167)*,
200 km (124 miles) away.

The Moscow house was
turned into a museum in 1921
on Lenin's orders and has been
preserved much as it would
have been when Tolstoy and
his family resided here.

On the ground floor, the
large table in the dining room
is still laid with crockery. The
evening meal in the Tolstoy
household always began
promptly at 6pm to the sum-
mons of the cuckoo clock
on the wall. Next door is the
"corner room" where, at one
time, the elder sons, Sergey,
Ilya and Lev, would retire to
play Chinese billiards.

**The simple desk in Tolstoy's study where he
wrote his final novel, *Resurrection***

LEO TOLSTOY

By the time Tolstoy was in
his 50s, he was an author
of international renown and
had written his two great
masterpieces *War and Peace*
(1865–9) and *Anna Karenina*
(1873–7). He continued to
write fiction, but later re-
nounced his earlier books
and the world they depicted.
Instead Tolstoy concentrated
on his highly individual brand
of Christian Humanism, a doctrine that included non-violence,
vegetarianism and total sexual abstinence. It was in this
period that he wrote the stories *The Death of Ivan Ilych* and
the *Kreutzer Sonata* and his last great novel, *Resurrection*,
which strayed so far from Orthodoxy that the Holy Synod
excommunicated him in 1901. Tolstoy left Moscow the same
year for Yasnaya Polyana, where he devoted himself totally to
mysticism and the education of the peasants on the estate.

**The dining room with a painting of
Tolstoy's favourite daughter Mariya**

The house exudes a sense of
ordered, comfortable family
life, but Tolstoy and his wife
frequently quarrelled violently,
largely on account of his wish
to renounce society and live as
simply as possible. The couple
were reconciled for a short
time when Vanya,
their much-loved
youngest child died
from scarlet fever at
the age of seven. His
memory is preserved
in his small bedroom
near the scullery,
where his high chair,
rocking horse and
books can be seen.

The bedroom of
Tolstoy's second
daughter, Tatyana, is
crammed with orna-
ments and keepsakes.
She was a talented
artist and her own
paintings and sketches
are hung on the walls.

The stairs to the first
floor open into the
salon, a large hall
where frequent guests

were treated to supper.
They included the young
Sergei Rachmaninov who
accompanied the bass,
Fyodor Shalyapin *(see
p83)*, on the piano here,
the artist Ilya Repin, whose
portrait of Tatyana now
hangs in the "corner
room", the music critic
Vladimir Stasov, and the
writer Maxim Gorky *(see
p95)* with whom Tolstoy
would play chess. The drawing
room next door was decorated
by Sofya Andreevna herself.

The bedroom of Tolstoy's
favourite child, Mariya, is
rather spartan, testifying to
her sympathy for her father's
ideals and way of life.

At the far end of the upstairs
passage is Tolstoy's study, a
spacious room overlooking the
garden. Reflecting his passion
for austerity, the room is simply
furnished in black leather. The
plain, solid desk where he
wrote his novel *Resurrection*
is lit by candles. Rather than
admit to being shortsighted,
Tolstoy sawed off the ends of
his chair legs to bring himself
closer to his papers. In the
adjoining washroom are dumb-
bells and a bicycle – evidence
of his interest in keeping fit.
Also on show are the tools he
used for his hobby of shoe-
making, with some of the
pairs he made. The back stairs
close by lead to the garden,
which is only accessible to
those taking a guided tour.

The luxurious interior of the Church of St Nicholas of the Weavers

Church of St Nicholas of the Weavers ⓭

Церковь Николая в Хамовниках
Tserkov Nikolaya v Khamovnikakh

Ulitsa Lva Tolstovo 2. **Map** 6 D4.
Tel *(499) 246 2719* Ⓜ *Park Kultury.*
⬜ *during services* 📷

Dedicated to the patron saint of weavers, sailors and farmers, this spectacular church was founded in 1679 by local weavers (*khamovniki*). Their aim was to surpass the Church of the Resurrection in Kadashi (*see p122*), which was built a few years before by rival weavers across the river.

While staying at their winter home nearby, Tolstoy and his family used to attend services here until his rift with the Church authorities. The church continued to function throughout the Communist era.

The exterior is decorated with vivid orange and green gables and topped with five golden domes, while the walls are decorated with patterned tiles imitating woven motifs. Inside the church there is an iconostasis featuring a 17th-century Icon of St Nicholas. A separate Icon of the Virgin, Helper of Sinners, is reputed to perform miracles.

New Tretyakov Gallery ⓮

Третьяковская галерея
Tretyakovskaya galereya

Krymskiy val 10. **Map** 6 F3. ***Tel*** *(499) 230 7788.* Ⓜ *Park Kultury, Oktyabrskaya.* ⬜ *10am–7:30pm Tue–Sun.*
📷 ♿ 🎧 *English.* **www**.tretyakov.ru

This huge white box of a building is an annexe of the Tretyakov Gallery (*see pp118–21*) in the centre of town. It is devoted to Russian art from the early 1900's to the present. Most of the canvases here belong to the official movement known as Socialist Realism and reflect the cultural straitjacket imposed by Stalin (*see p27*) in the 1930s. It had its roots in the Wanderers movement of the 1860s, which was based on the principle that art has, first and foremost, a social role to play, though lyricism and beauty in paintings were also important (*see p120*). In contrast, the hard-hitting art of the Communist era served the state's interests, reflecting socialist goals and achievements. A few examples of the titles given to the paintings say it all: *Life is Getting Better; Building New Factories; Unforgettable Meeting* (between Stalin and a spellbound young woman). Technological achievements were also immortalized in pictures such as *The First Russian Airship*.

Many people will find the Modernist paintings at the beginning of the exhibition more aesthetically pleasing. These include pictures by previously outlawed artists, such as the *Black Square* by Kazimir Malevich and works by Constructivists such as Aleksandr Rodchenko and the brothers Georgiy and Vladimir Stenberg.

Outside, on the Moskva river embankment, is the Graveyard of Fallen Monuments, a collection of some of the sculptures removed from around Moscow at the end of the Soviet era. Pride of place belongs to the huge statue of the secret police chief, Feliks Dzerzhinskiy, which was taken down from outside the KGB headquarters in Lubyanka Square (*see p112*) in 1991. A striking addition to the view from the Tretyakov's gardens is a huge statue of Peter the Great by Zurab Tsereteli, completed in 1997.

The Church of St Nicholas of the Weavers, topped by golden domes

The vast statue of Peter the Great, erected in 1997, viewed from the Graveyard of Fallen Monuments

The distinctive, colourful Church of St John the Warrior

Church of St John the Warrior ❿
Церковь Иоанна Воина
Tserkov Ioanna Voina

Ulitsa Bolshaya Yakimanka 46.
Map 6 F4. *Tel* (495) 238 2056.
Ⓜ *Oktyabrskaya.* ✪

The plans for this famous church, attributed to the architect Ivan Zarudniy, are said to have been personally approved by Peter the Great *(see p22)*. Building work took place from 1709–13 and the result is a notable example of Petrine Baroque, a style which had begun to flourish in St Petersburg, the tsar's new capital. The church's most eye-catching feature is a tiered octagonal tower, with an elegant balustrade and coloured roof tiles forming bold, geometric designs.

St John the Warrior is one of the few churches to have stayed open after the Revolution and a number of historic works of religious art were transferred here for safekeeping. These can still be seen in the church and include the 17th-century Icon of the Saviour, which hung in a chapel near the Saviour's Tower in the Kremlin. Across the road is the

The Old Cathedral, Donskoy Monastery

extremely striking Igumnov House, which was built in 1893 for a rich merchant by Nikolay Pozdeev. It is a typically flamboyant example of Russian-Revival architecture *(see p45)*, and now houses the French Embassy.

Donskoy Monastery ⓫
Донской монастырь
Donskoy monastyr

Donskaya ploshchad 1. *Tel* (495) 952 4901. Ⓜ *Shabolovskaya.* ◯ 7am– 7pm daily. ♿ grounds only. ✪ 📷

The Donskoy Monastery was founded in 1593 by Boris Godunov to honour the Icon of the Donskoy Virgin, credited with having twice saved Moscow from the Mongols. The first time was in 1380 when Prince Dmitriy Donskoy carried the icon into battle at Kulikovo *(see p161)*. Boris Godunov also used it to rally his troops in 1591 against the army of Khan Kazy Girei, which retreated after minor skirmishes.

The crescent moons, below many of the golden crosses on top of the monastery buildings, symbolize the defeat of Islam.

The modest scale of the original monastery is reflected

in the beautifully understated Old Cathedral with its bright blue dome and *kokoshniki* gables *(see p44)*. Two orthodox prelates are buried within: Archbishop Amvrosiy, killed by a mob during a plague riot in 1771, and Patriarch Tikhon, who was imprisoned by the Bolsheviks after the Revolution.

In the late 17th century the monastery acquired greater prestige under the patronage of the Regent Sophia and her lover Golitsyn. The fortified outer walls and New Cathedral are additions from this period.

Built in 1684–98 in the Moscow-Baroque style *(see p44)*, the New Cathedral is a towering brick building with five domes. Inside are a stunning seven-tiered iconostasis and some exuberant frescoes, painted in 1782–5 by Italian artist Antonio Claudio. The Icon of the Donskoy Virgin is now in the Tretyakov Gallery *(see pp118–21)*, but a copy is on show in the Old Cathedral.

The Donskoy Monastery's imposing 17th-century New Cathedral

Danilovskiy Monastery ⓬
Даниловский монастырь
Danilovskiy monastyr

Danilovskiy val 22. *Tel* (495) 958 0502. Ⓜ *Tulskaya.* ◯ 7am–8pm daily. ♿ 📷 www.saintdaniel.ru

Founded by Prince Daniil in 1298–1300, the Danilovskiy Monastery is the city's oldest. It was used as a factory and youth detention centre after the Revolution, but since 1988 it has been the headquarters of

THE RUSSIAN ORTHODOX CHURCH

Christianity was adopted as Russia's official religion in AD 988 when Vladimir I *(see p17)* married the sister of the Byzantine Emperor and had himself baptized in the Orthodox faith. In the 13th century monasteries became a focus for resistance against the invading Mongols. Thereafter the Church played a vital role in Russian life until the Revolution, when it was forced underground. As the Soviet Union broke up, the church revived and, in 1992, Boris Yeltsin became the first Russian leader to attend church services since 1917.

Delicate stone tracery on the Figured Gate at Tsaritsyno

the Russian Orthodox Church, which has offices in its more modern, plainer buildings.

The green-domed Church of the Holy Fathers of the Seven Ecumenical Councils is the oldest of the three churches within the fortified walls. It was founded by Ivan the Terrible *(see p18)* in the 16th century. The main church, on the first floor, has a 17th-century iconostasis with contemporary icons.

At the heart of the monastery is the elegant yellow Cathedral of the Trinity, designed by Osip Bove *(see p45)* in 1833 and completed five years later. The pretty pink bell tower in the northern wall contains the Gate Church of St Simeon the Stylite. It was built in 1730–32, but knocked down in the 1920s. The bells were sold to Harvard University, but have now been restored to the rebuilt gate and bell tower.

Kolomenskoe ⑬

See pp138–9.

Tsaritsyno ⑭

Царицыно
Tsaritsyno

Ulitsa Dolskaya 1. **Tel** (495) 355 4844. Ⓜ *Orekhovo, Tsaritsyno.* ◻ *11am–6pm Wed–Sun (Oct–Mar: 11am–5pm).*

Catherine the great *(see p23)* bought this tract of land in 1775 and changed its name from Chyornaya Gryaz (Black Mud) to Tsaritsyno (the Tsarina's Village). In doing so, she commissioned one of her most imaginative architects, Vasiliy Bazhenov *(see p44)*, to design and construct a lavish imperial palace which would rival any found in St Petersburg.

Bazhenov conceived an innovative palace complex combining Gothic, Baroque and even Moorish styles and Catherine approved the plans. She visited the site in 1785 and, although construction was well under way, proclaimed herself dissatisfied. Bazhenov's young colleague Matvey Kazakov *(see pp44–5)* was told to rebuild the palace but, after a further decade of construction, lack of funds left it still incomplete.

Today the grounds boast charming lakes and woodland walks. Some of the ruins have been restored, but the forlorn remainder have a beauty which the completed palace might never have matched. Although the shell of Kazakov's Grand Palace is the most imposing building on the estate, some of Bazhenov's smaller structures are equally impressive. Visitors can see the Figured Gate with its elegant Gothic-style towers and lancet windows, the Figured Bridge and the ornate two-storey Opera House, one of the few buildings Catherine approved. The extraordinary Bread Gate, with its arch of sharply pointed stone "teeth", leads to the kitchens, while the Octahedron was built as the servants' quarters. The attractive Church of Our Lady of the Life-Giving Spirit was added in the 19th-century.

A small museum on the estate displays icons, china, glass and some Fabergé eggs, as well as landscapes and architectural exhibits. However, only a fraction of the items in the cellars below the palace are on show at any one time.

The iconostasis in the Church of the Holy Fathers, Danilovskiy Monastery

Kolomenskoe ⑬
Коломенское
Kolomenskoe

The earliest known reference to Kolomenskoe village is in the will of Ivan I (see p18), dated 1339. By the 16th century Kolomenskoe was a favourite country estate of the tsars. The oldest surviving building is the Church of the Ascension, constructed in 1532. A superb wooden palace was built for Tsar Alexis Mikhailovich (see p19) in 1667–71, but it was demolished in the 18th century. After the Revolution the park was designated a museum of architecture, and wooden buildings, such as Peter the Great's cabin from Archangel, were moved here from all over Russia. Also located on the estate is the Front Gate Museum. Its exhibits include a model of Tsar Alexis' palace and Russian craft objects, such as tile paintings and woodcarvings.

The Falcon Tower was constructed in 1627. It was used as a water tower.

Refectory

★ Church of the Ascension
This magnificent church was erected by Basil III in 1532 to celebrate the birth of his son Ivan (later the Terrible). It is closed for interior work until at least the end of 2011.

The Pavilion is all that remains of Alexander I's palace, built in 1825.

Church of St George
The 16th-century Church of St George once stood on this site, but today only the church's bell tower still stands.

Mead Brewery

Front Gate Museum

The Front Gate was the ceremonial entrance to Tsar Alexis' palace. The chambers on either side of the gate now form the Front Gate Museum.

MODEL OF WOODEN PALACE

Kolomenskoe underwent a major expansion during the reign of Tsar Alexis Mikhailovich, father of Peter the Great. He added a new centrepiece, an astonishing wooden palace with fanciful barrel-shaped roofs, onion domes and carved ornamentation, which visiting diplomats described as the "eighth wonder of the world". It was demolished in 1768 on the orders of Catherine the Great. Fortunately she had a model made, which is now displayed in the Front Gate Museum.

STAR FEATURES

- ★ Church of the Ascension

- ★ Church of Our Lady of Kazan

Church of St John the Baptist

Located to the south of the main estate, this church was commissioned by Ivan the Terrible to celebrate his accession to the throne in 1547.

Church of St John the Baptist

VISITORS' CHECKLIST

Prospekt Andropova 39. **Tel** (499) 615 2768. Ⓜ *Kolomenskaya*. **Front Gate Museum & Churches** ◯ 10am–5pm Tue–Sun. 🍴 🎧 English (book in advance). 🎫 🍴 ◻ **Grounds** ◯ 10am–8pm daily. ♿

This wooden gate tower was brought to Kolomenskoe from the St Nicholas Monastery at Karelia in 1932. It was built in 1692 from interlocking sections without using a single nail.

Front Gate Museum annexe

Peter the Great's Cabin

This simple log cabin was built for Tsar Peter the Great in 1702 when he visited Archangel (on the north coast of Russia). It was brought to Kolomenskoe in 1934 and its four low-ceilinged rooms restored.

Bratsk Stockade Tower

These ancient oaks are said to have been planted by Peter the Great.

0 metres	25
0 yards	25

The Boris Stone (12th century) bears the inscription, "Strong, brave, holy Boris".

St Saviour's Gate is the main entrance to the complex.

Kolomenskaya metro

★ Church of Our Lady of Kazan

Completed in 1650 for Tsar Alexis, this stunning church is an early example of Moscow Baroque (see p44). It is now open again for worship. A replica of the Icon of Our Lady of Kazan, which is believed to have helped Russia drive out Polish invaders in 1612, can be found inside the church.

Krutitskoe Mission ⑮

Крутицкое подворье
Krutitskoe podvore

Krutitskaya ulitsa 11. **Map** 8 E5.
Tel *(495) 276 9724.* Ⓜ *Proletarskaya.*
Grounds ◯ *8am–8pm daily.* Ⓖ

The Metropolitan originally
resided in the Kremlin,
but after the creation of the
patriarchate in the 16th
century the bishops of
Krutitsy became metropolitans
(see p56). The Mission's name
derives from the Russian
krutoy, meaning steep, and
refers to the nearby bank of
the Moskva river.

The Baroque buildings seen
today are undergoing restoration and are dominated by
the bulky Cathedral of the
Assumption, which was built
in 1685. The entire edifice,
including the onion domes, is
built of bricks.

A covered gallery links the
cathedral to the Metropolitan's
Palace via a double-arched
gateway topped by a small
pavilion or *teremok*. The gallery and pavilion are by Osip
Startsev, who was famous in
Russia in the late 17th century
as a designer of religious
buildings. The northern façade
of the *teremok* is decorated
with intricately carved window
frames and turquoise tiles
with yellow floral motifs.

The Metropolitan's Palace
is a handsome, though plainer,
red brick building with pyra-
midal chimneys and an
impressive staircase at the rear.

Since falling into disrepair
early in the 19th century, the
Mission has served as a bar-
racks, a prison and, after the

Revolution, a workers' hostel:
their wooden living quarters
still survive. Now, the youth
movement of the Orthodox
Church is based here.

Kuskovo ⑯

See pp142–3.

Monastery of the Saviour and Andronicus ⑰

Спасо-Андрониковский
монастырь
*Spaso-Andronikovskiy
monastyr*

Andronevskaya ploshchad 10. **Map** 8
F2. Ⓜ *Ploshchad Ilyicha.* ◯ *11am–*
6pm Thu–Tue. **Museum Tel** *(495) 278*
1467. Ⓖ Ⓞ Ⓒ *(book in advance).*

Travelling back from the city
of Constantinople in 1360,
Metropolitan Aleksey survived
a storm at sea. To give thanks
he founded the Monastery of
the Saviour on the banks of
the Yauza river.
He then appoint-
ed the monk
Andronicus to
be the first abbot
and to oversee the
building works.

The best-known
monk to have
lived here was
Andrey Rublev,
Russia's most bril-
liant icon painter
(see p61). He is
thought to have
died and been buried here in
about 1430, but the location
of his grave is unknown.
Rublev is commemorated by

The Cathedral of the Saviour, with
characteristic *kokoshniki* gables

the monastery's Andrey Rublev
Museum of Old Russian Art.
There are no icons by Rublev
himself here, but some excellent copies of his works are
on show, along with genuine
pieces by his contemporaries.
Original Rublev icons can be
seen in the Tretyakov Gallery
(see pp118–21). The museum's
collections are on
show in two of the
monastery build-
ings. The 16th-
century Abbot's
House, decorated
with tiles and just
to the right of the
main entrance, dis-
plays decorative
arts of the 11th–
20th centuries. The
Baroque Church
of the Archangel
Michael, built in
1691–94, displays Russian art
of the 13th–17th centuries.
Highlights include the 17th-
century Icon of the Tikhvin
Virgin, originally from the
Donskoy Monastery *(see p136)*,
and paintings depicting the life
of St Nicholas of Zaraysk, one
of Russia's favourite saints. The
18th-century monks' building,
which contained monks' cells,
is being renovated and will
provide further gallery space.

The beautiful, single-domed
Cathedral of the Saviour was
built in either 1390 or 1425–7.
If the former date is correct,
this would make it the oldest
church in Moscow. The interior
was painted by Rublev but
only traces of his work survive,
around the altar windows.

**Icon of St John the
Baptist, 15th century**

Gateway at Krutitskoe, linking the cathedral to the Metropolitan's Palace

Izmaylovo Park ⑱

Парк Измайлово

Park Izmaylovo

Narodniy prospekt 17. **Tel** (495) 166 7909. Ⓜ *Izmaylovskiy Park, Shosse Entuziastov.* ◯ 24 hours. 🚻 🖵

One of the largest parks in Europe, Izmaylovo covers nearly 12 sq km (4.7 sq miles). It features attractions such as sports facilities, children's amusements, cafés and woods, as well as an outdoor theatre, a famous flea market *(see p193)*, a cathedral and the picturesque remains of one of the tsars' country estates.

Izmaylovo passed to the Romanov family in the 16th century and became one of their favourite hunting lodges. In 1663, Tsar Alexis *(see p19)* built an enormous wooden palace here and dedicated the land to experiments in animal and vegetable husbandry and various cottage industries.

Peter the Great later spent an idyllic childhood at Izmaylovo, secluded from palace intrigues. It was here that his lifelong fascination with the sea began, when he learned to sail an old boat on a lake. The boat was later nicknamed the "grandfather of the Russian navy".

The wooden palace has long since disappeared, demolished by Catherine the Great in 1767. However, about 500 m (550 yds) east of Izmaylovskiy Park metro, the remains of other buildings can be seen on an island near the sports stadium. The lake surrounding them was once part of a network of

17th-century Cathedral of the Intercession, Izmaylovo Park

37 ponds previously created by Tsar Alexis for breeding fish and irrigating experimental crops. He planted exotic species such as mulberry trees and cotton and ordered seeds from his ambassadors in England.

The island is reached over a small bridge. The iron archway at its far end was built in 1859 and led to three buildings commissioned by Nicholas I and designed by Konstantin Ton *(see p45)* in the 1840s for retired soldiers. Rising above the trees ahead, behind the remains of the estate's walls, are the five, formidable black domes of the Cathedral of the Intercession, built in 1671–9. The domes are tiled with metallic "scales". The *zabomary* gables *(see p44)* beneath them are beautifully decorated with "peacock's

eye" tiles, by Stepan Polubes, a late 17th-century Belorussian ceramicist working in Moscow.

On the cathedral's right is a tiered red-brick arch with a tent roof. Built in 1671, this is the Bridge Tower, all that remains of a 14-span bridge that once crossed the estate's extensive waterways. Its tower was used for meetings of the boyars' council under Tsar Alexis. The top tier of the bridge gives fine views over the whole estate.

On the opposite side of the cathedral from the Bridge Tower stands the white, triple-arched Ceremonial Gate. It was designed by Terentiy Makarov in 1682 and is one of two gates that originally led to the palace.

The flea market, just to the northwest of the lake, trails down the hill from the concrete tower blocks of the Izmaylovo Hotel, offering an amazingly eclectic variety of goods. Muscovites come here in large numbers to buy items such as second-hand household goods and vehicle parts. Tourists are likely to be greeted by a storm of shouts in English from people selling their wares.

Triple-arched Ceremonial Gate, the surviving entrance to the tsars' former estate, Izmaylovo Park

Kuskovo ⑯

Кусково

Kuskovo

Statue of Minerva

For over 200 years before the Revolution, Kuskovo was the country seat of one of Russia's wealthiest aristocratic families, the Sheremetevs. The present buildings were commissioned by Count Pyotr Sheremetev after his marriage to the heiress Varvara Cherkasskaya in 1743. Among their 200,000 serfs were the architects Fyodor Argunov and Aleksey Mironov who played a major role in Kuskovo's construction, probably under the supervision of professional architect Karl Blank. Apart from the elaborate gardens, the main attraction is the two-storey wooden palace, completed in 1777. A ceramics museum, with a Renowned collection of porcelain, occupies the Orangery.

★ Formal Gardens
The gardens were laid out in the French, geometrical style, which led to Kuskovo gaining a reputation as the Russian Versailles.

The Hermitage has distinctive rounded walls and is topped by a dome.

Church of the Archangel Michael
Constructed in 1737–8, the church is the oldest building on the estate. The statue on its dome is of the Archangel Michael. The wooden bell tower and golden spire were added in 1792.

Obelisk

Lake

The Dutch Cottage was built in 1749 in the homely style of 17th-century Dutch architecture, in red brick and with stepped gables. The tiled interiors house Russian ceramics and glassware.

STAR FEATURES

★ Wooden Palace

★ Grotto

★ Orangery

★ Formal Gardens

The Swiss Cottage resembles a traditional Alpine chalet. It was designed by Nikolay Benoit in 1870.

★ Wooden Palace
Surprisingly, this Neo-Classical palace is made entirely of wood, plastered and painted to resemble stone. Carriage ramps sweep up to the main portico, which is emblazoned with the crest of the Sheremetev family.

★ Orangery
With a central hall for dining and dancing, the Orangery was built in 1761–2. It is now a ceramics museum, based on the 18th–19th-century porcelain collection of Aleksey Morozov (see p96). Pieces on show include Wedgwood, Meissen and items from various Russian factories.

VISITORS' CHECKLIST

Ulitsa Yunosti 2. **Tel** (495) 370 0160. M Ryazanskiy prospekt, Vykhino. 133, 208 (see p227). mid-Apr–Sep: 10am–6pm Wed–Sun; Oct–mid-Apr: 10am–4pm Wed–Sun. last Wed of the month; when temperatures are below -10°C (14°F). tickets sold at main entrance for individual sights.

The Green Theatre was used to stage open-air plays and concerts for an audience of 50 guests.

Allegorical statue of the Greek river god Scamander

Statue of Minerva, Roman goddess of wisdom

Aviary

American Conservatory

Italian Cottage
Russian architect Yuriy Kologrivov studied in Italy prior to designing this pavilion. It was built in 1754–5 in the style of a late-Renaissance villa and now contains displays of 18th-century paintings.

Coach House

The Menagerie, a semi-circle of terracotta and white fenced pavilions, housed songbirds.

0 metres 50
0 yards 50

The kitchens were housed in this large, imposing building, constructed in 1756–7.

Entrance

★ Grotto
Designed by Fyodor Argunov in the mid-18th century, the Grotto is the most remarkable of Kuskovo's pavilions. The cool, spacious interior is decorated with shells and porcelain embedded in sand and stucco.

Main entrance of the Style-Moderne Yaroslavskiy station on Komsomolskaya ploshchad

Komsomolskaya Ploshchad ⑲

Комсомольская площадь
Komsomolskaya ploshchad

Map 4 D2. Ⓜ *Komsomolskaya.*

The three railway stations on this large square are long-standing rivals for the affection of Muscovites. The oldest, Leningradskiy station (formerly Nikolaevskiy station), opened in 1851, serving as the terminus of the line from St Petersburg to Moscow. The building was designed according to the tenets of historicism by Konstantin Ton *(see p45)*, architect of the Great Kremlin Palace *(see p63)*.

In complete contrast is the turreted Yaroslavskiy station, rebuilt in 1902 by architect Fyodor Shekhtel *(see p45)*. The station is a colourful Style-Moderne building with a tiled frieze and an unusual, steeply pitched roof. The Trans-Siberian Railway starts here.

Shekhtel's radical design for his station goaded his rival, Aleksey Shchusev *(see p45)*, into adopting an equally bold approach when designing the third station, Kazanskiy, on the opposite side of the square. Begun in 1912, the station has a tiered central tower modelled on the citadel in the Mongol capital Kazan. The terminal was completed in 1926 and serves the Urals.

The porticoed pavilion of Komsomolskaya metro station *(see pp39–41)* is also a striking

feature of the square. It is named after the Komsomol (Communist Youth volunteers) who helped to build it. It has a luxurious interior, lit by glittering chandeliers.

Komsomolskaya ploshchad itself is a seething mass of beggars, families with apparently everything they own in tow, street hawkers, drunks, drug dealers and, in the evenings, prostitutes. Over recent years it has assumed an unnerving atmosphere to say the least, so it is advisable not to linger here long, especially at night.

Vasnetsov House-Museum ⑳

Дом-музей ВМ Васнецова
Dom-muzey VM Vasnetsova

Pereulok Vasnetsova 13. **Map** 3 A2. **Tel** (495) 281 1329. Ⓜ *Sukharevskaya, Prospekt Mira.* ◯ 10am–5pm Wed–Sun. 🖼 🚫 🗺 🔲

A graphic artist, sculptor, painter, theatre designer and architect, Viktor Vasnetsov (1848–1926) was a member of the artists' colony set up by arts patron Savva Mamontov at Abramtsevo *(see p160)*. He is probably best known for the highly original façade of the Tretyakov Gallery *(see pp118–21)*, where many of his paintings are also housed.

Ornate roof of the wooden house designed by Viktor Vasnetsov

Vasnetsov designed this unusual house for himself and his family in 1893–4 and lived here until he died in 1926, at the age of 78. As an enthusiastic advocate of traditional Russian folk art and architecture, he employed peasant carpenters from Vladimir *(see pp166–7)* to build his remarkable, log-cabin-like, timber house with green roofs.

The ground-floor rooms display highly individual pieces of furniture, many designed by Vasnetsov and his similarly talented younger brother, Apollinariy (1856–1933). The stoves are decorated with colourful tiles made by fellow artists from Abramtsevo.

A spiral staircase hung with 17th-century chain mail and weaponry leads up to the artist's studio, which resembles a vaulted medieval hall. This is the perfect backdrop for Vasnetsov's arresting canvases, many of which take figures from Russian legends as their subjects. For example, *Baba Yaga* portrays Russia's forest witch indulging in her favourite occupation, stealing children. The enormous painting of *The Sleeping Princess*, painted in the last year of Vasnetsov's life, shows a scene from the classic fairy story of Sleeping Beauty.

Ostankino Palace ㉑

Московский музей-усадьба Останкино
Moskovskiy muzey-usadba Ostankino

1-ya Ostankinskaya ulitsa 5a. **Tel** (495) 286 6288. Ⓜ *VDNKh.* ◯ 10am–5pm Wed–Sun. 🔲 Oct–April. 🖼 ♿ *gardens only.* 🗺 *English.*

Like the estate at Kuskovo *(see pp142–3)*, Ostankino was built by the serf architects Pavel Argunov and Aleksey Mironov for the Sheremetevs, one of Russia's richest families. Count Nikolay Sheremetev was a prominent patron of the arts and built his palace around a theatre, where a company of 200 serf actors and actresses performed plays of his choosing. In 1800 the Count married Praskovia Zhemchugova-Kovaleva, one of the actresses. Secluded at their palace, they

Main façade of the Imposing, Neo-Classical Ostankino Palace

were able to shelter themselves from the disapproval of polite society, but sadly Praskovia died three years later. The count never recovered from the loss and left the palace, which fell into disuse.

Ostankino is a handsome palace, with a shallow green dome and impressive classical 18th century interiors. The main building has an admirably restrained Neo-Classical façade. It was built in wood in 1792–8 and skilfully plastered over to look like brick and stone. It demonstrates the remarkable workmanship of Sheremetev's serf craftsmen. The halls are a wonder of *trompe l'oeil* decor. Carved wooden mouldings are painted to resemble bronze, gold and marble, parquet floors are patterned in birchwood and mahogany, while a huge crystal chandelier hangs from the frescoed ceiling of the main hall. The pavilion also serves as a sculpture gallery and among the sculptures is a Roman marble head of Aphrodite from the 1st century AD.

The *pièce de résistance* of the palace is the theatre, a breathtaking, elliptical hall with a superb painted ceiling supported by rows of Corinthian columns. In 1796 the building was partly reconstructed to allow the installation of an ingenious mechanical device which raised the auditorium floor so that the theatre could

also be used as a ballroom. In the summer, concerts of classical music are still held here.

On the road leading from the estate is the ornate Church of the Trinity with a cluster of green domes. It was built in 1678–83 for the Cherkasskiy family, who owned Ostankino estate before the Sheremetevs.

Theatre auditorium, Ostankino Palace, once home to Count Sheremetev's serf actors

All-Russian Exhibition Centre ㉒

Всероссийский Выставочный Центр (ВВЦ)
Vserossiyskiy Vystavochniy Tsentr (VVTs)

Prospekt Mira. **Tel** *(495) 544 3400.*
Ⓜ VDNKh. **Pavilions** ⬜ *May–Oct: 10am–6pm Mon–Fri, 10am–7pm Sat–Sun; Nov–Apr: 10am–5pm Mon–Fri, 10am–6pm Sat–Sun.* Ⓖ **Botanical Gardens** ⬜ *10am–4pm (8pm summer).* **Space Museum** ⬜ *10am–6pm Wed–Sun.* 📷 Ⓖ ∅ 🗣 *English.*

One of the city's main tourist attractions in Soviet times, the former Exhibition of Economic Achievements of the USSR (VDNKh) has now become the All-Russian Exhibition Centre (VVTs), a vast park, shopping centre and exhibition site.

VVTs remains a fascinating place for a visit, especially for enthusiasts of Soviet architecture. There are scores of massive pavilions, including a Pavilion of the Peoples of the USSR, guarded by a statue of Lenin. Its interior once featured a huge illuminated map of the USSR, but is now divided into booths selling electrical goods and cosmetics.

The main entrance to the park is a huge triumphal arch, topped by the figures of a tractor driver and female collective farmer, holding up a sheaf of corn.

In the centre of the complex is the Fountain of the Republics, consisting of 15 gilded statues of maidens in national dress (representing the former Soviet republics) circling a golden wheat sheaf. Jets of water from the basin are sprayed 24 m (79 ft) into the air, and at night it is lit up by some 525 spotlights.

Nearby is the entrance to the **Botanical Gardens**, which contain a small but pleasant Japanese Garden where tea is served. There are also numerous ponds and picnic spots.

Heading back towards VDNKh Metro, it is hard to avoid the Space Obelisk. Over 100 m (328 ft) high, it represents a rocket lifting off. It was erected in 1964, three years after Yuriy Gagarin's historic flight. Underneath it is the **Space Museum**, one of Moscow's hidden treasures, containing Belka and Strelka (stuffed), the two dogs who were the first creatures to come back alive from space (Laika, more famous in the West, died), and *Vostok 1*, the tiny capsule in which Gagarin famously orbited the Earth.

Statue of tractor driver and farmer atop the main entrance of the VVTs

TWO GUIDED WALKS

Modern Moscow is, in many respects, the brainchild of Stalin. A sprawling city of around 10 million people, it is not a place that lends itself easily to a casual stroll. Stalin intended the city to awe, tearing down churches and any other buildings that got in the way of his plan for a Socialist megalopolis, and the capital's wide streets and imposing structures are a testament to his vision. Walking through Moscow, one can feel dwarfed by buildings that seem to have been designed for a larger race of being. One of the joys of life in the city, however, is finding a quiet, forgotten corner, an unexpected moment of calm amid the bustle of city life. The two walks that follow present two very different aspects of the Russian capital. The first explores Moscow's busy centre, passing some often neglected, yet fascinating sights from both Russia's recent and distant past including the former headquarters of the KGB. The second walk provides a journey through Russian literature, from the giant statue of Dostoevsky outside the Russian State Library, to Patriach's Pond, straight from the pages of a modern Soviet classic.

Statue of Pushkin, Russia's literary giant

CHOOSING A WALK

The Two Walks
This map shows the general area covered by the two guided walks in relation to the main sightseeing areas of Moscow.

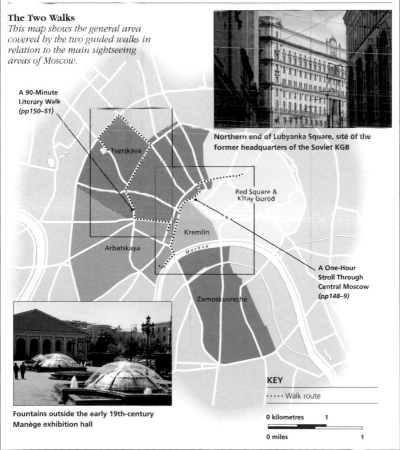

A 90-Minute Literary Walk (pp150–51)

Tverskaya

Arbatskaya

Kremlin

Moskva

Red Square & K'Itay Gorod

Zamoskvoreche

Northern end of Lubyanka Square, site of the former headquarters of the Soviet KGB

A One-Hour Stroll Through Central Moscow (pp148–9)

Fountains outside the early 19th-century Manège exhibition hall

KEY

····· Walk route

0 kilometres   1
0 miles   1

◁ **Resurrection Gate, a modern replica that serves as an entrance to Red Square**

A One-Hour Stroll Through Central Moscow

Like any major capital, Moscow is a busy place and full of life. This walk, along the the quieter embankments and older streets, is a chance to explore the city's ancient heart, while avoiding many of the busier sections. Taking in such varied sights as the recreated Cathedral of Christ the Redeemer, Red Square and the former KGB HQ, the route provides an excellent opportunity to appreciate Moscow's rich and eventful history of the distant, as well as more recent, past.

Cathedral of Christ the Redeemer, one of Moscow's main landmarks ①

Along the Moscow River

The gilded dome of the Cathedral of Christ the Redeemer ① *(see p74)* is immediately visible on exiting from Kropotkinskaya station. The original 19th-century cathedral was blown up on the orders of Stalin in 1931. This modern replica was completed in 1997. Explore the grounds to find a statue of Tsar Alexander I ②. After leaving the cathedral grounds turn left and walk along the embankment of the Moskva river, passing under Bolshoy Kamennyy Bridge. After the bridge turn left again in the direction of the Kremlin, and then cross the road at the traffic lights, under the watchful eyes of Moscow's traffic police. The guarded gate is Borovitskaya Tower ③, the presidential entrance to the Kremlin. When the President, or any other important figure, arrives traffic is held up throughout Moscow to allow the entourage, with its flashing blue lights, a clear road.

Around Alexander Gardens

Next, follow the pathway through Alexander Gardens ④ *(see p67)* past the Kremlin walls and turrets, including Trinity Tower ⑤ *(see p56)*, the tallest of the Kremlin's fortifications. The gardens contain a number of cafés and the paths are a favourite place for Muscovites to take a stroll when the weather is fine. Look out for the fountains with characters from Russian fairy tales set against the wall of the shopping complex at the northern end of the gardens. Close to the park's exit are the monuments to the Hero Cities of the Soviet Union ⑥ (Moscow, Leningrad, Kursk, etc.). They commemorate the bravery of the citizens of those cities that bore the brunt of the fighting during World War II. Next to these monuments is the Tomb of the Unknown Soldier, dedicated to the millions of Soviet soldiers who died in the battle against Fascism. Newly-married couples often come here to pay homage to the fallen. Leaving Alexander Gardens, look to the right for an unusual view of Red Square ⑦ *(see p106)*. Walking on, the statue of the earnest looking military man astride a horse is Marshal Georgiy Zhukov ⑧, the stout defender of Stalingrad and leader of the Soviet forces during the Battle of Kursk in 1943, the largest tank battle of World War II.

Continue past the statue of Zhukov for Resurrection Gate ⑨ *(see p105)* and another stunning view of Red Square. Walk through the gate: to the left is Kazan Cathedral ⑩ *(see p105)*, a 1990s replica of the original, which, like

Water jets of an equestrian fountain, Alexander Gardens ④

Biblioteka imeni Lenina Ⓜ

Aleksandrovskiy Sad Ⓜ

Borovitskaya Ⓜ

Kropotkinskaya Ⓜ

MAL. ZNAMENSKIY PER.

UL VOLKHONKA

UL. LENIVKA

UL. LEBYAZHIY PER.

PRECHISTENSKAYA NABEREZHNAYA

BERSENEVSKAYA NABEREZHNAYA

SOYMONOVSKIY PR.

MANEZ...

MOS...

0 metres   300

0 yards   300

KEY

• • • Walk route

Ⓜ Metro station

the Cathedral of Christ the Redeemer, was destroyed on Stalin's orders in 1936. Head back through Resurrection Gate and turn right.

From Ploshchcad Revolyutsii to Lubyanka

Walk across to Ploshchad Revolyutsii (Revolution Square) to find the chunky statue of Karl Marx ⑪. The inscription at the statue's base, urging the workers of the world to unite, grows more incongruous year by year as capitalism becomes

Kazan Cathedral, rebuilt after its destruction by the Communists ⑩

the main economic model in Russia. Opposite Marx is the world famous Bolshoy Theatre ⑫ (see pp190–91), which has recently undergone extensive internal and external reconstruction. Head towards the theatre, crossing the road via the underpass to the right. Teatralnaya ploshcad is a favourite place for local workers to sit and eat lunch

on summer days. It is also occasionally the site of demonstrations.

Next head up Teatralnyy proezd to No 5, Detskiy Mir ⑬ (see p193), which was the largest and most famous toy shop in Russia but which has been closed for repairs. A short distance away is Lubyanka Square (see p112), and, on it, the HQ of the former KGB ⑭. Here, during Communist Russia's darkest days, the state security agency carried out many of its interrogations. A plaque to Yuriy Andropov, the former Soviet General Secretary and KGB chief, is near the entrance. A statue of Feliks Dzerzhinskiy, founder of the Cheka (forerunners to the KGB), once stood in the square until it was toppled in 1991 by cheering crowds in one of the most symbolic events to take place during the death throes of the USSR. In a move that many have seen as equally symbolic, a plaque to Dzerzhinskiy has recently been placed within the grounds of what is now the HQ of the modern state security service, the FSB. To the right, on Lubyanskiy proezd, is the Mayakovsky Museum ⑲ (see p111), dedicated to the life of Vladimir Mayakovsky. One of Stalin's favourite poets, Mayakovsky eventually became disillusioned with Communism and committed suicide in this very building. It is a short walk from here to Lubyanka metro station.

Imposing statue of Marx in Revolution Square ⑪

TIPS FOR WALKERS

Starting point: Cathedral of Christ the Redeemer.
Length: 3 km (2 miles).
Getting there: Kropotkinskaya metro station.
Stopping-off points: There are plenty of cafés and places to sit in Alexander Gardens.

Statue of war hero Marshal Zhukov, next to the Historical Museum ⑧

A 90-Minute Literary Walk

Russia has long been revered for its writers and
Moscow is dotted with statues, monuments and other
reminders of them. This walk highlights not only the
well-known giants of Russian literature, such as
Dostoevsky, but also lesser known yet important
literary figures such as Pushkin, the father of Russian
literature, Yesenin, a young idealist poet who took his
own life, and Bulgakov, author of *The Master and
Margarita*, a novel that conjures up a strange reality in
which Moscow is visited by the devil himself. As well
as sights directly relating to Russian literature, this walk
also passes by other places of interest including
theatres and newspaper offices.

Ornate façade of the 19th-century
House of Friendship ⑤

Giant statue of Dostoevsky outside
the Russian State Library ③

The Republics' Tree to the
Morozov Mansion

Arriving at Borovitskaya metro
station, take the city exit. Next
to the stairs leading to the escalators is *The Republics' Tree* ①,
a mural depicting the peoples
of the 15 former Soviet republics in national costume. Take
the escalators to street level.
Turn left and follow the road
to the corner for a view of the
Manège ② *(see p94)*, an exhibition hall that was partially
destroyed in a mysterious fire
in 2005. To the left is the
Russian State Library ③ and,
outside it, the brooding figure
of Fyodor Dostoevsky (1821–
81), the prolific writer who
helped to shape the 20th-
century novel in works such as
Crime and Punishment (1866).
Further on, at No 5, is the
Shchusev Museum of Architecture ④, a former Bolshevik
HQ. Continuing on, cross the
road via the underpass to the
glitzy House of Friendship ⑤
(see p95). Next to it is the 19th-
century neo-Gothic Morozov
Mansion ⑥ *(see p96)*.

From Nikitskiy bulvar to
Pushkin Square

Turning into Nikitskiy bulvar,
cross the road to No 7b ⑦,
where Nikolai Gogol (1809–
52), author of the classic novel
Dead Souls (1842), lived out his
final years. It was here that he
wrote the second volume of
Dead Souls, but, having fallen
under the influence of a
religious fanatic, he destroyed
the manuscript. Cross back
over the road at the pedestrian
crossing, pass the Museum of
Eastern Peoples ⑧ at No 12a,
and then walk to the end of
the road. The building opposite
is ITAR-TASS ⑨, the Russian
state news agency and the
mouthpiece of the Communist
Party in Soviet times. To the left
is a statue of botanist and
thinker Kliment Timiryazev ⑩.
Carry on up Tverskoy bulvar
to the statue of the poet Sergey
Yesenin ⑪. Born in 1895, he
is best known for *Pugachev*
(1922), a verse tragedy dealing
with the peasant rebellion of
1773–75. Yesenin had a troubled life, including an unhappy
marriage to the American

dancer Isadora
Duncan, and killed
himself in 1925.
Facing each other,
slightly further up
the road at Nos
22 and 23
respectively,
are the MXAT
Gorky Art
Theatre ⑫, named
for Maxim Gorky, the
dramatist founder of
Socialist Realism, and the
Pushkin Theatre ⑬. At the
end of the road, take the
underpass and follow the
tunnel to the left to enter
Pushkin Square ⑭ where there
is a monument to Alexander
Pushkin (1799–1837). Com-
paratively little-known in the
West, Pushkin is a hero of
Russian literature. *Eugene
Onegin* (1830), his novel in
verse, is held by many critics
to be the greatest masterpiece
of Russian literature *(see p73)*.

Ground-floor window of ITAR-TASS, Russia's official news agency ⑨

Tverskaya ulitsa to Mayakovskaya Metro

Continue up Tverskaya ulitsa. On the right hand side of the street, at No 18a, look out for a plaque (in Russian) noting that this was where Lenin's wife worked on the *Pravda* newspaper ⑮.

Patriarch's Pond, one of the city's most popular picnic spots ⑳

Across the street, at No 21, stands the red-bricked Museum of the Revolution, now renamed the Museum of Modern History ⑯ *(see p97)*. At the end of Tverskaya ulitsa, use the underpass to cross over to the statue of Vladimir Mayakovsky ⑰ (1893–1930). A poet of the revolution, Mayakovsky was one of the few writers permitted to travel abroad during the Soviet crackdown. He was a favourite of Stalin, who proclaimed that indifference to his works was a crime *(see p111)*. South of the statue is the Tchaikovsky Concert Hall ⑱ *(see p200)*, named after the composer of *The Nutcracker*. Heading down Bolshaya Sadovaya ulitsa, walk into the courtyard at No 10 to pay a visit to the Bulgakov Flat-Museum ⑲ *(see p96)*. Never a supporter of the Soviet regime, most of Mikhail Bulgakov's work was supressed during his lifetime. Continue on, taking the first left to reach Patriarch's Pond ⑳. This is the setting for the opening of Bulgakov's *The Master and Margarita*, where Satan makes his first appearance. From here, head back to Mayakovskaya metro station.

Statue of the troubled poet Sergey Yesenin on Tverskoy bulvar ⑪

TIPS FOR WALKERS

Starting point: The Republics' Tree, Borovitskaya metro station.
Length: 4 km (2 miles).
Getting there: Borovitskaya.
Stopping-off points: Pushkin Square has stalls selling food. Patriarch's Pond is a good place for a picnic, with shops nearby. There are cafés along Nikitskiy bulvar and Tverskaya ulitsa.

KEY

• • • Walk route

Ⓜ Metro station

0 metres 300
0 yards 300

Golden and azure domes of the Cathedral of the Assumption, Trinity Monastery of St Sergius ▷

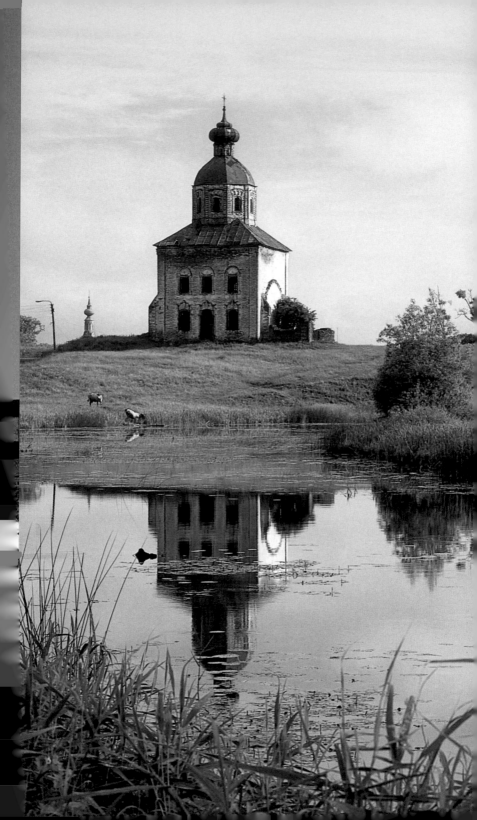

BEYOND MOSCOW

The magnificence of some of the palaces and churches outside Moscow and the historic interest of some of the towns make excursions there justly rewarding. Although parts of the landscape are unappealingly industrial, the large areas of true countryside are green, forested and dotted with villages of small wooden dachas.

Visitors may find it a good idea to take an organized tour *(see p206)* to out-of-town sights as public transport can be erratic, though perfectly feasible for those who prefer mixing with local daily life *(see p227)*. There are several places of historic and cultural importance within easy reach of the city. To the west is Borodino *(see p158)*, site of the great battle between Napoleon's army and Russian forces under the command of Field Marshal Mikhail Kutuzov. To the north is the magnificent Trinity Monastery of St Sergius *(see pp162–5)* and to the northeast the towns of the Golden Ring *(see p161)*. The political heyday of these towns was in the 12th and 13th centuries, before the rise of Moscow, and their churches and wooden buildings make them well worth exploring.

Also outside Moscow are houses lived in by two of Russia's most famous sons, Pyotr Tchaikovsky *(see p159)* and Leo Tolstoy *(see p134)*.

On Friday nights the trains and roads into the countryside are packed with families travelling to their dacha, a migration that leaves the capital rather deserted. Each dacha has a small plot of land that is used for growing fruit and vegetables. For some Muscovites this was, and often still is today, an essential source of food. In the last few years, brick houses have started to spring up where farmers used to grow crops, built for New Russians who have adopted Western commuter habits. However, many have been abandoned half built as construction firms have gone out of business in the fast-changing economic climate.

Field Marshal Mikhail Kutuzov

The Sacred Supper, painted in 1685, displayed in the Treasury at the Trinity Monastery of St Sergius

◁ The Church of the Prophet Elijah, one of many picturesque churches in the Golden Ring town of Suzdal

Exploring the Moscow Region

Despite the numerous attractions of Moscow, it is well worth spending time in the surrounding region. Several country estates lie within easy reach of the city and make for delightful one- or two-day trips. Among them are Yasnaya Polyana, where Leo Tolstoy *(see p134)* lived for many years, the house in Klin rented by Pyotr Tchaikovsky *(see p159)* and Abramtsevo Estate-Museum, a former artists' colony. However, the star attraction of the region is the Trinity Monastery of St Sergius. Once a place of pilgrimage for the tsars, this huge complex has several superb cathedrals.

Moscow is also an ideal base for visiting the Golden Ring towns, which include Pereslavl-Zalesskiy, Suzdal and Vladimir. Founded by Russians seeking shelter from invading tribes, these attractive settlements still have many historic buildings.

Tiles by artist Mikhail Vrubel on a bench at Abramtsevo

KEY

═══	Motorway
▬▬	Main road
═══	Minor road
▬▬	Scenic route
┅┅	Main railway
┄┄	Minor railway

Dmit

TCHAIKOVSKY HOUSE-MUSEUM ❸

Vysokovsk

Solnechnogorsk

Volokolamsk

Riga, Pskov

Zelenograd

Istra

Nakhabino

Khimki

Mytishc

Lobnj

ARKHANGELSKOE ❶

Zvenigorod

Ruza

Moskva

MOSCOW

Mamonov

Golicyno

Vnukovo

BORODINO ❷

Mozhaysk

Kubinka

Aprelevka

Podol'sk

Minsk, Kiev

Naro-Fominsk

Klimovsk

Chekhov

Serpukhov

The blue-domed Church of the Holy Spirit and the Chapel Over the Well, Trinity Monastery of St Sergius

SIGHTS AT A GLANCE

Abramtsevo Estate-Museum ❹
Arkhangelskoe ❶
Borodino ❷
Pereslavl-Zalesskiy ❻
Suzdal ❼
Tchaikovsky House-Museum ❸
Trinity Monastery of St Sergius pp162–5 ❺
Vladimir ❽
Yasnaya Polyana ❾

YASNAYA POLYANA

Orel

The beautiful Chamber of the Cross in Suzdal Museum, which is housed in a former archbishops' palace

The Cathedral of the Assumption, Vladimir's most famous monument

GETTING AROUND

While some sights on the map, such as Pereslavl-Zalesskiy, can be visited in a day, a trip to Suzdal, Vladimir or Yasnaya Polyana will take at least two days. Sights are served by a mixture of trains, buses and coaches *(see p227)*. For more adventurous travellers the extensive road network offers an alternative means of getting to sights, but this too has its problems *(see p226)*. One of the best ways to visit sights outside Moscow is on an organized tour *(see p206)*.

0 kilometres 30

0 miles 30

The southern, garden façade of the Neo-Classical, stucco-covered, wooden palace at Arkhangelskoe

Arkhangelskoe ❶

Архангельское

Arkhangelskoe

20 km (12 miles) W of Moscow.
Tel (495) 363 1375. ◯ *9am–6pm
Mon–Fri, 9am–7pm Sat–Sun.* ◉ *last
Wed of the month.* Ⓜ *Tushinskaya,
then bus (see p227).* 🎨 ♿ *pavilions
and grounds only.*

Most of the buildings on this
country estate date from the
18th and 19th centuries. The
charming Church of the
Archangel Michael was completed in 1667, however, and
gives the estate its name.

The Golitsyn family acquired
the estate in 1703. In the 1780s
Prince Nikolay Golitsyn began
a wholesale rebuilding, including a new palace which was
built to a design by the French
architect Charles de Guerne.
Constructed from wood, it was
covered with stucco to give the
effect of stone. When Golitsyn
died in 1809, the estate was
purchased by Prince Nikolay

Yusupov. Recently restored,
the palace's sumptuous rooms
are filled with fine furniture,
fabrics and antiques. There is
also an excellent art collection.

The formal gardens were laid
out in the 18th century. Within
them stand pavilions such as
the diminutive Caprice Palace,
built in 1819 for soirees. In
1910–16 a lavish mausoleum
was erected for the Yusupov
family, but it was never used
because of the Revolution.

Borodino ❷

Бородино

Borodino

130 km (80 miles) SW of Moscow.
Tel 8238 51522. ◯ *10am–5pm
Tue–Sun.* ◉ *last Fri of the month.* 🚃
*Mozhaisk or Borodino, then bus (see
p227).* 🎨 ♿ 🎫 *www.*borodino.ru

One of the fiercest military
confrontations of the 19th
century took place at Borodino
on 7 September 1812. For over
15 hours Napoleon
Bonaparte's Grande
Armée and the
Russian army, led
by Field Marshal
Mikhail Kutuzov,
fought each other to
a bloody impasse.
It is estimated that
40,000 Russian and
30,000 French sol-
diers were killed.
Napoleon called it
the "most terrible"
of all his battles, but
claimed victory on

the grounds that the Russians
were forced to continue their
retreat to Moscow. Posterity,
however, awarded the laurels
to the Russians. The French
followed the Russians, but
arrived to find the city and the
Kremlin deserted. The
Muscovites then started a
great fire (*see pp24–5*) in
the city, and faced with a
Russian winter in the
open, the French were
finally forced to retreat.

The battlefield covers
over 100 sq km (40sq
miles), but the main
places of interest are
reasonably accessible.
A museum, 1 km (½
mile) south of Borodino
village, recounts the
story of the battle with
the aid of models and
an illuminated map.
More than 30
monuments are
strewn around the
area. Russia's most
distinguished gen-
eral to fall in battle,
Prince Pyotr
Bagration, was
buried at the base of a column
dedicated to the fallen just
east of the museum. Nearby
is the inn, now a museum,
where Leo Tolstoy stayed to
research the background for
his epic novel *War and Peace.*

The small Empire-style
Spasskiy Church of 1822 was
the first monument to be constructed on the battlefield.
A re-enactment of the battle
takes place every 7 September.

Monument to th
fallen of Borodir

The gorgeously painted dome of the Yusupov
mausoleum, built in 1910–16, at Arkhangelskoe

Tchaikovsky House-Museum ❸

Дом-музей ПИ Чайковского
Dom-muzey PI Chaykovskovo

90 km (55 miles) NW of Moscow.
Ulitsa Tchaikovskaya 48, Klin.
Tel (495) 539 8196. ◯ 10am–6pm
Fri–Tue. ◉ last Mon of the month.
🚆 Klin (see p227). 🏷 🗿 www.
cbook.ru/tchaikovsky

The reception area in the house at Klin, containing Tchaikovsky's piano

In a letter to his brother Anatoly in May 1892 Pyotr Tchaikovsky wrote, "I have rented a house in Klin. What a blessing it is to know that no-one will come, either to interrupt my work, or my reading or walking". Previous stays in the village of Frolovskoe near Klin had inspired some of his best music, including the ballets *The Sleeping Beauty* and *The Nutcracker*, and the opera *The Queen of Spades* based on Pushkin's novel *(see p73)*. Tchaikovsky enjoyed Klin for only a few months, as he died in 1893. In 1894 his younger brother, Modest, opened the

Tchaikovsky's wooden house in Klin, in the quiet of the Russian countryside he loved so much

estate to visitors. The ground floor of the clapboard house is closed to the public, but on entering the composer's rooms on the first floor visitors find themselves in a bright, spacious reception area. The walls are covered with photos of his family, his classmates at law school and fellow musicians. The grand piano in the centre of the room was a gift from the Russian firm Becker. Though an excellent pianist, Tchaikovsky never performed in public. The winner of the Tchaikovsky International Competition *(see p200)* gives a recital here on the composer's birthday, 7 May.

Tchaikovsky was a great collector of souvenirs. On a shelf behind the piano is a Statue of Liberty inkpot, which he brought back from his triumphant conducting tour of the United States in 1891.

The bedroom is separated from the reception area by a curtain. Warm and intimate, it contains Tchaikovsky's diminutive slippers and a beautiful coverlet made by his niece. Tchaikovsky finished his *Sixth Symphony*, the *Pathétique*, at the table by the window.

Also open to visitors are the handsome wood-panelled library and the study where Modest Tchaikovsky worked as the Klin archivist until his death in 1916. A memorial room to the composer holds some of his personal possessions, including his top hat, gloves and evening clothes.

Tchaikovsky habitually took a stroll in the garden before breakfast and after lunch. His favourite flowers, lilies of the valley, are still planted here.

PYOTR TCHAIKOVSKY

Probably Russia's most famous composer, Tchaikovsky was born in 1840. After graduating initially in law, he studied music at the St Petersburg Conservatory. One of his teachers helped the young composer to get a job teaching music at the Moscow Conservatory *(see p94)* in 1866 where he then taught for the next 12 years. It was during this period that Tchaikovsky composed his first four symphonies and the ballet *Swan Lake* (1876). In 1877 he married a student from the Conservatory in an effort to suppress his homosexuality.

Statue of Pyotr Tchaikovsky at the Moscow Conservatory

However, the marriage was unhappy and short-lived. Tchaikovsky composed prolifically in the 1880s, completing such works as the ballet *The Sleeping Beauty* (1889) and the overture *The Year 1812* (1880). In 1892 he moved to Klin, outside Moscow. He died of cholera in November 1893, while overseeing the premiere of his final work, the *Sixth Symphony*, in St Petersburg. It is rumoured that he drank infected water as a dignified form of suicide after the exposure of his homosexual affair with a young aristocrat.

Iconostasis in the Church of the Saviour, Abramtsevo Estate-Museum

by Mamontov out of respect for his predecessor. Aksakov knew the novelists Nikolai Gogol and Ivan Turgenev, and, here, in the red sitting-room, Gogol would read aloud from his masterpiece, *Dead Souls*. The dining room features a beautiful, tiled corner fireplace and a profusion of paintings. The gaze, however, is drawn to a copy of Valentin Serov's arresting portrait of Vera, Savva Mamontov's daughter, seated at the dining table. Entitled *Girl with Peaches* (1887), the original can be found in the Tretyakov Gallery *(see p121)*.

Trinity Monastery of St Sergius ⑤

See pp162–5.

Abramtsevo Estate-Museum ④
Музей-усадьба Абрамцево
Muzey-usadba Abramtsevo

60 km (35 miles) NE of Moscow. 🚇 *Khotkova or Sergiev Posad, then bus (see p227).* **Tel** *8254 32470.* 🕐 *10am–5pm Wed–Sun.* 🔴 *last Thu of the month.* 📷 🚫 📷 *English (book in advance).*

In the second half of the 19th century this delightful rural retreat became a hive of cultural activity. Until his death in 1859, the house was owned by the writer Sergey Aksakov, whose sons were leading Slavophile thinkers. The estate's creative legacy was continued in 1870 when it was acquired by Savva Mamontov, an industrialist and art patron. Mamontov's generosity and zeal led to the establishment of an artists' colony here, and to a re-evaluation of traditional Russian folk art and craftwork. The work of local peasant craftsmen, whose children were educated in the estate's school, was a source of inspiration for many of the artists.

Dotted around the estate are a number of remarkable buildings. The artists' studio, with a spectacular carved roof, was designed in 1872 by Viktor Gartman. Displayed here are ceramics by the two distinguished artists Valentin Serov and Mikhail Vrubel. The

teremok, meanwhile, is a free improvization on the typical peasant hut *(izba)*, and was originally built as a bathhouse by Ivan Ropet in 1873. It was later used as a guesthouse. Inside are the original wooden furnishings and ornaments, such as statuettes, kitchen utensils and a tiled stove.

The House on Chicken Legs stands on stilts. Designed by Viktor Vasnetsov, it is now a popular children's attraction, recalling the witch of Russian folklore, Baba Yaga, whose house in the forest is built on giant chicken legs.

A woodland path leads to the most remarkable building on the estate. The Church of the Saviour Not Made by Human Hand is modelled on the medieval churches of Novgorod, but was brought up to date by the addition of bands of painted majolica tiles to its walls of white-washed brick. The church was built in 1881–2, to a design by Viktor Vasnetsov; the mosaic floor is also his work, while the icons were painted by Vasnetsov, Ilya Repin and his wife Vera, Vasiliy Polenov and Nikolay Nevrev. A small oratory holds Savva Mamontov's remains and those of his son Andrey, who died, aged 19, in 1891.

The manor house still contains Aksakov's original Empire-style furnishings, left

Pereslavl-Zalesskiy ⑥
Переславль-Залесский
Pereslavl-Zalesskiy

135 km (85 miles) NE of Moscow. 🚶 *43,400.* 🚇 *Sergiev Posad, then bus (see p227).*

Founded as a fortress in 1152 by Yuriy Dolgorukiy, and overlooking Lake Pleshcheevo, Pereslavl-Zalesskiy was an independent princedom until 1302, when it came under the control of Moscow. Peter the Great *(see p22)* developed plans for the Russian navy here. Sights of interest include the 12th-century **Cathedral of the Transfiguration** and the **Goritskiy Monastery of the Assumption**, founded in the 14th century but dating mainly from the 17th–18th centuries.

Cathedral of the Goritskiy Monastery of the Assumption, Pereslavl-Zalesskiy

The History of the Golden Ring

The first important cities in Russia were Novgorod in the north and Kiev in the south, which were situated on trade routes connecting the Baltic and the Black Sea. From the 11th century, as hostile tribes invaded Kievan Rus *(see p17)* and many Russians were forced northward, new settlements were founded such as Rostov, Yaroslavl, Vladimir and Suzdal. Like Novgorod and Kiev, these towns flourished on trade from Western

16th-century icon from the Golden Ring

Europe, Byzantium and Central Asia, while Sergiev Posad, location of the Trinity Monastery of St Sergius *(see pp162–5)*, became an important centre for the Orthodox Church. Moscow was also founded during this era *(see p17)* and, by the 16th century, had become Russia's capital. By this time the cluster of towns northeast of Moscow had paled into insignificance, although in the 1960s their historic importance brought them the title the Golden Ring.

THE GOLDEN RING

Kostroma
Yaroslavl
Rostov
Pereslavl-Zalesskiy
Ivanovo
Sergiev Posad
Suzdal
Vladimir
MOSCOW

Prince Vladimir Monomakh *(see p59) founded a small trading settlement in the late 11th century It was named Vladimir in 1108. Monomakh's son, Yuriy Dolgorukiy (see p17), expanded the town and it was later the capital of Northern Rus.*

A campaign *by Suzdal against Novgorod in 1169 is the subject of this icon. Created by the 15th-century Novgorod School (see p61), it recalls Suzdal's strength before Moscow became pre-eminent.*

Andrey Bogolyubskiy, *the son of Yuriy Dolgorukiy, moved his court to Vladimir in 1157, where his craftsmen were to recreate the splendour of Kiev. His boyars later murdered him for being a dictator.*

Angels denote that the campaign against the Mongols was blessed.

Dmitriy Donskoy

The Battle of Kulikovo *(see p18), in 1380, was a turning point in the history of the Golden Ring. The Mongols made many inroads into the area, sacking Suzdal in 1238 and demanding tribute from the Russians. Dmitriy Donskoy (see p18) won a decisive victory against them at Kulikovo, with a blessing, it is said, from monk Sergius of Radonezh (see p165).*

Many churches *were built in the towns of the Golden Ring, a sign of their comparative wealth. Some wooden churches are preserved in a museum at Suzdal (see p166).*

Trinity Monastery of St Sergius ❺

Троице-Сергиева Лавра
Troitse-Sergieva Lavra

Founded around 1345 by Sergius of Radonezh *(see p165)*, the Trinity Monastery of St Sergius in the town of Sergiev-Possad is one of Russia's most important religious centres and places of pilgrimage. In 1608–10, during the Time of Troubles *(see p19)*, the monks survived a siege by the Polish army and in the 1680s the young Peter the Great found refuge here during the Streltsy Rebellion *(see p22)*. The monastery was closed down by the Communists in 1919, but was allowed to open again in 1946, when it became headquarters of the Russian Orthodox Church. The headquarters transferred to new premises at the Danilovskiy Monastery *(see pp136–7)* in 1988.

The Church of the Virgin of Smolensk was built in 1745 to house the Icon of the Smolensk Virgin.

The bell tower was begun in 1741 and completed 28 years later. Spectacular views can be obtained from its gallery.

Carpenters' Tower

Hospital with Church of SS Zosima and Savvatiy

Obelisk

Treasury

Chapel Over the Well
This delightful, Moscow-Baroque (see p44) *chapel was built in the late 17th century to mark the site of a holy spring.*

Sacristy

★ **Trinity Cathedral**
Built in 1422–3 over the grave of St Sergius, this splendid church contains an iconostasis painted by a team of artists led by Andrey Rublev (see p61).

Palace of the Metropolitans
This grand palace was completed in 1778. It was the residence of the metropolitans and patriarchs in 1946–88.

Water Tower

Church of the Holy Spirit

★ **Church of St Sergius and Refectory**
The monks' refectory was built in 1686–92 with the Church of St Sergius at its eastern end. The colourful façade features pillars with vine leaf decoration and chequered walls. The interior is equally lavish.

Tsars' Apartments
These apartments were built in the late 17th century for Tsar Alexis Mikhailovich. He often visited the monastery with a retinue of over 500 courtiers. The building now houses a theological college.

VISITORS' CHECKLIST

75 km (47 miles) NE of Moscow.
Tel 8254 45356. from Yaroslavskiy station (see p227). **Trinity
Cathedral** 6am–5pm daily.
Museum 10am–5pm
Wed–Mon. **Grounds** 5am–9pm daily.
www.stsl.ru

School buildings

Library

**The Duck
Tower** was
given its unusual
name because of
the legend that Peter
the Great used to shoot
ducks from its windows.

| 0 metres | 25 |
| 0 yards | 25 |

Drying
Tower

Усыпальница Годуновыхъ

Godunov's Tomb
Tsar Boris Godunov is buried with members of his family in this simple tomb. It was originally inside the cathedral, but later alterations put it outside. In Soviet times the tomb was opened and it was discovered that Boris Godunov's skull was missing.

Beautiful Tower –
main entrance

To train station

**The Gate Church
of St John the
Baptist** stands
over the main
entrance. It was
built in 1692–99
by the wealthy
Stroganov family.

★ Cathedral of the Assumption
Commissioned in 1559 by Ivan the Terrible to commemorate the capture of Kazan, this is the monastery's main cathedral. Its sumptuous interior was decorated by artists from Yaroslavl over a century later.

STAR FEATURES

★ Cathedral of the
Assumption

★ Trinity Cathedral

★ Church of St Sergius
and Refectory

Exploring the Trinity Monastery of St Sergius

In the 14th century, Sergius of Radonezh built a small wooden church in the forests to the north of Moscow and consecrated it to the Holy Trinity. Many pilgrims were attracted to the site by reports of Sergius' piety. He organized them into a community and the Trinity Monastery was born. The monastery expanded as it gained wealth and influence and today the huge complex is enclosed by white walls around 1.6 km (1 mile) long. Its stunning churches, grouped around the spectacular Cathedral of the Assumption, are among the most beautiful in Russia.

The fortified Trinity Monastery of St Sergius seen from the southeast

The superb 17th-century iconostasis in the Cathedral of the Assumption

the heart of the monastery. Ivan the Terrible commissioned the cathedral in 1559 to celebrate his defeat of the Mongols at Kazan *(see p19)*. It was completed 26 years later to a design inspired by Aristotele Fioravanti's Cathedral of the Assumption *(see pp58–9)* in the Kremlin. Painters from the acclaimed Yaroslavl school of artists, led by Dmitriy Grigorev, took just 100 days to decorate the lofty interior in 1684. Their names are inscribed beneath a fresco of the Last Judgement on the west wall. The sumptuous five-tiered iconostasis dates from the same period but incorporates a number of icons from the 16th century.

Trinity Cathedral
This exquisite white cathedral is decorated with *kokoshniki* gables *(see p44)* above a triple-banded frieze and is the oldest stone building in the monastery. It was built over the tomb of St Sergius in 1422, the year of his canonization. St Sergius' remains are now

Church of St Sergius and Refectory
The monks' refectory was built in 1686–92 using money donated by Peter the Great and his half-brother, Ivan V, in gratitude for the refuge given them by the monastery during the Streltsy Rebellion *(see p22).*

Baroque pillars on the Church of St Sergius and the Refectory

The exterior walls are divided into a series of panels, topped by carved scallop shells and separated by pillars decorated with sculpted vines. Each panel is painted so that it looks as though it has three-dimensional facets similar to those of the Faceted Palace *(see p62)*

in the Kremlin. The refectory's main façade features a covered terrace with a wealth of ornamentation. At the eastern end of the refectory is the Church of St Sergius. Its iconostasis was brought here from Moscow's Church of St Nicholas on Ilinka in 1688. Delicate fretwork on the iconostasis seems to be metal, but is actually made of wood.

Cathedral of the Assumption
This magnificent cathedral, with its central golden cupola surrounded by four blue, star-spangled domes, is located at

Christ in Majesty (1425–7) in the Trinity Cathedral's iconostasis encased in a silver shrine inside the cathedral and are still a focus for visiting pilgrims.

The original decoration of the interior was the work of master artists Andrey Rublev and Daniil Chernyy. Most of their frescoes have since been painted over. Their iconostasis has survived, but Rublev's icon *The Trinity* (1420s) is a copy. The original is in the Tretyakov Gallery *(see pp118–21)*. Also in the iconostasis are two icons by renowned painter Simon Ushakov: *The Holy Face* (1674) and *Christ Enthroned* (1684).

Open rotunda over the holy spring, next to the Chapel Over the Well

Other Churches

There are five smaller churches within the monastery walls. The oldest is the Church of the Holy Spirit, built in 1476 by craftsmen from Pskov *(see p44)*, a town to the northwest of Moscow. The infirmary and its adjoining tent-roofed Church of SS Zosima and Savvatiy were constructed in 1635–8.

The Chapel Over the Well was built at the end of the 17th century over a holy spring. The open rotunda next to it was added in the 19th century. Pilgrims still come to fill bottles with holy water from the spring beneath the rotunda.

Just in front of the Church of St Sergius stands the small Church of St Micah. This single-domed church is named after one of St Sergius' pupils, who is buried beneath it.

The Baroque Church of the Virgin of Smolensk, a small, blue and white rotunda, was

---

THE HOLIEST MONK

Sergius of Radonezh (c.1319–92) was born into a noble family but, with his brother, withdrew from the world and founded the Trinity Monastery.

Sergius was instrumental in encouraging Russia's princes to unite against the Mongol invaders and, in 1380, Prince Dmitriy Donskoy, commander of the Russian army, asked for his blessing before attacking the Mongols at Kulikovo *(see p161)*. The Russian victory, along with the discovery that Sergius' body was miraculously unharmed in a Mongol attack on the monastery in 1408, led to Sergius' canonization in 1422.

A 16th-century icon of the appearance of the Virgin and Saints Peter and Paul to Sergius of Radonezh

---

built in 1745. The last of the monastery's churches to be constructed, it houses the Icon of the Smolensk Virgin.

Palaces and Museums

Gifts from the tsars are among the monastic treasures in the former Sacristy and Treasury. Visitors can see jewelled icon covers, exquisite crosses, icons, gospels in gilded covers, vestments and some wonderful tapestries, including the pall from the coffin of St Sergius.

Built in the late 17th century for Tsar Alexis Mikhailovich, the Tsar's Apartments are now used as a theological college. Parts of the slightly shabby exterior are painted to appear

faceted. In the southwest corner of the monastery is the 18th-century Palace of the Metropolitans. It was the first of the buildings to come back into religious use when the Soviets allowed the patriarchs and metropolitans to return in 1946.

Towers and Gate Churches

The Trinity Monastery was originally fortified in the reign of Ivan the Terrible *(see p18)*. Its formidable walls are 12 m (39 ft) high and date, in their present form, from the early 17th century. The monastery's main gate is in the Beautiful Tower. The frescoes on its archway depict the life of St Sergius. Behind the Beautiful Tower is the red-brick Gate Church of St John the Baptist.

At the north end of the walls is the Duck Tower, so called because Peter the Great shot ducks from its windows. The spire, with its carved duck, and the upper tiers were added in 1672–86.

The soaring, five-tiered, blue and white bell tower was built between 1741 and 1769.

One of the frescoes depicting scenes from St Sergius' life, on the archway of the Beautiful Tower

Suzdal ➐
Суздаль
Suzdal

200 km (124 miles) NE of Moscow.
🏛 *12,100.* 🚉 *Vladimir, then bus.*
🚌 *(see p227).* ⛴ *Sun.*

Nestling on the banks of
the Kamenka river, Suzdal
is the best preserved of the
Golden Ring *(see p161)* towns.
Its clusters of 17th- and 18th-
century whitewashed churches,
built by local merchants, and
its streets of low, wooden
houses with traditional carved
eaves and windows mean that
it is also one of the most
attractive towns in the area.
　The first records of Suzdal
date from 1024. Shortly afterwards the founder of Moscow,
Prince Yuriy Dolgorukiy *(see
p17)*, built the town's kremlin
on a grassy rampart above the
river. Its dominant building is
the **Cathedral of the Nativity**
with its blue, star-spangled
domes. Although it was built
in the 13th century, most of
the current building dates from
the 16th century. The south
and west doors are of gilded
copper, etched with biblical
scenes. Frescoes dating from
the 13th to the 17th centuries
cover the interior walls.

**The Cathedral of the Nativity, in
the grounds of Suzdal's kremlin**

Next to it stands the former
archbishop's palace, now the
Suzdal Museum. Its collection
of icons and ancient art is
housed in the main room, the
magnificent Chamber of the
Cross, one of the largest un-
supported vaults in Russia. To
the northeast, on Suzdal's main
street, a long, arcaded building
dating from 1806–11 was the
former merchants' quarters.
　Suzdal also contains five important religious foundations,
including the **Monastery of St
Euthymius**. Once the richest
in the area, with more than
10,000 serfs at its disposal, the
monastery has a commanding
position in the north of Suzdal,
overlooking the town.
Its fortified walls are
almost 6 m (20 ft)
thick. The monks'
cells now house the
**Museum of Arts
and Crafts**, which
has an impressive
collection, including
religious paintings
and jewellery.
　To the south of
the monastery is the
**Aleksandrovskiy
Convent**. It was
originally founded in
1240, but it burned
down and was rebuilt
in the 17th century.
Its Cathedral of the
Ascension was built at
this time by Nataliya
Naryshkina, mother
of Peter the Great.
　Rising from the
meadows directly
across the river here
is the **Convent of
the Intercession**.
Founded in the 14th

**Icon of St Nicholas, dating from the 15th
century, in the Suzdal Museum**

century, it was completed
in the reign of Basil III in
1510–14. Its retreat houses
offer overnight lodgings.
　On the southwest edge of
town is the **Suzdal Museum
of Wooden Architecture** an
open-air exhibition of wooden
buildings brought from all
over Russia. Particularly impressive is the Church of the
Transfiguration, built in 1756.
With domes made with over-
lapping shingles, it was built
without using any metal nails.

🏛 **Suzdal Museum**
Ul Kremlyovskaya. *Tel 809231
20444.* 🕐 *Wed–Mon.* 🖼 📷
English (book in advance).

🏛 **Museum of Arts and Crafts**
Ul Lenina. *Tel 809231 20444.* 🕐 *Tue–
Sun.* 🖼 📷 *English (book in advance).*

🏛 **Suzdal Museum of
Wooden Architecture**
Ul Kremlyovskaya. *Tel 809231 20444.*
🕐 *Wed–Mon.* 🖼 📷 *English (book
in advance).*

**The Golden Gate, the entrance to
Vladimir from the Moscow road**

Vladimir ➑
Владимир
Vladimir

170 km (106 miles) NE of Moscow.
🏛 *360,000.* 🚉 🚌 *(see p227).* ⛴
Daily. **www.**vladimir.ru

Founded on the Klyazma
river by Prince Vladimir
Monomakh *(see p161)* in the
late 11th century, Vladimir
really began to flourish during
the rule of his son, Prince
Yuriy Dolgorukiy *(see p17)*. In
1157 Dolgorukiy's heir, Prince
Andrey Bogolyubskiy, brought
his court here and made it the
capital of the new principality
of Vladimir-Suzdal. The town's
heyday was in the 12th and

The 12th-century Cathedral of the Assumption in Vladimir

gallery on the west wall.
A short distance away is the **Cathedral of St Dmitriy**, built in 1194–7 by Prince Vsevolod III. A single-domed church of white limestone, its exterior is covered with more than a thousand bas-reliefs featuring griffons, centaurs, prancing lions and fantastic birds and plants, as well as a portrait of Vsevolod and his family. Over the window on the south wall is a carving of Alexander the Great ascending to heaven, a symbol of princely authority.

Yasnaya Polyana ●
Ясная Поляна
Yasnaya Polyana

180 km (112 miles) S of Moscow. **Tel** 0872 339118. ◯ *10am–5:30pm Wed–Sun.* ▢ *Tula, then bus.* 🚌 *(see p227).* 📷

The beloved country estate of Leo Tolstoy *(see p134)*, Yasnaya Polyana is located in a peaceful valley surrounded by forests. Tolstoy was born on the estate in 1828. From the mid-1850s he spent the summers here with his wife and children, and the family moved here permanently in 1901. The house and its contents are much as they were in Tolstoy's day. The rooms on show include the study, where Tolstoy wrote *War and Peace* and *Anna Karenina*. Other buildings on the estate include the Dom Volkonskovo, where the serfs lived, and a pavilion for the guests. A small literary museum is housed in the former peasants' school that Tolstoy established.

early 13th centuries and most of the architectural monuments worth seeing date from this period. Like Suzdal, Vladimir was later eclipsed by Moscow in political importance, but it remained a significant trading centre. Today, Vladimir looks like any industrial city of the Soviet era, although, fortunately, the chemical plants and tyre factories are situated at some distance from the picturesque old part of the town, with its fine views.

When approaching Vladimir by the Moscow road, the visitor will still enter the city through the splendid **Golden Gate**. This was constructed in 1164, and combines the functions of both triumphal arch and defensive bastion. The icons above the archway were whitewashed by the Communists and have only recently been restored. The gate now contains a small exhibition on military history.

A short stroll down the main street takes the visitor past the 19th-century trading arcades and shops to the **Cathedral of the Assumption**, Vladimir's most famous monument. Built in 1158–60, high above the

A detail of the carved bas-reliefs on the Cathedral of St Dmitriy

banks of the Klyazma, it was originally decorated with prodigious quantities of gold and silver, precious gems, majolica tiles and white stone carvings. Craftsmen came from all over Russia, Poland and the Holy Roman Empire to contribute to what was then the tallest building in Russia. The coronation of many of Russia's princes, including Dmitriy Donskoy *(see p18)* and Aleksandr Nevskiy *(see p17)*, took place here.

The cathedral was damaged by fire in 1185, and when it was repaired, four domes were added. When, in the 15th century, Ivan III wanted to build the Cathedral of the Assumption in Moscow *(see pp58–9)*, he instructed his Italian architect, Aristotele Fioravanti, to use the cathedral of the same name in Vladimir as his model.

The famous Icon of the Virgin of Vladimir *(see p61)* used to hang in the cathedral, but it is now in the Tretyakov Gallery *(see p121)*. However, some superb frescoes by medieval masters Andrey Rublev and Daniil Chernyy are still visible under the choir's

Leo Tolstoy's house on his beloved family estate, Yasnaya Polyana

TRAVELLERS' NEEDS

WHERE TO STAY 170–177

RESTAURANTS, CAFÉS AND BARS 178–191

SHOPS AND MARKETS 192–197

ENTERTAINMENT IN MOSCOW 198–203

WHERE TO STAY

The hotel situation in Moscow has improved considerably since Russia became an independent state in 1992. New hotels have been built and grand old residences renovated. These works are likely to continue as Yuriy Luzhkov, the city's dynamic mayor, has made new accommodation a priority. Despite the improvements, there is still a great shortage of hotels of all types in the city. Worse still, as with much in modern Russian life, expansion tends

A mosaic by Aleksandr Golovin on the Metropol's façade *(see p88)*

to have taken place at the top end of the market and there is a shortage in the mid-price range. The selection of hotels on pages 174–7 is divided into central or further afield locations and arranged in price order. Prices are liable to rapid change so should always be checked. There are websites that act as accommodation agencies and it is possible to make a reservation at most hotels directly by phone or fax. The best method, however, is to book through a travel agent in advance.

TYPES OF HOTEL

In theory there are more than 200 hotels in Moscow. Many of these, however, are little more than hostels for professional delegations, with names such as The Oncological Research Centre Hotel. With occasional exceptions, therefore, the foreign visitor is in effect confined to hotels that fall into three broad categories: luxury hotels, the newer, mid-price hotels and the cheaper, plainer ex-Soviet hotels, which were formerly run by the state.

Luxury hotels are often foreign-owned or run as joint Russian-Western ventures. Many occupy historic buildings (some pre- and some post-Revolution), and have rooms combining period furniture with modern facilities. Service is similar to that in the best hotels in the West, but a double room rarely costs less than

The spacious lobby at the luxurious Baltschug Kempinski *(see p175)*

the equivalent of $300 a night. Hotels of this type are often referred to as Western-style.

There is comparatively little available in the mid-price range. For example, the Hotel Moskva (www.hotel-moskva.ru), which was demolished recently, used to be a valuable landmark overlooking Red Square and represented

excellent value for money. Legend has it that when Stalin was presented with the two possible designs for the hotel, he unwittingly approved them both. The hotel was built with an amalgamation of both styles, as no-one on Stalin's staff wanted to point out his mistake. The Moskva is currently being rebuilt, but when it eventually re-opens, it will be as a five-star luxury hotel.

A number of smaller, more modern hotels are gradually emerging to accommodate the mid-price bracket and these are being supplemented by the redevelopment and reinvention of a number of other prominent ex-Soviet hotels. The iconic Hotel Ukraine (www.hotel-ukrainia.ru) *(see p173)* is still closed for redevelopment but will reopen as a top-end hotel. Fans of Soviet-era service and design will be disappointed to learn that the old Intourist hotel on Tverskaya has been replaced by a luxury Ritz-Carlton.

Of the remaining ex-Soviet hotels, those that have not been redeveloped are generally lacklustre and the service can seem to take little account of what guests actually want. Nevertheless, the rooms are usually clean and of a good size. These hotels can also offer a fascinating insight into how the elite in the Soviet era used to live. It is planned that service will be standardized with the advent of a common system of hotel accreditation.

A spacious, elegantly appointed room in the National *(see p89)*

◁ Restaurant beneath the vaulted glass ceiling of the Metropol Hotel *(see p174)*

Guest sitting room adjoining a bedroom at the Danilovskaya *(see p176)*

LOCATION OF HOTELS

Most of the luxury hotels are within 15 minutes' drive or metro ride of the centre, while ex-Soviet hotels tend to be a little further out. Unfortunately, there are few moderately priced hotels right in the city centre.

For all types of hotel, the price is unlikely to be affected very much by location. However, when choosing a hotel, visitors should think about how they want to get around the city and take into consideration whether or not they will have a car, whether they want to get to the main sights on foot, or if their ability to read Cyrillic script is adequate to allow them to use buses and the metro with confidence.

Opulent dining room at the Savoy *(see p175)*

MAKING A RESERVATION

During the Soviet era all accommodation had to be arranged before going to Russia. To obtain a tourist visa, you must still pre-book a room *(see p208)*. However, once in Moscow, it is possible to walk into any hotel and book a room on the spot. In practice, though, it is best to make arrangements before arriving. Many of the more expensive hotels may be booked up well in advance, particularly in the event of a major exhibition, which might make reservations for a full week problematic. In ex-Soviet hotels, there might be difficulties for foreign visitors arriving unannounced. Almost all the hotels listed here will accept reservations by fax or phone (many will not accept reservations by e-mail). All the luxury hotels have staff who speak good English, but it is advisable to book rooms at ex-Soviet hotels by fax, asking for written confirmation. Luxury hotels will usually ask for a credit card number as a deposit.

FACILITIES

All luxury hotels provide the facilities that would be found in an expensive hotel in the West. These include television (often satellite), business facilities, such as a message-taking service and meeting room, mini-bars, a laundry service and 24-hour room service. All rooms have a bathroom with a bath or shower, or both. Fitness facilities and swimming pools are increasingly widespread, although they are not necessarily up to Western standards in cheaper establishments. Not all hotels have air conditioning, which can be a drawback in summer.

Rooms in an ex-Soviet hotel always contain a television, a fridge and a telephone. International calls from rooms are expensive and may not be easy to make if they have to be booked through the operator. En-suite bathrooms with a bath or shower are also standard. Ex-Soviet hotels, particularly the cheaper places, are not likely to have sophisticated room service, although a laundry service can usually be arranged.

Many ex-Soviet hotels still have a *dezhurnaya* (concierge) sitting at a desk on each floor. As one of their duties, these sometimes rather fearsome women look after guests' keys while they are out. Visitors should make sure they do not lose the card given to them when the keys are handed in, as it sometimes has to be shown to get back in through the main entrance. Friendly relations with the *dezhurnaya* will increase the chances of receiving good service or obtaining food and drink at unusual hours.

All hotels have bars and restaurants. The luxury hotels contain some of the city's finest restaurants, but do not expect to find a bargain here. Ex-Soviet hotels tend to be less flexible about meal times, and the food is much less exciting. Continental breakfasts are the norm in luxury hotels. In ex-Soviet establishments guests usually help themselves from a large buffet which includes eggs, *budterbrod* (sandwiches), salads and confectionary. Breakfast is not usually included in the room service and is typically only available between 7am and 8am.

The Sovietskiy's elegant Yar restaurant, where mirrored walls add to the feeling of spaciousness *(see p175)*

PAYMENT

The general shortage of accommodation in Moscow means that, almost without exception, hotel rooms in the city are over-priced. The rates given in this book are the standard rates quoted by the hotels. However, very few guests actually pay the full rate. Business guests usually have cheaper rates negotiated at the expensive hotels by their companies and most tourists book through an agent, again at more favourable rates. It is worth remembering that it is rarely economical to book any hotel room personally. Travellers interested in a particular hotel should ask a travel agent to enquire about special rates, or find an agent that has already dealt with the hotel. Leisure weekend discounts are available at many luxury hotels, since most of their clients are business people who stay only during the week.

Luxury hotels generally quote prices in a foreign currency (usually US dollars). However, it is illegal to pay in any currency other than roubles. The easiest way to pay in these hotels is undoubtedly with a credit card, which eliminates the need to carry around large amounts of money. Check in advance before trying to pay by travellers' cheques as luxury hotels may have a hidden surcharge. Ex-Soviet hotels do not normally quote prices in dollars and most take only cash (in roubles). Some will take credit cards, though none accept travellers' cheques.

Luxury hotels frequently quote prices exclusive of VAT and city tax; this can add more than 30 per cent to the bill. Visitors should also note that tax rates in Russia are liable to change at short notice.

Breakfast is rarely included in room prices and can be a significant addition to the bill. The cost of making phone calls (international or local) from a hotel room can be high. The local phone network *(see p214)* is cheaper.

Stylish and modern, the bar area of the Palace Hotel *(see p176)*

TRAVELLING WITH CHILDREN

Russians idolize their children, but this rarely seems to translate into hotel facilities for families. In most hotels it should be possible to have an extra bed put in a room for an additional fee, and most luxury hotels will provide babysitters. Generally, however, hotels are more interested in business guests or tour groups, so do not expect to find extensive facilities for children or favourable room rates for families.

Corner suite at the designer hotel Golden Apple Deluxe *(see p176)*

The Marco Polo Presnya, centrally located in a quiet street *(see p174)*

DISABLED TRAVELLERS

Few hotels in Moscow have wheelchair access, and those that do generally have few facilities. Disabled travellers should check in advance with their travel agents or the hotels, making sure to enquire about any specific needs.

SECURITY

While many of the dangers of life in Moscow are exaggerated, hotels (particularly those owned by foreign companies) take security very seriously. Do not be surprised to see security staff with walkie-talkies patrolling the entrances of even the most refined establishments. Luxury hotels all

The Stalinist-Gothic tower of the Ukraine *(see p170)*

have safe-deposit boxes and hotel guests generally have few problems with personal safety.

Ex-Soviet hotels also have a very good record on security. Porters keep undesirables out, and the *dezhurnaya (see p171)* on each floor keeps a close eye on her own patch.

However, as in other cities, tourists are often targets for petty criminals. Take particular care when leaving the hotel, as pickpockets are known to hang around outside tourist hotels.

STAYING WITH FAMILIES

For a revealing insight into Russian culture, staying with a family can be a worthwhile option, especially for visitors who plan to stay for a month or more. The system is similar to the European bed and breakfast and prices generally include breakfast only (meals other than breakfast can occasionally be provided at a cost). Your hosts are likely to be extremely hospitable, and will probably be keen to talk about life in Russia.

Moscow Bed and Breakfast and **Interchange** have a range of options for staying with a Russian family.

BUDGET ACCOMMODATION

Options for travellers on a tight budget are very limited. Some of the cheaper ex-Soviet hotels have rooms for the equivalent of less than $100. The service may be rather sullen and the rooms a little shabby, but they should be clean. Their restaurants may be uninspiring at best.

Bed and Breakfast rents out apartments with cleaning included, most of them close to Belorusskaya metro. Flats for one person cost the equivalent of about $50 a night; the rate decreases for people sharing. There are a very limited number of hostels in

Moscow. Places such as **Godzillas**, **Traveller's Guest House** and **Sherstone** are of a good standard and specifically cater for travellers on a tight budget. They offer dormitory accommodation from the equivalent of $20, $35 and $40 a night respectively. The service is friendly and the dormitories are clean.

DIRECTORY

STAYING WITH FAMILIES

Interchange (in UK)
Tel 020 8681 3612.
Fax 020 8760 0031.

Moscow Bed and Breakfast
Tel (495) 457 3508.
Fax (495) 457 3508.

BUDGET ACCOMMODATION

Bed and Breakfast
Tel (499) 147 0021.

Godzillas
Bolshoy Karetnyy 6, Apt 5, 1st fl.
Map 3 A3.
Tel (495) 699 4223.
Fax (495) 699 1691.
www.godzillashostel.com

Hostel Asia
3/2 Zelenodolskaya ulitsa, 5th fl.
Tel (495) 378 0001.
Fax (495) 378 2866.
www.hostels.ru/asia/

Hostel Snail
Selskokhozyaistvennaya st, 15/1,
Office 339.
Tel (495) 795 2335.
Fax (495) 189 0297.
www.hostel-snail.ru

Prakash Guest House
Profsoyuznaya ulitsa 83, korpus 1,
podezd 2.
Tel (495) 334 2598.
Fax (495) 334 2598.

Sherstone
8 Gostinichnyi proezd,
Building 1, 3rd floor, Office 324.
Tel (495) 580 9090.
www.sherstone.ru

Travellers' Guest House
Bolshaya Pereyaslavskaya ulitsa 50, 10th floor.
Tel (495) 631 4059.
Fax (495) 680 7686.
www.tgh.ru

Choosing a Hotel

The hotels in this guide have been chosen for their good value, facilities and location. The list covers a variety of areas and price categories with additional information to help you choose a hotel that best meets your needs. Hotels within the same area and price category are listed alphabetically. For map references see pages 238–45.

PRICE CATEGORIES
Price categories for a standard double room with bathroom per night, including breakfast, and service charges:

ⓈⓈ under US$125
ⓈⓈ US$125–US$250
ⓈⓈⓈ US$250–US$375
ⓈⓈⓈⓈ US$375–US$500
ⓈⓈⓈⓈⓈ US$500 and over

CITY CENTRE

ARBATSKAYA Arbat Арбат
ⓈⓈⓈ
Plotnikov pereulok 12 **Tel** *(495) 777 1938* **Fax** *(495) 921 4161* **Rooms** *102*   **Map** *6 D2*

For those who want somewhere reasonably quiet and central, the Arbat is a good option. Though the rooms are large, the bathrooms and furnishings, as with so many ex-Soviet hotels, have a tired look. There is a nice veranda where guests can sit and have a drink outside in summer. Not ideal for public transport. **http://arbat.bookin.ru**

TVERSKAYA Akvarel Акварель
ⓈⓈ
Stoleshnikov pereulok 12/3 **Tel** *(495) 502 9430* **Fax** *(495) 502 9431* **Rooms** *23*   **Map** *3 A4*

The Akvarel is conveniently located within a quiet alley in the heart of the city. The interior is modern and understated; rooms are spacious, modern and bright. A welcome alternative to the cavernous ex-Soviet hotels, the facilities are suitable for business visitors and tourists alike. **www.hotelakvarel.ru**

TVERSKAYA Peking Пекин
ⓈⓈ
Bolshaya Sadovaya ulitsa 5/1 **Tel** *(495) 234 2647* **Fax** *(495) 234 2461* **Rooms** *130*   **Map** *2 D3*

The impressive interior of this hotel matches its grandiose exterior. The prices for the rooms vary, depending on whether you want basic amenities or high-end luxury. The excellent Peking restaurant is the largest Chinese restaurant in Moscow, and is held in high regard. **www.hotelpekin.ringnet.ru**

TVERSKAYA Marriott Grand Марриот Гранд
ⓈⓈⓈⓈ
Tverskaya ulitsa 26 **Tel** *(495) 935 8500* **Fax** *(495) 937 0001* **Rooms** *392*   **Map** *2 E3*

This luxury establishment offers every modern amenity, including computer terminals in all the rooms. The conference facilities and meeting rooms attract business travellers. The hotel's three restaurants serve a mix of Russian and Western cuisine. Prices vary, depending on availability. **www.marriott.com**

TVERSKAYA Ararat Park Hyatt Арарат Парк Хаятт
ⓈⓈⓈⓈⓈ
Neglinnaya ulitsa 4 **Tel** *(495) 783 1234* **Fax** *(495) 783 1235* **Rooms** *216*   **Map** *3 A5*

The Ararat is conveniently located for the shops and sights, and boasts a wonderful view of the Bolshoy Theatre (*see pp90–91*) and Kremlin (*see pp52–67*) from its terrace. The hotel is elegant yet relaxed, with large, understated rooms. The hotel's atrium is a marvel of glass and chrome. **www.moscow.park.hyatt.com**

TVERSKAYA Marco Polo Presnya Марко Поло Пресня
ⓈⓈⓈⓈⓈ
Spiridonevskiy pereulok 9 **Tel** *(499) 244 3631* **Fax** *(499) 926 5402* **Rooms** *68*   **Map** *2 E4*

This quiet and comfortable hotel is situated in a lovely residential area, not too far from the shops and sights. The interior is a little worn-out and service could be more attentive, but it offers a low-key alternative to the grandeur of other Moscow luxury hotels. **www.presnja.ru**

TVERSKAYA National Националь
ⓈⓈⓈⓈⓈ
Mokhovaya ulitsa 15/1 **Tel** *(495) 258 7000* **Fax** *(495) 258 7100* **Rooms** *206*   **Map** *2 F5*

The National is firmly established as one of Moscow's top luxury hotels. The pricier rooms contain antique furniture and rugs. Rooms get smaller and less impressive the higher up they are, and the Kremlin view comes at a premium. **www.national.ru**

TVERSKAYA Ritz Carlton Ритц Карлтн
ⓈⓈⓈⓈⓈ
Tverskaya ulitsa 3 **Tel** *(495) 225 8888* **Fax** *(495) 225 8400* **Rooms** *334*   **Map** *2 F5*

The Ritz-Carlton in Moscow opened in 2008 in a newly-constructed building situated opposite the Red Square. All the amenities you would expect from a top hotel are available, including an on-site spa, swimming pool, fitness facilities, 24-hour room service, Internet access and Bulgari bath products. **www.ritzcarlton.com**

RED SQUARE AND KITAY GOROD Metropol Метрополь
ⓈⓈⓈⓈⓈ
Teatralnyy proezd 1/4 **Tel** *(495) 501 7800* **Fax** *(495) 501 7810* **Rooms** *365*   **Map** *3 A5*

The Metropol is a wonderful example of Style Moderne (*see p45*) from the turn of the 20th century. Its spectacular interior is adorned with mosaics, golden chandeliers and stained glass. The hotel restaurant is lit by great rings of lamps on long gilded stalks. Many of the rooms are similarly lavish. **www.metmos.ru**

Key to Symbols *see back cover flap*

RED SQUARE AND KITAY GOROD Savoy Савой

⑤⑤⑤⑤⑤

Ulitsa Rozhdestvenka 3 **Tel** *(495) 620 8500* **Fax** *(495) 625 0596* **Rooms** *90*   **Map** *3 A4*

Tucked away on a quiet side street, the Savoy's unassuming exterior belies its luxurious interior. The rich fittings and subdued lighting give it an atmosphere akin to a gentlemen's club from a past era. Corridors double as an art gallery, while the bedrooms have high ceilings, reproduction furniture and modern facilities. **www.savoy.ru**

ZAMOSKVORECHE Baltschug Kempinski Балчуг Кемпински
⑤⑤⑤⑤⑤

Ulitsa Balchug 1 **Tel** *(495) 287 2000* **Fax** *(495) 287 2002* **Rooms** *234*   **Map** *7 B2*

Hidden within a handsome late-19th century building is a luxurious, modern interior. The bedrooms are smart and elegant. Rooms on the riverside offer magnificent views of the Kremlin and St Basil's Cathedral *(see pp108–9)*. Taxi and transfer services are available from the hotel's fleet of luxury cars. **www.kempinski-moscow.com**

FURTHER AFIELD

NORTH OF THE CENTRE Godzilla's Hostel Годзиллас Хостел
⑤

Bolshoy Karetnyy Pereulok **Tel** *(495) 699 4223* **Fax** *(495) 699 1691* **Rooms** *90 beds*   **Map** *3 A3*

This amusingly-named hostel is located in a quiet side street in a simple but adquate 1950 building, and is a popular budget option. Beds are in private rooms or dorms and the staff are friendly and very helpful. There are also three kitchens, where guests can prepare their own food. **www.godzillashostel.com**

NORTH OF THE CENTRE Hilton Leningradskaya Хилтон Ленингра́дская
⑤

Ulitsa Kalanchevskaya 21/40 **Tel** *(495) 955 6655* **Fax** *(495) 975 1802* **Rooms** *329*   **Map** *4 D2*

Designed by architect L. Polyakov in 1954, this hotel is one of the most famous in the city. Rooms on the top floors have wonderful views and the hotel is just 15 minutes from Red Square by metro. Having undergone major redevelopment, room rates are expected to rise. **www.leningradskaya.ru**

NORTH OF THE CENTRE Izmailovo Delta Измайлово Дельта
⑤

Ismaylovskoe shosse 71 **Tel** *(495) 737 7070* **Rooms** *7,500*

The Izmailovo Delta is part of a development of four huge hotels built for the 1980 Moscow Olympics. The rooms are basic but comfortable, and the hotel has good facilities, including saunas, a casino and cabaret entertainment. Located near Izmailovo Market *(see p193)*, the centre is accessible by metro in 15 minutes. **www.izmailovo.ru**

NORTH OF THE CENTRE Sherston Шерстон
⑤

Gostinichnly proezd 8 **Tel** *(495) 580 9090* **Fax** *(495) 482 3190* **Rooms** *295*

Some distance from the centre, but easily accessible by metro, the Sherston has clean, though somewhat ordinary, rooms. It is ideal for visitors on a tight budget who don't mind travelling to the main sights and are not expecting too many luxuries. A hostel is located on the third floor *(see p173)*. **www.sherston.ru**

NORTH OF THE CENTRE Tourist Турист
(⑤)

Ulitsa Selkokhozyaystvennaya 17/2 **Tel** *(495) 980 7394* **Rooms** *450*

Convenient for the Russian Academy of Science, this hotel has been a popular venue for visiting athletes since it opened in 1955. The complex unites five separate hotels, the best being Building 5. Rooms are basic but clean. A true Soviet experience offering unrivalled value for money. **www.hoteltourist.com**

NORTH OF THE CENTRE Zarya Заря
⑤

Gostinichnaya ulitsa 4/9 **Tel** *(495) 788 7272* **Fax** *(495) 482 2211* **Rooms** *181*

Located not far from the centre, this hotel's basic rooms are of a decent size and are bright and clean. There is a wide range of rooms, from the run-down economy class to luxurious studios. A café, with a Salvador Dali theme, serves Russian and European cuisine. **www.maximahotels.ru**

NORTH OF THE CENTRE Holiday Inn Lesnaya Холидей Инн Лесная
⑤⑤

Lesnaya ulitsa 15 **Tel** *(495) 783 6500* **Fax** *(495) 785 6501* **Rooms** *301*   **Map** *2 D2*

Contemporary and understated, the Holiday Inn Lesnaya is typical of the chain. Even if the hotel lacks the charm and character of its peers, the service is good. Although close to the metro, the location is not ideal as the area is busy and noisy. The hotel is convenient for reaching Sheremetevo airport. **www.holiday-inn.com**

NORTH OF THE CENTRE Irbis Ирбис
⑤⑤

Gostinichnaya ulitsa 1 **Tel** *(495) 788 7277* **Fax** *(495) 482 2211* **Rooms** *97*

The Irbis is a plain but well-equipped business hotel situated near the All-Russian Exhibition Centre *(see p145)* and the Ostankino Palace *(see pp144–5)*. Rooms are basic but comfortable. Sheremetevo airport is just a 30 minute drive away. **www.maximahotels.ru**

NORTH OF THE CENTRE Kosmos Космос
⑤⑤

Prospekt Mira 150 **Tel** *(495) 234 1000* **Fax** *(495) 615 8880* **Rooms** *1,777*   **Map** *3 B1*

Opened in 1980, in time for the Moscow Olympics, the Kosmos is a distinctive city landmark. The cavernous lobby is dated but the rooms are of a good size and get plenty of light. Those on the top floors have splendid views. The lower ground floor features a late-night bar and a bowling alley. **www.hotelcosmos.ru**

NORTH OF THE CENTRE Novotel Новотель
Sheremetevo 2 Airport **Tel** *(495) 626 5900* **Fax** *(495) 626 5904* **Rooms** *488*

As you would expect from an airport hotel, the Novotel is clean, bright and efficient. Rooms are a good size and are well-equipped. For visitors stuck at the airport for any length of time, the facilities at the Novotel eclipse anything available in the airport itself, although it is unsuitable for commuting to the centre. **www.novotel.ru**

NORTH OF THE CENTRE Sovetskiy Советский
Leningradskiy prospekt 32/2 **Tel** *(495) 960 2000* **Fax** *(495) 250 8003* **Rooms** *100*   **Map** *1 B1*

Built in Stalinist style, the Sovetskiy is wonderfully grandiose. The bedrooms are large with high moulded ceilings, wooden floors and period furniture, although bathrooms can be a bit shabby. The hotel's restaurant is a spectacular mirrored hall. The hotel is a 15 to 20 minute drive from the city centre. **www.sovetsky.ru**

NORTH OF THE CENTRE Art Арт отель
3-ya Peschanaya ulitsa 2 **Tel** *(495) 725 0905* **Fax** *(495) 955 2310* **Rooms** *86*

Clean and well maintained, Art resembles an up-market American motel. Rooms are of a decent size with modern, functional furniture. The beer garden provides a pleasant place to sit outside, weather permitting. The hotel is 20 minutes from the city centre by car. **www.arthotel.ru**

NORTH OF THE CENTRE Holiday Inn Vinogradovo Холидей Инн Виноградово
Dmitrovskoye shosse 171 **Tel** *(495) 937 0670* **Fax** *(495) 937 0672* **Rooms** *154*

Situated in the countryside north of Moscow, the Vinogradovo is a five minute drive from Sheremetevo airport. Offering good sports and fishing facilities and picturesque ponds, it makes a good alternative to the Novotel *(see below)*. Rooms are modern and of a good standard, if a little uninspiring. **www.holiday-inn.com**

NORTH OF THE CENTRE Korston Корстон
Kosyigina ulitsa 15 **Tel** *(495) 939 8888* **Fax** *(495) 939 8008* **Rooms** *320*

The Korston is situated on Sparrow Hills and contains restaurants offering Japanese, Chinese, Korean, Italian, Russian and Greek cuisine. Facilities are extensive and include a casino, bowling alley, Turkish baths and karaoke club. Rooms are dated, but well-equipped and of a good size. **www.korston.ru**

NORTH OF THE CENTRE Le Meridien Country Club Ле Меридиен Кантри Клаб
Nakhabino, Krasnogorsky District **Tel** *(495) 626 5911* **Fax** *(495) 626 5921* **Rooms** *131*

Just 45 minutes from the city centre, this hotel offers a luxurious retreat from the urban sprawl. It primarily caters to golfing enthusiasts as it boasts Russia's only 18-hole championship course (home to the Russian Open). The hotel's Country Club is a favourite weekend retreat for the city's elite. **www.lemeridien.mcc.com**

NORTH OF THE CENTRE Palace Шератон Палас
1-ya Tverskaya-Yamskaya ulitsa 19 **Tel** *(495) 931 9700* **Fax** *(495) 931 9703* **Rooms** *218*   **Map** *2 D2*

Occupying a modern building with a simple façade of granite and mirrored glass, this hotel has modern facilities and efficient, friendly staff. Although short on the glamour of Moscow's older hotels, its facilities are great value. The entrance leads out onto an extension of Tverskaya ulitsa. **www.sheratonpalace.ru**

NORTH OF THE CENTRE Renaissance Ренессанс
Olimpiyskiy prospekt 18/1 **Tel** *(495) 931 9000* **Fax** *(495) 931 9076* **Rooms** *472*   **Map** *3 A1*

The Renaissance Hotel is modern and comfortable. Although it is a little lacking in character, it has excellent facilities, including a good swimming pool. Rooms are small and fitted with functional furniture. Bars, restaurants and shops are available. The metro station is about ten minutes' walk. **www.renaissancehotels.com**

NORTH OF THE CENTRE Golden Apple Голден Эппл
Ulitsa Malaya Dmitrovka 11 **Tel** *(495) 980 7000* **Fax** *(495) 980 7001* **Rooms** *92*   **Map** *2 F3*

The Golden Apple hotel is unique. A homage to design, the hotel's interior is dressed in wood, marble and slate, while bedrooms are modern with high ceilings. The floors are colour-coded. The whole experience is elegant and suitable for business visitors and tourists alike. **www.goldenapple.ru**

NORTH OF THE CENTRE Sretenskaya Сретенская
Sretenka ulitsa 15 **Tel** *(495) 933 5544* **Fax** *(495) 933 5545* **Rooms** *38*   **Map** *3 B3*

The interior of the Sretenskaya is rich with references to traditional Russian life and the rooms are comfortable, bright and modern. The atmosphere is relaxed and friendly, and facilities are admirable for a small hotel. It is located in a nice area, although public transport to the sights is not ideal. **www.hotel-sretenskaya.ru**

SOUTH OF THE MOSKVA Aerotel Аэротель
Domodedovo Airport **Tel** *(495) 795 3868* **Fax** *(495) 795 3569* **Rooms** *294*

Located just a few minutes away from Domodedovo, this typical airport hotel lacks character but has good facilities. It is extremely convenient for business travellers who only intend to stay in Moscow one or two nights. **www.airhotel.ru**

SOUTH OF THE MOSKVA Danilovskaya Даниловская
Bolshoy Starodanilovskiy pereulok 5 **Tel** *(495) 954 0503* **Fax** *(495) 954 0750* **Rooms** *116*

A five storey block in the grounds of the Danilovskiy Monastery *(see pp136–7)*, this hotel is run by the Russian Orthodox Church. Portraits of Moscow's patriarchs hang in the corridors and religious icons decorate the rooms. It has clean, quiet rooms but is not within walking distance of the main sights. **www.danilovsky.ru**

Key to Price Guide *see p174* **Key to Symbols** *see back cover flap*

SOUTH OF THE MOSKVA Katerina Катерина

Shluzovaya naberezhnaya 6 **Tel** *(495) 933 0401* **Fax** *(495) 795 2423* **Rooms** *120* **Map** *8 D5*

Located on the bank of the Moskva river, this hotel is decorated in a contemporary Swedish style. The hotel offers a range of services to suit those visiting Moscow on business as well as tourists. The restaurant offers European and Russian fare and there are two bars. Rooms are clean and warm with modern furniture. **www.katerina.msk.ru**

SOUTH OF THE MOSKVA Sputnik Спутник

Leninskiy prospekt 38 **Tel** *(495) 930 2287* **Fax** *(495) 930 1988* **Rooms** *317*

Located on Leninskiy prospekt, the Sputnik is convenient for the centre, with fairly good public transport links. The cheaper rooms can be rather small. The Sputnik usually caters for domestic business visitors. Good Indian restaurant on site. Breakfast is only available early. **www.hotelsputnik.ru**

SOUTH OF THE MOSKVA President Президент

Ulitsa Bolshaya Yakimanka 24 **Tel** *(495) 239 3800* **Fax** *(495) 271 2800* **Rooms** *209* **Map** *7 A4*

Opened in 1983, the President was favoured by top Communist Party officials and the atmosphere still lingers. Security is extremely tight, making this a popular choice for visiting foreign statesmen. Inside, this hotel has all the hallmarks of late Soviet architecture at its most monumental. **www.president-hotel.ru**

SOUTH OF THE MOSKVA Swissôtel Krasnye Holmy Красные Холмы

Kosmodamianskaya naberezhnaya 52/6 **Tel** *(495) 787 9800* **Fax** *(495) 787 9898* **Rooms** *235*

Located on the edge of the centre, the Swissôtel is relatively new to the Moscow hotel scene, but is considered to be one of the city's best. The two restaurants are excellent, as are the business facilities. The light and modern rooms are well-equipped. At 34 storeys high, the view from Swissôtel is stunning. **www.swissotel.com**

SOUTH OF THE MOSKVA Tatiana Татьяна

Stremyannyy pereulok 11 **Tel** *(495) 721 2500* **Fax** *(495) 721 2521* **Rooms** *72* **Map** *7 C5*

The Hotel Tatiana, located in the south of Zamoskvoreche, offers guests an elegant interior, along with comfortable, well-equipped rooms of a good size. The restaurant is elegant, with marble floors and dark-wood furniture. Facilities for the business traveller and tourist are commendable. **www.hotel-tatiana.ru**

SOUTHWEST OF THE CENTRE Belgrade Белград

Smolenskaya ulitsa 8 **Tel** *(495) 248 1643* **Fax** *(495) 248 2814* **Rooms** *235* **Map** *5 C1*

The service in the Belgrade can be rather perfunctory, a reminder of pre-democracy standards, but the restaurant serves good Eastern European food and the hotel fulfils a useful role as a functional and economical ex-Soviet hotel near the centre of Moscow. Location is good, though public transport links are less so. **www.hotel-belgrad.ru**

SOUTHWEST OF THE CENTRE Proton Протон

Novozavodskaya ulitsa 22 **Tel** *(495) 797 3300* **Fax** *(495) 797 3380* **Rooms** *84*

Proton is primarily a business hotel, offering excellent facilities and service. The leisure facilities are also excellent and include a fitness suite, billiards room and sauna. Located close to a park, the hotel is a good alternative to central business hotels, although its location is not ideal for sightseeing. **www.protonhotel.ru**

SOUTHWEST OF THE CENTRE Radisson Рэдиссон

Ploshchad europa 2 **Tel** *(495) 941 8020* **Rooms** *410* **Map** *5 B2*

Located on the bank of the Moskva river, the Radisson has excellent facilities. Panoramic views complement the modern and well-equipped rooms. The hotel is located close to the metro and visitors can, weather permitting, take a cruise down the river to the centre of the city. **www.radisson.com**

SOUTHWEST OF THE CENTRE Yunost Юность

Hamovnichevsky val 34 **Tel** *(495) 900 8292* **Fax** *(495) 242 0284* **Rooms** *187* **Map** *5 B5*

The Yunost was built in 1961 by Soviet architect Jury Arndt and was connected to the Soviet youth organization Komsomol. Rooms are bright and airy, although bathrooms are less impressive. The Sparrow Hills market, selling a good range of souvenirs, is nearby.

SOUTHWEST OF THE CENTRE Kebur Palace Кебур Палас

Ostozhenka ulitsa 32 **Tel** *(495) 733 9070* **Fax** *(495) 733 9054* **Rooms** *63* **Map** *6 E3*

This small and friendly hotel is well-located in a quiet part of the old city near the Cathedral of the Saviour (see *p140*). Rooms are basic, but clean and bright and many overlook a pretty cobbled courtyard. Prices also include use of the pool and sauna. There is a popula Georgian restaurant next door. **www.keburpalace.ru**

SOUTHWEST OF THE CENTRE Crowne Plaza

Krasnopresnenskaya naberezhnaya 12 **Tel** *(495) 252 2122* **Fax** *(495) 253 2051* **Rooms** *547* **Map** *5 A1*

This is a spiralling complex of hotel rooms, offices, shops and restaurants. It is popular with the business community, although its location is relatively inaccessible for visitors keen on sightseeing. Various bars and restaurants lead off the foyers. **www.crowneplaza.ru**

SOUTHWEST OF THE CENTRE Golden Ring Золотое кольцо

Smolenskaya ulitsa 5 **Tel** *(495) 725 0100* **Fax** *(495) 725 0101* **Rooms** *293* **Map** *5 C2*

Convenient for the centre, the Golden Ring has rooms of a good size that are well-equipped and have good access for disabled visitors. A range of cuisine, including Russian, Alsace and Japanese, is available in the hotel's restaurants. **www.hotel-goldenring.ru**

RESTAURANTS, CAFÉS AND BARS

Although eating out was a rare privilege during the Soviet era, and, in the years immediately after perestroika (restructuring), an unaffordable luxury, Russia has been experiencing something of a restaurant boom in recent years. New places open and close every week and include anything from cheap student cafés to exclusive sushi restaurants. All the major cuisines are represented including Russian and modern European, Indian and Chinese,

Logo of Russkoe Bistro chain

as well as restaurants serving dishes from former Soviet Republics, such as Georgia, Armenia and Uzbek. The hungry visitor should have little trouble finding a place that matches his or her appetite and budget. The following pages will help to locate some of the best-quality food and most exciting cuisine on offer in all price categories. A detailed review of selected restaurants is provided on pages 184–9, and ideas for light meals on pages 190–91.

Yakitoria *(see p191)*, one of a popular chain of sushi restaurants

WHERE TO EAT

Most of Moscow's better known restaurants are to be found in central Moscow; most, therefore, are relatively easy to reach by metro. Tverskaya ulitsa *(see p89)* has the highest concentration and variety of restaurants, from Russian and Georgian to Italian and Japanese, as well as a now ubiquitous branch of McDonald's *(see p190)*. There is also plenty of choice along Ulitsa Arbat *(see pp70–71)* and, on Triumfalnaya ploshchad, Russkoe Bistro *(see p191)* is one of many popular new chains offering fast food Russian style.

READING THE MENU

In restaurants specializing in international cuisine, the menu is usually in Russian and English, or available separately in English. Waiting staff speak English in most restaurants geared towards foreigners. In smaller, local eateries, a knowledge of the

Cyrillic alphabet will help with deciphering the menu, as many ingredients are phonetic transcriptions of their English equivalents.

TYPES OF CUISINE

There are surprisingly few good, exclusively Russian restaurants in Moscow. Russians have never made a habit of dining out, nor has Russian cuisine ever enjoyed the reputation of, say, French or Italian. Much of the best Russian food is either wholesome dishes and soups from recipes passed down from generation to generation, or cured and salted fish, as well as caviar, for which preparation is more

Café sign, listing a selection of Russian dishes

important at its source, as opposed to in restaurants. Georgian or Armenian cooking, both of which are delicious and relatively inexpensive, are a better option. Mediterranean and other Western European restaurants, especially Italian ones, are now increasingly popular in Moscow. Chinese and Indian food is generally overpriced, bland and of variable quality. There are a few excellent Asian restaurants, however, particularly Japanese, with sushi being the most fashionable cuisine of the past decade in Moscow. Prices are high as the city is utterly landlocked and fresh fish has to be flown in daily.

WHAT TO DRINK

Vodka is the alcoholic drink most often associated with Russia. However, in the years since perestroika beer has become more widely available as an accompaniment to meals. Most restaurants now offer imported and local beer on tap, along with a variety of bottled beers. Russian beer is light and generally very good. Imported beer is often overpriced. The better European restaurants have commendable wine lists,

The Central House of Writers *(see p186)*, one of Moscow's most exclusive restaurants

Outdoor café in Tverskaya, a good place to watch the world go by

though good imported wine tends to be quite expensive. It is a shame to visit Moscow without sampling a bottle of Georgian wine *(see p183)* in one of its many Georgian eateries. This is an excellent accompaniment to Georgian food, although it can some-times overpower the subtler flavours of European cuisine.

PAYMENT AND TIPPING

One of the drawbacks of eating out in Moscow is that some restaurants, usually the less touristy ones, only take cash. This situation is gradually changing, but it is still a consideration when deciding where to eat. Generally restaurants that serve Western or Asian cuisine will accept credit cards, but it is a good idea to call ahead and check exactly which cards are accepted and whether a surcharge is taken. Prices vary enormously from

Cosy interior of Cafe Margarita *(see p191)*, a traditional café

the cheapest local cafeteria *(stolovaya)*, where a meal might cost the equivalent of around US$5, to the Central House of Writers, where dinner will be over US$75.

Tipping is not as ingrained in Russia as elsewhere. Keeping to international standards of 10–15 per cent if you are satisfied is appropriate, although regardless of the total spent in a restaurant it is unnecessary to leave more than a few hundred roubles. In Russian-style restaurants or cafés it is acceptable to leave small change, or nothing at all. Service is rarely included in the bill.

OPENING TIMES

Dinner is the main meal of the day, but many restaurants in Moscow have now adopted the concept of the business lunch. These often take the form of a fixed price menu and can be excellent value. They are usually served from noon to 4pm. Most restaurants start serving dinner at around 6pm and stop taking orders at 10:30pm; some family-run Georgian establishments close their kitchens as early as 9pm. Increasingly, restaurants are staying open until the early hours of the morning, and some are even open around the clock.

MAKING A RESERVATION

Most international and tourist-oriented restaurants take reservations and some of the most popular require them. Generally, it is best

to book ahead whenever possible. However, some of the most popular Georgian and Caucasian restaurants do not take reservations and these can be busy, especially at weekends.

ETIQUETTE

Casual or semi-formal dress is acceptable in almost every Moscow restaurant. Russians tend to overdress rather than underdress, however, so it is probably safer to err on the formal side. Children are a rare sight at expensive restaurants and most menus do not have special dishes for them. Moscow does have a few family-style restaurants, and many of the Western-owned restaurants provide children's menus.

VEGETARIANS

Much of Russian cuisine consists of meat dishes. Even salads often contain meat, so the best option for vegetarians is often a beetroot or tomato platter. Georgian cuisine, featuring numerous excellent bean and aubergine dishes, is usually a better bet. Restaurants are increasingly taking into account the demands of vegetarian visitors. European, Chinese and Japanese restaurants usually have some items suitable for vegetarians. There are a few vegetarian restaurants in the city, and the standard of these is rising.

SMOKING

There are generally areas for non-smokers in restaurants. However, smoking during meals is considered accept-able in Russia and smokers sometimes pay scant regard to non-smoking areas.

DISABLED PERSONS

Few restaurants in Moscow have facilities for disabled visitors. Some restaurants are located in basements and would therefore pose a prob-lem. It is always best to phone in advance to check if there is full disabled access.

The Flavours of Moscow

Russia's culinary reputation centres on warming stews, full of wintery vegetables such as cabbage, beetroot and potatoes. Yet Moscow was once the capital of a vast empire stretching from Poland to the Pacific and this is reflected in the variety of food on offer in the city. Aubergines (eggplants) and tomatoes, imported from the Caucasus in the south, bring in the flavours of the Mediterranean, while spices from Central Asia lend an exotic touch. On the stalls of the city's Central Market, crayfish and caviar sit alongside honey from Siberia and melons and peaches from Georgia.

Wild mushrooms

Caviar, the roe of sturgeon from Russia's warm southern waters

pickles. There is a refreshing soup, *solianka*, in which pickled cucumbers impart a delicious salty taste. Pickled mushrooms in sour cream make a regular appearance on restaurant menus, as do a variety of fresh berry juices.

In a country where food shortages are a fairly recent memory, very little is wasted. *Kvas*, a popular, mildly alcoholic drink is frequently made at home by fermenting stale bread with sugar and a scattering of fruit. Summer visitors should make a point of trying the delicious cold soup *okroshka*, which is based on *kvas*.

Russia is also a land with hundreds of rivers and lakes, and has a long tradition of fish cookery. Dishes range from simple soups, such as *ukha*, to caviar and sturgeon, and salmon cooked in a bewildering variety of ways.

RUSSIAN COUNTRYSIDE

Many Muscovites have small country houses within easy reach of the city, and spend weekends from spring to early winter lovingly tending their immaculate vegetable gardens, or combing the countryside for wild berries and mushrooms. Much of this bountiful harvest is made into preserves and

Blinis   Pickled mushrooms   Spiced feta   Rye bread   Gherkins

Pickled herring   Salted fish   Soured cream

A typical spread of *zakuski* (cold appetizers)

LOCAL DISHES AND SPECIALITIES

Borscht (beetroot soup) and *blinis* (buttery pancakes) with caviar are perhaps two of the most famous Russian dishes – one a peasant dish which varies with the availability of ingredients and the other a staple for the week leading up to Lent, when rich food would be eaten to fatten up before the fast. Much of Russia's cuisine is designed to make use of what is readily to hand or is warming and filling. A popular main course is *kulebiaka*, a hearty fish pie, larded with eggs, rice, dill and onion and encased in a buttery crust. Another is beef stroganoff with its creamy mushroom sauce, created in 18th-century St Petersburg by the chef of the wealthy Stroganoff family.

Beetroot

Borscht *Made with meat or vegetable stock, this beetroot soup is usually served with dill and soured cream.*

Market vegetable stall in central Moscow

THE CAUCASUS

The former Soviet states of the Caucasus – Georgia, Azerbaijan and Armenia – are renowned for their legendary banquets, where the tables are laden with an enormous quantity and variety of food and drink. These regions still supply Russia's cities with a tempting range of fine subtropical produce. Limes, lemons, oranges, walnuts, figs, pomegranates, peaches, beans, salty cheeses and herbs are all shipped in season to Moscow's markets and its many Georgian restaurants. The cuisine of Georgia, with its focus on freshly grilled meats, pulses, vegetables, yogurt, herbs and nut sauces – including the hallmark walnut sauce, *satsivi* – is famously healthy and

Georgians are particularly known for their longevity.

CENTRAL ASIA

From the Central Asian republics of the old Soviet Union, which include

Freshly picked lingonberries from Russia's bumper autumn harvest

Uzbekistan, Turkmenistan and Tajikistan, come a range of culinary traditions based on the nomadic lifestyles of Russia's one-time overlords, the Mongol or Tartar Hordes. The meat of fat-tailed sheep, which thrive in the desert air, is used to make communal piles of *plov* (pilaf) around which guests sit, eating in the traditional manner with their hands. Served in Moscow's Uzbek restaurants, it shares the menu with delicious flat breads, spicy noodle soups, *manti* (tasty dumplings reminiscent of Chinese cuisine) and a variety of melons and grapes, which proliferate in the desert oases, and apricots and nuts, grown in the mountains.

ZAKUSKI

A traditional Russian meal generally begins with *zakuski*, a selection of cold appetizers. These may include pickled mushrooms (*gribi*), gherkins (*ogurtsi*), salted herrings (*seliodka*), an assortment of smoked fish, blinis topped with caviar, various vegetable pâtés (sometimes known as vegetable caviars), stuffed eggs (*yaitsa farshirovanniye*), spiced feta cheese (*brinza*), beetroot salad (*salat iz svyokla*) and small meat pies (*pirozhki*), accompanied by rye bread and washed down with shots of vodka. A bowl of steaming soup often follows, before the main course reaches the table.

Kulebiaka *Rich, buttery puff pastry is wrapped around a mix of fish, hard-boiled eggs, rice, onion and chopped dill.*

Pelmeni *These meat-stuffed dumplings may be served in a clear broth, or with tomato sauce or soured cream.*

Kissel *A mix of red berries is used to make this soft, fruity jelly, which is served topped with a swirl of fresh cream.*

What to Drink in Moscow

A glass of flavoured vodka

Russia is renowned for vodka, which has been manufactured there since the 14th or 15th century and was possibly originally invented by Muscovite monks. Vodka produced in Moscow has always been considered to be the finest. Peter the Great *(see p22)* was particularly fond of pepper and anise vodkas and devised modifications to the distillation process which greatly improved the quality of the finished drink.

Tea is Russia's other national drink. Traditionally made using a samovar and served black, tea has been popular in Russia since the end of the 18th century when it began to be imported from China.

A 19th-century Russian peasant family drinking vodka and tea at their *izba*

Stolichnaya   **Moskovskaya**   **Stolichnaya Cristall**

CLEAR VODKA

Russian vodka is produced from grain, usually wheat, although some rye is also used. Stolichnaya is made from wheat and rye and is slighly sweetened. Probably the best known of the Russian vodkas, its name means "from the capital city". Moskovskaya is a high-quality, slightly fizzy vodka, while Kubanskaya, originally produced by the Cossacks, is slightly bitter. The Cristall distillery in Moscow has been hailed as the finest in Russia and produces super-premium versions of several vodkas, including Stolichnaya and Moskovskaya, as well as its own vodka, Cristall. Vodka is almost always served with food in Russia, often with a traditional range of accompaniments called *zakuski (see p181)*. These specialities are usually spicy or salty and their strong flavours complement vodka perfectly.

Kubanskaya

FLAVOURED VODKA

The practice of flavouring vodka has entirely practical origins. When vodka was first produced commercially in the Middle Ages, the techniques and equipment were so primitive

Pertsovka

that it was impossible to remove all the impurities. This left unpleasant aromas and flavours, which were disguised by adding honey together with aromatic oils and spices. As distillation techniques improved, flavoured vodkas became a speciality in their own right. Limonnaya, its taste deriving from lemon zest, is one of the most traditional, as is Pertsovka, flavoured with red chilli pepper pods. Okhotnichya (hunter's vodka) has a wider range of flavourings including juniper, ginger and cloves. Starka (old vodka) is a mixture of vodka, brandy, port and an infusion of apple and pear leaves, aged in oak barrels.

Limonnaya   **Okhotnichya**   **Starka**

MAJOR WINE REGIONS

■ Vine-growing region	■ Russia
■ Moldova	□ Georgia
■ Ukraine	□ Armenia
	■ Azerbaijan
	— International boundaries

Georgian wines　　*Shampanskoe*

WINE

The former Soviet Union was one of the world's largest producers of wine *(vino)*. Many of its major wine regions, however, are now within independent republics, but their vintages are still popular in Moscow. A wide range of indigenous grape varieties is cultivated in the different regions, along with many types found in other parts of the vine-growing world. Georgia and Crimea (in southeastern Ukraine) have traditionally produced the best wines, although Georgian wines are difficult to find in Moscow due to frosty relations between Georgia and Russia. Moldova produces white, sparkling wines in the south and central regions, and the south is also known for its red wines. Since 1799 Moldova has also produced vast amounts of a sweet, sparkling wine called *shampanskoe.*

OTHER ALCOHOLIC DRINKS

Originally a by-product of wine-making, brandy *(konyak)* only began to be made commercially in Russia in the 19th century. Among the ex-Soviet republics, Georgia and Armenia both produce brandy. Armenian is considered the finer, with a vanilla fragrance resulting from ageing it in barrels made of 70–100-year-old oak. Although beer *(pivo)* is becoming more popular, it is still served in relatively few restaurants and cafés. Good Russian beers include Zhigulevskoe, Baltika, Kolos and Moskovskoe. Various imported beers are also available.

Baltika beer　　**Armenian brandy**

OTHER DRINKS

Made from Barley and Rye, *kvas* is a sweet, mildly alcoholic drink consumed by adults and children alike. Russia has a huge range of mineral waters *(mineralnaya voda)*, including many with unusually high mineral contents. Those from the Caucasus, Siberia and Georgia are especially prized. Also available are fruit juices *(sok)* sweetened drinks made by boiling fruit with sugar and water *(kompot)*. The cranberry equivalent is called *mors*.

Mineral water　　*Kvas*　　*Mors*

TEA

Russian tea is served black with a slice of lemon and is traditionally drunk from a tall glass, called a *stakan*, or a cup. The tea *(chay)* is often sweetened with jam *(varenye)* instead of sugar. The boiling water for making tea traditionally comes from a samovar. The water is used to brew a pot of strong tea, from which a little is poured into the glasses. This is then diluted with more boiling water.

A glass of tea, with jam (varenye) to sweeten it

THE SAMOVAR

Traditionally made from brass or copper, samovars were once used to provide boiling water for a variety of domestic purposes. Nowadays they are often made of stainless steel and are used for boiling water to make tea. Occasionally eggs are put in the top of the samovar to cook in the boiling water. The word samovar comes from *samo* meaning "itself" and *varit* meaning "to boil".

Choosing a Restaurant

The restaurants in this guide have been selected across a wide price range for their exceptional food, good value, and their convenient and/or interesting locations. The chart below lists the restaurants by area, and the entries are alphabetical within each price category. For the map references, *see pages 238–45*.

PRICE CATEGORIES
Price categories for a three-course meal for one with a glass of wine, including service:

⑤ under US$45
⑤⑤ US$45–US$55
⑤⑤⑤ US$55–US$65
⑤⑤⑤⑤ US$65–US$75
⑤⑤⑤⑤⑤ US$75 and over

ARBATSKAYA

5-Spice 5 Специй
⑤⑤   Map 6 D2
Pereulok Sivtev Vrazhek 3/18 **Tel** *(495) 697 1283*

Specialising in Cantonese food and dishes from the Northern Provinces, 5-Spice enjoys a reputation as one of the best Chinese restaurants in Moscow. Centrally located, the restaurant is a short walk from Kropotkinskaya metro station and the Cathedral of Christ the Redeemer *(see p74)*. Pleasant interior and good service. **www.5spice.ru**

Mekhana Bansko Механа Банско
⑤⑤   Map 5 C1
Smolenskaya ploshchad 9/1 **Tel** *(495) 691 3132*

A friendly, family-run Bulgarian restaurant. Favourites on the menu include diverse meat dishes along with vegetables and feta cheese. The *banitsa* (pies with spinach, meat, cheese, pumpkin and walnuts) are highly recommended. Traditional Bulgarian entertainment in the evenings. Reservations are advised at weekends.

Cutty Sark Катти Сарк
⑤⑤⑤   Map 2 D5
Novinskiy bulvar 12 **Tel** *(495) 691 3350*

Located fairly close to the New Arbat, Cutty Sark is a seafood restaurant, designed to resemble an ocean-going yacht. It serves fresh seafood from all over the world, and has separate sushi and oyster bars and a good selection of wines. The service is attentive, and there is a special VIP cigar room.

Rus' Русь
⑤⑤⑤   Map 6 E1
Ulitsa Arbat 12 **Tel** *(495) 691 9626*

Built in the style of a log cabin, the Rus' boasts a traditional Russian menu, including such delicacies as *solyanka* (fish soup) and black caviar. Although it lacks a non-smoking area, the ventilator is extremely effective. Ideally located, the Rus' is popular with Russian celebrities from the worlds of politics and entertainment.

San Marco Сан Марко
⑤⑤⑤   Map 6 E1
Ulitsa Arbat 25 **Tel** *(495) 697 1770*

San Marco is a cosy family restaurant right on the old Arbat and located in a restored 19th-century building. Perfectly-prepared pizzas and pasta, a summer veranda and friendly staff make this one of the best places in the city for all things Italian.

Vostochnaya Komnata Восточная Комната
⑤⑤⑤   Map 5 C1
Smolenskaya Ploschad 3/5 **Tel** *(495) 937 8423*

Vostochnaya Komnata means Eastern Room in English, and if offers authentic Indian food in the heart of Moscow. The curries and dahl on offer are popular with both expats and Russians alike. Also, somewhat incongruously, there is Georgian food on the menu. The restaurant can get busy at weekends.

Praga Прага
 ⑤⑤⑤⑤⑤   Map 6 E1
Ulitsa Arbat 2/1 **Tel** *(495) 690 6171*

Located right between the New and Old Arbats, Praga is one of the most famous restaurants in the city, featuring Russian, Japanese, European, Caucasian and Brazilian cuisine. A special historical menu is available, with dishes made according to Tsarist recipes, such as the dressed sturgeon. The numerous dining rooms make this restaurant unique. **www.praga.ru**

TVERSKAYA

Maki Café Макикафе
⑤   Map 2 F4
Glinishchevskiy pereulok 3 **Tel** *(495) 692 9731*

Maki Café offers an eclectic menu and a tasteful minimalist interior of exposed concrete and polished metal. Guests can enjoy Japanese, French, Italian and Russian dishes. Located on a quiet street just off Tverskaya ulitsa, the restaurant is reasonably priced and the food is of a good quality. Booking is recommended at weekends.

Key to Symbols *see back cover flap*

Café Ararat Кафе Арарат

$)$)

Neglinnaya ulitsa 4 **Tel** *(495) 783 1234*   **Map** *3 A5*

The Café Ararat is situated inside the Ararat Park Hyatt Hotel and offers Armenian specialities based on authentic recipes, with ingredients delivered from various regions of Armenia. It is a replica of the original Café Ararat, a landmark of 1960s Moscow, and has a wide selection of vintage Armenian brandies and wines.

Mayak Маяк

$)$)

Bolshaya Nikitskaya Ulitsa 19 **Tel** *(495) 291 7503*   **Map** *2 D5*

Offering good value Russian and European food, Mayak is a popular meeting place for actors and artists. There's a wonderfully bohemian atmosphere, and it is definitely worth a visit if you are in the area. The soups and fish dishes are excellent. Its on the first floor of the Mayakovsky Theatre.

Tibet Kitchen Тибет

$)$)

Kamergerskiy pereulok 5/6 **Tel** *(495) 923 2422*   **Map** *2 F5*

Tibetan cuisine in a somewhat Buddhist interior, decorated with an altar and Tibetan dolls. Try the spicy soups and the chicken, meat and seafood dishes served in a variety of delicious sauces. No-one should leave without tasting the dumplings and salty Tibetan tea. Conveniently located for the Bolshoy Theatre *(see pp90–91)*.

Akademiya Академия

$)$)$)

Kamergerskiy Pereulok 2 **Tel** *(495) 692 9649*   **Map** *2 D5*

Situated right on the pedestrian strip of Kamergerskiy Pereulok, a ten minute walk from Red Square, this restaurant is a great place to eat good Italian food (pizza, pasta) and people-watch at the same time. There is also very good ice-cream. Drinks are expensive, however.

Champagne Café Шампань Кафе

$)$)$)

Bolshaya Nikitskaya ulitsa 12 **Tel** *(495) 629 5325*   **Map** *2 F5*

Set in Venetian-style halls with stained glass windows, the Champagne Café offers an extensive list of champagnes and wines, and features a fusion menu of Italian, French and other European culinary traditions. Seafood dishes can be prepared to order. There is live music on Thursdays and Fridays.

Il Tartufo Трюфель

$)$)$)

Malyy Gnezdnikovskiy pereulok 12/27 **Tel** *(495) 629 6688*   **Map** *2 F4*

Close to Tverskaya, the Il Tartufo restaurant offers all things Italian, from truffles to Fiorentina steak. A cosy restaurant with fine food, the Il Tartufo also has a delicatessen store on the premises selling pastas, olive oils, cheeses and truffles. The walls are covered in photos taken by the restaurant's very own truffle supplier, Luigi from Acqualana.

Mari Vanna Мари Vanna

$)$)$)

Spiridonevskiy Pereulok 10 **Tel** *(495) 650 6500*   **Map** *2 E4*

This is one of Moscow's most unusual restaurants. Designed to replicate a 1930s Soviet flat, it offers delicious home cooking. From soups to *pelmeni (see p181)* everything is perfectly prepared and authentic. There are only a small number of vegetarian options however. There is no sign outside the 20th-century building, just ring the doorbell.

New Tandoor Нью Тандур

$)$)$)

Tverskaya ulitsa 30/2 **Tel** *(495) 699 8062*   **Map** *2 E3*

Tandoor serves Indian and Chinese food prepared by native Indian and Chinese chefs. The Indian menu is highly recommended and includes excellent tomato soup, tandoori dishes, warm naan breads and much more. The pleasant interior and attentive service help to compensate for the rather small portions.

Teatro Театро

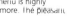

$)$)$)

Teatralnyy proezd 1/4 **Tel** *(495) 927 6067*   **Map** *3 A5*

Located close to the Kremlin *(see pp52–67)*, inside the Metropol Hotel, Teatro boasts an Italian Chef, who serves his own take on Italian food, and flies in ingredients from abroad. The Art Deco interior also has a VIP room that can accommodate 14 guests. Reservations are recommended. Live piano music from Tuesdays to Thursdays.

Godunov Годуновъ

$)$)$)$)

Teatralnaya ploshchad 5 **Tel** *(495) 698 5609*   **Map** *3 A5*

Once part of the Zaikonospassky Monastery, and built during the rule of Boris Godunov, the Godunov serves excellent *borshch* and other rich soups, delicious game, *pirozhki* and a good choice of vegetarian main dishes. Russian dishes are slightly adapted to western tastes. There is traditional Russian entertainment in the evenings.

Moskovsky московский

$)$)$)$)

Ulitsa Mokhovaya 15/1 **Tel** *(495) 658 7068*   **Map** *6 F1*

Situated opposite the Kremlin *(see pp52–67)*, in one of Moscow's most famous hotels, the Moskovsky has possibly the finest panoramic view of any restaurant in the city. The menu is a mix of Russian aristocratic, French and Mediterranean fare, and includes a fine selection of desserts. In the evenings there is live classical music.

Paper Moon Пэйпер мун

$)$)$)$)

Ulitsa Petrovka 17 **Tel** *(495) 980 7350*   **Map** *3 A4*

Paper Moon is known for the quality of its Italian and Adriatic food, which is served in a modern and elegant interior. The Italian-owned chain has restaurants in Milan, New York, Istanbul and Tel Aviv. Great location and service, and one of the best wine lists in the city. Booking is recommended.

Polo Club Поло Клуб
Ulitsa Petrovka 11/20 **Tel** *(495) 937 1024*

$$$$

***Map** 3 A4*

Conveniently located for the Kremlin *(see pp52–67)* and Red Square *(see p106)*, Polo Club is a steak house with an enviable reputation. It is situated on the second floor of the Marriott Royal Aurora Hotel and has a good seafood menu and a large selection of desserts. The international wine list is extensive and well chosen.

Roberto Роберто
Strastnoy bulvar 16 **Tel** *(495) 921 3839*

$$$$

***Map** 2 F3*

Genuine Italian cuisine served in a pleasant environment. Excellent *carpaccio* (thinly sliced raw beef), pastas and delicious tiramisu desserts. It is located just off Pushkinskaya ploshchad and is widely held to be one of the best Italian restaurants in Moscow. Booking is recommended but not essential.

Sergei Сергей
Kamergerskiy pereulok 3a **Tel** *(495) 629 5793*

$$$$

***Map** 2 F5*

Located just off Tverskaya ulitsa, in the pedestrian zone of Kamergerskiy pereulok, Sergei offers a mixture of Russian and European food. This is an especially attractive option for the summer as guests can spend an evening relaxing and watching the crowds walk by, while enjoying some fine food. Retreat to the cosy interior in winter.

Tesoro Тезоро
Romanov pereulok 4 **Tel** *(495) 937 7730*

$$$$

***Map** 2 F5*

Located in a quiet side street, Tesoro is a pleasant combination of an Italian restaurant and pizzeria. Dinner with wine in the restaurant can be quite expensive, but the cheaper pizzeria serves excellent minestrone soup, generous pasta servings, tasty pizzas and delicious desserts at modest prices. The terrace is lovely in summer.

Uncle Guilly's Гиляй
Stoleshnikov pereulok 6 **Tel** *(495) 933 5521*

 $$$$

***Map** 2 F4*

Uncle Guilly's is proud of its status as Moscow's top steak house. There is much more to its menu, however, which features a wide range of dishes at reasonable prices. The restaurant has three rooms, the Library, Mill Room, and in the basement, the Printing Press, which was the site of an archaeological dig and contains various 'finds'.

Café Des Artistes Кафе дез Артист
Kamergerskiy pereulok 5/6 **Tel** *(495) 692 4042*

 $$$$$

***Map** 2 F5*

This Swiss-run restaurant serves European cuisine with a French twist. Excellent vegetable soups, gourmet meat dishes, delicious desserts and a large choice of wines mean that the restaurant is held in high regard by expats and the Russian nouveau-riche alike. It can have a fairly stiff atmosphere, although the service is good.

Pushkin Пушкин
Tverskoy bulvar 26a **Tel** *(495) 739 0033*

$$$$$

***Map** 2 E4*

Pushkin offers a unique Russian dining experience in an elegant interior. The first floor's décor harks back to its origins as an 18th-century pharmacy, and serves Russian dishes. The second floor was once a library and offers pricier and even more exquisite Russian cuisine. In summer, enjoy the view of Tverskaya ulitsa from the rooftop terrace.

Scandinavia Скандинавия
Bolshoy Palashevskiy pereulok 7 **Tel** *(495) 937 5630*

$$$$$

***Map** 2 E4*

This spacious Swedish-run restaurant is located in a side street, a pleasant stroll from Pushkinskaya ploshchad, and is especially popular in summer, when guests can dine under chestnut trees in the pretty courtyard. The quality European cuisine, with some Swedish specialities, includes some excellent steaks and desserts.

RED SQUARE AND KITAY GOROD

Jagannat Джаганнат
Ulitsa Kuznetskiy Most 11 **Tel** *(495) 628 3580*

$

***Map** 3 A4*

This is a vegetarian restaurant, a rare thing indeed in Moscow. Service is slow, but you fill find tasty Indian, Mexican and European food. No alcohol is served but the ginger beer is delicious. There is also a café and a New Age shop on the premises. It's located 15 minutes from the Kremlin.

Khodzha Nasreddin v Khive Ходжа Насреддин в Хиве
Ulitsa Pokrovka 10 **Tel** *(495) 917 0444*

 $

***Map** 3 C5*

The delicious Uzbek cuisine on offer here is served amid a stunning blue, turquoise and white décor devoted to the ancient Uzbek city of Khiva. On the second floor guests can dine in Eastern fashion, reclining on cushions at low tables. Clowns and fairy tales help keep children entertained on weekend afternoons.

1 Red Square Красная площадь, дом 1
Red Square 1/2, in the Historical Museum **Tel** *(495) 925 3600*

 $$$

***Map** 7 A1*

The food here is cooked according to old Russian recipes found in the Historical Museum archives, such as mushrooms pickled in barrels at the bottom of a lake and *kedrach* (cedar nut vodka). The aristocratic tradition is evident in the glorious interior. Located just off Red Square, it is an ideal venue to sample the best of Russian cuisine.

Maharaja Махараджа ⬛🔲🔲Ⓥ🔲 $$$

Ulitsa Pokrovka 2/1 **Tel** *(495) 921 9844*   **Map** *3 C5*

Though more expensive than its competitors, Maharaja is a safe bet for delicious Indian food. The restaurant offers tasteful décor and a quiet, low-key atmosphere. Portions are small, but the service is attentive. The location is fairly central, although the restaurant is located in the basement of a building. Most of the waiters speak English.

Noev Kovcheg Ноев Ковчег 🔲🔲🔲🔲Ⓥ🔲 $$$

Malyy Ivanovskiy pereulok 9 **Tel** *(495) 917 0717*   **Map** *7 C1*

Noev Kovcheg ("Noah's Ark") offers an extensive, authentic Armenian menu, with a detailed explanation of each dish in English. The bean stew and grilled cheese appetizers are excellent, as is the acclaimed Armenian cognac. The busy restaurant often features the unobtrusive sounds of national music and is recommended for vegetarians.

Villa Вилла 🔲🔲Ⓥ🔲 $$$

Myasnitskaya ulitsa 48 **Tel** *(495) 925 4715*   **Map** *3 B4*

Villa has a Mediterranean menu offering fresh fish and shellfish, as well as an aquarium with live lobsters. All the seafood is flown in twice a week from France. It has over 300 varieties of wine in its cellar. Decorated in an Art Deco style, it also has a huge open fireplace and live piano and singing in the evenings.

Portofino Портофино 🔲Ⓥ🔲 $$$$

Ulitsa Bolshaya Lubyanka 16/4 **Tel** *(495) 923 0286*   **Map** *3 B4*

Named after the Italian city of the same name, Portofino has an Italian chef and a Mediterranean/Italian menu specialising in mushroom recipes. It has three dining areas, each of which is individually decorated. The restaurant is well worth a visit, especially for vegetarians, who will appreciate the tasty mushroom-based meals on offer.

Nostalgie Ностальжи 🔲🔲🔲Ⓥ🔲 $$$$$

Chistoprudnyy bulvar 12a **Tel** *(495) 916 9478*   **Map** *3 C4*

Nostalgie has one of the best wine lists in Moscow, which goes well with the haute cuisine prepared by a French chef. The restaurant looks out over ponds and is far from stuffy despite its high tariff; there is a special programme for children at the weekend. Reservations are recommended.

ZAMOSKVORECHE

Discovery Дискавери 🔲🔲 $$

Novokuznetskaya ulitsa 24/2 **Tel** *(495) 953 3803*   **Map** *7 B3*

Discovery is located in an old merchant's townhouse and offers a Mediterranean menu. With fireplaces and a library, it has a relaxed, if busy atmosphere, somewhat reminiscent of a clubhouse. The second floor was designed to resemble a luxury yacht. Worth checking out to see another side of Moscow's restaurant culture.

Uncle Vanya Дядя Ваня 🔲🔲🔲 $$

Ulitsa Pyatniskaya 20 **Tel** *(495) 951 0586*   **Map** *7 B2*

Uncle Vanya is a traditional Russian restaurant very close to Trotyakov Gallery (see pp118–21). In the day there is quiet background music, and in the evenings live piano concerts. The menu excels at Russian favourites. Portions are large, although it is possible to order smaller meals. The borshch is particularly tasty.

Dorian Gray Дориан Грей 🔲🔲Ⓥ🔲 $$$$

Kadashevskaya naberezhnaya 6/1 **Tel** *(499) 238 6401*   **Map** *7 A3*

Dorian Gray is a riverside restaurant with a stunning view of the Kremlin (see pp52–67), and has a traditional and elegant Italian menu. Pay a visit for what is probably the best Tiramisu in Moscow. The excellent pasta dishes and beautiful presentation are complemented by attentive and professional service.

Oblomov Обломов 🔲🔲🔲🔲Ⓥ🔲 $$$$$

Monetchikovskiy pereulok 5 **Tel** *(495) 953 6828*   **Map** *7 B4*

The first floor of Oblomov is occupied by a cheaper café "Pizhon" with an Art Deco interior, serving European cuisine. The second and third floors are the actual restaurant, and specialise in French and Russian food. The Eastern Room on the third floor has water pipes and live belly dancers.

Sea Time Море Времени 🔲🔲🔲 $$$$

Ulitsa Bolshaya Polyanka 51a **Tel** *(495) 953 4913*   **Map** *7 A4*

This fine seafood restaurant is conveniently located for the Tretyakov Gallery (see pp 118–21). The crab is flown in from eastern Russia to produce Kamchatka Crab, one of the restaurant's highly recommended specialities. There is a 15 per cent discount from noon to 4pm, making it an ideal place for lunch. Live music in the evening.

Suliko Сулико 🔲🔲🔲🔲Ⓥ🔲 $$$$

Ulitsa Bolshaya Polyanka 42/2 **Tel** *(499) 238 2888*   **Map** *7 A4*

Suliko has a large and tasty Georgian menu and an interior of mini-fountains, fake plants and figurines. There is loud evening entertainment from a Georgian choir in the main hall; ask to be seated in one of the smaller rooms if you want to avoid this. The "Green Room" has an all-you-can-eat buffet from noon to 4pm daily, wine included.

FURTHER AFIELD

NORTH OF THE CENTRE Budvar Будва
Ulitsa Pokrovka 23 **Tel** *(495) 923 3364* **Map** *4 D4* ⑤

Budvar, a Yugoslavian restaurant, is famed for its service. Diners can enjoy fresh, unpretentious and satisfying food, such as schnitzel and chorba, and can select from a good range of Yugoslavian wines. The portions are generous and prices reasonable. It can get busy, so anyone wanting a romantic setting may be disappointed.

NORTH OF THE CENTRE Bungalo Bar Бунгало Бар
Ulitsa Zemlyanoy val 6 **Tel** *(495) 916 2432* **Map** *4 D4* ⑤

Bungalo Bar offers reasonably priced Ethiopian fare and authentic décor, which includes a rhinoceros! The menu includes some great vegetarian options and spicy dishes (the menu carries spice warnings). The European dishes are best avoided. Some of the more exotic options are well worth trying. Good service.

NORTH OF THE CENTRE Kavkazskaya Plenitsa Кавказская пленница
Prospekt Mira 36 **Tel** *(495) 680 5111* **Map** *3 B1* ⑤⑤

This brightly decorated Georgian restaurant takes as its theme a popular Russian comedy show from the 1970s. In summer you can dine on the open-air terrace facing the restaurant's lovely garden. There is a good range of Georgian favourites, and children's entertainers at weekends. The service is good.

NORTH OF THE CENTRE Muscat Мускат
Novoslobodskaya ulitsa 11 **Tel** *(495) 973 5174* **Map** *2 E1* ⑤⑤

One of the better Arabic restaurants in Moscow, Muscat offers a tempting range of Algerian, Moroccan and Tunisian dishes with a handful of European alternatives. It is one of the few places in Moscow that serves good hummus. Located within walking distance of Novoslobodskaya Metro station on the Circle Line. Good for vegetarians.

NORTH OF THE CENTRE Skazka Vostoka Сказка востока
Frunzenskaya Naberezhnaya 22 **Tel** *(499) 766 8343* **Map** *6 D5* ⑤⑤

This is a good value restaurant set on a boat moored on the Moscow River. Spicy Georgian and Azeri food is the draw, with a fair amount of vegetarian options. This is one of the city's most romantic dining options too, due to the setting. It's open 24 hours.

NORTH OF THE CENTRE Tofu Тофу
Ulitsa Malaya Dmitrovka 2 **Tel** *(495) 299 3073* **Map** *2 F3* ⑤⑤

A great option for vegetarians, Tofu serves a mixture of Asian cuisines, ranging from Chinese to Korean. The interior is decorated in classical Oriental style. The service is friendly, and the drinks menu includes sake and plum wine. Located off Tverskaya ulitsa, this is a good option for an evening meal after exploring the city centre.

NORTH OF THE CENTRE Yapona Mama Япона Мама
Tsvetnoy bulvar 11/3 **Tel** *(495) 921 6098* **Map** *3 A3* ⑤⑤

Located not far from the metro, Yapona Mama ("Japanese Mother") is a marvel of glass and exposed concrete. The two levels are supplemented by a rooftop terrace for outside dining, weather permitting. The restaurant offers good service in a stylish environment, and some of the best sushi in Moscow. A few non-Japanese dishes are also served.

NORTH OF THE CENTRE Capri Капри
Prospekt Akademika Sakharova 7 **Tel** *(495) 607 5253* **Map** *3 C3* ⑤⑤⑤

Capri is a gourmet restaurant with an Italian chef and an emphasis on Italian meat and seafood dishes. It also has a sushi bar and a coffee house in the grounds. Its two main dining areas are decorated to resemble a 19th-century *palazzo*, with furniture in a Louis XVI style. There is live music in the evening from Tuesday to Thursday.

NORTH OF THE CENTRE Market Маркет
Ulitsa Sadovaya-Samotechnaya 18 **Tel** *(495) 609 4131* **Map** *3 A2* ⑤⑤⑤

Boasting a chef from Shanghai, Market is an Asian seafood restaurant, with a heated veranda for outside dining. A special oyster menu is laid on for certain national holidays. Although it is located a fair distance from the centre, the restaurant is worth visiting, if only for the efficient and friendly service.

NORTH OF THE CENTRE Natura Viva Натура Вива
Dolgorukovskaya ulitsa 19 **Tel** *(495) 609 2845* **Map** *2 E2* ⑤⑤⑤

Natura Viva boasts organically produced fruit and meat from Australia and Argentina respectively, as well as herb teas from the mountain regions of Elbrus. The restaurant consists of three floors. The first floor is more of a café, the second a restaurant in a colonial style. The third floor resembles an attic lounge.

NORTH OF THE CENTRE Simple Pleasures Симпл Плэжерс
Ulitsa Sretenka 22/1 **Tel** *(495) 607 1521* **Map** *3 B3* ⑤⑤⑤

Simple Pleasures has an elegant minimalist interior, including one room with an open fireplace. Its eclectic menu ranges from Mediterranean to South American, taking in French and Spanish cuisine along the way. The restaurant has a solid, if unspectacular, wine list. There is live music in the evening – usually unobtrusive blues.

Key to Price Guide *see p184* **Key to Symbols** *see back cover flap*

NORTH OF THE CENTRE Tzimmes Цимес

Ulitsa Novoslobodskaya 3 **Tel** *(495) 973 0873*   **Map** *2 E1*

Tzimmes is a Jewish restaurant offering genuine home-made Jewish food. The restaurant's décor is rustic in style and harks back to village life from the early 20th century. A special winter menu includes many warming favourites. There is live Jewish music in the evening and a children's club at the weekend. Formal dress code.

NORTH OF THE CENTRE Carre Blanc Карре Бланк

Seleznevskaya ulitsa 19/2 **Tel** *(495) 258 4403*   **Map** *2 F1*

With an ever-evolving menu and a beautiful summer courtyard, Carre Blanc is held by some to be the best restaurant in Moscow. Certainly the best French restaurant in the city, it offers superb seafood, attentive service and a tremendous range of superb dishes. Tapas is served on Thursdays.

SOUTHWEST OF THE CENTRE Genatsvale VIP Генацвале VIP

Ulitsa Ostozhenka 14/2 **Tel** *(495) 695 0393*   **Map** *6 E3*

A Georgian restaurant, offering delicious *khachapuri* (hot cheese-filled bread), *lobio* (beans with walnuts and spices), and other Georgian musts. The extensive wine list concentrates on Georgian vintages. The cheaper Genatsvale, at No 12/1, has an almost identical menu and a much simpler interior, and there's also a new venue at No 11 Novyy Arbat.

SOUTHWEST OF THE CENTRE U Pirosmani У пиросмани

Novodevichiy proezd 4 **Tel** *(499) 255 7926*   **Map** *5 A5*

This Georgian restaurant has picturesque views of Novodevichiy Convent *(see pp130–31)*. Meat dishes are prepared in a variety of ways including *chanahi* (lamb with aubergine or egg-plant, served in a clay dish) and *abhazuri* (meat mixed with pomegranates). Delicious vegetable starters, salads and Georgian breads.

SOUTHWEST OF THE CENTRE Traktir Khlestakov Трактир Хлестаков

3-ya Frunzenskaya ulitsa 9/1 **Tel** *(499) 766 8692*   **Map** *5 C5*

This theatre-like restaurant is named after a play by the Russian writer Nikolai Gogol, and features 19th-century décor, waiters attired in traditional costumes, a parrot and canaries. The menu, arranged as a five-act play, offers authentic Russian cuisine. The food, wine and service are good quality.

SOUTHWEST OF THE CENTRE Sky Lounge Скай Лаунж

Leninskiy prospect 32a **Tel** *(495) 938 5775*   **Map** *6 F5*

Sky Lounge is situated on the 22nd floor of the Russian Academy of Sciences, and the views from the restaurant are spectacular. The food attains equally lofty heights and is a successful mixture of Asian and European fare. At weekends the restaurant invites fashionable DJs from around the world to spin lounge music.

SOUTHWEST OF THE CENTRE Vanil Ваниль

Ulitsa Ostozhenka 1/9 **Tel** *(495) 602 3341*   **Map** *6 E2*

Vanil offers a fusion of French and Japanese cuisine in an elegant and modern interior and includes some excellent dishes prepared from the finest ingredients. The service is discreet and thoughtful and the wine list is very good. The restaurant features a gorgeous summer veranda with beautiful views of the Cathedral of the Saviour *(see p140)*.

WEST OF THE CENTRE Avocado Авокадо

Christoprudnyy Bulvar 12/2 **Tel** *(495) 241 6217*   **Map** *3 C4*

Avocado, which is situated near the Chistye Prudy metro, is famed for its vegetarian versions of world cuisine. From *pelmeni (see p181)* to soups, pasta to curries, everything on the menu is healthy and tasty. The interior is nothing special, but window tables provide good opportunities for people-watching.

WEST OF THE CENTRE Ermak Ермак

Nizhniye Mnevnik ulitsa 41 **Tel** *(499) 191 2523*

Rustic décor gives Ermak the feel of a 15th-century Russian cottage. Guests can enjoy such rare delicacies as Siberian river fish. The restaurant is "child-friendly", with a special children's menu and live entertainment at the weekend. There are live performances of Russian folk music at the weekends.

WEST OF THE CENTRE China Garden Китайский Сад

Krasnopresnenskaya naberezhnaya 12 **Tel** *(495) 976 0586*   **Map** *1 B5*

Located on the ground floor of Moscow's World Trade Centre, China Garden was one of the very first privately owned Chinese restaurants in the city and serves Szechwan, Peking and Cantonese dishes. The service is very good and friendly, and the majority of the staff speak English. A good place for a peaceful meal.

WEST OF THE CENTRE Izola Изола

Naberezhnaya Tarasa Shevchenko 23a **Tel** *(495) 730 4400*   **Map** *5A1*

A Mediterranean-cum-Italian restaurant with Spanish and Chilean wines. Some way from the centre, but close to the homes of the Moscow elite, it is a good place for people-watching and affords excellent views of the Moskva river. The interior is wonderful, with stained glassed windows and handmade mosaics.

WEST OF THE CENTRE Shinok Шинок

Ulitsa 1905 Goda 2 **Tel** *(495) 651 8101*   **Map** *1 A3*

Decorated in the style of a Ukrainian peasant house, this rustically-themed restaurant comes complete with farm animals and traditionally dressed waitresses. A shop, called "Grandmother's Chest", is part of the package and sells antique kitchenware. The Ukrainian food is expensive but delicious, and the service reasonable.

Light Meals and Snacks

Moscow has plenty of cafés, bistros, restaurants, bars and fast-food outlets catering for every taste and budget. Russian food, particularly its traditional soups and salads, is perfect for a light meal. A tempting variety of patisserie-style confectionary is also a feature of Russian cuisine, and afternoon tea can be a real occasion, especially in traditional Russian and Central Asian cafés. Pizza, pasta and sushi are in plentiful supply in a wide variety of environments, from bars and cafés to up-market restaurants. Many restaurants offer a good value "business lunch" or discount on their á la carte menu between 12pm and 4pm. For a quick bite, snacks such as pancakes and baked potatoes can be obtained from street vendors. The best stalls can be found in Moscow's busiest shopping streets, such as Tverskaya ulitsa and the Novyy Arbat.

RUSSIAN

Traditional Russian cafés and bistros are usually rustically decorated, but can be rather smoky. The menu consists of soups such as borscht, and hearty salads including silodka pod shuboi (pickled herring with shredded beetroot). Pirozhki, pastries stuffed with anything from cabbage to liver (see p181), are good fillers. Excellent examples of such offerings can be ordered at **Elki-Palki** and **Café Margarita**, while **Maki Café** and **Art Club Nostalgie** offer both European and Russian food. For a quick meal, the chain restaurants **Moo Moo** and **Russkoe Bistro** serve fast food, Russian style. For Russian food on the move the best option are the blini stalls, which can be found all over the city serving buckwheat pancakes with a variety of sweet and savoury fillings.

GEORGIAN, ARMENIAN, UZBEK AND VEGETARIAN

Moscow's ethnic restaurants often have striking Central Asian décor. Guests may well find themselves sitting on cushions at low tables. The food tends to be simple, well-cooked and reasonably priced. Staples from the former Soviet republics of Georgia, Armenia and Uzbekistan, such as dolmas (meat and rice wrapped in vine leaves), shashlyk (shish kebabs) and lobio (a thick spicy bean soup), are

well worth trying. Meals usually involve a soup, grilled meats and a fresh salad. Of the Uzbek restaurants, **Kish Mish** and **Khodzha Nasreddin v Khive** offer good-value, tasty food. **Shesh Besh** serves generous portions of Azeri food, while **Genatsvale** has a superb range of Georgian favourites. **Korchma Taras Bulba** is an excellent place to sample Ukrainian cooking.

While vegetarians will find they are better provided for at ethnic restaurants than at Russian eateries, they may still find their options are limited. **Jagannat** is a wholly vegetarian restaurant, serving Indian, Japanese and Chinese meals.

FAST FOOD, PIZZA AND PASTA

Restaurant chains tend to predominate for pizza, pasta and fast food. **Il Patio** serves tasty pizzas at a range of locations, while **Propaganda** has pasta and salad dishes. For American food, **Starlight Diner** and the **American Bar and Grill** both offer authentic burgers. Branches of **Rosticks**, a fried chicken chain, can be found in most shopping centres. Stalls selling warming baked potatoes with a variety of toppings are dotted around the city.

PASTRIES AND SWEETS

Russian restaurants and cafés usually have a good range of pastries and sweets, the best of which feature meringue and

fruit. European style cafés such as **Coffee House**, **Zen Coffee** and **Shokoladnitsa** have more international offerings. Russian ice cream is sold in cafés and kiosks and is truly excellent. For picnic supplies, try the delicious cakes and pastries on offer from Yeliseev's Food Hall (see p89).

PUBS AND BARS

Moscow's pubs and bars offer a good range of light meals. So-called art cafés, often featuring live music (see p201), also have excellent menus. In the evening these cafés may be busy, with some form of art-happening taking centre stage, but at lunchtime they usually have a calmer atmosphere. Two good choices are **Kult** and **Kitaiskiy Lyotchik Djao Da**, which both serve good-value, bistro-style food. **Durdin** and **Tinkoff** stock their own micro-brewed beers, and have an excellent menu. These, along with **The Real McCoy**, offer "business lunches" for just $6. **Sally O'Brien's** is Moscow's premier Irish bar and provides a range of wholesome pub food. The **Albion Pub** is also a good choice and benefits from a wider menu.

SUSHI

Sushi is readily available in Moscow, and can be enjoyed in Japanese restaurants, sushi bars, nightclubs and "art cafés". Despite being landlocked, the sushi on offer in the capital is generally fresh and well prepared, though it can sometimes be a little bland.

The **Yakitoria** chain has branches throughout the city. It has traditional Japanese décor and offers good sushi at reasonable prices. **Yapona Mama** is more minimalist in ambience and serves sushi along with a variety of hot dishes, including European ones. Both are reasonably priced. Some cafés and bars, such as the **Maki Café** and **The Discreet Charm of the Bourgeoisie**, offer sushi on the menu alongside Italian and French dishes.

DIRECTORY

RUSSIAN

Art Club Nostalgie
Арт клуб ностальжи
Chistoprudnyy bulvar 12a.
Map 3 C4.
Tel (495) 925 7675.
www.nostalgie.ru

Café Margarita
Кафе Маргарита
Malaya Bronnaya ulitsa 28.
Map 2 E4.
Tel (495) 699 6534.

Elki-Palki
Елки-Палки
Bolshaya Dmitrovka ulitsa 23/8.
Map 2 F4.
Tel (495) 600 0965.

Maki Café
Макикафе
Glinishchevsky pereulok 3.
Map 2 F4.
Tel (495) 692 9731.

Moo Moo
Му-му
Ulitsa Arbat 45/24.
Map 6 D1.

Russkoe Bistro
Русское Быстро
Tverskaya ulitsa 16.
Tel (495) 690 0834.
Map 2 F5.

GEORGIAN, ARMENIAN, UZBEK AND VEGETARIAN

Genatsvale
Генацвале
Ulitsa Ostozhenka 12/1
(entry from the yard).
Map 6 E3.
Tel (495) 956 9997.

Jagannat
Джаганнат
Ulitsa Kuznetskiy most 11.
Map 3 A4.
Tel (495) 628 3580.

Khodzha Nasreddin v Khive
Ходжа Насреддин в Хиве
Ulitsa Pokrovka 10.
Map 3 C5.
Tel (495) 917 0444.

Kish Mish
Кишмиш
Ulitsa Novyy Arbat 28.
Tel (495) 691 2010.
Map 5 C1.

Korchma Taras Bulba
Корчма Тарас Бульба
Pyatnitskaya ulitsa 14.
Map 7 B3.
Tel (495) 200 6082.

Shesh Besh
Шеш-беш
Pyatnitskaya ulitsa 24/1.
Map 7 B3.
Tel (495) 959 5862.

FAST FOOD, PIZZA AND PASTA

American Bar and Grill
Американ Бар Грилл
Ulitsa Zemlyanoy val 59.
Map 8 E2.
Tel (495) 912 3615.

Il Patio
Иль Патио
Ulitsa Smolenskaya 3.
Map 6 F2.
Tel (495) 290 5070.

Propaganda
Пропаганда
Bolshoy Zlatoustinskiy pereulok 7. **Map** 3 B5.
Tel (495) 924 5732.
www.propaganda
moscow.com

Rosticks
Ростикс
1st Tverskaya-Yamskaya ulitsa 2/1.
Map 2 E3.
Tel (495) 251 4950.
www.rostiks.rosinter.ru

Starlight Diner
Старлайт лайнер
Bolshaya Sadovaya ulitsa 16.
Map 2 E3.
Tel (495) 690 9638.

PASTRIES AND SWEETS

Coffee House
Кофе Хауз
Manezhnaya ploshchad 1.
Map 3 A5/7 A1.
Tel (495) 796 3290.
www.coffeehouse.ru

Ulitsa Petrovka 19/1.
Tel (495) 787 7041.
Map 3 A4.

Gogolevskiy bulvar 3/2.
Tel (495) 202 3104.
Map 6 E2.

Shokoladnitsa
Шоколадница
Ulitsa Stary Arbat 29.
Map 6 D1.
Tel (495) 241 0620.
www.shoko.ru

Klimentovskiy pereulok 10.
Map 7 B3.
Tel (495) 951 3703.

Bolshaya Nikitskaya ulitsa 14.
Map 2 F5.
Tel (495) 203 1261.

Zen Coffee,
Зен кофе
Kamergersky pereulok 5/6, Building 4.
Map 2 F5.
Tel (495) 692 5114.

PUBS AND BARS

Albion Pub
Альбион
Manezhnaya ploshchad 1 (enter from Alexander Gardens).
Map 3 A5/7 A1.
Tel (495) 995 9545.

Durdin
Дурдинь
Bolshaya Polyanka ulitsa 5b.
Map 7 A3
Tel (495) 953 5200.

Kitaiskiy Lyotchik Djao Da
Китайский Летчик Джао Да
Lubyansky proezd 25/12.
Map 3 B5.
Tel (495) 924 5611.

Kult
Культ
Ulitsa Yauzskaya 5.
Map 8 D2.
Tel (495) 917 5706.

Sally O'Brien's
Bolshaya Polyanka 1/3.
Map 7 A3.
Tel (495) 959 0175.
www.sallyobriens.ru

The Real McCoy
Риал Маккой
Kudrinskaya ploshchad 1.
Map 1 C5.
Tel (495) 255 4144.
www.mccoy.ru

Tinkoff
Тинкофф
Protochnyy pereulok 11.
Map 5 C1.
Tel (495) 777 3300.

SUSHI

The Discreet Charm of the Bourgeoisie
Скромное обаяние буржуазии
Bolshaya Lubyanka ulitsa 24
Map 3 B4.
Tel (495) 923 0848.

Maki Café
Макикафе
Glinishchevsky pereulok 3.
Map 2 F4.
Tel (495) 292 9731.

Yakitoria
Якитория
Ulitsa Petrovka 16.
Map 3 A4.
Tel (495) 924 0609.

1st Tverskaya Yamskaya ulitsa 29/1.
Tel (495) 250 5385.
Map 2 E3.

Yapona Mama
Япона Мама
Tsvetnoi bulvar 11/3.
Map 3 A3.
Tel (495) 921 6098.

SHOPS AND MARKETS

Russian doll

Russia's appetite for Western goods means that Moscow now offers most of the shopping facilities of a large, modern Western city. There are supermarkets, department stores stocking imported goods and exclusive boutiques with French and Italian designer clothes and shoes for the new rich.

Moscow's most interesting shopping districts are located within the Garden Ring. The main department

stores are clustered around the city centre near Red Square, while the best souvenir and antique shops can be found along ulitsa Arbat (see pp70–71), a charming old pedestrian street. For the more adventurous a trip to the weekend flea market at Izmaylovo Park is a must. Here it is possible to buy everything from Russian dolls and Soviet memorabilia to handmade rugs from Central Asia and antique jewellery.

A display counter in the sumptuously decorated Yeliseev's Food Hall (see p194)

OPENING HOURS

Moscow's shops and businesses rarely open before 10am and often not until 11am. Most stay open until around 7pm. Many shops, especially old, state-run stores, close for an hour at lunchtime, either from 1pm to 2pm, or from 2pm to 3pm. Shops are usually open all day on Saturdays, and nowadays many are also open on Sundays, although often for shorter hours.

Markets generally operate from 10am to 4pm but it is necessary to go in the morning to get the best choice of goods.

HOW TO PAY

Until recently many food shops, department stores and state-run souvenir (berezhka) shops used the kassa system of payment. This involved visiting several cashier's desks and could be confusing for the uninitiated.

Nowadays, the kassa system is pretty rare in Moscow and there are hundreds of Western-type shops of all sizes. Throughout the city there are several chain stores, for example, Sedmoi Kontinent, Kopeika, Perekrestok and Ramstor. The latter offers a huge range of products from food to clothes. There are also a few hypermarkets.

The only legal currency in Russia is the rouble and most shops will not accept other currencies. Vendors at the tourist markets may quote prices in US dollars. However, this will not guarantee a discount and visitors should bear in mind that it is illegal. Now that the rampant inflation of the early 1990s is under control there should rarely be pressure to pay in hard currency.

Western-style supermarkets and shops, as well as some up-market Russian boutiques, accept the main credit cards.

A new Western boutique in Moscow's largest department store, GUM

Some shops still display prices in US dollars or, very occasionally, in units that have a fixed rate of exchange with roubles. If so the price will be converted into roubles, at a higher than average exchange rate, before payment is made. Paying by credit card avoids this as credit card slips are nearly always made out in US dollars.

Prices for most goods include 15 per cent VAT. Only staples such as locally produced milk and bread are exempt.

There are a few duty-free shops in the centre of Moscow and at Sheremetevo 2 airport.

DEPARTMENT STORES

The most famous department store in Russia is the State Department Store, known by its acronym, **GUM** (see p107). Its beautiful edifice houses three arcades of shops under a glass roof. It was built at the end of the 19th century, just before the Revolution put an end to such luxurious capitalism. During Soviet times GUM stocked the same goods as other department stores in the city and was very dingy and run-down. It has recently been renovated and now houses several top Western chains, as well as speciality shops and boutiques. Items such as cosmetics, medicines, cameras and electronic goods are all available along with clothes and household goods.

Moscow's other large department store is **TsUM**, the Central Department Store. Formerly cheaper and a little shabbier than GUM, it has now been

Replica icons on sale at the Trinity Monastery of St Sergius *(see pp162–5)*

and a little shabbier than GUM, it has now been thoroughly renovated and is too expensive for most ordinary Muscovites.

Detskiy Mir (Children's World) on Teatralnyy proezd is the largest children's store in Russia, but it is currently closed for repairs and may be turned into elite apartments. An alternative for imported and Russian educational toys, audiotapes, cartoon books and board games is **Malenkiy Genii** (Little Genius).

Souvenirs on sale at the flea market in Izmaylovo Park

BAZAARS AND MARKETS

Many Muscovites buy their cheese, meat, and fresh fruit and vegetables at one of a number of big produce markets dotted around the city. One of the biggest and most picturesque food markets is the **Danilovskiy Market**, which takes its name from the nearby Danilovskiy Monastery *(see pp136–7)*. The market at **Metro Universitet** has a wide variety of fresh produce; there is sometimes a market across the road (by the circus) in which vendors from far flung Russian regions sell produce and souvenirs. Down the road is the larger **Cherkizovskiy Market** which sells everything from produce to clothing. Also well worth a visit is the colourful **Basmannyy Market**, which is in the heart of the former Nemtskaya Sloboda (German Settlement).

Izmaylovo Market is a flea market held every weekend at Izmaylovo Park *(see p141)*. It is a treasure trove of old and new. All the usual souvenirs are on sale, including Soviet memorabilia and painted Russian *matryoshka* dolls *(see p196)*, as well as antique silver and jewellery, icons, samovars, china and glassware, fur hats, amber and some of the best Central Asian rugs in Russia. In recent years many local artists and crafts people have also set up their stalls here.

Gorbushka, an indoor market, sells a variety of electrical goods, along with DVDs and CDs.

MUSEUM SHOPS

There is a small, but excellent, souvenir shop at the **Museum of Modern History**. Its stock includes old Soviet posters, stamps and badges, amber and lacquer boxes. Both the **Pushkin Museum of Fine Art** *(see pp78–81)* and the **Tretyakov Gallery** *(see pp118–121)* sell a good selection of art books with English commentaries.

BARGAINING ETIQUETTE

Many market vendors come from long-established trading families and expect buyers to haggle. It may seem a daunting prospect, but bargaining down the price of an item can be extremely satisfying, although visitors are unlikely to get the better of these adept salesmen. Most vendors at souvenir markets speak enough English to bargain. Little, if any, English will be spoken at other markets, so a

few Russian words will certainly come in handy.

Occasionally sales people will refuse to drop their price. Try thanking them and turning to leave, to see if they will cut the price further. Their final price, whether bargained down or not, is usually reasonable by Western standards.

A stall selling fresh vegetables and herbs at the Danilovskiy Market

BUYING ANTIQUES

It is very difficult to take any items made before 1945 out of Russia *(see p200)*. All outgoing luggage is x-rayed by customs officials to check for precious metals, works of art, rugs and icons, and complete documentation for all these objects is required before they can be exported. Permission to export antiques and art can only be obtained from the **Ministry of Culture**. This process takes at least two weeks and an export tax of 50 per cent of the ministry's assessment of the antiques value will have to be paid.

It is safest to restrict purchases to items less than 50 years old. However, customs inspectors at the airport may still want to see receipts and documentation that proves the age of the objects.

Samovars and other items for sale in one of the many antiques shops along ulitsa Arbat

Where to Shop in Moscow

The days of Soviet era queues and shortages are long gone. Moscow is a modern city, full of shops, and just about everything that is available in the West is available here. The Arbat and Tverskaya are the main shopping drags, and are filled with shoppers visiting chic boutiques and other meccas of consumerism. However, high import duties, transportation costs and the relative lack of competition can make some consumer goods more expensive than in the West. The colourful Russian arts and crafts available at many locations throughout the city are popular with visitors as are exotic goods from the ex-Soviet Republics of Central Asia and memorabilia from the Soviet era.

VODKA AND CAVIAR

Russia is the best place in the world to buy vodka and caviar, but buyers must be careful. Caviar should not be bought in the street and it is advisable to buy it in tins rather than jars. Even tins should be kept refrigerated at all times. Caviar is available from most supermarkets but, for a real Russian shopping experience, go to the slightly run-down **Yeliseev's Food Hall** *(see p89)*. A pre-Revolutionary delicatessen, it was known as Gastronom No. 1 in Soviet times, and boasts chandeliers and stained-glass windows.

There is a great deal of bootleg vodka about, which can be highly poisonous. It is essential to ensure that there is a pink tax label stuck over the top of any bottle of vodka and none should ever be bought on the street. Popular vodkas such as Stolichnaya and Moskovskaya *(see p182)* are available from most supermarkets including **Sedmoi Kontinent**.

Vodka and caviar are also available at the duty-free shops at the airports *(see p216)*, but are much cheaper in town.

Russians never mix vodka, but instead eat snacks or drink juice immediately after a 'shot', to cool the aftertaste and increase endurance.

ARTS AND CRAFTS

Low labour costs mean that handmade goods are generally cheaper here than in the West and they make exotic and interesting souvenirs to take home. The best places to buy are the markets, such as the **Izmaylovo Market** *(see p193)*, and souvenir shops on ulitsa Arbat *(see pp70–71)*. Lacquer trays and bowls, painted china and *matryoshka* dolls can be bought at **Arbatskaya Lavitsa**. Handmade lace and embroidery are on sale in **Russkaya Vyshivka**, while for Russian jewellery and amber visitors should try **Samotsvety**.

A good range of arts and crafts is also available at shops elsewhere in the city, such as **Russkiy Uzory**. **Russkaya Galereia** has an exhibition of paintings for sale, as well as jewellery and lacquer boxes. For more unusual souvenirs, try **Dom Farfora**, which sells hand-painted tea sets and Russian crystal, and the **Salon of the Moscow Cultural Fund**, which has samovars, old lamps and some whimsical sculptures and mobiles.

ANTIQUES

The new Russian rich are hungry for antiques and dealers know the value of goods, so the bargains of a few years ago are no longer available. It is also worth noting that exporting objects made before 1945 from Russia involves a lot of expense and effort *(see p193)*. However, it is still well worth exploring the many wonderful shops full of treasures.

Ulitsa Arbat has many of the best antique shops in Moscow. **Serebryaniy Ryad** offers a good selection of icons, silver, jewellery and china, while **Ivantsarevich** has a variety of interesting Soviet porcelain.

For larger pieces and furniture visitors should go to the **Aleksandr Art Gallery**, and **Rokoko** which sells goods for people for a commission. **The Foreign Book Store**, which is principally a bookshop, also sells furniture and a lot of china, lamps and bric-a-brac.

FASHION AND ACCESSORIES

There are many boutiques in the centre of town around **GUM** *(see p107)*, **TsUM** *(see p192)* and **Okhotnyy Ryad**, and along Tverskaya ulitsa *(see p89)*. The centre also has two good arcades. **Petrovskiy Passage** sells clothes and shoes as well as furniture and electrical goods. **Gallery Aktyor**, a modern, three-storey arcade, contains Western and designer stores selling clothes, French perfumes and jewellery from Tiffany and Cartier. Clothes by Russian designers are gradually appearing in Moscow's shops; **Masha Tsigal** near TsUM sells clothes, handbags and sunglasses.

On the edge of the city centre is the **Atrium** shopping centre, which contains a variety of boutiques and stores, along with cafés, bars and a cinema. On the outskirts of the city are the **Mega** shopping complexes at Teply Stan and Khimki.

A wide range of authentic Russian fur hats are old in Petrovskiy Passage and on the second floor of GUM.

BOOKS AND MUSIC

For English-language books, **Dom Inostrannoi Knigi** is probably the best shop to visit. The enormous **Moscow House of Books** sells a good range of English-language books, and also old icons and Soviet propaganda posters. **Biblio Globus** is well worth having a browse in, while the **Moskva Trade House** deals in Russian and foreign books, as well as selling stamps, small antiques and paintings. For vintage and specialist music try **Transylvania**, just off Tverskaya ulitsa.

DIRECTORY

DEPARTMENT STORES

GUM
ГУМ
Krasnaya ploshchad 3.
Map 3 A5.
Tel (495) 921 5763.

Malenkiy Genii
Маленький Гении
Bolshoy Kozikhinskiy
pereulok 6.
Map 2 E4.
Tel (495) 291 2147.

Okhotnyy Ryad
Охотный Ряд
Mokhovaya ulitsa.
Map 3 A5.
Tel (495) 737 8449.

TsUM
ЦУМ
Ulitsa Petrovka 2.
Map 3 A4.
Tel (495) 292 1157.

BAZAARS AND MARKETS

Basmannyy Market
Басманный рынок
Baumanskaya ulitsa 47/1.

Cherkizovskiy Market
Черкизовский рынок
Lomonosovskiy prospekt.

Danilovskiy Market
Даниловский рынок
Mytnaya ulitsa 74.

Gorbushka
Горбушка
Barklaya ulitsa 8.

Izmaylovo Market
Рынок Измайлово
Izmaylovskoe shosse.

MUSEUM SHOPS

Museum of Modern History
Музей современной
истории
Muzey sovremennoy istorii
Tverskaya ulitsa 21.
Map 2 E4.
Tel (495) 699 5217.

Pushkin Museum of Fine Art
Музей изобразительных
искусств имени АС
Пушкина
*Muzey izobrazitelnykh
iskusstv imeni AS Pushkina*
Ulitsa Volkhonka 12.
Map 6 F2.
Tel (495) 697 7998.

Tretyakov Gallery
Третьяковская галерея
Tretyakovskaya galereya
Lavrushinskiy pereulok 12.
Map 7 A3.
Tel (495) 951 1362.

VODKA AND CAVIAR

Sedmoi Kontinent
Седьмой Континент
Bolshaya Gruzinskaya ul 63.
Map 2 D2.
Tel (495) 721 3874.

Yeliseev's Food Hall
Елисеевский гастроном
Yeliseevskiy gastronom
Tverskaya ulitsa 14.
Map 2 F4.
Tel (495) 209 0760.

ARTS AND CRAFTS

Arbatskaya Lavitsa
Арбатская Лавица
Ulitsa Arbat 27
Map 6 E1.
Tel (495) 290 5689.

Dom Farfora
Дом фарфора
Leninskiy prospekt 36.
Tel (495) 137 6023.

Russkaya Galereia
Ulitsa Vozdvizhenka 5.
Map 6 E1.
Tel (495) 203 1306.

Russkaya Vyshivka
Русская вышивка
Ulitsa Arbat 31.
Map 6 D1.
Tel (495) 241 2841.

Russkiy Uzory
Русские узоры
Ulitsa Petrovka 16.
Map 3 A4.
Tel (495) 923 1883.

Salon of the Moscow Cultural Fund
Салон Московского
фонда культуры
*Salon Moskovskovo
fonda kultury*
Pyatnitskaya ulitsa 16.
Map 7 B3.

Tel (495) 951 3302.

Samotsvety
Самоцветы
Ulitsa Arbat 35.
Map 6 D1.
Tel (495) 241 0765.

ANTIQUES

Aleksandr Art Gallery
Александр Арт Галерея
Traditsiya i lichnost
Ulitsa Arbat 2,
2nd floor. **Map** 6 E1.
Tel (495) 690 6294.

Ivantsarevich
Иванцаревич
Ulitsa Arbat 4.
Map 6 F1.
Tel (495) 691 7444.

Ministry of Culture
Министерство культуры
Malyy Gnezdnikovskiy
97/6.
Tel (495) 629 2008.

Rokoko
Рококо
Frunzenskaya nab 54.
Tel (495) 242 3684.

Serebryaniy Ryad
Серебряный Ряд
Arbat 23.
Map 6 D1.
Tel (495) 691 7308.

FASHION AND ACCESSORIES

Atrium
Атриум
33 Zemlyanoi Val.
Tel (495) 775 2356.

Gallery Aktyor
Галерея Актер
Tverskaya ulitsa 16/2.
Map 2 F4.
Tel (495) 290 9832.

Masha Tsigal
Маша Цигал
Pokrovka Ulitsa 11.
Map 3 C5.
Tel (495) 915 8464.

Mega
Мега
Mega Teply Stan
Kaluzhskoe shosse,
Teply Stan.
Tel (495) 933 7450.

Mega Khimki
Leningradskoye shosse,
Khimki.
Tel (495) 221 1390.

Petrovskiy Passage
Петровский Пассаж
Ulitsa Petrovka 10.
Map 3 A4.
Tel (495) 928 5012.

BOOKS AND MUSIC

Biblio Globus
Библио Глобус
Miasnitskaya ul. 6.
Map 3 B5.
Tel (495) 781 1900.

Dom Inostrannoi Knigi
Дом Иностранной Книги
Ulitsa Kuznetskiy most 18.
Map 3 A4.
Tel (495) 628 2021.

The Foreign Book Store
Иностранная Книга
Inostrannaya kniga
Malaya Nikitskaya ul 16/5.
Map 2 D5.
Tel (495) 290 4082.

Moskva Trade House
Торговый дом Москва
Torgovyy dom Moskva
Tverskaya ulitsa 8.
Map 2 F4.
Tel (495) 629 6483.

Moscow House of Books
Московский
Дом книги
Moskovskiy Dom knigi
Ulitsa Novyy Arbat 8.
Map 6 D1.
Tel (495) 789 3591.

Transylvania
Трансильвания
Tverskaya ulitsa 6/1, 5.
Map 2 F5.
Tel (495) 629 8786.

What to Buy in Moscow

Intricate wooden box

It is easy to find interesting and beautiful souvenirs in Moscow. Traditional crafts were encouraged by the State in the old Soviet Union, so many age-old skills were kept alive. Artisans today continue to produce items ranging from small, low-cost, enamelled badges through to more expensive hand-painted Palekh boxes, samovars and worked semi-precious stones. Other popular items are lacquered trays and bowls, chess sets, wooden toys and *matryoshka* dolls. Memorabilia from the Soviet era also make good souvenirs and Russia is definitely the best place to buy the national specialities, vodka and caviar.

Vodka and Caviar

An enormous variety of both clear and flavoured vodkas (such as lemon and pepper) is available (see p182). They make excellent accompaniments to black caviar (ikra) and red caviar (keta), which are often served with blini.

Flavoured vodka

Clear vodka

Red caviar

Black caviar

Samovar

Used to boil water to make tea, samovars (see p183) come in many sizes. A permit is needed to export a pre-1945 samovar.

Malachite egg

Amber ring

Semi-precious Stones

Malachite, amber, jasper and a variety of marbles from the Ural mountains are used to make a wide range of items – everything from jewellery to chess sets and inlaid table tops.

Wooden Toys

These crudely carved wooden toys often have moving parts. They are known as bogorodskie toys and make charming gifts.

Matryoshka Dolls

These dolls fit one inside the other and come in a huge variety of styles. The traditional dolls are the prettiest, but the models painted to represent Soviet political leaders are also very popular.

Chess Sets

Chess is an extremely popular pastime in Russia. Chess sets made from all kinds of materials, including malachite, are available. This beautiful wooden set is painted in the same folkloric style as the traditional matryoshka dolls.

LACQUERED ARTIFACTS

Painted wooden or papier-mâché artifacts make popular souvenirs and are sold all over the city. The exquisite hand-painted, lacquered Palekh boxes can be very costly, but the eggs decorated with icons and the typical red, black and gold bowls are more affordable.

Palekh Box

The art of miniature painting on papier-mâché items originated in the late 18th century. Artists in the four villages of Palekh, Fedoskino, Mstera and Kholuy still produce these hand-painted marvels. The images are based on Russian fairytales and legends.

Painted wooden egg

Bowl with Spoon
The brightly painted bowls and spoons usually known as "Khokhloma" have a lacquer coating, forming a surface which is durable, but not resistant to boiling liquids.

Russian hand-painted tray

Tuners   **Strings**

Traditional Musical Instruments
Russian folk music uses a wide range of musical instruments. This gusli is similar to the Western psaltery, and is played by plucking the strings with both hands. Also available are the balalaika and the garmon, which resembles a concertina.

Russian Shawl
These brilliantly coloured, traditional woollen shawls are good for keeping out the cold of a Russian winter. Mass-produced polyester versions are also available, mostly in big department stores, but they will not be as warm.

Soviet Memorabilia
A wide array of memorabilia from Soviet times can be bought. Old banknotes, coins, pocket watches and all sorts of Red Army kit, including belt buckles and badges, can be found, together with more recent watches with cartoons of KGB agents on their faces.

Pocket watch

Gzhel Vase
Ceramics with a distinctive blue and white pattern are produced in Gzhel, a town near Moscow. Ranging from figurines to household crockery, they are popular with Russians and visitors alike.

Badge with Soviet symbols

Red Army leather belt

ENTERTAINMENT IN MOSCOW

Moscow offers many forms of entertainment, from great theatre productions, operas and ballets to a wide choice of lively nightlife venues. Attending a performance at the Bolshoy (see pp90–91) remains a must for opera and ballet buffs, although the main stage is closed while undergoing refurbishment. Other theatres put on an enormous range of productions, including musicals

A neon sign advertising one of Moscow's casinos (see p202)

and shows for children. Moscow has several cinemas screening foreign-language films. They usually show the latest releases only a few weeks after they are premiered in the West. The city also has over 300 nightclubs and many late-night bars, some of which have live bands. In addition, there is plenty of free entertainment from street performers, especially on ulitsa Arbat (see pp70–71).

A performance of the opera *Boris Godunov* at the Bolshoy Theatre

PRACTICAL INFORMATION

Moscow does not have any conventional tourist information offices. However, listings for events such as films, plays, concerts and exhibitions, together with extensive lists of restaurants and nightclubs can be found in the Friday edition of the English-language newspaper *The Moscow Times*. Restaurants and nightclubs are also listed in the English-language *Moscow News*. Both are free and available at large hotels. Those who can read Russian can take advantage of the magazines *Afisha* and *Dozug*, both of which have comprehensive listings sections.

Visitors should note that the safest way to get back from late-night events is in an official taxi booked in advance (see p220).

BOOKING TICKETS

By far the easiest way to book tickets for a concert, a ballet, an opera or the theatre is through one of

the main international hotels, even for visitors not staying there. Both Western-style and Russian-run hotels will usually offer this service. However, tickets bought in this way are often more expensive than those available elsewhere. Ticket-booking desks in

hotels accept payment by major credit cards, but many will charge a fee for doing so. Visitors who speak Russian will be able to buy cheaper tickets from a theatre ticket kiosk (teatralnaya kassa). These kiosks are scattered all round the city and in metro stations. A particularly useful ticket agency is located on Theatre Square (see p88).

Another alternative is to book tickets at the venues. Although these tickets are usually the cheapest, it can require a lot of

Posters for theatre performances

THE MOSCOW STATE CIRCUS

Russians have always loved the circus. In the 18th and 19th centuries it was the most popular theatrical entertainment. Troupes travelled round the country performing mostly satirical shows. Today the renowned Moscow State Circus has its permanent home in Moscow. It is famous for its clowns, the breathtaking stunts of its acrobats and trapeze artists and its performing animals. The latter often include tigers jumping through burning hoops and bears riding bicycles, and animal-lovers should be aware that they may find some acts distressing. The original venue, now known as the **Old Circus**, was built in 1880 by Albert Salamonskiy for his private troupe. Salamonskiy's Circus became the Moscow State Circus in 1919. The **New Circus** was built in 1973. Both venues are now in use.

The big top of the New Circus, second venue of the Moscow State Circus patience to obtain them since ticket offices are often open at unpredictable hours.

There are ticket touts outside most events, especially those at the Bolshoy Theatre. However, there is a risk that their tickets are counterfeit and they will almost certainly be overpriced.

CHILDREN'S ENTERTAINMENT

Traditional Russian entertainments for children have always included the puppet theatre, the zoo and the circus. Moscow has two puppet theatres: the **Obraztsov Puppet Theatre** (see p200), which puts on matinee performances for children, and the **Moscow Puppet Theatre**. The **Nataliya Sats Children's Musical Theatre** performs excellent shows, great for children of all ages.

The **Russian Academic Youth Theatre** (see p88) puts on a range of performances suitable for children from the age of seven.

Moscow Zoo is a great favourite but, unfortunately, the

animals often look underfed and cramped in their cages.

At **Arlecchino Children's Club** children can play with toys and computer games or be entertained by clowns.

Miracle City at Gorky Park is an outdoor, Western-style amusement complex, which opens from late spring until late October. Children under 1.2 m (4 ft) tall are given free entry to all the children's rides, which include merry-go-rounds, trains and mini racing cars. There are also more high-octane rides, such as roller coasters.

Also in Gorky Park is the **Buran Shuttle**, a space shuttle that, since its one unmanned test flight, has been converted into a simulator. Would-be astronauts can also sample the tubes of foods, such as soups and pâtés, that cosmonauts typically eat.

A scene from the story of Noah's Ark being performed at the Moscow Puppet Theatre

Paddle boats, one of the many attractions on offer in Gorky Park

SPECTATOR SPORTS

Traditionally, the most popular sports in Russia are football and hockey. Important matches and championships are held at the **Dynamo Central House of Sports**, the **Luzhniki Stadium** and the **Olympic Sports Complex**. On the whole, Moscow's football grounds are safe, although hooliganism is beginning to become a problem. Krylatskoye also has a race course and a canal where rowing races take place. The Olympic Sports Complex is Moscow's main venue for tennis tournaments.

DIRECTORY

CHILDREN'S ENTERTAINMENT

Arlecchino Children's Club
Детский клуб Арлекино
Verkhnyaya Radishchevskaya ul 19/3, stroenie 1.
Map 8 E3.
Tel (495) 915 1106.

Buran Shuttle
Космический корабль Буран
Gorky Park, ulitsa Krymskiy val 9.
Map 6 F4.
Tel (495) 637 0832.

Miracle City
Миргрд
Gorky Park, ulitsa Krymskiy val 9.
Map 6 F4.
Tel (495) 636 3112.

Moscow Puppet Theatre
Московский кукольный театр
Spartakovskaya ulitsa 26.
Map 4 F2. **Tel** (495) 261 2197.

Moscow Zoo
Зоопарк
Bolshaya Gruzinskaya ul 1.
Map 1 C4. **Tel** (495) 252 3580.

Nataliya Sats Children's Musical Theatre
Детский музыкальный театр имени Наталии Сац
Vernadskovo prospekt 5.
Near Sparrow Hills (see p129). **Tel** (495) 930 7021.

New Circus
Новый цирк
Vernadskovo prospekt 7.

Near Sparrow Hills (see p129). **Tel** (495) 930 0272.

Obraztsov Puppet Theatre
Кукольный театр имени Образцова
Ulitsa Sadovaya-Samotechnaya 3. **Map** 3 A2. **Tel** (495) 299 5373.

Old Circus
Старый цирк
Tsvetnoy bulvar 13. **Map** 3 A3. **Tel** (495) 625 0668.
www.circusnikulin.ru

Russian Academic Youth Theatre
Российский академический молодёжный театр
Teatralnaya ploshchad 2.
Map 3 A5.
Tel (495) 292 0069.

SPECTATOR SPORTS

Dynamo Central House of Sports
Динамо – Центральный дворец спорта
Lavochkina ulitsa 32.
Tel (495) 453 6501.

Luzhniki Stadium
Лужники
Luzhnenskay Nab 24.
Tel (495) 637 0764.

Olympic Sports Complex
Спортивный олимпийский комплекс
Olimpiyskiy prospekt 16.
Map 3 A1.
Tel (495) 288 1533.

The Arts in Moscow

From June until late September most of Moscow's concert halls and theatres close and the city's orchestras, theatre and ballet companies perform elsewhere in Russia and abroad. However, for the rest of the year the city has a rich and varied cultural scene. The Bolshoy Theatre (see pp90–91), Moscow's oldest and most famous opera and ballet house, offers an impressive repertoire. Numerous drama theatres put on a variety of plays in Russian, ranging from the conventional to the avant-garde. For non-Russian speakers there is a wide choice of events, ranging from folk dance and gypsy music to classical concerts by top international musicians. Evening performances at most venues begin at 7pm or 7:30pm, while matinées generally start around midday.

Moscow's most prestigious classical music gathering is the annual Svyatoslav Richter December Nights Festival (see p35). Held in the Pushkin Museum of Fine Arts (see pp78–81), the concerts attract a star-studded array of Russian and foreign musicians.

In summer both indoor and outdoor concerts are held outside Moscow at Kuskovo (see pp142–3) on Tuesday and Thursday evenings.

THEATRE

Moscow has more than 60 theatres, most of which are repertory. This means that a different production is staged every night. Listings can be found in the Friday edition of The Moscow Times or in The Exile (see p215).

BALLET AND OPERA

There are numerous venues in Moscow where visitors can see high-quality ballet and opera. Undoubtedly the most famous is the **Bolshoy Theatre**, originally built in 1780. Despite two major fires, the building remains impressive and stands on its original site. Today the Bolshoy is still the best venue in Moscow in which to see opera and ballet. Its magnificent main auditorium accommodates some 2,500 people. World-famous ballets, including Giselle by Adolphe Adam and Swan Lake and The Nutcracker by Pyotr Tchaikovsky, have been danced here by the company. The theatre's operatic repertoire includes a number of works by Russian composers. Among them are Boris Godunov by Modest Mussorgsky, The Queen of Spades and Eugene Onegin by Pyotr Tchaikovsky, and Sadko by Nikolai Rimsky-Korsakov.

Another much younger company, the Kremlin Ballet Company, can be seen at the **State Kremlin Palace** (see p56) in the Kremlin. This gigantic steel and glass building, originally constructed in 1961 as a convention hall for the Communist Party, has a 6,000-seat auditorium. It is a prime venue for those wishing to see visiting Western opera singers, as well as for ballet.

Less grandiose, but nevertheless high-quality, operas and ballets are performed at the **Helicon Opera**, the **Novaya Opera** and the **Stanislavskiy and Nemirovich-Danchenko**

Musical Theatre. As its name implies, the **Operetta Theatre** performs operettas, while the **Gnesin Music Academy Opera Studio** stages more experimental productions.

CLASSICAL MUSIC

Moscow has a strong tradition of classical music and has long been home to several top international music events. One of Moscow's most famous classical music venues is the **Tchaikovsky Concert Hall**. The main feature of this large circular auditorium is a giant pipe organ, which has 7,800 pipes and weighs approximately 20 tonnes. It was made in Czechoslovakia and was installed in 1959.

The **Moscow Conservatory** (see p94) is both an educational establishment and a venue for concerts of classical music. It was founded in 1866 and Pyotr Tchaikovsky (see p159), then a young composer at the beginning of his brilliant career, taught here for 12 years. Nowadays the conservatory has more than 1,000 music students at any one time.

The Bolshoy Zal (Great Hall) is used for orchestral concerts, both by the conservatory's resident orchestra and visiting orchestras. The Malyy Zal (Small Hall) is used for recitals by smaller ensembles. Over the years many prominent musicians have performed here and every four years the conservatory plays host to the prestigious Tchaikovsky International Competition (see p33).

The **Moscow Arts Theatre** (see p92) stages a wide repertoire, but it is particularly famous for its productions of Anton Chekhov's plays, such as The Seagull. In contrast, the **Lenkom Theatre** produces musicals and plays by contemporary Russian writers. Russia's first drama theatre, the **Malyy Theatre**, across the street from the Bolshoy, played a major role in the development of Russian theatre.

The **Obraztsov Puppet Theatre** (see p199) is as entertaining for adults as it is for children. It was founded in 1931 and is named after its first director, Sergey Obraztsov. The theatre's repertoire is outstanding and most of the plays can be enjoyed without a knowledge of the Russian language. Evening performances may only be open to those over the age of 18.

Performances at the **Gypsy Theatre** consist of traditional gypsy dancing and singing. Performances of Russian folk dancing are held at various venues throughout Moscow.

The **Taganka Theatre**, favourite of Russian president Vladimir Putin, has some excellent productions such as works by Mikhail Bulgakov. The **Mossoviet Theatre** is also among the city's best, showing alternative interpretations of Shakespeare and excellent productions of Russian classics.

FILM

The Russian film industry flourished under the Soviet regime and Lenin (see p28) himself recognized the value of films for conveying messages. Specially commissioned films shown throughout Russia on modified trains, for example, informed much of the rural population that there had been a revolution in the capital.

Until the Soviet Union's collapse in 1991, the film industry was run by the state. Films were subsidized and their subject matter closely monitored. Russian film-makers now have artistic freedom, but suffer from a shortage of funding. Cinemas show both Hollywood blockbusters and Russian releases. After a period of stagnation, Russian cinema is enjoying a real boom, and domestically produced films are now more popular than imports.

Many cinemas have out-of-date equipment, muffled sound and uncomfortable seats, but two central Russian-language cinemas, the **Rossiya** and the **Udarnik**, offer digital sound and good facilities. The **Arts Cinema** is one of the oldest in Moscow. Its sound system is not as good as those at the Rossiya and the Udarnik, but it remains one of the city's most popular cinemas. It shows the latest Russian releases and Western films in Russian. For English language cinema, the **Oktyabp** and **35mm** are the only options within the city centre. The Oktyabp is a modern multi-screen cinema showing foreign language films in Hall 11. There are also a number of cafés on the premises. 35mm screens various films in English. Outside the centre **Kinostar De Lux** at Mega in Khimki (see p195) offers screenings in a modern Western-style cinema.

Films from Europe and India can be seen in their original languages at the **Illuzion** and the **Cinema Centre**. The latter is also the venue for the Moscow International Film Festival (see p33).

Tickets for films can only be bought at the cinemas themselves. At most, payment is in cash.

DIRECTORY

BALLET AND OPERA

Bolshoy Theatre
Большой театр Teatralnaya ploshchad 1. **Map** 3 A4.
Tel (495) 250 7317.
www.bolshoi.ru

Gnesin Music Academy Opera Studio
Оперная студия академии музыки имени I Нёсиных
Povarskaya ulitsa 30/36.
Map 2 D5.
Tel (495) 290 2422.

Helicon Opera
Геликон опера
Bolshaya Nikitskaya ulitsa 19. **Map** 2 E5.
Tel (495) 290 0971.
www.helikon.ru

Novaya Opera
Новая опера
Novyy Arbat 11. **Map** 6 D1. **Tel** (495) 694 0868.
www.novayaopera.ru

Operetta Theatre
Театр оперетты
Ulitsa Bolshaya Dmitrovka 6. **Map** 3 A4.
Tel (495) 292 1237.

State Kremlin Palace
Государственный Кремлёвский дворец
Gosudarstvennyy Kremlevskiy Dvorets
Kremlin. **Map** 7 A1.
Tel (495) 917 2336.

Stanislavskiy and Nemirovich-Danchenko Musical Theatre
Музыкальный театр имени Станиславского и Немировича-Данченко
Ulitsa Bolshaya Dmitrovka 17.
Map 2 F4.
Tel (495) 629 2835.

CLASSICAL MUSIC

Moscow Conservatory
Московская консерватория
Bolshaya Nikitskaya ulitsa 1. **Map** 2 F5.
Tel (495) 629 9401.
www. mosconsv.ru

Tchaikovsky Concert Hall
Концертный зал имени ПИ Чайковского
Triumfalnaya ploshchad 4/31.
Map 2 E3.
Tel (495) 299 3681.

THEATRE

Gypsy Theatre
Театр ромэн
Teatr romen
Leningradskiy prospekt 32/2.
Map 1 B1.
Tel (495) 251 8522.

Lenkom Theatre
Театр Ленком
Ulitsa Malaya Dmitrovka 6. **Map** 2 F3.
Tel (495) 299 0708.
www.lenkom.ru

Malyy Theatre
Малый театр
Teatralnaya ploshchad 1/6.
Map 3 A5.
Tel (495) 923 2621.

Moscow Arts Theatre
МХАТ имени АП Чехова
MKhAT imeni AP Chekhova
Kamergerskiy pereulok 3.
Map 2 F5.
Tel (495) 229 8760.

Mossoviet Theatre
Театр им. Моссовета
Bolshaya Sadovaya 16.
Map 2 D3.
Tel (495) 699 2035.

Taganka Theatre
Театр на Таганке
Zemlyanoy val 76.
Map 4 D4.
Tel (495) 915 1015.

FILM

35mm
Ulitsa Pokrovka 47/24.
Map 4 D4.
Tel (495) 917 5492.

Arts Cinema
Художественный кино
Khudozhestvennyy kino
Arbatskaya ploshchad 14.
Map 6 E1.
Tel (495) 291 5598.

Cinema Centre
Киноцентр
Druzhinnikovskaya ulitsa 15.
Map 1 C5.
Tel (495) 205 7306.
www.kinocenter.ru

Illuzion
Иллюзион
Kotelnicheskaya naberezhnaya 1/15
Map 8 D2.
Tel (495) 915 4339.

Kinostar De Lux
Mega Khimki, Mega Teply Stan.
Tel (495) 775 4477.

Oktyabp
Октябрь
Novyy Arbat 24.
Map 6 D1.
Tel (495) 545 0505.
www.karo.ru

Rossiya
Россия
Pushkinskaya ploshchad 2.
Map 2 F4.
Tel (495) 229 2111.

Udarnik
Ударник
Ulitsa Serafimovicha 2.
Map 7 A3.
Tel (495) 795 3795.

Music and Nightlife

Under the Communist regime, Moscow's nightlife was practically non-existent and those clubs and bars that did exist were for a privileged elite. Today, nightlife in Moscow is booming. Foreign bands, DJs and performers of all types now visit the city regularly, while the quality of the domestic scene has improved markedly. The variety of venues is similarly impressive and ranges from bars where you can see local rock bands to glitzy casinos and late-night clubs playing the latest techno music. The Russian take on modern dance music is noteworthy, as Russians like to party hard and long into the night. Venues can be packed and prices high, but it is an experience not to be missed.

ROCK VENUES

After years of being isolated from major Western pop and rock acts, Muscovites can at last get to see big-name artists in the flesh. Many of the more famous acts from abroad, as well as the best in local talent, play at clubs such as **Apelsin**, **Tochka** and **Sixteen Tons**. Apelsin is a fairly commercial venue with its own sushi bar and bowling alley attached. Tochka caters more to the student crowd, while Sixteen Tons favours alternative and indie music.

Among the smaller venues, **Bunker**, **Kitaiskiy Lyotchik Djao Da**, **Gogol**, **Art Garbage** and **Ikra** showcase less well known acts. Djao Da is good for acoustic music; Bunker, Ikra and Art Garbage are slightly larger and have a more sophisticated feel.

Major rock concerts usually take place at either **Olympiiskiy Stadium** or **Luzhniki Stadium**.

JAZZ, BLUES AND LATIN VENUES

Moscow has a vibrant jazz and blues scene, with clubs such as **B2** featuring a live act most evenings. B2 is a one-stop shop for a night out and also has a pool hall, sushi bar and a disco. Other clubs worth checking out are **Woodstock MKhat** and **Roadhouse**; both put on good live music, including acts from abroad. Moscow's best club for jazz and blues is **Le Club**, but it's also the priciest.

Cabana, a Brazilian bar and restaurant, is a good bet for Latin American bands and hosts lively Salsa nights, as does **Che**. Head to **Zhisn Zemelyatin Lyudi**, a friendly venue, which has live swing bands several times a week.

NIGHTCLUBS AND DISCOS

The range of clubs to be found in Moscow is now on a par with other major capital cities and new clubs open every month. As elsewhere, nothing really gets going until around 11pm. Entrance is usually cheaper or free before this time although the queues can be long. Most clubs don't close until 4am; some are open until 6am at weekends.

Domestic preference is still for bass-heavy house music, with trance also becoming popular. For those who love more mainstream pop and disco, there are large clubs such as **XIII** offering a relaxed vibe and midweek student nights. Foreign DJs often perform at clubs such as **Propaganda** and **Fabrique**. Propaganda is one of the best known clubs, and plays a variety of styles from the latest electronic sounds to old school disco. Fabrique plays mostly house music. House music is blended with more up-tempo Latin beats at **Karma Bar**, while **Kult** offers more urban grooves, including drum & bass and four-to-the-floor techno.

A number of Moscow's leading clubs, such as **A Priori** and **Slava**, cater to Moscow's "new-rich", with prices and cover charges to match. Slava is located away from the centre in a large complex and is worth a visit, if only to spot the partying catwalk models and Russian gangsters.

The welcoming **Doug and Marty's Boar House** and **Papa Johns** are more akin to low-key boozers than full-on nightclubs.

Keep in mind that many of Moscow's clubs have an unspoken dress code. Gone are the days when simply being Western was enough to gain entry to any club and the more upmarket venues are likely to look unfavourably on anyone wearing trainers and jeans. At some of the smaller clubs, however, such as Kult, looking too neat could also result in getting turned away by the doormen.

ART CAFÉS

Some of the city's more unusual clubs are the so-called "art cafés", such as **Art Garbage** or **Bilingua**, which promote an eclectic mix of entertainment. One night there might be live music, and the next an alternative fashion show or an avant-garde film. **Krizis Zhana** has live music and poetry in a cramped but friendly setting. The bohemian **FAQ Café** is a warren of cosy rooms and features concerts on weekends. Many of the art cafés are also good places to visit for a relaxed meal (see p191).

CASINOS

Moscow has some fantastic casinos. Visitors should exercise caution, however, as there are also numerous unsavoury ones, which are best avoided. New Russians love to gamble, and entrance fees and chip prices can be steep. Even if you don't intend to play, it can be entertaining to visit and soak up the atmosphere. Casinos worthy of note include **Shangri La**, which has excellent entertainment, **New York**, **Jazz Town** and the **Udarnik Casino**. None are cheap, but all are safe and foreigner-friendly.

DIRECTORY

ROCK VENUES

Apelsin
Апельсин
Malaya
Gruzinskaya 15.
Map 1 B4.
Tel (495) 253 0253.

Art Garbage
Запасник
Starosadskiy
pereulok 5/6.
Map 3 C5.
Tel (495) 928 8745.
www.art-garbage.ru

Bunker
Бункер
Tverskaya ulitsa 12.
Map 2 F4.
Tel (495) 200 1506.

Gogol
Stoleshnikov
pereulok 11.
Map 3 A4.
Tel (495) 514 0944.
www.gogolclubs.ru

Ikra
Икра
Ulitsa Kazakova 8.
Map 4 E4.
Tel (495) 262 1182.

Kitaiskiy Lyotchik Djao Da
Китайский Летчик
Джао Да
Lubyansky proezd 25/12.
Map 3 B5.
Tel (495) 924 5611.
www.jao-da.ru

Luzhniki Stadium
Лужники (Большая арена)
Luzhnetskaya
Nabarezhnaya 24.
Tel (495) 637 0764.

Olympiiskiy Stadium
Олимпийский Стадион
Olympiyskiy Prospekt 16.
Map 3 B1.
Tel (495) 688 5322.

Sixteen Tons
Шестнадцать тонн
Presnenskiy val 6.
Map 1 B4.
Tel (495) 253 5300.
www.16tons.ru

Tochka
Точка
Leninskiy prospekt.
Map 6 F5.
Tel (495) 737 7666.

JAZZ, BLUES AND LATIN VENUES

B2
Б2
Bolshaya Sadovaya
ulitsa 8.
Map 2 D3.
Tel (495) 650 9918.
www.b2club.ru

Cabana
Кабана
Raushskaya nab 4.
Map 7 B2.
Tel (495) 638 5006.

Che
Че
Nikolskaya ulitsa 10/2
Map 3 A5.
Tel (495) 921 7477.

Le Club
Bolshaya Radishevskaya
ulitsa 21. **Map** 8 F3.
Tel (495) 915 1042.

Roadhouse
Дом у Дороги
Ulitsa Dovatora 8
Map 3 B5.
Tel (495) 245 5543.
www.roadhouse.ru

Woodstock MKhat
Kamergerskiy
pereulok 3
Map 2 F5.
Tel (495) 292 0934.

Zhisn Zemelyatin Lyudi
Жизнь замечательных
людей
Sadovaya-
Chernogryazskaya 8/23.
Map 4 D3.
Tel (495) 608 2934.

NIGHTCLUBS AND DISCOS

XIII
Myasnitskaya ulitsa 13.
Map 3 B4.
Tel (495) 928 4747.

A Priori
Bolshaya Molchanovka
ulitsa 12/1.
Map 6 E1.
Tel (495) 291 7783.

Doug and Marty's Boar House
Zemlyanoy val ulitsa 26.
Map 8 E1.
Tel (495) 917 0150.

Fabrique
Sadovnicheskaya
ulitsa 33.
Map 7 B2.
Tel (495) 953 6576.

Karma Bar
Карма-бар
Pushechnaya ulitsa 3.
Map 3 A4.
Tel (495) 924 5633.

Krizis Zhanra
Кризис жанра
Ulitsa Pokrovka 16/16.
Tel (495) 623 2595.

Kult
Культ
Ulitsa Yauzskaya 5.
Map 8 D2.
Tel (495) 917 5706.

Papa Johns
Папа Джонс
Ulitsa Myasnitskaya 22.
Map 3 B4.
Tel (495) 755 0564.

Propaganda
Пропаганда
Bolshoy Zlatoustinskiy
pereulok 7.
Map 3 B5.
Tel (495) 924 5732.
www.propaganda
moscow.com

Slava
Слава
Shosse Entuziastov 58.
Tel (495) 672 3333.

ART CAFÉS

Art Garbage
Запасник
Starosadskiy
pereulok 5/6.
Map 3 C5.
Tel (495) 928 8745.

Bilingua
Krivokolennyy
pereulok, 10/5.
Map 3 B4.
Tel (495) 623 9660.
www.bilingua-club.ru

Bunker
Бункер
Tverskaya ulitsa 12.
Map 2 F4.
Tel (495) 200 1506.

FAQ Café
Gazetnyy pereulok 9/2.
Map 2 F5.
Tel (495) 629 0827.
www.faqcafe.ru

CASINOS

Jazz Town
Taganskaya
ploshchad 12.
Map 8 E3.
Tel (495) 912 5726.

New York
Казино Нью-Йорк
Bolshaya Sadovaya
ulitsa 5/1 (inside the
Peking Hotel).
Map 2 D3
Tel (495) 924 9333.

Shangri La
Pushkinskaya
ploshchad 2.
Map 2 F4.
Tel (495) 229 0003.
www.shangrila.ru

Udarnik Casino
Казино Ударник
Serafimovicha ulitsa 2.
Map 7 A3.
Tel (495) 258 8150.

SURVIVAL
GUIDE

PRACTICAL INFORMATION 206–215

GETTING TO MOSCOW 216–219

GETTING AROUND MOSCOW 220–227

PRACTICAL INFORMATION

Moscow is not as difficult for visitors to find their way around as it may seem at first. Certainly, the city is vast, street names and signs are in Cyrillic, and the traffic can be formidably heavy, especially in the centre. On the other hand, there is an excellent metro system, and passers-by and people working in hotels, restaurants and shops will usually help foreigners. However, it is a good idea for visitors to familiarize themselves with the Cyrillic alphabet in order to decipher signs.

**Sign for the
Intourist agency**

With tourism still a fledgling industry in Moscow, some tourist facilities, such as information services, are fairly basic. The first port of call for visitors wanting information about events and practicalities should be their hotel. Surprisingly, Moscow can be one of the most expensive cities in the world to visit. While public transport is cheap, hotels, restaurants and theatre tickets can cost more than their Western equivalents. It is always worth enquiring about the price before booking something.

Information desk run by concierge in the Baltschug Kempinski Hotel

TOURIST INFORMATION

There are no conventional tourist information offices in Moscow, so hotels are the main source of guidance for visitors. Concierges in Western-style hotels, such as the Radisson-Slavyanskaya, National, Baltschug Kempinski and Metropol (see pp174–7), will provide assistance. All the large hotels, both Western-style and Russian-run, will book theatre tickets, but will add commission. Most also have a flight-booking service, accepting payment by credit card, or will put visitors in touch with a travel agency. The advice of Russian-run hotels on sights and restaurants is often indifferent, but the English-language press (see p215), particularly The Moscow Times and The Exile, has details of most exhibitions, events and opening hours.

GUIDED TOURS AND EXCURSIONS

Hotels can book places on group guided tours and day trips in several languages. Alternatively, agencies, such as **Intourist** in the UK, offer a wide range of themed tours, including trips around the city and special trips to more out-of-the-way places. **Patriarshiy Dom Tours** in Moscow

organizes tours in English, including trips around the KGB Museum, the Kremlin and State Armoury, as well as hiking expeditions. Tours should generally be booked at least 48 hours in advance.

ADMISSION CHARGES

Many museums and theatres charge foreigners considerably higher admission fees than Russians, although still well within European and North American norms. Those that do include the Tretyakov Gallery (see pp118–21), the State Armoury (see pp64–5), the Pushkin Museum of Fine Arts (see pp78–81) and the Bolshoy Theatre (see pp90–91). Schoolchildren and students (see p208) are entitled to discounts. Credit cards are never accepted at sights.

The ticket office, recognizable by the кacca (kassa) sign, is often some distance away from the entrance to the sight; staff at the entrance will point you in its direction.

**Tour operator in Red Square
signing up visitors for excursions**

Tour bus operated by the Intourist agency

A woman leaving church after a service, appropriately dressed in a headscarf

OPENING HOURS

Most museums have standard opening hours, from 10 or 10:30am to 6pm, but ticket offices may close earlier than the museums. The majority of museums close one day a week and one day a month for cleaning. All museums open on Sundays. Some cathedrals and churches are always open, but others only open for services.

Sign for open (*otkryto*)

Sign for closed (*zakryto*)

VISITING CHURCHES

Attending an Orthodox church service is a fascinating experience. The most important services take place on Saturday evenings and Sunday mornings, and on religious holidays. In general, services run for several hours. Russian churches do not have any chairs, and the congregation is expected to stand. It is acceptable for visitors to drop in on a service for a while, but certain dress rules

must be observed. Shorts are not acceptable. Men must remove their hats, while women should cover their chest and shoulders and preferably wear a headscarf or hat. Although acceptable in town churches, women wearing trousers are likely to be refused entry to monasteries.

LANGUAGE

Cyrillic is the alphabet of the Russian language. It is named after Cyril *(see p17)*, the monk who in 860–70 invented the alphabet from which it developed. Various systems for transliterating Cyrillic into Roman characters *(see p252)* exist, but they do not differ enough to cause confusion.

Many Russians who regularly come into contact with visitors can speak some English. However, a knowledge of even one or two words of Russian *(see pp260–64)* on the part of visitors will be taken as a sign of respect and much appreciated.

ETIQUETTE

Russian manners and attitudes are becoming more Westernized, but the linguistic distinction between the formal "you" *(vy)* and informal "you" *(ty)* remains strictly in force. On public transport, young men are expected to give up their seats to the elderly or families with young children.

Smoking and drinking are popular pastimes. Frequent toasts are required to justify the draining of glasses. When invited to someone's home, the toast *za khozyayku* (to the hostess) or *za khozyaina* (to the host) should always be offered by the visitor.

Many Russians are superstitious. Most prefer not to shake hands across the threshold of a doorway and, if someone accidentally steps on a friend's toes, the injured party pretends to step back on the perpetrator's toes.

Sign on a block of flats giving a *podezd* number

PAYING AND TIPPING

Roubles are the only valid currency in Russia *(see p213)*. Some large shops and hotels may display prices in US dollars or euros, but all cash payments must be in roubles only. Credit cards are accepted in some restaurants and most hotels, but rarely in shops, except for those selling imported goods at much higher prices than abroad.

Tipping is a matter of choice, but baggage handlers at the airport and train stations may ask exorbitant sums. Visitors should simply pay what they consider to be appropriate.

ADDRESSES

Russian addresses are given in the following order: post code, city, street name, house *(dom)* number and, finally, apartment *(kvartira)* number. If a flat is part of a complex, a *korpus (k)* number will also be given to indicate which block it is in. When visiting a flat, it is useful to know which entrance *(podezd)* to the block to use.

After the Revolution of 1917, many streets were renamed to avoid imperial connotations or to commemorate new Soviet heroes. Since perestroika most streets in the centre have officially reverted to their pre-1917 names. This initially caused confusion as people would use the Soviet names, forgetting that street signs now show the original ones. However, such post-Soviet confusion is now a thing of the past.

Six-figure post (or index) code

Street name

House number

Apartment number

Name

VISAS

Visitors from almost all countries will need a visa. Only those from CIS member states (excluding the Baltic states) are exempt. All visitors travelling to Moscow should check their requirements before departing; those arriving by train will also need a transit visa for Belarus. Visa formalities are confusing. In the UK there are three types: business (for visitors who have been invited by an organization), private (for those who have been invited to stay at a private address) and tourist (for those intending to stay at a hotel or hotels).

For those on package tours tourist visas will be arranged by the tour companies. For independent travellers, the easiest way to obtain a visa is to pay a modest fee and get a specialist agent, such as **Russia Direct** or **Visa Express**, based in the UK, or **Peace Travel Services** in Florida, to arrange it. Moscow-based **Visa House** can also arrange visas for visitors of any nationality.

Alternatively, apply to the Russian embassy. Independent tourist visa applications must be supported with appropriate documentation (be sure to find out exactly what this is) as well as proof of pre-booked hotel accommodation. Holders of a private visa have to show an invitation endorsed by **OVIR**, the Visa and Registration Department, at their host's local police station.

Visas normally take around ten days to process but, if speed is important, both Peace Travel Services and Visa Express offer an express service for an extra fee. The cost of a visa depends on the length of its validity as well as how soon it is required. Britons pay from about £65 for a short-term, single-entry visa issued well in advance. US subjects can expect to pay around $180.

While tourist visas cannot be extended, private and business visa extensions can be sought by the individual or organization that issued the invitation. Overstaying, however, can lead to a hefty fine or having to remain until an extension is obtained.

Igumnov House, built in 1893, now the home of the French Embassy

IMMIGRATION AND CUSTOMS

Passports and visas are thoroughly checked at immigration desks. All visitors have to fill out a customs declaration form on arrival, which is available in various languages (some airlines hand them out on the plane). On the form you are asked to state how much currency you have and any valuables you may have with you. The form is rarely checked, but should be kept for the duration of your stay and handed back together with another declaration form at departure.

It is illegal to take roubles out of Russia (nor are they allowed in). There are no limits on how much foreign hard currency may be brought in, but visitors will be expected to have less when they leave (to prove they have been buying rather than selling). Valuables such as jewellery and computers should be declared on the customs form on entry, otherwise duty may be levied on them on leaving. Departure customs are generally stricter then in other countries, particularly in regard to art and antiques (*see p193*).

REGISTRATION

Officially, all foreigners are supposed to register with OVIR, the Visa and Registration Department, within three days of their arrival. Hotels can do this for guests. Non-registration is rarely a problem, but sometimes people are fined or ordered to get their paperwork in order, if the authorities become suspicious of them.

EMBASSIES AND CONSULATES

Every country that has diplomatic relations with Russia has an embassy or consulate in Moscow. Anyone intending to reside in Russia for longer than three months is advised to register with their own one. Should a visitor be robbed, hospitalized, imprisoned or otherwise rendered helpless, the embassy or consular officials will then be able to help, for instance with interpretation, or at least to give advice. They can re-issue passports and, in some cases, provide emergency money.

DISABLED TRAVELLERS

Moscow has few facilities for the disabled. Public transport is difficult to access; steps and narrow doors are everywhere and lifts are rare. It is adviseable to phone in advance to check if a tourist sight has full disabled access.

International Student Identity Card

STUDENT TRAVELLERS

As well as being accepted for discounts in museums, international student cards can also be used to obtain discounts on rail and air travel booked through **STAR Travel**.

TRAVELLING WITH CHILDREN

Russians adore children, and those accompanying visitors to Moscow are likely to attract plenty of compliments. On the other hand, it is not unknown for Russian grannies *(babushki)* to be overly inquisitive and even to offer critical, though well-meaning, remarks on the way they are dressed.

Children under six travel free on public transport, but older ones pay the full price. Museums are free for toddlers and babies, and offer concessions to schoolchildren.

Children playing on a cannon at the Armoury in the Kremlin

PUBLIC TOILETS

Few cafés and bars have facilities, and public toilets on the street are not pleasant. It is often best to find the nearest foreign hotel or a pay toilet in, say, a department store. These are usually very cheap. Though the lady who takes the money also hands out rations of toilet paper here, it is always a good idea to carry your own.

ELECTRICAL APPLIANCES

The electrical current in Russia is 220 V. Two-pin plugs are needed, but some of the old Soviet two-pin sockets do not take modern European plugs, which have thicker pins. Hotels all have modern sockets. Adaptors are best bought before travelling, but those for old-style plugs are found only in Russia. US appliances need a 220:110 current adaptor.

Toilet (*tualet*) sign

Men's toilets   Women's toilets

PHOTOGRAPHY

There are no longer any serious restrictions on what visitors are allowed to photograph (unless you want to take aerial pictures). Expect to have to pay for the right to take photos or use a video camera in museums.

TIME DIFFERENCE

Moscow time is three hours ahead of Greenwich Mean Time (GMT). Russia has recently come into line with the rest of Europe, putting its clocks forward by an hour at the end of March, and back again in October.

CONVERSION TABLE

Imperial to Metric
1 inch = 2.54 centimetres
1 foot = 30 centimetres
1 mile = 1.6 kilometres
1 ounce = 28 grams
1 pound = 454 grams
1 pint = 0.6 litres
1 gallon = 4.6 litres

Metric to Imperial
1 centimetre = 0.4 inches
1 metre = 3 feet, 3 inches
1 kilometre = 0.6 miles
1 gram = 0.04 ounces
1 kilogram = 2.2 pounds
1 litre = 1.8 pints

DIRECTORY

TOURIST INFORMATION AND GUIDED TOURS

Intourist
7 Princedale Road,
London, W11 4NW.
Tel 020 7792 5240.
www.intourist.co.uk

Patriarshiy Dom Tours
Vspolniy per 6. **Map** 2 D4.
Tel (495) 795 0927.
www.russiatravel-
pdtours.netfirms.com

VISA FORMALITIES

OVIR
ОВИР
Pokrovka ulitsa 42.
Map 4 D4. **Tel** (495) 200
8427. ⬤ Wed, Sat, Sun.

Peace Travel Services
1648 Taylor Rd #222,
Port Orange, FL, 32128.
Tel 702 420 5135.
www.go-russia.com

Russia Direct
39 Palmerston Place,
Edinburgh, EH12 5AU.
Tel 0131 476 7727.
www.russiadirect.net

Visa Express
31 Corsham Street, 2nd
Floor, London, N1 6DR.
Tel 020 7490 8142.
www.visaexpress.co.uk

Visa House
22 Bolshaya Nikitskaya,
Office 18, Moscow.
Map 2 E5. **Tel** (495) 721
1021.
www.visahouse.com

EMBASSIES AND CONSULATES

Australia
10 A / 2 Podkolokolny per.
Map 7 D1.
Tel (495) 956 6070.
www.aus.ru

Canada
Starokonyushenny per 23.
Map 6 E2.
Tel (495) 956 6666.
www.canadaeuropa.
gc.ca/russia

Ireland
Grokholskiy per 5.
Map 3 C2.
Tel (495) 937 5900.

New Zealand
Ul Povarskaya 44.
Map 2 D5.
Tel (495) 956 3579.
www.nzembassy.msk.ru

South Africa
Granatny per 1/ 9.
Map 2 F5.
Tel (495) 540 1177.
www.saembassy.ru

UK
Smolenskaya Nab 10.
Map 5 C1.
Tel (495) 956 7200.
www.britishembassy.gov.
uk

US
Bolshoy Deviatinsky
pereulok 8. **Map** 2 D5.
Tel (495) 728-5000.
www.usembassy.ru

STUDENT TRAVEL

STAR Travel
Mokhovaya ulitsa 9, (room
001). **Map** 6 F1.
Tel (495) 797 9555.

Personal Security and Health

Despite lurid worldwide reporting on the mafia, crime in Moscow is no worse than in any big city. Petty crime should be the visitor's only concern, but even this can usually be avoided if sensible precautions are taken. For language reasons, it is a good idea to have a card with your Russian address written on it for use in taxis and emergencies. Medical insurance is essential. Although many medicines are readily available, local healthcare compares poorly with Western care and English-speaking services and medical evacuation are very expensive.

PROTECTING YOUR PROPERTY

Every visitor should take out travel insurance. Once in Moscow, visitors can avoid pickpockets by not carrying money in open pockets or displaying large sums of money in public; bags should be kept closed and roubles kept apart from foreign currency and credit cards. It is advisable to carry a small sum of money for purchases, and to keep the rest separately or at the hotel.

It is best not to stop for gypsies who sometimes frequent Tverskaya ulitsa and the central metro stations, apparently begging. Hold tight to valuables and walk determinedly on without aggression.

Travellers' cheques have the advantage that they are insured against loss or theft. However, if they are stolen this should be reported immediately to the issuing company as they can easily be "laundered" in Russia.

It is absolutely essential to report thefts to the police in order to obtain certificates for insurance claims. It is best to report first to hotel security staff who can usually provide interpreters or deal with the whole matter. Embassies will deal with serious situations.

GAI policeman checking documents

PERSONAL SAFETY

The greatest danger for visitors comes from thieves who might become violent if they encounter resistance. As in any country, it is advisable to hand over belongings if they are demanded with menace.

The mafia, though widespread, has scant contact with foreigners, particularly tourists, who are generally much poorer than Russian businessmen.

Women on their own may be approached by kerb-crawlers, who are best ignored, and may be proposi-

tioned if alone in bars and restaurants. At night, it is safer to use taxis booked in advance rather than those hailed on the street. The metro is also safe.

Other threats come from local drivers, who see pedestrians as a nuisance, and from manhole covers, which have a tendency to rock wildly or collapse when stepped on.

POLICE

Several kinds of police operate on Moscow's streets. They change uniforms according to the weather, wearing fur hats and big coats in winter. The normal police or *militsiya*, who always carry guns, are the most frequently seen.

The riot police or OMON *(otryad militsii osobgo naznacheniya)* are rarely seen on the streets and dress in camouflage.

Totally separate are the traffic police, or GIBDD *(gosudarstvennaya inspekcia bezopasnosti dorozhnovo dvizhenia)*. Recognizable by their striped truncheons, they may stop any vehicle to check the driver's documents.

Both the *militsiya* and GIBDD supplement their incomes by picking people up on minor offences, such as jay-walking. It is usually best to pay the "fine", which is about the equivalent of five or ten dollars.

Militsiya

Fire engine with distinctive white stripe

МЕДЭП
МЕДИЦИНСКАЯ ЭКСТРЕННАЯ ПОМОЩЬ

☎ 143-63-43

Ambulance

МИЛИЦИЯ

Police car

Pharmacy, identified by the word *apteka*

PHARMACIES

Pharmacies in Russia are all signed by the word **Аптека** (*apteka*) and usually have a green cross hanging outside. The best ones are on ulitsa Novyy Arbat, Tverskaya ulitsa and Kutuzovskiy prospekt. These sell many imported medications, some with the instructions still in the original language. Prescriptions are not necessary for any purchase, and antibiotics and other strong medications can be purchased over the counter. All the assistants are trained pharmacists and can suggest a Russian alternative to visitors who name the drug they are seeking. However, visitors with specific requirements, particularly insulin, should bring enough with them for their whole stay. Moscow has a number of all-night pharmacies (*see directory*).

Sign for a pharmacy

MEDICAL TREATMENT

Most hotels have their own doctor and this should be the first port of call for anyone who falls ill. There are several companies, notably the **European Medical Centre** and the **American Medical Center**, that specialize in dealing with foreigners. They can provide everything that travellers are likely to need, from basic treatment where they are staying to dental care, x-rays, ultra-sound scans and even medical evacuation home. Their charges are very high, but they are all used to dealing with foreign insurance policies.

Slightly cheaper is **Assist-24**, which has English-speaking Russian doctors who are well able to deal with minor medical emergencies. **US Dental Care** provides a full range of dental treatment.

For those in need of immediate attention, without the time to contact any of the above, the casualty department of the **Botkin Hospital** is the safest bet. The staff can give injections and stitches and carry out general first aid, but no English is spoken.

Anyone waking up in a local hospital should contact their embassy or one of the above medical centres. They can arrange a move or oversee care.

HEALTH PRECAUTIONS

Visitors should not drink the tap water in Moscow, but stick to bottled water and avoid fruit and raw vegetables that may have been washed in tap water. Food in a foreign country often unsettles the stomach and eating the meat and sausage pies (*pirozhki*) sold on the streets is a sure route to a stomach upset.

In past years diphtheria has increased among the local population. It is advisable to be inoculated against this before going to Russia.

MOSQUITOES AND TICKS

Mosquitoes (*komari*) are the bane of everyone's life from June to late September. Plug-in chemical mosquito coils are available and are particularly good at night. Alternatives are sprays, or oil repellants used in vaporizers or burnt in candles.

A more serious issue is encephalitis-bearing ticks. These are found in rural and wooded areas from late spring to late summer. Always wear insect repellant and cover exposed skin. If you find a tick, remove it with tweezers.

DIRECTORY

EMERGENCY SERVICES

Fire (*pozhar*)
Tel 01.

Police (*militsiya*)
Tel 02.

Ambulance
(*skoraya pomoshch*)
Tel 03.

MEDICAL SERVICES

American Medical Center
Американский медицинский центр
Amerikanskiy meditsinskiy tsentr
Grokholskiy pereulok 1.
Map 3 B2. **Tel** (495) 933 7700.
www.amcenter.ru

Assist-24
Ассист-24
Dokukina 16/1.
Tel (495) 937 6450.

Botkin Hospital
Боткинская больница *Botkinskaya bolnitsa*
2-oy Botkinskiy proezd 5.
Map 1 A1.
Tel (495) 945 0033.

European Medical Centre
Европейский медицинский центр
Yevropeyskiy meditsinskiy tsentr
Spiridonievskiy pereulok 5.
Stroenie 1
Map 2 D4.
Tel (495) 933 6655.

US Dental Care
Американский стоматологический центр
Amerikanskiy stomatologicheskiy tsentr
Bolshaya Dmitrovka 7/5, Bldg 2.
Map 2 F4.
Tel (495) 933 8686.
www.usdentalcare.com

ALL-NIGHT PHARMACIES

Kutuzovskiy pr 14.
Map 5 A2.
Tel (495) 643 1601.

Ulitsa Zemlyanoy val 1/4.
Map 4 E4.
Tel (495) 917 1640.

Nikolskaya ul 19/21.
Map 3 A5.
Tel (495) 921 4942.

Banking and Local Currency

Moscow is slowly moving into the credit card age and major Western cards can now be used to pay in hotels, top restaurants and some shops. Everywhere else, however, cash is the norm, and roubles are the only legal currency. The city is well provided with exchange points where visitors can turn their currency (US dollars still being the most popular), travellers' cheques or credit cards into roubles. Rates of commission vary. Since bank exchange rates are so good, money should never be changed on the street. Apparently "better" offers from private individuals will lead to visitors being cheated.

CHANGING MONEY

Roubles cannot be obtained outside Russia, but there are numerous exchange offices all over Moscow, including at the airports. Some offices are open 24 hours a day.

A passport has to be shown when changing money. Any defect on foreign bank notes, especially vertical tears or ink or water stains, makes them invalid in Russia and they will be refused at the exchange. Make sure that all notes brought into Russia are in good condition and that any US dollars were issued after 1990.

On completing a currency transaction, an exchange slip is issued. All slips should be kept as they must be attached to the customs declaration filled in on arrival in Russia (see p208) and presented at customs on leaving the country.

A sign for a currency exchange office (obmen valyuty)

USING BANKS

There are only a few foreign banks in Russia and they mostly do not offer over-the-counter services. Most Russian banks, however, do have on-the-spot exchange services. They take a variety of currencies, credit cards for cash advances, and some take travellers' cheques. **Alfa-Bank** and **Sberbank** offer the best rates. For anyone wishing to have money sent to a bank in Russia, these two banks are also the most reliable. It is always advisable to check other banks' reliability.

Western Union will transfer money to Russia for you through Alfa-Bank, Guta Bank, Bank Moskvy and **American Express**, but they are expensive and primarily of use to businesspeople.

Many independent exchange offices in Russia accept only US dollars and euros.

Official currency exchange slip

CREDIT CARDS

It is now possible to obtain cash, both roubles and US dollars, with a credit card through the larger banks and from automatic cash dispensers at some banks and in major hotels. The local commission is between 2 and 5 per cent, plus whatever the card company

Automatic cash dispenser

charges. The most commonly accepted card is VISA, with Diners, MasterCard, Eurocard and American Express much less widely recognized. The cash dispensers at Alfa-Bank take MasterCard, Eurocard and VISA and charge no local commission, making them a popular option with visitors.

Lost or stolen credit cards should be reported immediately to the credit card company in the home country. No local security service is offered.

DIRECTORY

BANKS

Alfa-Bank
Альфа-Банк
Mashi Poryvaevoi ulitsa 7.
Map 4 D2.
Tel (495) 974 2515.

American Express
Usacheva ul 33, building 1.
Map 5 B5.
Tel (495) 933 8400.

Sberbank
Сбербанк
Ulitsa Bolshaya Yakimanka 18.
Map 7 A4.
Tel (495) 238 4920.

Vneshtorgbank
Внешторгбанк
Kuznetskiy most 16.
Map 3 A4.
Tel (495) 101 1887.

CASH DISPENSERS

Alfa-Bank
Альфа-Банк
Pokrovka 3/7.
Map 3 C5.
(accepts VISA, MasterCard, Eurocard)

American Express
Sadovaya-Kudrinskaya ul 21a.
Map 2 D4.
(accepts American Express only)

Radisson-Slavyanskaya Hotel
Гостиница РздиссонСлавянская
Gostinitsa Redisson-Slavyanskaya
Berezhkovskaya nab 2.
Map 5 B2.
(accepts VISA, MasterCard, American Express)

TRAVELLERS' CHEQUES

Banks charge at least 3 per cent to cash travellers' cheques. Only large banks, such as Alfa-Bank and Sberbank, offer this service. The cheapest alternative is American Express cheques, with a 2 per cent commission if cashed at the American Express office. Travellers' cheques can only be used as payment for goods or services in a few large hotels, and are acceptable only in US dollars and euros, or sometimes British pounds. In most cases euro cheques are usually preferred.

LOCAL CURRENCY

The Russian currency is the rouble (or ruble), written рубль or abbreviated to р or руб. The higher denominations of roubles are currently available in banknotes, which all bear images of well-known Russian cities, the lower denominations in coins. The kopek, of which there are 100 in a rouble, is issued in coins.

In 1998 the rouble was revalued owing to its stronger value and lower inflation rate. Values were divided by 1,000 (with 1,000 roubles becoming 1 rouble).

Banknotes

There are five denominations of banknote, with face values of 10, 50, 100, 500 and 1,000 roubles, and they have the same designs as their pre-revaluation equivalents. When changing money check that the notes correspond to those shown here.

10 roubles

50 roubles

100 roubles

500 roubles

1,000 roubles

Coins

The revaluation of the Russian rouble in 1998 led to the revival of the long-redundant but much-loved kopek. Traditionally, the rouble had always consisted of 100 kopeks. In addition to coins for 1, 2 and 5 roubles, there are now coins valued at 1, 5, 10 and 50 kopeks. Any coins issued before 1997, prior to revaluation, are essentially valueless. Visitors should therefore always examine change they receive and refuse to accept any of these old coins.

1 rouble

2 roubles

5 roubles

1 kopek

5 kopeks

10 kopeks

50 kopeks

Communications

Much of Moscow's antiquated phone system has been brought up to date in the last few years and there is now a good city-wide service. Many hotel and public phones have direct dialling all over the world, but phones in private homes may not have this facility. The same period has seen an explosive increase in the number of magazines, newspapers and television channels. Sadly, Russia's postal system has not improved at the same rate.

A sign outside a post office (*pochta*) that has public telephones (*telefon*)

TELEPHONE SERVICES

Comstar satellite phone boxes, which are blue, are installed at airports, in business centres, in most hotel foyers and in some restaurants. They accept credit cards or phonecards on sale in major hotels, restaurants and clubs, but calls are expensive. Moscow's local system is much cheaper. It is possible to call abroad on a direct line from one of the Moscow State Telephone Network (MITC) blue and white cardphones, located on streets and in some metro stations. Cards for the phones come in 25, 50, 100, 120, 200, 400 and 1,000 units, and are available from kiosks and post offices. To make an international call, at

MITC phone box

Token for a local phone

least 100 units are needed. International and inter-city calls are cheaper between 10pm and 8am and at all hours at weekends. The **Central Telegraph Office** has rows of local and international phones and calls are paid for at the counter.

At present, local calls from private phones are free, as they are covered by the cost of the line rental. This system may well change in the future, however, as there is increased pressure from the phone network to introduce a charge-by-the-minute system for calls.

Instructions on how to use an MITC cardphone are given below. Comstar phones work in the same way if used with a phonecard. The instructions automatically come up first in English. If using a credit card with a Comstar phone, insert it into the top left-hand slot and remove it again in one action. Wait 15 seconds for card verification before dialling. For non-card local phones, lift the receiver and dial the number. When someone answers, drop the token into the slot.

REACHING THE RIGHT NUMBER

- Local directory enquiries (Moscow only): dial 09.
- Inter-city call booking via operator: dial 07.
- There is as yet no international directory enquiries service.
- International call booking: dial 8 (tone) 194.
- Direct international dialling:
  UK: dial 8 (tone) 1044, then area code omitting first 0, then number.
  USA: dial 8 (tone) 101 followed by the area code and number.
  Australia: dial 8 (tone) 1061, then area code omitting first 0, then number.
  New Zealand: dial 8 (tone) 1064, then area code omitting first 0, then number.
  Irish Republic: dial 8 (tone) 10353, then area code omitting first 0, then number.
- AT&T Calling Card number: dial 755 5042.

USING AN MITC PHONECARD OPERATED PHONE

Russian phonecards

1 Lift the receiver and check that you have a dialling tone.

2 MITC phones offer instructions in Russian, English, French and German. They always appear in Russian first. Press this button to switch between languages. Instructions are given both on the display and through the earpiece.

3 When instructed, push your phonecard into the slot in the direction of the arrow marked on the card. Wait for card verification.

4 Dial the number. The ringing tone consists of long tones; the engaged signal of shorter tones.

5 Press this button at any time to increase the volume.

6 When someone answers, press this button to speak.

7 To end a call, replace the receiver and pull out the card.

POSTAL SERVICES

Post offices such as the **Main Post Office** and those in hotels sell ordinary and commemorative Russian stamps, postcards, envelopes and phonecards. The smaller post offices are marked почта (*pochta*), and are most plentiful in the centre of the city. They generally have big glass windows and have blue post boxes outside.

International post is often slow and is probably best avoided except for postcards. **Post International**, which also offers poste restante, provides the same service as courier companies. **American Express** runs its usual poste restante service for card holders.

Use a courier service for important documents, such as **DHL Worldwide Express**, **Federal Express** and **TNT Express Worldwide**. Anything other than paper, especially computer discs, is checked by customs, which can delay dispatch by an extra day or so.

FAX, TELEX, TELEGRAM, AND E-MAIL SERVICES

Many hotels and the **Main Post Office** offer fax, telex and telegram services. Telegrams in foreign languages can also be sent from the **Central Telegraph Office**. In addition to postal services, **Independent Postal Service** offers fax and e-mail services, while Internet cafés such as **Netland** and **Time Online** allow you to browse the Internet and send e-mails.

TELEVISION AND RADIO

Hotels have long offered Eurosport, CNN, BBC World Service TV and NBC channels. Russian-language television is dominated by imported soap operas, which are generally dubbed into Russian rather than subtitled. The best national news in Russian is on NTV and the best local news on TV-Tsentr. For English-language radio

Romanesque-inspired façade of Moscow's grand Main Post Office

broadcasts the best are still the BBC World Service and the Voice of America, which are broadcast on medium and shortwave. Ekho Moskvy provides an excellent news service in Russian.

Good pop stations include Radio Maximum (103.7 FM) and Local Europe Plus (106.2 FM) both of which play Western music, and Russkoe Radio (105.7 FM) which plays Russian music. Orfey (72.14 FM) plays classical music without adverts.

Postbox

NEWSPAPERS AND MAGAZINES

Moscow has one major English-language daily newspaper, *The Moscow Times*, published from Tuesday to Saturday. It covers both domestic and foreign news and has listings of exhibitions and events in its Friday edition. The Saturday edition has weekly television listings.

The English language version of *The Moscow News* is also a weekly and has listings. All of these papers are free and can be found in airports, clubs, restaurants and other places where foreigners

English- and Russian-language newspapers

gather. There is also a Russian language version of the UK listings magazine *Time Out*, which has extensive listings as well as articles. It can be bought at most newsstands.

To keep up with world events, however, you are better off going online or tuning into foreign radio.

DIRECTORY

TELEPHONE SERVICES

Central Telegraph Office
Центральный телеграф
Tverskaya ul 7.
Map 2 F5. *Tel* (495) 924 9004.
⬚ 8am–9pm. www.ctel.msk.ru

POSTAL SERVICES

American Express
Ulitsa Usacheva 33.
Map 5 B5. *Tel* (495) 933 8400.

Independent Postal Service
Malaya Dmitrovka 28/1.
Map 2 E3. *Tel* (495) 733 9073.
⬚ 9am–8pm Mon–Fri, 10am–5pm Sat, noon–5pm Sun.

Main Post Office
Главный почтамт
Malaya Dmitrovka 29.
Map 3 C4. *Tel* (495) 733 9073.
⬚ 8am–8pm Mon–Fri, 8am–7pm Sat, 9am–7pm Sun, noon–6pm public hols.

Post International
Myasnitskaya ulitsa 13/18a,
office 222. *Tel* (495) 825 8787

COURIER SERVICES

DHL Worldwide Express
Valovaya Ulitsa 21.
Map 7 B5. *Tel* (495) 956 1000.
www.dhl.ru

Federal Express
Gogolevskiy Bulvar 17.
Map 6 E2. *Tel* (495) 787 5555.
www.fedex.com/ru

TNT Express Worldwide
Ulitsa Svobody 31.
Map 6 E1. *Tel* (495) 797 2777.
www.tnt.ru/english

INTERNET CAFÉS

Netland
2 Rozhdestvenka ulitsa.
Map 3 A4. *Tel* (495) 781 0923.

Time Online
Manezhnaya ploshad. **Map** 7 A1.
Tel (495) 363 0060. ⬚ 24 hours.

GETTING TO MOSCOW

The quickest and most comfortable way to get to Moscow is by plane. Travelling overland, especially by road, can be difficult and often involves crossing numerous borders and negotiating roadworks and pot-holed roads. However, if cost is the priority, rail or coach are possibilities, especially for visitors arriving from St Petersburg or a neighbouring country,

A plane owned by the Russian airline Aeroflot

such as Ukraine or Belarus. It is essential that visitors plan their journey before applying for a visa *(see p208)* since the Russian authorities require detailed information about travel arrangements, including which cities visitors will use to enter and leave Russia. Whichever route is chosen, it is worth shopping around to find the best deal as prices fluctuate greatly throughout the year.

Exterior of Sheremetevo 2, Moscow's main international airport

ARRIVING BY AIR

There is a reasonable choice of flights to Moscow from the UK. Three carriers – **British Airways**, **Aeroflot** and **Transaero** – operate direct flights, while several other airlines, including **SAS**, **KLM** and **Austrian Airlines** run a variety of flights via a number of destinations. Transaero, which now flies direct from London, is the only reliable Russian alternative to Aeroflot. Both Transaero and Aeroflot operate long-haul flights from the USA, Australia and Canada. Despite popular belief that Aeroflot's flights are of an inferior quality, its Moscow to London route is a reasonable option, and its first-class service is excellent.

Cheap trips are advertised in the travel sections of many newspapers and magazines. There are also several agencies in London and New York that book trips to Russia. Some, such as **Eastways Travel Service**, sell only flights, while others, such as **Russian National Group**, also book hotel accommodation or offer inclusive package deals. These can be cheaper than

booking flights and accommodation separately. Some agencies also arrange visas for travellers *(see p208)*.

MAIN AIRPORTS

Moscow has two main air terminals, each servicing various domestic and international locations. The major international terminal for many years was **Sheremetevo 2**, but now many airlines have relocated to **Domodedovo**, the more modern international airport in the south of the city. Improvements have been promised for many years at the shabby Sheremetevo 2, but little has been done.

Sheremetevo 2 is situated about 28km (17 miles)

Airport signs, Sheremetevo 2

northwest of the city centre. It has one terminal, with flights divided between its right and left wings. Central notice boards in both the departure and arrivals lounges indicate which wing each flight is expected at or leaving from.

At Domodedovo, departure and arrival times are clearly displayed on monitors near the check in desks. Visitors are required to fill in customs declarations upon departure and arrival at both airports.

Tourists can expect a long wait when arriving at Sheremetevo 2. Things are generally a lot better at Domodedovo, although at peal times there can be large queues. Exchange offices, duty free stores and the like can be found at both airports.

OTHER AIRPORTS

Moscow has three other airports. **Sheremetevo 1**, close to Sheremetevo 2, is used mainly for domestic flights, including those from St Petersburg. It also handles all Transaero flights and some Aeroflot charters from abroad. Flights destined for the nearer parts of Russia and other CIS member states often leave from **Vnukovo** airport, which is located in the southwest of Moscow. **Bykovo**, to the west, is Moscow's smallest airport and is used only by small, old-fashioned planes as it does not have the modern runways needed by larger aircraft. Bykovo serves the less important routes within Russia and, in summer, also receives some charter flights.

BUS AND METRO LINKS INTO THE CITY CENTRE

KEY

- ▬ Metro line 2
- ▬ Bus/minibus route
- ▬▬ Walk

Rechnoy Vokzal metro, at the end of metro line 2

Sign at departure point of express bus to Rechnoy Vokzal bus station

GETTING INTO THE CITY

Although the easiest way of getting into the city from either Domodedovo or Sheremetevo 2 is by taxi there are other options. From Sheremetevo 2, around 7 km (4 miles) from the centre of Moscow, a bus runs from the arrivals hall to the air terminal (*aerovokzal*), taking about 35 minutes. The air terminal is about 15 minutes' walk from either Aeroport or Dinamo metro stations. Another bus route runs to Rechnoy Vokzal bus station, close to Rechnoy Vokzal metro. Both ser-vices run from 6:25am to 11:30pm.

Buses and mini-buses leave from Domodedovo from outside the domestic terminal, situated next to international arrivals. Bus services run from 5:45am–11:30pm. Both services go to Domodedovo metro station. There is also an hourly express train service to Paveletskiy station, from where you can easily connect with the metro system.

Sheremetevo 1 has both bus and mini-bus services, which also go to Rechnoy Vokzal bus station or the air terminal. Both services run from 6:25am until 11:30pm. The minibuses seem to also run all night, but their schedule is erratic. The

destination of each bus is indicated by a sign displayed in its front window.

For those preferring to travel by taxi (*see p212*) there are several things to remember. Firstly, it is much easier for travellers to book a cab prior to arriving, either through a travel agency or hotel. Airport taxis are expensive (the equivalent of US$50–60 to the city centre) and not all of them are official. These unofficial drivers are generally safe, but it is better to walk outside to the rank of official taxis. These yellow cars have black chequered designs on the roof. The taxi meters installed in most of them are rarely used so it is vital to negotiate a price for the trip beforehand. No tips are necessary. The journey into the city centre should take about 30–40 minutes if the roads are clear.

A minibus that takes people from Sheremetevo 1 to Rechnoy Vokzal bus station or the air terminal

Passengers waiting to board a bus from Sheremetevo 2 to Rechnoy Vokzal bus station

Rank of unofficial taxis outside the arrivals hall at Sheremetevo 2, waiting for fares into the city

ARRIVING BY TRAIN

Moscow can be reached by train from Paris, Brussels, Berlin and several other European capitals, but the trip will take at least a day and a night and you will need a transit visa for Belarus. Be prepared for a lengthy wait at the Russian border while all of the train's wheels are changed to fit the wider Russian tracks.

Three of Moscow's main railway stations are situated on Komsomolskaya ploshchad

Restaurant car of the Budapest train arriving at Kievskiy station

(*see p144*), also known as ploshchad Trekh Vokzalov (Square of the Three Railway Stations). **Yaroslavskiy** and **Kazanskiy** serve domestic routes only. **Leningradskiy** is the terminus for trains from St Petersburg and Finland. Of the other stations, **Rizhskiy** serves the Baltic and **Kievskiy** serves Eastern Europe, while **Belorusskiy** handles trains from Western Europe and Poland. **Paveletskiy** and **Kurskiy** stations are the points of arrival for trains from southern Russia and parts of the Ukraine.

The imposing main entrance to Belorusskiy station

Soviet crest on the exterior of Kievskiy railway station

Tickets for all trains have to be booked in advance. Owing to the long distances covered, the majority are overnight sleepers, but some standard trains operate on the shorter routes. Trains fall into four categories: express (*ekspressy*) trains, which travel the direct route between Moscow and St Petersburg only; fast (*skorye*) trains, which operate on long journeys and stop at only a few stations; passenger (*passazhirskie*) trains, which also operate on long routes, but stop at most or all stations; and suburban (*prigorodnye*) trains (*see p227*).

ARRIVING BY COACH

It is possible to get to Moscow by coach, but it is only usually worth it if visitors are travelling from a neighbouring country or are on a tight budget. There are coach routes to Moscow from the Czech Republic, Poland, Hungary and Slovakia. Some run via the Ukraine, while others enter Russia via Belarus. Sometimes a change of coach is necessary and the onward journey from either country takes 12–16 hours as the roads to Moscow from Belarus and the Ukraine are not well maintained.

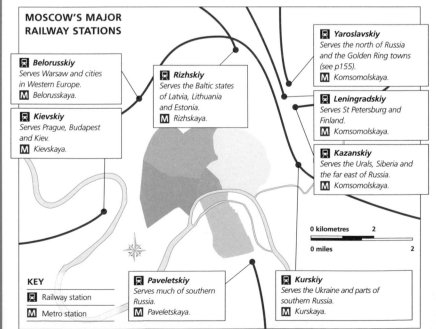

MOSCOW'S MAJOR RAILWAY STATIONS

🚉 **Belorusskiy**
Serves Warsaw and cities in Western Europe.
Ⓜ Belorusskaya.

🚉 **Kievskiy**
Serves Prague, Budapest and Kiev.
Ⓜ Kievskaya.

🚉 **Rizhskiy**
Serves the Baltic states of Latvia, Lithuania and Estonia.
Ⓜ Rizhskaya.

🚉 **Yaroslavskiy**
Serves the north of Russia and the Golden Ring towns (see p155).
Ⓜ Komsomolskaya.

🚉 **Leningradskiy**
Serves St Petersburg and Finland.
Ⓜ Komsomolskaya.

🚉 **Kazanskiy**
Serves the Urals, Siberia and the far east of Russia.
Ⓜ Komsomolskaya.

0 kilometres   2

0 miles   2

KEY

🚉 Railway station

Ⓜ Metro station

🚉 **Paveletskiy**
Serves much of southern Russia.
Ⓜ Paveletskaya.

🚉 **Kurskiy**
Serves the Ukraine and parts of southern Russia.
Ⓜ Kurskaya.

TRAVELLING TO MOSCOW FROM ST PETERSBURG

The easiest way of getting to Moscow from St Petersburg is by train. Express trains run from Moskovskiy station in St Petersburg to Leningradskiy station in Moscow. It is easiest to organize a ticket through a hotel or travel agent.

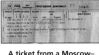

A ticket from a Moscow–St Petersburg express

The best night-time trains are Nos. 1 (called the *Red Arrow*) and 3 from St Petersburg to Moscow, and Nos. 2 and 4, from Moscow to St Petersburg.

САНКТ-ПЕТЕРБУРГ

МОСКВА

Sign indicating the *Aurora* train from St Petersburg to Moscow

All these services leave at midnight and arrive at 8:30 the next morning and are usually on time. Other trains, including Nos. 47 and 159 (the *Aurora*) are almost as good, especially for those who prefer to make the trip in the day. On all these trains travellers should be wary of thieves. Most compartments have locks, which should be used at night.

Ticket prices vary depending on class and the services which are included, and prices rise in the high season. There is a choice between *sidyashchyy* (sitting) tickets and a variety of more expensive sleeper options. Bedlinen costs extra. Food may be available, but visitors are advised to bring their own. The alternative to taking the train is flying. The

Compartment on the *Red Arrow* St Petersburg–Moscow express

flight only takes 50 minutes, but allow plenty of time to get to and from the airports, especially in Moscow (*see p217*). Planes depart from Pulkovo 1 airport in St Petersburg and arrive at Sheremetevo 1 (*see p216*). The air fare is considerably more expensive than the train.

DIRECTORY

TRAVEL AGENCIES

Andrews Travel House
23 Pembridge Square, London, W2 4DR.
Tel 020 7727 2838.

BTI Russia
Stoleshnikov pereulok 14, Building 1, Moscow.
Tel (495) 961 3434.
www.btirussia.com

Eastways Travel Service
6 Brick Lane, London, E1 6RS. *Tel* 020 7247 3823.

Russian National Group
224 West 30th St, Suite 701, NY 10001.
Tel (877) 221 7120.
www.russia-travel.com

AIRLINES

Aeroflot
Аэрофлот
Leningradskyy prospekt 37.
Map 3 A4.
Tel (495) 223 5555.
Tel 020 7355 2233 *in UK.*
www.aeroflot.ru

Austrian Airlines
Smolenskaya ulitsa 5.
Map 5 C2. *Tel* (495) 995 0995. *Tel* 020 7434 7300 (UK). www.aua.com

British Airways
4th Lesnoy Pereulok 4 (5th floor). **Map** 2 D1.
Tel (495) 363 2525.
Tel 0844 493 0787 (UK).
www.britishairways.com

KLM
Ulitsa Usacheva 33, fl 1
Map 5 A5. *Tel* (495) 658 3000. *Tel* 020 8750 9000 (UK). www.klm.com

SAS
1 Tverskaya-Yamskaya ulitsa 5. **Map** 2 D3.
Tel (495) 775 4747.
Tel 0870 6072 7727 (UK).
www.sas-airlines.com

Transaero
Трансаэро
Bolshaya Polyanka ulitsa 47.
Tel (495) 788 80 80.
www.transaero.ru

MOSCOW AIRPORTS

Sheremetevo 1 & 2
Шереметьево 1 & 2
Tel (495) 578 0901.

Bykovo
Быково
Tel (495) 558 4738.

Domodedovo
Домодедово
Tel (495) 933 6666.

Vnukovo
Внуково
Tel (495) 436 2813.

TRAIN STATIONS

Belorusskiy
Белорусский
Ploshchad Tverskoy Zastavy 7. **Map** 1 C2.
Tel (495) 973 8191.

Kazanskiy
Казанский
Komsomolskaya pl 2.
Map 4 D2. *Tel* (495) 624 6556.

Kievskiy
Киевский
Ploshchad Kievskovo vokzala. **Map** 5 B2.
Tel (495) 640 1115.

Kurskiy
Курский
Ulitsa Zemlyanoy val 29.
Map 4 E5. *Tel* (495) 917 3152.

Leningradskiy
Ленинградский
Komsomolskaya pl 3. **Map** 4 D2. *Tel* (495) 262 9143

Paveletskiy
Павелецкий
Paveletskaya ploshchad 1.
Map 7 C5. *Tel* (495) 635 0522.

Rizhskiy
Рижский
Ploshchad Rizhskovo vokzala.
Tel (495) 971 1588.

Savelouskiy
Савеловский
Ploshchad Savelovskovo vokzala.
Tel (495) 685 9005.

Yaroslavskiy
Ярославский
Komsomolskaya ploshchad 5. **Map** 4 D2.
Tel (495) 921 5914.

General Enquiries
Tel (495) 666 9333.

Ticket Bookings
Tel (495) 666 8333.

BUS STATIONS

Moscow Bus Station
Московский автовокзал
Moskovskiy avtovokzal
Nr Shchelkovskaya metro, Uralskaya ulitsa 2.
Tel (495) 468 0400.

GETTING AROUND MOSCOW

Moscow's vast metro network, which has stops close to all the major sights, is the most reliable way of travelling around the city. However, it can get extremely crowded. Moscow is also served by buses, trolleybuses and trams. Services are relatively frequent, although delays are now more common than they were in the Soviet era. A knowledge of the Cyrillic alphabet will help with reading signs on these serv-

Indicates a pedestrian area

ices. Suburban buses are particularly useful for travelling around Moscow's outlying districts, beyond the reach of the metro network, and bus routes often start at a major metro station. Trams run as far as the outskirts of the city, but services are gradually being reduced. Trolleybuses are a good means of transport in the city centre, covering the popular routes. Taxis are the most flexible, but most expensive, way of getting around.

The Kremlin, at the heart of Moscow (see pp52–67), must be explored on foot

WALKING

Moscow's centre is very spread out and so not easily negotiable on foot. However, the area within the Boulevard Ring, where many sights are located, offers a few good opportunities for walking. At the heart of the city are Red Square *(see p106)* and the Kremlin, which are only accessible on foot. Visitors should allow three hours to cover this area including all the cathedrals in the Kremlin.

Pedestrian subway sign

Across the river from here, beautiful Zamoskvoreche *(see pp114–25)* is another district which pedestrians will enjoy.

Muscovites themselves are not great walkers but, in the evenings or at weekends, they can often be seen taking a stroll around the Old Arbat *(see pp70–71)*, a district of the city frequented by artists, musicians and street performers. Other places to take a walk are Tverskaya ulitsa *(see p89)*, numerous parks – in

particular Gorky Park *(see p129)*, Izmaylovo Park *(see p141)* and Sokolniki Park – and by the Moskva river.

When embarking on a walk around the city, it is a good idea to wear sturdy shoes, and preferably old ones as Moscow can be dirty. Traffic is heavy and major roads can often be crossed via subways (although, as in other cities, it is wise to be vigilant when doing so alone). Alternatively use a zebra crossing if a green light shows: drivers in Moscow do not stop at zebra crossings without lights. It is not advisable for anyone, but especially a woman, to walk around any part of the city alone late at night. The best walking tours in English are organized by Patriarshi Dom Tours *(see p206)*.

TAXIS

For safety reasons it is best to travel only by official taxis: yellow cabs with a black chequered design on their roofs. They can be booked through the **Moscow Taxi** company, although operators are unlikely to speak English, or alternatively through a hotel. They usually arrive within half an hour. Taxis to the airport should be booked well in advance. Some hotels have their own taxi ranks, but the taxis that wait there can be very expensive. It is possible to flag down an official taxi on the street. Some switch on a green light, either on

Official yellow Moscow taxi

HOT AIR BALLOONS

Taking a trip in a hot air balloon has recently become a popular pastime among well-off New Russians and visitors to the city, especially in the summer. **Avgur** launches its balloons near the Istra river in Zvenigorod outside Moscow. Rides last for about two hours, taking three passengers, who can include children, in addition to the pilot. Trips are expensive, but offer fantastic views of the city including the "Seven Sisters", Stalinist-Gothic skyscrapers *(see p45)*.

Hailing a private car for a ride, a common practice among Russians

their window or on their roof, to indicate they are for hire. Others do not, but if they are for hire they will stop. All official taxis have meters, but some are out-of-date and the driver may prefer to negotiate the fare. It is crucial either to agree on a fare, or to be sure that the driver turns on the meter, before setting off.

Russians themselves prefer to use private taxis (*chastniki*) to official ones. Any car can be hailed and a fee agreed for a journey. Other cars may therefore stop when an official taxi is hailed. Private taxis are cheap and generally safe. However, it is not advisable for visitors to the city who do not speak Russian to use them.

MOSCOW RIVER CRUISES

River boats are extremely popular in summer. They operate from May to October and cover quite a long stretch of the Moskva river. They stop at 10 or so points along the river and you can hop on and off, but must purchase a new ticket each time. All riverboats have two decks and on sunny days the upper deck is great for combining sunbathing with sightseeing.

River cruises pass several major sites and are a good way to get a feel for the city's layout. The main pick-up point for these cruises is opposite Kievskiy station. Major stops are near Moscow State University at Sparrow Hills (*see p129*), Gorky Park and

near Red Square (Bolshoy Ustinskiy most). **Moscow River Line** is the main company running these cruises. It also hires boats out and organizes parties on them.

DIRECTORY

Moscow Taxi
Московское такси
Moskovskoe taksi
Tel (495) 991 6173.
www.taxi749.com

Moscow River Line
Московское речное Пароходство
Moskovskoe pechnoe parohodstvo
Tel (495) 459 7150.

Avgur
Авгур
Ulitsa Stepana Shutova 4.
Tel (495) 359 1001/1065.

Double decker river boat, a good way to view the sights along the river

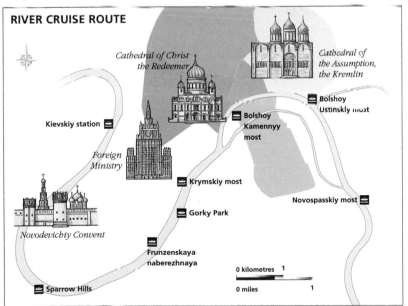

RIVER CRUISE ROUTE

Cathedral of Christ the Redeemer

Cathedral of the Assumption, the Kremlin

Kievskiy station

Foreign Ministry

Bolshoy Ustinskiy most

Bolshoy Kamennyy most

Krymskiy most

Novospasskiy most

Gorky Park

Novodevichiy Convent

Frunzenskaya naberezhnaya

0 kilometres 1

0 miles 1

Sparrow Hills

The Metro

Moscow metro symbol

Moscow is a sprawling, hectic city. One of its great assets, however, is its excellent metro network, which extends from the centre right out to many of its suburbs. During the rush hour, in particular, heavy traffic means that it is often faster to travel by metro than by car, let alone any other form of public transport. For years all transport in the Soviet Union was extremely cheap and metro fares are still very good value. At present passengers pay the same fare regardless of the length of their journey. However, the city authorities have announced plans to introduce new variable fares at some point in the future.

The metro system is extremely reliable, with trains running frequently throughout the day. Constructed as part of Stalin's grand plan for rebuilding Moscow, it is also a tourist attraction in its own right *(see pp38–41)*.

Main entrance to Tretyakovskaya metro, an interchange station

CHANGING LINES

For those unused to the complexity of Moscow's metro system, journeys can be made even more confusing by the fact that stations where it is possible to change between metro lines often have two or more separate names, one for each line involved. On the metro map *(see p224)* these interchange stations are bracketed together For instance, near the centre of the city there is an interchange between four lines – 1, 3, 4 and 9 – each of which is served by a different station. Correspondingly, four station names are given on the map: Biblioteka imeni Lenina, Arbatskaya, Aleksandrovskiy Sad and Borovitskaya.

When changing lines at an interchange station it is therefore important to know the name of the station on the other line. It is then easy to reach the right platform by following the *(perekhod)* – or "interchange" – signs indicating this name.

The ornate, cavernous interior of Arbatskaya metro

THE NETWORK

The Moscow metro network is well planned and extensive, consisting of 10 lines which cover the whole city except its outermost suburbs. One feature worth noting is the circular line connecting all the mainline railway stations *(see p218)*. Changing between the metro and a mainline station is generally easy as both have the same name, but with a slightly different ending. Belorusskiy railway station, for instance, links to Belorusskaya metro, and Kievskiy railway station to Kievskaya metro. However, Komsomolskaya, also on the circle line, is the exception. It

Emergency intercom to driver

links to three mainline railway stations – Leningradskiy, Kazanskiy and Yaroslavskiy.

The metro lines are colour-coded and numbered from 1 to 10, and all signs are in Cyrillic only. Trains arrive frequently, generally every 1–2 minutes on weekdays, while services are slightly less frequent at weekends. During the rush hour the interval between trains is usually under a minute.

The Moscow metro is on the whole safe and reliable. All the stations are staffed, although metro attendants are unlikely to speak anything except their mother tongue. Travellers who have a heavy bag or a suitcase will have to pay an added charge.

Metro train ready to depart from Mayakovskaya metro

TICKETS AND TRAVEL CARDS

There is no such thing as a one-day travel card in Moscow. Instead, there are tickets for one, two, five, 10, 20 or 60 rides, or passes for three months or a year. As the fare for a single journey is still a flat rate, whether it is a couple of stops or the length of the network, it is a very simple system to use. This also means that it is possible to change as many times as necessary if exploring the metro's architectural highlights (see pp38–41). Buy enough tickets for your stay at one time to avoid waiting in the ticket counter, or **касса** (kassa) queues, which can be long during the morning and evening rush hours.

The usual type of ticket is a magnetic card (magnitnaya karta) which works on a phonecard principle. When a card is inserted into the barrier, the passenger is allowed through if the card is valid, and the number of journeys left will be reduced by one. This number will then flash up on the display.

There are also new 'smart cards' which work on the same principal, but rather than being inserted into the barrier, are simply swiped across a yellow detector which reads the information. Any number of people can travel on the same ticket or card since they all pay exactly the same fee for their journey.

There are no child tickets for the Moscow metro, but children under six travel free of charge. Metro ticket counters also sell phonecards and tickets for trolleybuses, buses and trams (see p225).

Magnetic card being inserted into the barrier at a metro station

MAKING A JOURNEY BY METRO

1 Study the metro map (see p224) and plan your journey in advance as the station names on each platform are not visible from inside the train. It is well worth learning the pronunciation of the station names as the driver will announce which station you are approaching. It is also a good idea to count the number of stops.

2 Purchase a magnetic card from the **касса** (kassa), the counter situated just inside the metro station. Insert the card into the automatic barrier to gain access to the train platforms. Each time the card is used the details are printed on the back so the number of journeys remaining can be monitored.

3 To find the right platform follow signs headed к **поездам до станции** (k poezdam do stantsiy), which show the stops in each direction from the station you are at. These signs are sometimes colour coded.

Stops in one direction

4 On the platform, consult the signs showing all the stops of the line you are using. Trains always stop at each one. Look at the vertical lists beneath each interchange station. These show which subsequent stations you reach by changing at that point.

Colour of intersecting line   **Stops on other lines**   **Line**

5 Look at the digital board showing the time that has elapsed since a train last left the station. On weekdays another one will usually arrive within one or two minutes.

Current time   **Minutes and seconds since last train**

6 If you change to a different line during your journey, follow the signs marked with either **переход** (perekhod) or на **станцию** (na stantsiyu) and the appropriate station name. Once at your destination follow signs for **выход** (vykhod) to locate the exit.

Interchange sign

Exit and interchange sign

THE MOSCOW METRO

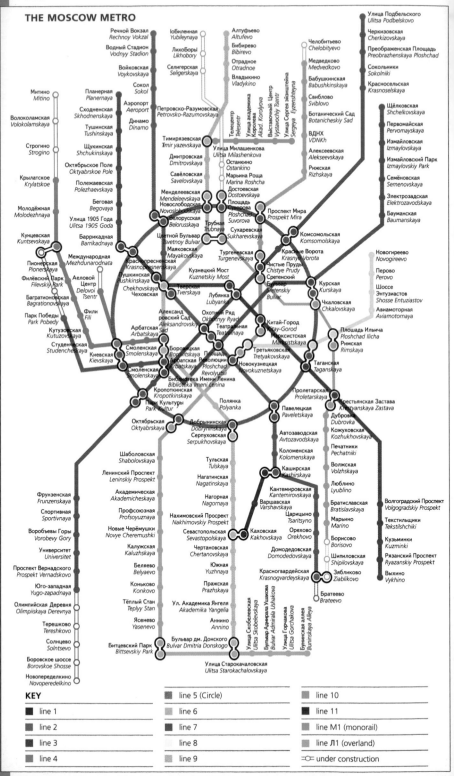

KEY

■ line 1	■ line 5 (Circle)	■ line 10
■ line 2	■ line 6	■ line 11
■ line 3	■ line 7	■ line M1 (monorail)
■ line 4	■ line 8	■ line Л1 (overland)
	■ line 9	⊏○⊐ under construction

Travelling by Tram, Trolleybus and Bus

Moscow has extensive bus, trolleybus and tram routes, and some of the most useful ones are identified on the transport map on the inside back cover of this book. Some routes link in with the metro network *(see pp222–4)*, often starting at one metro station and terminating at another. Main avenues are generally served by both buses and trolleybuses. Trams are less useful but, as a sedate form of transport, they are great for sightseeing. Busy routes can get extremely crowded during the morning and evening rush hours, and traffic is often slow-moving at these times. Moscow's newer, more remote suburbs are well served by these forms of transport. Stops are clearly signed and are at frequent intervals, though tram stops are occasionally further apart.

Queue of people waiting at a bus stop in central Moscow

TRAMS

Although trams remain Moscow's most traditional means of transport, services are now being cut back and some old tracks have been removed altogether. However, they provide a bumpy, entertaining ride for children, and interest and variety for visitors.

The surviving tram services run frequently, especially those operating in the suburbs,

linking metro stations and apartment blocks. Tram stops are marked by a transparent sign labelled "Tp" in Cyrillic and usually have a semi-circular shelter with a bench. Trams have one or two carriages, each with three doors. It was customary to get on through the rear door and leave through the front, but this practice is no longer observed.

Tram route A, which starts at Chistye Prudy metro, is useful for visitors to the city as it passes close to quite a few of Moscow's central sights.

TROLLEYBUSES

Trolleybuses are very useful for travelling around the city centre. Even though they are less comfortable and Muscovites prefer travelling by bus, most of the routes are still packed during rush hours. Stops are marked by a plaque with the Cyrillic letter T.

Trolleybuses are blue, red or yellow. Those with two cars have three working doors and those with a single car have two working doors. As with trams, there is no established etiquette as to which door to use when getting on or off.

Trolleybus b travels around the Garden Ring and is good for getting to know the city. Trolleybus

15 cuts across the whole city centre, starting at Suvorov ploshchad next to Novoslobodskaya metro and terminating at the Luzhniki Central Stadium *(see pp202–203)*.

BUSES

Buses are most useful for travelling in Moscow's suburbs where distances between metro lines are much greater than in the centre. Bus stops are marked by white and yellow plaques showing the cyrillic letter A and are the same distance apart as trolleybus stops. Public buses are yellow, red, or red and white. Bus services in the city centre are limited, and there are none running along Tverskaya ulitsa. However, several bus routes run up Kutuzovskiy prospekt past the Borodino Panorama Museum, the Triumphal Arch and Victory Park *(see pp128–9)*.

Ticket for tram, bus and trolleybus

Insert ticket here

Push large knob to punch ticket

Punching machine for validating tram, trolleybus and bus tickets

TICKETS AND TRAVEL CARDS

One-day travel cards are not available in Moscow, but monthly cards can be bought at metro stations: these cover the metro alone; tram, bus and trolleybus (separately or in any combination); or all four modes of transport. Individual tickets for bus, trolleybus and tram are identical and can be bought in metro stations or at nearby kiosks, or from drivers, but then cost a little more. They must be inserted into the punching machine on any bus, trolleybus or tram to be valid.

A yellow and white Moscow tram

A yellow Moscow bus

Trolleybus, powered by an overhead cable and running on a fixed route

Driving in Moscow

Driving in Moscow can be quite gruelling for the uninitiated. Most driving regulations, and many principles
that would be considered common sense elsewhere, are
ignored. For instance, although the majority of drivers
will stop at red lights, some carry on regardless. Cars
travel in disorderly lanes and veer dangerously to avoid
pot holes. Drivers tend to be aggressive and inconsiderate
about giving way to one another. Road signs mostly follow international conventions but, as all major roads are
sign-posted in Russian only, it is well worth drivers famil-
iarizing themselves with Cyrillic place-names in advance.

**Petrol station belonging to one of
several chains operating in Moscow**

DRIVING REGULATIONS

Driving regulations in
Moscow are complex.
GIBDD, Russia's traffic police
(see p210), have the right to
stop drivers at any time and
ask for documents.
They can issue fines
on the spot for
infringements
such as not
having a fire
extinguisher or
first-aid kit and
not wearing seat
belts. It is com-
pulsory for both
drivers and front-
seat passengers to
wear seat belts, although many
people do not. Drivers are not
allowed to drink any alcohol
at all and fines for drink-
driving can be very
high. It is illegal to
make U-turns on
many of Moscow's
main streets.
   Priority is always
given to traffic com-
ing from the right
unless a yellow, dia-
mond-shaped sign
indicates otherwise.
   The buying of
driving licences is
common in Russia,
so visitors should
not assume that all
road users are quali-
fied and responsible.

**Priority to
traffic on
the right
cancelled**

PARKING AND PETROL

Parking is expensive in most
of central Moscow. There
are no meters; instead, drivers
pay attendants in grey uniforms
on either arriving or leaving.
Parking time is by half-hour
periods, with no time limit.
Fines for parking in restricted
areas (marked with the international signs) are high. All
petrol is leaded. A98 (super-
plus) and A95 (super) are
suitable for foreign cars; A92
is for Russian-made cars.

CAR HIRE

There are several well-known
companies which operate in
Moscow. **Hertz** and **Europcar**
have offices at Sheremetevo 2
airport and in the city centre.
Other car-hire companies in
Moscow include **National Car
Rental** and **Avis**. Visitors
hiring a car need international
insurance and must show an
international driving licence
and their passport and credit
card when collecting it. Some
of the larger international
hotels also arrange car hire.

**Multiple lanes of traffic on Teatralniy proezd,
one of Moscow's busiest roads**

WINTER DRIVING

Most drivers use studded
tyres in winter as roads
are often icy and covered
with snow. Driving in these
conditions can be dangerous
and is not advisable unless
visitors have had experience
in other northern climates.

DRIVING OUTSIDE
MOSCOW

The roads leading out of
Moscow are in reasonable
condition, but Kutuzovskiy
prospekt is particularly well-
maintained because it is used
by government officials and
the New Russians who own
a *dacha* in this area. It is vital
to have a good map because
side roads to small villages
can easily be missed.

Directory

CAR HIRE

Avis
Meshchanskaya ullitsa 7/21.
Map 3 B2. *Tel (495) 684 1937.*
www.avis.com

Europcar
Moscow Mozhayskoe shosse 166.
Tel (495) 775 7565.
Domodedovo Airport Arrival Hall.
Tel (495) 363 6418.
www.europcar.com

Hertz
Leningradskoe shosse 16/9.
Tel (495) 937 3274.
Sheremetevo 2 airport. *Tel (495)
578 5646.* **www**.hertz.com

National Car Rental
Bolshaya Kommunisticheskaya
ulitsa 1/5. *Tel (495) 698 6146.*

City Wheels Moscow
Pohodnil proezd 123,
Tel (495) 645 2067. **www.**
citywheels.ru

RESCUE SERVICES

Angel Rescue Service
Ангел
Signalyyy proezd 5. *Tel (495) 747
0022.*

**Emergency Service
Station (24 hours)**
Ryazanski pereulok 13.
Map 4 D3. *Tel (495) 667 0113.*

Excursions from Moscow

Arrangements to visit sights outside Moscow *(see pp126–67)* can be made through either a hotel or a travel agency, or the trip can be made independently by train, bus or car. Most of the places mentioned below are not far from Moscow and can be visited on a day trip. A few, such as Suzdal and Vladimir, take two days. Patriarshiy Dom Tours *(see p206)* offers a wide range of excursions to the major sights around Moscow. It is advisable to enquire in good time as reservations with them have to be made 48 hours before departure.

Inside the carriage of one of Moscow's suburban trains

USING TRAINS AND BUSES

Suburban trains *(prigorodnye poezda)* to the nearer sights can be caught at the appropriate mainline station *(see p218)*. They usually depart from a station annexe and are cheap as foreigners pay the same fare as Russians. More distant sights are served by passenger trains *(passazhirskie poezda)*.

Suburban buses *(prigorodnye marshruty)* to several closer excursion sights leave from Moscow Bus Station at Shchelkovskaya metro station in the northeast of the city. Towns further from Moscow are served by inter-city buses *(mezhdugorodnye avtobusy)*.

An inter-city bus, which can be used to make long-distance trips

ONE-DAY TRIPS

Both Novodevichiy Convent *(see pp130–1)* and Kolomenskoe *(see pp138–9)* are south of the city centre, the former close to Sportivnaya metro, the latter to Kolomenskaya metro. Kuskovo *(see pp142–3)*, in eastern Moscow, is also best reached by metro, to Ryazanskiy Prospekt or Vykhino. A short bus ride will then take visitors to the estate.

Arkhangelskoe *(see p158)*, 20 km (12 miles) to the west of the city centre, is served by Tushinskaya metro and then a bus. By car it is on a straight route out along Volokolamskoe shosse or Rublevskoe shosse.

It takes around two hours to travel to the village and battle-field of Borodino *(see p158)* by train from Belorusskiy station, by bus from Moscow Bus Station or by car, leaving the city on Mozhayskoe shosse.

The Tchaikovsky House-Museum *(see p159)* is two hours northwest of the city by car on Leningradskoe shosse, by train from Leningradskiy station, or by bus from Moscow Bus Station.

Abramtsevo Estate-Museum *(see p160)* is situated to the northeast of Moscow just off Yaroslavskoe shosse. Trains leave from Yaroslavskiy station and buses from Moscow Bus Station. The journey takes an hour or so.

The Trinity Monastery of St Sergius *(see pp162–5)* is also to the northeast along Yaroslavskoe shosse and the journey also takes just over an hour. It is possible to get there by train or by bus from Yaroslavskiy station, and by bus from Moscow Bus Station.

Pereslavl-Zalesskiy *(see p160)* can be reached by car along Yaroslavskoe shosse, by train from Yaroslavskiy station, or by bus from Moscow Bus Station. The trip takes approximately two hours.

TWO-DAY TRIPS

Suzdal *(see p166)*, 200 km (124 miles) northeast of Moscow, is reached by leaving the city on Gorkovskoe shosse. Buses to Suzdal leave from Moscow Bus Station and take about four hours.

Vladimir *(see pp166–7)* is also situated northeast of the city along Gorkovskoe shosse. The 170 km (106-mile) trip can be made by bus from Moscow Bus Station, by train or by car in about three hours.

Yasnaya Polyana *(see p167)* is 180 km (112 miles) south of Moscow on the Simferopolskoe shosse. Trains run from Kurskiy station and coaches from Moscow Bus Station. Both take almost four hours.

It is worth considering combining a trip to Vladimir and Suzdal; buses run daily between the two. Patriarshiy Dom runs tours to both towns with an overnight stopover, and day trips to Yasnaya Polyana.

Train arriving at Sergiev Posad for the Trinity Monastery of St Sergius

MOSCOW STREET FINDER

The key map below shows the areas of Moscow covered by the *Street Finder*. The map references given throughout the guide for sights, restaurants, hotels, shops or entertainment venues refer to the maps in this section. All the major sights have been marked so they are easy to locate. The key below shows other features marked

A Moscow family out sightseeing

on the maps, such as post offices, metro stations and churches. The *Street Finder* index lists street names in transliteration, followed by Cyrillics (on maps, Cyrillics are only given for major roads). This guide uses the reinstated old Russian street names, not the Soviet versions *(see p207)*. Places of interest are listed by their English names.

0 kilometres 1

0 miles 1

KEY TO STREET FINDER

◼ Major sight	🚢 River boat pier	⊠ Post office	
◼ Place of interest	🚖 Taxi rank	═ Railway line	
◻ Other building	✚ Hospital	45» House number (main street)	
🚆 Train station	🚓 Police station		
Ⓜ Metro station	✝ Orthodox church	**SCALE OF MAP PAGES**	
🚊 Main tram stop	✝ Non-Orthodox church		
🚎 Main trolleybus stop	✡ Synagogue	0 metres 300	
🚌 Main bus stop	☪ Mosque	0 yards 300	

Street Finder Index

1 Maya, Park im
1 МАЯ, ПАРК ЙМ 4F5

1-ya Borodinskaya ulitsa
1-Я БОРОДИНСКАЯ УЛИЦА 5B2

1-ya Brestskaya ulitsa
1-Я БРЕСТСКАЯ УЛИЦА 2D2

1-ya Dubrovskaya ulitsa
1-Я ДУБРОВСКАЯ УЛИЦА 8F5

1-ya Frunzenskaya ulitsa
1-Я ФРУНЗЕНСКАЯ УЛИЦА 6D5

1-ya Miusskaya ulitsa
1-Я МИУССКАЯ УЛИЦА 2D1

1-ya Tverskaya-Yamskaya ulitsa
1-Я ТВЕРСКАЯ-ЯМСКАЯ УЛИЦА 2D2

1-ya Yamskovo Polya, ulitsa
1-Я ЯМСКОГО ПОЛЯ, УЛИЦА 1C1

1-yy Rabegorodskiy pereulok
1-ЫЙ ВАБЛЕГОРОДСКИЙ ПЕРЕУЛОК 6F3, 7A4

1-yy Basmannyy pereulok
1-ЫЙ БАСМАННЫЙ ПЕРЕУЛОК 4E3

1-yy Botkinskiy proezd
1-ЫЙ БОТКИНСКИЙ ПРОЕЗД 1A1

1-yy Bryanskiy pereulok
1-ЫЙ БРЯНСКИЙ ПЕРЕУЛОК 5B2

1-yy Goncharnyy pereulok
1-ЫЙ ГОНЧАРНЫЙ ПЕРЕУЛОК 8D3

1-yy Kadashevskiy pereulok
1-ЫЙ КАДАШЕВСКИЙ ПЕРЕУЛОК 7B3

1-yy Kazachiy pereulok
1-ЫЙ КАЗАЧИЙ ПЕРЕУЛОК 7A4

1-yy Khvostov pereulok
1-ЫЙ ХВОСТОВ ПЕРЕУЛОК 7A4

1-yy Kolobovskiy pereulok
1-ЫЙ КОЛОБОВСКИЙ ПЕРЕУЛОК 3A3

1-yy Koptelskiy pereulok
1-ЫЙ КОПТЕЛЬСКИЙ ПЕРЕУЛОК 3C2

1-yy Koteinicheskiy pereulok
1-ЫЙ КОТЕЛЬНИЧЕСКИЙ ПЕРЕУЛОК 8D3

1-yy Kozhevnicheskiy pereulok
1-ЫЙ КОЖЕВНИЧЕСКИЙ ПЕРЕУЛОК 8D5

1-yy Krutitskiy pereulok
1-ЫЙ КРУТИЦКИЙ ПЕРЕУЛОК 8E5

1-yy Lesnoy pereulok
1-ЫЙ ЛЕСНОЙ ПЕРЕУЛОК 2D1

1-yy Lyusinovskiy pereulok
1-ЫЙ ЛЮСИНОВСКИЙ ПЕРЕУЛОК 7A5

1-yy Neopalimovskiy pereulok
1-ЫЙ НЕОПАЛИМОВСКИЙ ПЕРЕУЛОК 5C3

1-yy Nikoloshchepovskiy pereulok
1-ЫЙ НИКОЛОЩЕПОВСКИЙ ПЕРЕУЛОК 5C1

1-yy Novokuznetskiy pereulok
1-ЫЙ НОВОКУЗНЕЦКИЙ ПЕРЕУЛОК 7B4

1-yy Novyy pereulok
1-ЫЙ НОВЫЙ ПЕРЕУЛОК 4F1

1-yy Obydenskiy pereulok
1-ЫЙ ОБЫДЕНСКИЙ ПЕРЕУЛОК 6E2

1-yy Samotechnyy pereulok
1-ЫЙ САМОТЕЧНЫЙ ПЕРЕУЛОК 2F2

1-yy Shchemilovskiy pereulok
1-ЫЙ ЩЕМИЛОВСКИЙ ПЕРЕУЛОК 2F1

1-yy Shibaevskiy pereulok
1-ЫЙ ШИБАЕВСКИЙ ПЕРЕУЛОК 5C5

1-yy Shlyuzovoy pereulok
1-ЫЙ ШЛЮЗОВОЙ ПЕРЕУЛОК 8D4

1-yy Smolenskiy pereulok
1-ЫЙ СМОЛЕНСКИЙ ПЕРЕУЛОК 5C1

1-yy Spasonalivkovskiy pereulok
1-ЫЙ СПАСОНАЛИВКОВСКИЙ ПЕРЕУЛОК 7A4

1-yy Truzhenikov pereulok
1-ЫЙ ТРУЖЕНИКОВ ПЕРЕУЛОК 5B3

1-yy Tverskoy-Yamskoy pereulok
1-ЫЙ ТВЕРСКОЙ-ЯМСКОЙ ПЕРЕУЛОК 2E3

1-yy Vrazhskiy pereulok
1-ЫЙ ВРАЖСКИЙ ПЕРЕУЛОК 5B3

1-yy Zachatevskiy pereulok
1-ЫЙ ЗАЧАТЬЕВСКИЙ ПЕРЕУЛОК 6E3

1-yy Zemelnyy pereulok
1-ЫЙ ЗЕМЕЛЬНЫЙ ПЕРЕУЛОК 1A3

2-oy Botkinskiy proezd
2-ОЙ БОТКИНСКИЙ ПРОЕЗД 1A1

2-oy Bryanskiy pereulok
2-ОЙ БРЯНСКИЙ ПЕРЕУЛОК 5B2

2-oy Kadashevskiy pereulok
2-ОЙ КАДАШЕВСКИЙ ПЕРЕУЛОК 7B3

2-oy Kazachiy pereulok
2-ОЙ КАЗАЧИЙ ПЕРЕУЛОК 7B4

2-oy Khvostov pereulok
2-ОЙ ХВОСТОВ ПЕРЕУЛОК 7A4

2-oy Kozhevnicheskiy pereulok
2-ОЙ КОЖЕВНИЧЕСКИЙ ПЕРЕУЛОК 8D5

2-oy Krutitskiy pereulok
2-ОЙ КРУТИЦКИЙ ПЕРЕУЛОК 8E5

2-oy Lesnoy pereulok
2-ОЙ ЛЕСНОЙ ПЕРЕУЛОК 2D1

2-oy Neopalimovskiy pereulok
2-ОЙ НЕОПАЛИМОВСКИЙ ПЕРЕУЛОК 5C3

2-oy Novokuznetskiy pereulok
2-ОЙ НОВОКУЗНЕЦКИЙ ПЕРУЛОК 7B4

2-oy Obydenskiy pereulok
2-ОЙ ОБЫДЕНСКИЙ ПЕРЕУЛОК 6E2

2-oy Raushskiy pereulok
2-ОЙ РАУШСКИЙ ПЕРЕУЛОК 7C2

2-oy Shchemilovskiy pereulok
2-ОЙ ЩЕМИЛОВСКИЙ ПЕРЕУЛОК 2F2

2-oy Shlyuzovoy pereulok
2-ОЙ ШЛЮЗОВОЙ ПЕРЕУЛОК 8D4

2-oy Smolenskiy pereulok
2-ОЙ СМОЛЕНСКИЙ ПЕРЕУЛОК 5C2

2-oy Spasonalivkovskiy pereulok
2-ОЙ СПАСОНАЛИВКОВСКИЙ ПЕРЕУЛОК 7A5

2-oy Truzhenikov pereulok
2-ОЙ ТРУЖЕНИКОВ ПЕРЕУЛОК 5B3

2-yy Vrazhskiy pereulok
2-ОЙ ВРАЖСКИЙ ПЕРЕУЛОК 5C3

2-ya Borodinskaya ulitsa
2-Я БОРОДИНСКАЯ УЛИЦА 5B1

2-ya Brestskaya ulitsa
2-Я БРЕСТСКАЯ УЛИЦА 2D2

2-ya Dubrovskaya ulitsa
2-Я ДУБРОВСКАЯ УЛИЦА 8F5

2-ya Miusskaya ulitsa
2-Я МИУССКАЯ УЛИЦА 2D2

2-ya Tverskaya-Yamskaya ulitsa
2-Я ТВЕРСКАЯ-ЯМСКАЯ УЛИЦА 2D2

2-ya Zvenigorodskaya ulitsa
2-Я ЗВЕНИГОРОДСКАЯ УЛИЦА 1A4

3-iy Golutvinskiy pereulok
3-ИЙ ГОЛУТВИНСКИЙ ПЕРЕУЛОК 6F3, 7A3

3-iy Kadashevskiy pereulok
3-ИЙ КАДАШЕВСКИЙ ПЕРЕУЛОК 7B3

3-iy Kotelnicheskiy pereulok
3-ИЙ КОТЕЛЬНИЧЕСКИЙ ПЕРЕУЛОК 8D3

3-iy Krutitskiy pereulok
3-ИЙ КРУТИЦКИЙ ПЕРЕУЛОК 8E5

3-iy Lesnoy pereulok
3-ИЙ ЛЕСНОЙ ПЕРЕУЛОК 2D2

3-iy Monetchikovskiy pereulok
3-ИЙ МОНЕТЧИКОВСКИЙ ПЕРЕУЛОК 7B4

3-iy Neopalimovskiy pereulok
3-ИЙ НЕОПАЛИМОВСКИЙ ПЕРЕУЛОК 6D3

3-iy Samotechnyy pereulok
3-ИЙ САМОТЕЧНЫЙ ПЕРЕУЛОК 2F1

3-iy Shlyuzovoy pereulok
3-ИЙ ШЛЮЗОВОЙ ПЕРЕУЛОК 8D4

3-iy Smolenskiy pereulok
3-ИЙ СМОЛЕНСКИЙ ПЕРЕУЛОК 5C1

3-iy Zachatevskiy pereulok
3-ИЙ ЗАЧАТЬЕВСКИЙ ПЕРЕУЛОК 6E3

3-ya Frunzenskaya ulitsa
3-Я ФРУНЗЕНСКАЯ УЛИЦА 5C5

3-ya Tverskaya-Yamskaya ulitsa
3-Я ТВЕРСКАЯ-ЯМСКАЯ УЛИЦА 2D2

ABBREVIATIONS & USEFUL WORDS

ul	ulitsa	street
pl	ploshchad	square
pr	prospekt	avenue
per	pereulok	small street/ passage/lane
	most	bridge
	podezd	entrance
	proezd	small street/ passage/lane
	sad	garden
	shosse	road
	stroenie	building
	tupik	cul-de-sac

3-ya Yamskovo Polya, ulitsa
3-Я ЯМСКОГО ПОЛЯ, УЛИЦА   **1C1**

4-ya Tverskaya-Yamskaya ulitsa
4-Я ТВЕРСКАЯ-ЯМСКАЯ УЛИЦА   **2D2**

4-yy Dobryninskiy pereulok
4-ЫЙ ДОБРЫНИНСКИЙ ПЕРЕУЛОК   **7A5**

4-yy Krutitskiy pereulok
4-ЫЙ КРУТИЦКИЙ ПЕРЕУЛОК   **8E5**

4-yy Lesnoy pereulok
4-ЫЙ ЛЕСНОЙ ПЕРЕУЛОК   **2D1**

4-yy Monetchikovskiy pereulok
4-ЫЙ МОНЕТЧИКОВСКИЙ ПЕРЕУЛОК   **7B4**

4-yy Rostovskiy pereulok
4-ЫЙ РОСТОВСКИЙ ПЕРЕУЛОК   **5C2**

5-yy Kotelnicheskiy pereulok
5-ЫЙ КОТЕЛЬНИЧЕСКИЙ ПЕРЕУЛОК   **8D3**

5-yy Monetchikovskiy pereulok
5-ЫЙ МОНЕТЧИКОВСКИЙ ПЕРЕУЛОК   **7B5**

6-oy Rostovskiy pereulok
6-ОЙ РОСТОВСКИЙ ПЕРЕУЛОК   **5C2**

7-oy Rostovskiy pereulok
7-ОЙ РОСТОВСКИЙ ПЕРЕУЛОК   **5C3**

1905 goda, ulitsa
1905 ГОДА, УЛИЦА   **1A3**

A

Abelmanovskaya ulitsa
АБЕЛЬМАНОВСКАЯ УЛИЦА   **8F4**

Akademika Sakharova, prospekt
АКАДЕМИКА САХАРОВА, ПРОСПЕКТ   **3C3**

Akademika Tupoleva, naberezhnaya
АКАДЕМИКА ТУПОЛЕВА, НАБЕРЕЖНАЯ   **4F5**

Akvarium, sad
АКВАРИУМ, САД   **2E3**

Aleksandra Lukyanova, ulitsa
АЛЕКСАНДРА ЛУКЬЯНОВА, УЛИЦА   **4E3**

Aleksandra Nevskovo, ulitsa
АЛЕКСАНДРА НЕВСКОГО, УЛИЦА   **2D2**

Alexander Gardens   **7A1**

Ananevskiy pereulok
АНАНЕВСКИЙ ПЕРЕУЛОК   **3C3**

Andronevskaya naberezhnaya
АНДРОНЬЕВСКАЯ НАБЕРЕЖНАЯ   **8F2**

Anny Severyanovoy, ulitsa
АННЫ СЕВЕРЬЯНОВОЙ, УЛИЦА   **1A5**

Aptekarskiy pereulok
АПТЕКАРСКИЙ ПЕРЕУЛОК   **4F3**

Arbat Square   **6E1**

Arbat, ulitsa
АРБАТ, УЛИЦА   **6D1**

Arbatskaya ploshchad
АРБАТСКАЯ ПЛОЩАДЬ   **6E1**

Aristarkhovskiy pereulok
АРИСТАРХОВСКИЙ ПЕРЕУЛОК   **8E2**

Arkhangelskiy pereulok
АРХАНГЕЛЬСКИЙ ПЕРЕУЛОК   **3C4**

Armyanskiy pereulok
АРМЯНСКИЙ ПЕРЕУЛОК   **3B4**

Arsenal   **3A5, 7A1**

Ashcheulov pereulok
АЩЕУЛОВ ПЕРЕУЛОК   **3B3**

Astrakhanskiy pereulok
АСТРАХАНСКИЙ ПЕРЕУЛОК   **3C1**

B

Bakhrushin Theatre Museum   **7C5**

Bakhrushina, ulitsa
БАХРУШИНА, УЛИЦА   **7C4**

Balchug, ulitsa
БАЛЧУГ, УЛИЦА   **7B2**

Barashevskiy pereulok
БАРАШЕВСКИЙ ПЕРЕУЛОК   **4D5**

Barrikadnaya ulitsa
БАРРИКАДНАЯ УЛИЦА   **1C4**

Barykovskiy pereulok
БАРЫКОВСКИЙ ПЕРЕУЛОК   **6E2**

Basmannyy pereulok
БАСМАННЫЙ ПЕРЕУЛОК   **4E3**

Basmannyy tupik
БАСМАННЫЙ ТУПИК   **4D3**

Baumana, sad im A
БАУМАНА, САД ИМ А   **4E3**

Baumanskaya ulitsa
БАУМАНСКАЯ УЛИЦА   **4F2**

Begovaya alleya
БЕГОВАЯ АЛЛЕЯ   **1B1**

Begovaya ulitsa
БЕГОВАЯ УЛИЦА   **1A2**

Begovoy proezd
БЕГОВОЙ ПРОЕЗД   **1A2**

Bely House-Museum   **6D2**

Berezhkovskaya naberezhnaya
БЕРЕЖКОВСКАЯ НАБЕРЕЖНАЯ   **5A4**

Bernikov pereulok
БЕРНИКОВ ПЕРЕУЛОК   **8D2**

Bernikovskaya naberezhnaya
БЕРНИКОВСКАЯ НАБЕРЕЖНАЯ   **8D2**

Bersenev pereulok
БЕРСЕНЕВ ПЕРЕУЛОК   **6F3**

Bersenevskaya naberezhnaya
БЕРСЕНЕВСКАЯ НАБЕРЕЖНАЯ   **6F2**

Blagoveshchenskiy pereulok
БЛАГОВЕЩЕНСКИЙ ПЕРЕУЛОК   **2E3**

Bobrov pereulok
БОБРОВ ПЕРЕУЛОК   **3B4**

Bogoslovskiy pereulok
ВОГОСЛОВСКИЙ ПЕРЕУЛОК   **2E4**

Bogoyavlenskiy pereulok
БОГОЯВЛЕНСКИЙ ПЕРЕУЛОК   **3A5, 7B1**

Bolotnaya naberezhnaya
БОЛОТНАЯ НАБЕРЕЖНАЯ   **7A3**

Bolotnaya ploshchad
БОЛОТНАЯ ПЛОЩАДЬ   **7A2**

Bolotnaya ulitsa
БОЛОТНАЯ УЛИЦА   **7B2**

Bolshaya Andronevskaya ulitsa
БОЛЬШАЯ АНДРОНЬЕВСКАЯ УЛИЦА   **8F2**

Bolshaya Bronnaya ulitsa
БОЛЬШАЯ БРОННАЯ УЛИЦА   **2E4**

Bolshaya Dekabrskaya ulitsa
БОЛЬШАЯ ДЕКАБРЬСКАЯ УЛИЦА   **1A3**

Bolshaya Dmitrovka, ulitsa
БОЛЬШАЯ ДМИТРОВКА, УЛИЦА   **2F4**

Bolshaya Dorogomilovskaya ulitsa
БОЛЬШАЯ ДОРОГОМИЛОВСКАЯ УЛИЦА   **5B2**

Bolshaya Gruzinskaya ulitsa
БОЛЬШАЯ ГРУЗИНСКАЯ УЛИЦА   **1C4**

Bolshaya Kommunisticheskaya ulitsa
БОЛЬШАЯ КОММУНИСТИЧЕСКАЯ УЛИЦА   **8E3**

Bolshaya Lubyanka, ulitsa
БОЛЬШАЯ ЛУБЯНКА, УЛИЦА   **3B4**

Bolshaya Molchanovka, ulitsa
БОЛЬШАЯ МОЛЧАНОВКА, УЛИЦА   **6D1**

Bolshaya Nikitskaya ulitsa
БОЛЬШАЯ НИКИТСКАЯ УЛИЦА   **2D5**

Bolshaya Ordynka, ulitsa
БОЛЬШАЯ ОРДЫНКА, УЛИЦА   **7B3**

Bolshaya Pereyaslavskaya ulitsa
БОЛЬШАЯ ПЕРЕЯСЛАВСКАЯ УЛИЦА   **3C1**

Bolshaya Pionerskaya ulitsa
БОЛЬШАЯ ПИОНЕРСКАЯ УЛИЦА   **7C5**

Bolshaya Pirogovskaya ulitsa
БОЛЬШАЯ ПИРОГОВСКАЯ УЛИЦА   **5A5**

Bolshaya Polyanka, ulitsa
БОЛЬШАЯ ПОЛЯНКА, УЛИЦА   **7A3**

Bolshaya Sadovaya ulitsa
БОЛЬШАЯ САДОВАЯ УЛИЦА   **2D3**

Bolshaya Serpukhovskaya ulitsa
БОЛЬШАЯ СЕРПУХОВСКАЯ УЛИЦА   **7B5**

Bolshaya Spasskaya ulitsa
БОЛЬШАЯ СПАССКАЯ УЛИЦА   **3C2**

Bolshaya Tatarskaya ulitsa
БОЛЬШАЯ ТАТАРСКАЯ УЛИЦА   **7C3**

Bolshaya Yakimanka, ulitsa
БОЛЬШАЯ ЯКИМАНКА, УЛИЦА   **6F4, 7A4**

Bolshie Kamenshchiki, ulitsa
БОЛЬШИЕ КАМЕНЩИКИ, УЛИЦА   **8E3**

Bolshoy Afanasevskiy pereulok
БОЛЬШОЙ АФАНАСЬЕВСКИЙ ПЕРЕУЛОК   **6E1**

Bolshoy Balkanskiy pereulok
БОЛЬШОЙ БАЛКАНСКИЙ ПЕРЕУЛОК   **3C2**

Bolshoy Cherkasskiy pereulok
БОЛЬШОЙ ЧЕРКАССКИЙ ПЕРЕУЛОК   **3B5, 7B1**

Bolshoy Chudov pereulok
БОЛЬШОЙ ЧУДОВ ПЕРЕУЛОК   **6D4**

Bolshoy Demidovskiy pereulok
БОЛЬШОЙ ДЕМИДОВСКИЙ ПЕРЕУЛОК   **4F4**

Bolshoy Devyatinskiy pereulok
БОЛЬШОЙ ДЕВЯТИНСКИЙ ПЕРЕУЛОК   **1C5**

Bolshoy Drovyanoy pereulok
БОЛЬШОЙ ДРОВЯНОЙ ПЕРЕУЛОК   **8E2**

Bolshoy Fakelnyy pereulok
БОЛЬШОЙ ФАКЕЛЬНЫЙ ПЕРЕУЛОК   **8F3**

Bolshoy Gnezdnikovskiy pereulok
БОЛЬШОЙ ГНЕЗДНИКОВСКИЙ ПЕРЕУЛОК   **2F4**

Bolshoy Golovin pereulok
БОЛЬШОЙ ГОЛОВИН ПЕРЕУЛОК   **3B3**

Bolshoy Kamennyy most
БОЛЬШОЙ КАМЕННЫЙ МОСТ   **6F2, 7A2**

Bolshoy Karetnyy pereulok
БОЛЬШОЙ КАРЕТНЫЙ ПЕРЕУЛОК   **3A3**

Bolshoy Kazennyy pereulok
БОЛЬШОЙ КАЗЕННЫЙ ПЕРЕУЛОК   **4D5**

Bolshoy Kharitonevsky p ereulok
БОЛЬШОЙ ХАРИТОНЬЕВСКИЙ ПЕРЕУЛОК   3C4

Bolshoy Kiselnyy pereulok
БОЛЬШОЙ КИСЕЛЬНЫЙ ПЕРЕУЛОК   3A4

Bolshoy Kislovskiy pereulok
БОЛЬШОЙ КИСЛОВКИЙ ПЕРЕУЛОК   2F5

Bolshoy Kondratevskiy pereulok
БОЛЬШОЙ КОНДРАТЬЕВСКИЙ ПЕРЕУЛОК   1C2

Bolshoy Kozikhinskiy pereulok
БОЛЬШОЙ КОЗИХИНСКИЙ ПЕРЕУЛОК   2E4

Bolshoy Kozlovskiy pereulok
БОЛЬШОЙ КОЗЛОВСКИЙ ПЕРЕУЛОК   3C3

Bolshoy Krasnokholmskiy most
БОЛЬШОЙ КРАСНОХОЛМСКИЙ МОСТ   8D4

Bolshoy Levshinskiy pereulok
БОЛЬШОЙ ЛЕВШИНСКИЙ ПЕРЕУЛОК   6D2

Bolshoy Moskvoretskiy most
БОЛЬШОЙ МОСКВОРЕЦКИЙ МОСТ   7B2

Bolshoy Nikolopeskovskiy pereulok
БОЛЬШОЙ НИКОЛОПЕСКОВСКИЙ ПЕРЕУЛОК   6D1

Bolshoy Nikolovorobinskiy pereulok
БОЛЬШОЙ НИКОЛОВОРОБИНСКИЙ ПЕРЕУЛОК   8D1

Bolshoy Novopeskovskiy pereulok
БОЛЬШОЙ НОВОПЕСКОВСКИЙ ПЕРЕУЛОК   5C1

Bolshoy Ordynskiy pereulok
БОЛЬШОЙ ОРДЫНСКИЙ ПЕРЕУЛОК   7B4

Bolshoy Ovchinnikovskiy pereulok
БОЛЬШОЙ ОВЧИННИКОВСКИЙ ПЕРЕУЛОК   7B3

Bolshoy Palashevskiy pereulok
БОЛЬШОЙ ПАЛАШЕВСКИЙ ПЕРЕУЛОК   2E4

Bolshoy Patriarshiy pereulok
БОЛЬШОЙ ПАТРИАРШИЙ ПЕРЕУЛОК   2D4

Bolshoy Poluyaroslavskiy pereulok
БОЛЬШОЙ ПОЛУЯРОСЛАВСКИЙ ПЕРЕУЛОК   8E1

Bolshoy Predtechenskiy pereulok
БОЛЬШОЙ ПРЕДТЕЧЕНСКИЙ ПЕРЕУЛОК   1B4

Bolshoy Rogozhskiy pereulok
БОЛЬШОЙ РОГОЖСКИЙ ПЕРЕУЛОК   8F3

Bolshoy Savvinskiy pereulok
БОЛЬШОЙ САВВИНСКИЙ ПЕРЕУЛОК   5B4

Bolshoy Sergievskiy pereulok
БОЛЬШОЙ СЕРГИЕВСКИЙ ПЕРЕУЛОК   3A3

Bolshoy Simonovskiy pereulok
БОЛЬШОЙ СИМОНОВСКИЙ ПЕРЕУЛОК   8F5

Bolshoy Spasoglinishchevskiy pereulok
БОЛЬШОЙ СПАСОГЛИНИЩЕВСКИЙ ПЕРЕУЛОК   3B5, 7CI

Bolshoy Strochenovskiy pereulok
БОЛЬШОЙ СТРОЧЕНОВСКИЙ ПЕРЕУЛОК   7B5

Bolshoy Sukharevskiy pereulok
БОЛЬШОЙ СУХАРЕВСКИЙ ПЕРЕУЛОК   3B3

Bolshoy Tatarskiy pereulok
БОЛЬШОЙ ТАТАРСКИЙ ПЕРЕУЛОК   7C4

Bolshoy Theatre   3A4

Bolshoy Tishinskiy pereulok
БОЛЬШОЙ ТИШИНСКИЙ ПЕРЕУЛОК   1B3

Bolshoy Tolmachevskiy pereulok
БОЛЬШОЙ ТОЛМАЧЕВСКИЙ ПЕРЕУЛОК   7A3

Bolshoy Trekhgornyy pereulok
БОЛЬШОЙ ТРЕХГОРНЫЙ ПЕРЕУЛОК   1B5

Bolshoy Trekhsvyatitelskiy pereulok
БОЛЬШОЙ ТРЕХСВЯТИТЕЛЬСКИЙ ПЕРЕУЛОК   3C5, 8D1

Bolshoy Ustinskiy most
БОЛЬШОЙ УСТЬИНСКИЙ МОСТ   7C2

Bolshoy Vlasevskiy pereulok
БОЛЬШОЙ ВЛАСЬЕВСКИЙ ПЕРЕУЛОК   6D2

Bolshoy Zlatoustinskiy pereulok
БОЛЬШОЙ ЗЛАТОУСТИНСКИЙ ПЕРЕУЛОК   3B5

Bolshoy Znamenskiy pereulok
БОЛЬШОЙ ЗНАМЕНСКИЙ ПЕРЕУЛОК   6E1

Borisoglebskiy pereulok
БОРИСОГЛЕБСКИЙ ПЕРЕУЛОК   2D5

Borodinskiy most
БОРОДИНСКИЙ МОСТ   5B2

Borovitskaya ploshchad
БОРОВИЦКАЯ ПЛОЩАДЬ   6F1

Botanicheskiy pereulok
БОТАНИЧЕСКИЙ ПЕРЕУЛОК   3C2

Botanicheskiy sad MGU
БОТАНИЧЕСКИЙ САД МГУ   3B2

Brodnikov pereulok
БРОДНИКОВ ПЕРЕУЛОК   7A4

Bryanskaya ulitsa
БРЯНСКАЯ УЛИЦА   5A2

Bryusov pereulok
БРЮСОВ ПЕРЕУЛОК   2F5

Burdenko, ulitsa
БУРДЕНКО, УЛИЦА   5C3

Butikovskiy pereulok
БУТИКОВСКИЙ ПЕРЕУЛОК   6E3

Butyrskiy val, ulitsa
БУТЫРСКИЙ ВАЛ, УЛИЦА   2D1

C

Cathedral of Christ the Redeemer   6F2
Cathedral of the Annunciation   7A2
Cathedral of the Archangel   7A2
Cathedral of the Assumption   7A1

Chaplygina, ulitsa
ЧАПЛЫГИНА, УЛИЦА   4D4

Chayanova, ulitsa
ЧАЯНОВА, УЛИЦА   2D2

Chekhov House-Museum   2D5

Chistoprudnyy bulvar
ЧИСТОПРУДНЫЙ БУЛЬВАР   3C4

Chistyy pereulok
ЧИСТЫЙ ПЕРЕУЛОК   6D2

Chugunnyy most
ЧУГУННЫЙ МОСТ   7B2

Church of St Clement   7B3
Church of St John the Warrior   6F4, 7A4
Church of St Nicholas in Pyzhy   7B3
Church of St Nicholas of the Weavers   6D4
Church of the Consolation of All Sorrows   7B3
Church of the Deposition of the Robe   7A1
Church of the Resurrection in Kadashi   7B3
Church of the Trinity in Nikitniki   7C1
Confectionery Shop   7B3
Convent of SS Martha and Mary   7B4
Convent of the Nativity of the Virgin   3A4

D

Daev pereulok
ДАЕВ ПЕРЕУЛОК   3B3

Dashkov pereulok
ДАШКОВ ПЕРЕУЛОК   6D3

Degtyarnyy pereulok
ДЕГТЯРНЫЙ ПЕРЕУЛОК   2E3

Delegatskaya ulitsa
ДЕЛЕГАТСКАЯ УЛИЦА   2F2

Denezhnyy pereulok
ДЕНЕЖНЫЙ ПЕРЕУЛОК   6D2

Denisovskiy pereulok
ДЕНИСОВСКИЙ ПЕРЕУЛОК   4F4

Derbenevskaya naberezhnaya
ДЕРБЕНЕВСКАЯ НАБЕРЕЖНАЯ   8E5

Desyatiletiya Oktyabrya, ulitsa
ДЕСЯТИЛЕТИЯ ОКТЯБРЯ, УЛИЦА   5B5

Devichevo Polya, proezd
ДЕВИЧЬЕГО ПОЛЯ, ПРОЕЗД   5C3

Dinamovskaya ulitsa
ДИНАМОВСКАЯ УЛИЦА   8E5

Dmitrovskiy pereulok
ДМИТРОВСКИЙ ПЕРЕУЛОК   3A4

Dobroslobodskaya ulitsa
ДОБРОСЛОБОДСКАЯ УЛИЦА   4F3

Dobrovolcheskaya ulitsa
ДОБРОВОЛЬЧЕСКАЯ УЛИЦА   8F2

Dobryninskiy pereulok
ДОБРЫНИНСКИЙ ПЕРЕУЛОК   7A3

Dokuchaev pereulok
ДОКУЧАЕВ ПЕРЕУЛОК   3C2

Dolgorukovskaya ulitsa
ДОЛГОРУКОВСКАЯ УЛИЦА   2E2

Donskaya ulitsa
ДОНСКАЯ УЛИЦА   6F5

Dostoevskovo, pereulok
ДОСТОЕВСКОГО, ПЕРЕУЛОК   2F1

Dostoevskovo, ulitsa
ДОСТОЕВСКОГО, УЛИЦА   2F1

Dovatora, ulitsa
ДОВАТОРА, УЛИЦА   5B5

Druzhinnikovskaya ulitsa
ДРУЖИННИКОВСКАЯ УЛИЦА   1C5

Dubininskaya ulitsa
ДУБИНИНСКАЯ УЛИЦА   7C5

Durasovskiy pereulok
ДУРАСОВСКИЙ ПЕРЕУЛОК   4D5, 8D1

Durova, ulitsa
ДУРОВА, УЛИЦА   3A1

E

Efremova, ulitsa
ЕФРЕМОВА, УЛИЦА   5C5

Elanskovo, ulitsa
ЕЛАНСКОГО, УЛИЦА   5C4

Elektricheskiy pereulok
ЭЛЕКТРИЧЕСКИЙ ПЕРЕУЛОК   1C3

Elizavetinskiy pereulok
ЕЛИЗАВЕТИНСКИЙ ПЕРЕУЛОК   4F4

Ermolaevskiy pereulok
ЕРМОЛАЕВСКИЙ ПЕРЕУЛОК   2D4

Eropkinskiy pereulok
ЕРОПКИНСКИЙ ПЕРЕУЛОК — 6D3

F

Faceted Palace — 7A2
Fadeeva, ulitsa
ФАДЕЕВА, УЛИЦА — 2E2
Faleevskiy pereulok
ФАЛЕЕВСКИЙ ПЕРЕУЛОК — 7A2
Filippovskiy pereulok
ФИЛИППОВСКИЙ ПЕРЕУЛОК — 6E1
Frunzenskaya naberezhnaya
ФРУНЗЕНСКАЯ НАБЕРЕЖНАЯ — 6D5
Furmannyy pereulok
ФУРМАННЫЙ ПЕРЕУЛОК — 4D4

G

Gagarinskiy pereulok
ГАГАРИНСКИЙ ПЕРЕУЛОК — 6D2
Gasheka, ulitsa
ГАШЕКА, УЛИЦА — 2D3
Gavrikova, ulitsa
ГАВРИКОВА УЛИЦА — 4E1
Gazetnyy pereulok
ГАЗЕТНЫЙ ПЕРЕУЛОК — 2F5
Georgievskiy pereulok
ГЕОРГИЕВСКИЙ ПЕРЕУЛОК — 2F5
Gilyarovskovo, ulitsa
ГИЛЯРОВСКОВО, УЛИЦА — 3B2
Glazovskiy pereulok
ГЛАЗОВСКИЙ ПЕРЕУЛОК — 6D2
Glinishchevskiy pereulok
ГЛИНИЩЕВСКИЙ ПЕРЕУЛОК — 2F4
Glubokiy pereulok
ГЛУБОКИЙ ПЕРЕУЛОК — 1B5
Glukharev pereulok
ГЛУХАРЕВ ПЕРЕУЛОК — 3C2
Gogolevskiy bulvar
ГОГОЛЕВСКИЙ БУЛЬВАР — 6E2
Golikovskiy pereulok
ГОЛИКОВСКИЙ ПЕРЕУЛОК — 7B3
Goncharnaya ulitsa
ГОНЧАРНАЯ УЛИЦА — 8D2
Goncharnyy proezd
ГОНЧАРНЫЙ ПРОЕЗД — 8D3
Gorkovo, park im
ПАРК КУЛЬТУРЫ И ОТДЫХА ИМЕНИ М ГОРКГО — 6E4
Gorky House-Museum — 2E5
Gorky Park — 6E4
Gorlov tupik
ГОРЛОВ ТУПИК — 2D1
Gorokhovskiy pereulok
ГОРОХОВСКИЙ ПЕРЕУЛОК — 4E4
Granatnyy pereulok
ГРАНАТНЫЙ ПЕРЕУЛОК — 2D5
Great Kremlin Palace — 7A2
Grokholskiy pereulok
ГРОХОЛЬСКИЙ ПЕРЕУЛОК — 3B2
Gruzinskiy pereulok
ГРУЗИНСКИЙ ПЕРЕУЛОК — 1C2
Gruzinskiy val, ulitsa
ГРУЗИНСКИЙ ВАЛ, УЛИЦА — 1C2
GUM — 3A5, 7B1
Gusyatnikov pereulok
ГУСЯТНИКОВ ПЕРЕУЛОК — 3C4
Gvozdeva, ulitsa
ГВОЗДЕВА, УЛИЦА — 8E4

H

History of Moscow Museum — 3B5
Hotel Metropol — 3A5
Hotel National — 2F5, 7A1
House of Friendship — 6E1
House of Unions — 3A5

I

Ilinka, ulitsa
ИЛЬИНКА, УЛИЦА — 3B5, 7B1
Ipatevskiy pereulok
ИПАТЬЕВСКИЙ ПЕРЕУЛОК — 3B5, 7B1
Ivan the Great Bell Tower — 7A1
Ivanovskaya Hill — 3C5

K

Kadashevskaya naberezhnaya
КАДАШЕВСКАЯ НАБЕРЕЖНАЯ — 7A3
Kalanchevskaya ulitsa
КАЛАНЧЕВСКАЯ УЛИЦА — 4D2

Kalanchevskaya ploshchad
КАЛАНЧЕВСКАЯ ПЛОЩАДЬ — 4D2
Kalashnyy pereulok
КАЛАШНЫЙ ПЕРЕУЛОК — 2E5
Kaloshin pereulok
КАЛОШИН ПЕРЕУЛОК — 6D1
Kaluzhskaya ploshchad
КАЛУЖСКАЯ ПЛОЩАДЬ — 6F4, 7A5
Kamennoy Slobody, pereulok
КАМЕННОЙ СЛОБОДЫ, ПЕРЕУЛОК — 6D1
Kamergerskiy pereulok
КАМЕРГЕРСКИЙ ПЕРЕУЛОК — 2F5
Kapelskiy pereulok
КАРЕЛЬСКИЙ ПЕРЕУЛОК — 3B1
Karetnyy ryad, ulitsa
КАРЕТНЫЙ РЯД, УЛИЦА — 2F3
Karmanitskiy pereulok
КАРМАНИЦКИЙ ПЕРЕУЛОК — 6D1
Kazakova, ulitsa
КАЗАКОВА, УЛИЦА — 4E4
Kazan Cathedral — 3A5, 7A1
Kazanskiy pereulok
КАЗАНСКИЙ ПЕРЕУЛОК — 7A4
Kazarmennyy pereulok
КАЗАРМЕННЫЙ ПЕРЕУЛОК — 4D5, 8D1
Khilkov pereulok
ХИЛКОВ ПЕРЕУЛОК — 6E3
Khlebnyy pereulok
ХЛЕБНЫЙ ПЕРЕУЛОК — 2D5
Khodynskaya ulitsa
ХОДЫНСКАЯ УЛИЦА — 1A3
Khokhlovskiy pereulok
ХОХЛОВСКИЙ ПЕРЕУЛОК — 3C5
Kholzunova, pereulok
ХОЛЬЗУНОВА, ПЕРЕУЛОК — 5C4
Khomutovskiy tupik
ХОМУТОВСКИЙ ТУПИК — 4D3
Khrushchevskiy pereulok
ХРУЩЕВСКИЙ ПЕРЕУЛОК — 6E2
Khrustalnyy pereulok
ХРУСТАЛЬНЫЙ ПЕРЕУЛОК — 7B1
Kievskaya ulitsa
КИЕВСКАЯ УЛИЦА — 5A2
Kievskovo Vokzala, ploshchad
КИЕВСКОГО ВОКЗАЛА, ПЛОЩАДЬ — 5B2
Kitaygorodskiy proezd
КИТАЙГОРОДСКИЙ ПРОЕЗД — 7C1
Klimashkina, ulitsa
КЛИМАШКИНА, УЛИЦА — 1B3
Klimentovskiy pereulok
КЛИМЕНТОВСКИЙ ПЕРЕУЛОК — 7B3
Kolokolnikov pereulok
КОЛОКОЛЬНИКОВ ПЕРЕУЛОК — 3B3
Kolpachnyy pereulok
КОЛПАЧНЫЙ ПЕРЕУЛОК — 3C5
Kolymazhnaya, ulitsa
КОЛЫМАЖНЫЙ ПЕРЕУЛОК — 6E1
Komissariatskiy most
КОМИССАРИАТСКИЙ МОСТ — 7C2
Komissariatskiy pereulok
КОМИССАРИАТСКИЙ ПЕРЕУЛОК — 7C3
Kompozitorskaya ulitsa
КОМПОЗИТОРСКАЯ УЛИЦА — 6D1
Komsomolskaya ploshchad
КОМСОМОЛЬСКАЯ ПЛОЩАДЬ — 4D2
Komsomolskiy prospekt
КОМСОМОЛЬСКИЙ ПРОСПЕКТ — 5C5
Komsomolskoy Ploshchadi, proezd
КОМСОМОЛЬСКОЙ ПЛОЩАДИ, ПРОЕЗД — 4D1
Konyushkovskaya ulitsa
КОНЮШКОВСКАЯ УЛИЦА — 1C5
Kooperativnaya ulitsa
КООПЕРАТИВНАЯ УЛИЦА — 5B5
Korobeynikov pereulok
КОРОБЕЙНИКОВ ПЕРЕУЛОК — 6E3
Koroviy val, ulitsa
КОРОВИЙ ВАЛ, УЛИЦА — 7A5
Kosmodamianskaya naberezhnaya
КОСМОДАМИАНСКАЯ НАБЕРЕЖНАЯ — 7C2
Kostikova, ulitsa
КОСТИКОВА, УЛИЦА — 1A4
Kostomarovskaya naberezhnaya
КОСТОМАРОВСКАЯ НАБЕРЕЖНАЯ — 8F2
Kostomarovskiy pereulok
КОСТОМАРОВСКИЙ ПЕРЕУЛОК — 8F1
Kostyanskiy pereulok
КОСТЯНСКИЙ ПЕРЕУЛОК — 3B3
Kotelnicheskaya naberezhnaya
КОТЕЛЬНИЧЕСКАЯ НАБЕРЕЖНАЯ — 8D3
Kozhevnicheskaya ulitsa
КОЖЕВНИЧЕСКАЯ УЛИЦА — 8D5

Kozhevnicheskiy proezd
КОЖЕВНИЧЕСКИЙ ПРОЕЗД   8D5

Kozitskiy pereulok
КОЗИЦКИЙ ПЕРЕУЛОК   2F4

Krasina, ulitsa
КРАСИНА, УЛИЦА   2D3

Krasnaya ploshchad
КРАСНАЯ ПЛОЩАДЬ   3A5, 7B1

Krasnaya Presnya, ulitsa
КРАСНАЯ ПРЕСНЯ, УЛИЦА   1B4

Krasnokholmskaya naberezhnaya
КРАСНОХОЛМСКАЯ НАБЕРЕЖНАЯ   8D4

Krasnopresnenskaya naberezhnaya
КРАСНОПРЕСНЕНСКАЯ НАБЕРЕЖНАЯ   1B5, 5A1

Krasnopresnenskoy Zastavy, ploshchad
КРАСНОПРЕСНЕНСКОЙ ЗАСТАВЫ, ПЛОЩАДЬ   1A4

Krasnoproletarskaya ulitsa
КРАСНОПРОЛЕТАРСКАЯ УЛИЦА   2F2

Krasnoprudnaya ulitsa
КРАСНОПРУДНАЯ УЛИЦА   4E2

Krasnoselskiy, tupik
КРАСНОСЕЛЬСКИЙ, ТУПИК   4E1

Kremlevskaya naberezhnaya
КРЕМЛЁВСКАЯ НАБЕРЕЖНАЯ   7A2

Krestyanskiy tupik
КРЕСТЬЯНСКИЙ ТУПИК   8E4

Krestyanskoy Zastavy, ploshchad
КРЕСТЬЯНСКОЙ ЗАСТАВЫ, ПЛОЩАДЬ   8F4

Krivoarbatskiy pereulok
КРИВОАРБАТСКИЙ ПЕРЕУЛОК   6D1

Krivokolennyy pereulok
КРИВОКОЛЕННЫЙ ПЕРЕУЛОК   3B4

Kropotkinskiy pereulok
КРОПОТКИНСКИЙ ПЕРЕУЛОК   6D3

Krutitskaya naberezhnaya
КРУТИЦКАЯ НАБЕРЕЖНАЯ   8E5

Krutitskaya ulitsa
КРУТИЦКАЯ УЛИЦА   8E5

Krutitskiy val, ulitsa
КРУТИЦКИЙ ВАЛ, УЛИЦА   8F5

Krutitskoe Mission
КРУТИЦКОЕ   8E5

Krymskaya naberezhnaya
КРЫМСКАЯ НАБЕРЕЖНАЯ   6E4

Krymskiy most
КРЫМСКИЙ МОСТ   6E4

Krymskiy tupik
КРЫМСКИЙ ТУПИК   6F4

Krymskiy val, ulitsa
КРЫМСКИЙ ВАЛ, УЛИЦА   6F4

Kseninskiy pereulok
КСЕНЬИНСКИЙ ПЕРЕУЛОК   6D4

Kudrinskaya ploshchad
КУДРИНСКАЯ ПЛОЩАДЬ   1C5

Kursovoy pereulok
КУРСОВОЙ ПЕРЕУЛОК   6F3

Kutuzovskiy prospekt
КУТУЗОВСКИЙ ПРОСПЕКТ   5A2

Kuznetskiy most, ulitsa
КУЗНЕЦКИЙ МОСТ, УЛИЦА   3A4

L

Lavrov pereulok
ЛАВРОВ ПЕРЕУЛОК   8E4

Lavrskiy pereulok
ЛАВРСКИЙ ПЕРЕУЛОК   3A2

Lavrushinskiy pereulok
ЛАВРУШИНСКИЙ ПЕРЕУЛОК   7A3

Lebyazhiy pereulok
ЛЕБЯЖИЙ ПЕРЕУЛОК   6F2

Lenin Mausoleum
ЛЕНИН   7A1

Leningradskiy prospekt
ЛЕНИНГРАДСКИЙ ПРОСПЕКТ   1B1

Leninskiy prospect
ЛЕНИНСКИЙ ПРОСПЕКТ   6F5

Lenivka, ulitsa
ЛЕНИВКА, УЛИЦА   6F2

Leontevskiy pereulok
ЛЕОНТЬЕВСКИЙ ПЕРЕУЛОК   2E5

Lermontov House-Museum
ЛЕРМОНТОВ   2D5, 6D1

Lermontovskaya ploshchad
ЛЕРМОНТОВСКАЯ ПЛОЩАДЬ   4D3

Lesnaya ulitsa
ЛЕСНАЯ УЛИЦА   2D2

Lesnoryadskaya ulitsa
ЛЕСНОРЯДСКАЯ УЛИЦА   4F1

Lesnoryadskiy pereulok
ЛЕСНОРЯДСКИЙ ПЕРЕУЛОК   4F1

Letnikovskaya ulitsa
ЛЕТНИКОВСКАЯ УЛИЦА   8D5

Likhov pereulok
ЛИХОВ ПЕРЕУЛОК   2F3

Lopukhinskiy pereulok
ЛОПУХИНСКИЙ ПЕРЕУЛОК   6E2

Lubyanka Square   3B4

Lubyanskaya ploshad
ЛУБЯНСКАЯ ПЛОЩАДЬ   3B5

Lubyanskiy proezd
ЛУБЯНСКИЙ ПРОЕЗД   3B5, 7C1

Lubyanskiy prospekt
ЛУБЯНСКИЙ ПРОСПЕКТ   3B5

Lukov pereulok
ЛУКОВ ПЕРЕУЛОК   3B3

Luzhkov most
ЛУЖКОВ МОСТ   7A3

Lva Tolstovo, ulitsa
ЛЬВА ТОЛСТОГО, УЛИЦА   6D4

Lyalin pereulok
ЛЯЛИН ПЕРЕУЛОК   4D4

Lyusinovskaya ulitsa
ЛЮСИНОВСКАЯ УЛИЦА   7B5

M

Makarenko, ulitsa
МАКАРЕНКО, УЛИЦА   4D4

Malaya Bronnaya ulitsa
МАЛАЯ БРОННАЯ УЛИЦА   2D4

Malaya Dmitrovka, ulitsa
МАЛАЯ ДМИТРОВКА, УЛИЦА   2E3

Malaya Dorogomilovskaya ulitsa
МАЛАЯ ДОРОГОМИЛОВСКАЯ УЛИЦА   5A2

Malaya Gruzinskaya ulitsa
МАЛАЯ ГРУЗИНСКАЯ УЛИЦА   1B4

Malaya Kommunisticheskaya ulitsa
МАЛАЯ КОММУНИСТИЧЕСКАЯ УЛИЦА   8E3

Malaya Lubyanka, ulitsa
МАЛАЯ ЛУБЯНКА, УЛИЦА   3B4

Malaya Nikitskaya ulitsa
МАЛАЯ НИКИТСКАЯ УЛИЦА   2D5

Malaya Ordynka, ulitsa
МАЛАЯ ОРДЫНКА, УЛИЦА   7B4

Malaya Pionerskaya ulitsa
МАЛАЯ ПИОНЕРСКАЯ УЛИЦА   7C5

Malaya Pirogovskaya ulitsa
МАЛАЯ ПИРОГОВСКАЯ УЛИЦА   5B5

Malaya Polyanka, ulitsa
МАЛАЯ ПОЛЯНКА, УЛИЦА   7A4

Malaya Trubetskaya ulitsa
МАЛАЯ ТРУБЕЦКАЯ УЛИЦА   5B4

Malaya Yakimanka, ulitsa
МАЛАЯ ЯКИМАНКА, УЛИЦА   7A3

Malye Kamenshchiki, ulitsa
МАЛЫЕ КАМЕНЩИКИ, УЛИЦА   8E4

Malyy Demidovskiy pereulok
МАЛЫЙ ДЕМИДОВСКИЙ ПЕРЕУЛОК   4E4

Malyy Drovyanoy pereulok
МАЛЫЙ ДРОВЯНОЙ ПЕРЕУЛОК   8E2

Malyy Gnezdnikovskiy pereulok
МАЛЫЙ ГНЕЗДНИКОВСКИЙ ПЕРЕУЛОК   2F4

Malyy Golovin pereulok
МАЛЫЙ ГОЛОВИН ПЕРЕУЛОК   3B3

Malyy Ivanovskiy pereulok
МАЛЫЙ ИВАНОВСКИЙ ПЕРЕУЛОК   7C1

Malyy Kamennyy most
МАЛЫЙ КАМЕННЫЙ МОСТ   7A3

Malyy Karetnyy pereulok
МАЛЫЙ КАРЕТНЫЙ ПЕРЕУЛОК   2F3

Malyy Kazennyy pereulok
МАЛЫЙ КАЗЕННЫЙ ПЕРЕУЛОК   4D4

Malyy Kharitonevskiy pereulok
МАЛЫЙ ХАРИТОНЬЕВСКИЙ ПЕРЕУЛОК   3C3

Malyy Kislovskiy pereulok
МАЛЫЙ КИСЛОВСКИЙ ПЕРЕУЛОК   2E5

Malyy Kozikhinskiy pereulok
МАЛЫЙ КОЗИХИНСКИЙ ПЕРЕУЛОК   2E4

Malyy Krasnokholmskiy most
МАЛЫЙ КРАСНОХОЛМСКИЙ МОСТ   8D4

Malyy Levshinskiy pereulok
МАЛЫЙ ЛЕВШИНСКИЙ ПЕРЕУЛОК   6D2

Malyy Moskvoretskiy most
МАЛЫЙ МОСКВОРЕЦКИЙ МОСТ   7B2

Malyy Novopeskovskiy pereulok
МАЛЫЙ НОВОПЕСКОВСКИЙ ПЕРЕУЛОК   5C1

Malyy Poluyaroslavskiy pereulok
МАЛЫЙ ПОЛУЯРОСЛАВСКИЙ ПЕРЕУЛОК   8E1

Malyy Rzhevskiy pereulok
МАЛЫЙ РЖЕВСКИЙ ПЕРЕУЛОК   2D5

Malyy Savvinskiy pereulok
МАЛЫЙ САВВИНСКИЙ ПЕРЕУЛОК   5A4

Malyy Sukharevskiy pereulok
МАЛЫЙ СУХАРЕВСКИЙ ПЕРЕУЛОК   3A3

Malyy Tatarskiy pereulok
МАЛЫЙ ТАТАРСКИЙ ПЕРЕУЛОК   7C4

Malyy Tishinskiy pereulok
МАЛЫЙ ТИШИНСКИЙ ПЕРЕУЛОК 1C3
Malyy Tolmachevskiy pereulok
МАЛЫЙ ТОЛМАЧЕВСКИЙ ПЕРЕУЛОК 7A3
Malyy Trekhsvyatitelskiy pereulok
МАЛЫЙ ТРЕХСВЯТИТЕЛЬСКИЙ ПЕРЕУЛОК 3C5, 8D1
Malyy Vlasevskiy pereulok
МАЛЫЙ ВЛАСЬЕВСКИЙ ПЕРЕУЛОК 6D2
Malyy Znamenskiy pereulok
МАЛЫЙ ЗНАМЕНСКИЙ ПЕРЕУЛОК 6F1
Mamonovskiy pereulok
МАМОНОВСКИЙ ПЕРЕУЛОК 2E4
Mandelshtama, park im
МАНДЕЛЬШТАМА, ПАРК ИМ 5C5
Manège 6F1, 7A1
Manezhnaya ploshchad
МАНЕЖНАЯ ПЛОЩАДЬ 7A1
Manezhnaya ulitsa
МАНЕЖНАЯ УЛИДА 6F1, 7A2
Mansurovskiy pereulok
МАНСУРОВСКИЙ ПЕРЕУЛОК 6D3
Mantulinskaya ulitsa
МАНТУЛИНСКАЯ УЛИЦА 1A5
Marksistskaya ulitsa
МАРКСИСТСКАЯ УЛИЦА 8E3
Marksistskiy pereulok
МАРКСИСТСКИЙ ПЕРЕУЛОК 8F4
Maronovskiy pereulok
МАРОНОВСКИЙ ПЕРЕУЛОК 6F4
Maroseyka, ulitsa
МАРОСЕЙКА, УЛИЦА 3B5
Martynovskiy pereulok
МАРТЫНОВСКИЙ ПЕРЕУЛОК 8E2
Mashkova, ulitsa
МАШКОВА, УЛИЦА 4D4
Mayakovsky Museum 3B5
Mayakovskovo, pereulok
МАЯКОВСКОГО, ПЕРЕУЛОК 8E3
Melnikov House 6D1
Melnitskiy pereulok
МЕЛЬНИЦКИЙ ПЕРЕУЛОК 8E1
Menshikov's Tower 3C4
Merzlyakovskiy pereulok
МЕРЗЛЯКОВСКИЙ ПЕРЕУЛОК 2E5
Meshchanskaya ulitsa
МЕЩАНСКАЯ УЛИЦА 3B2
Milyutinskiy pereulok
МИЛЮТИНСКИЙ ПЕРЕУЛОК 3B4
Mira, prospekt
МИРА, ПРОСПЕКТ 3B2
Miusskaya ploshchad
МИУССКАЯ ПЛОЩАДЬ 2D2
Miusskiy pereulok
МИУССКИЙ ПЕРЕУЛОК 2D1
Mokhovaya ulitsa
МОХОВАЯ УЛИЦА 6F1
Molochnyy pereulok
МОЛОЧНЫЙ ПЕРЕУЛОК 6E3
Monastery of the Epiphany 3A5, 7B1
Monastery of the Saviour and Andronicus 8F2
Morozov Mansion 2D4
Moscow Arts Theatre 2F4
Moscow Conservatory 2E5
Moscow Old University 2F5, 7A1
Moskvoretskaya naberezhnaya
МОСКВОРЕЦКАЯ НАБЕРЕЖНАЯ 7B2
Moskvoretskaya ulitsa
МОСКВОРЕДКАЯ УЛИЦА 7B1
Mozhayskiy val, ulitsa
МОЖАЙСКИЙ ВАЛ, УЛИЦА 5A2
Museum of Private Collections 6F2
Museum of the Revolution 2E4
Myasnitskaya ulitsa
МЯСНИЦКАЯ УЛИЦА 3B4
Mytnaya, ulitsa
МЫТНАЯ, УЛИЦА 7A5

N

Narodnaya ulitsa
НАРОДНАЯ УЛИЦА 8D4
Nashchokinskiy pereulok
НАЩОКИНСКИЙ ПЕРЕУЛОК 6E2
Nastasinskiy pereulok
НАСТАСЬИНСКИЙ ПЕРЕУЛОК 2E3
Nastavnicheskiy pereulok
НАСТАВНИЧЕСКИЙ ПЕРЕУЛОК 8F1
Neglinnaya ulitsa
НЕГЛИННАЯ УЛИЦА 3A4
Nesvizhskiy pereulok
НЕСВИЖСКИЙ ПЕРЕУЛОК 5C4

Nevolnyy pereulok
НЕВОЛЬНЫЙ ПЕРЕУЛОК 5C2
New Tretyakov Gallery 6F3
Nikitskie vorota, ploshchad
НИКИТСКИЕ ВОРОТА, ПЛОЩАДЬ 2E5
Nikitskiy bulvar
НИКИТСКИЙ БУЛЬВАР 2E5
Nikitskiy pereulok
НИКИТСКИЙ ПЕРЕУЛОК 2F5
Nikolaeva, ulitsa
НИКОЛАЕВА, УЛИЦА 1B5
Nikoloyamskaya naberezhnaya
НИКОЛОЯМСКАЯ НАБЕРЕЖНАЯ 8E2
Nikoloyamskaya ulitsa
НИКОЛОЯМСКАЯ УЛИЦА 8D2
Nikoloyamskiy pereulok
НИКОЛОЯМСКИЙ ПЕРЕУЛОК 8E2
Nikolskaya ulitsa
НИКОЛЬСКАЯ УЛИЦА 3A5
Nikolskiy pereulok
НИКОЛЬСКИЙ ПЕРЕУЛОК 3B5, 7B1
Nikonovskiy pereulok
НИКОНОВСКИЙ ПЕРЕУЛОК 2F2
Nizhniy Susalnyy pereulok
НИЖНИЙ СУСАЛЬНЫЙ ПЕРЕУЛОК 4E4
Nizhniy Taganskiy tupik
НИЖНИЙ ТАГАНСКИЙ ТУПИК 8D3
Nizhnyaya Krasnoselskaya ulitsa
НИЖНЯЯ КРАСНОСЕЛЬСКАЯ УЛИЦА 4F2
Nizhnyaya Syromyatnicheskaya ulitsa
НИЖНЯЯ СЫРОМЯТНИЧЕСКАЯ УЛИЦА 8F1
Nizhnyaya Taganskaya ploshchad
НИЖНЯЯ ТАГАНСКАЯ ПЛОЩАДЬ 8D3
Nizhnyaya ulitsa
НИЖНЯЯ УЛИЦА 1C2
Novaya Basmannaya ulitsa
НОВАЯ БАСМАННАЯ УЛИЦА 4D3
Novaya ploshchad
НОВАЯ ПЛОЩАДЬ 3B5
Novinskiy bulvar
НОВИНСКИЙ БУЛЬВАР 2D5
Novoarbatskiy most
НОВОАРБАТСКИЙ МОСТ 5B1
Novodevichiy Convent 5A5
Novodevichiy proezd
НОВОДЕВИЧИЙ ПРОЕЗД 5A4
Novodevichya naberezhnaya
НОВОДЕВИЧЬЯ НАБЕРЕЖНАЯ 5A5
Novokhokhlovskaya ulitsa
НОВОХОХЛОВСКАЯ УЛИЦА 2E1
Novokonyushennyy pereulok
НОВОКОНЮШЕННЫЙ ПЕРЕУЛОК 5C3
Novokrymskiy prospekt
НОВОКРЫМСКИЙ ПРОСПЕКТ 6E3
Novokuznetskaya ulitsa
НОВОКУЗНЕЦКАЯ УЛИЦА 7B3
Novolesnaya ulitsa
НОВОЛЕСНАЯ УЛИЦА 2D1
Novolesnoy pereulok
НОВОЛЕСНОЙ ПЕРЕУЛОК 2D1
Novopresnenskiy pereulok
НОВОПРЕСНЕНСКИЙ ПЕРЕУЛОК 1C4
Novoryazanskaya ulitsa
НОВОРЯЗАНСКАЯ УЛИЦА 4E3
Novoslobodskaya ulitsa
НОВОСЛОБОДСКАЯ УЛИЦА 2E1
Novospasskiy most
НОВОСПАССКИЙ МОСТ 8E5
Novospasskiy pereulok
НОВОСПАССКИЙ ПЕРЕУЛОК 8E4
Novospasskiy proezd
НОВОСПАССКИЙ ПРОЕЗД 8E4
Novovagankovskiy pereulok
НОВОВАГАНЬКОВСКИЙ ПЕРЕУЛОК 1B5
Novyy Arbat, ulitsa
НОВЫЙ АРБАТ, УЛИЦА 5C1

O

Obolenskiy pereulok
ОБОЛЕНСКИЙ ПЕРЕУЛОК 5C4
Obukha, pereulok
ОБУХА, ПЕРЕУЛОК 8E1
Ogorodnoy Slobody pereulok
ОГОРОДНОЙ СЛОБОДЫ ПЕРЕУЛОК 3C4
Okhotnyy ryad, ulitsa
ОХОТНЫЙ РЯД, УЛИЦА 3A5
Old English Court 7B1
Olimpiyskiy prospekt
ОЛИМПИЙСКИЙ ПРОСПЕКТ 3A2
Olkhovskaya ulitsa
ОЛХОВСКАЯ УЛИЦА 4E2

Olsufevskiy pereulok
ОЛСУФЬЕВСКИЙ ПЕРЕУЛОК   5C4

Orlikov pereulok
ОРЛИКОВ ПЕРЕУЛОК   4D3

Orlovo Davydovskiy pereulok
ОРЛОВО ДАВЫДОВСКИЙ ПЕРЕУЛОК   3B1

Oruzheynyy pereulok
ОРУЖЕЙНЫЙ ПЕРЕУЛОК   2E3

Ostozhenka, ulitsa
ОСТОЖЕНКА, УЛИЦА   6E3

Ovchinnikovskaya naberezhnaya
ОВЧИННИКОВСКАЯ НАБЕРЕЖНАЯ   7B2

Ozerkovskaya naberezhnaya
ОЗЕРКОВСКАЯ НАБЕРЕЖНАЯ   7C3

Ozerkovskiy pereulok
ОЗЕРКОВСКИЙ ПЕРЕУЛОК   7C3

Ozerkovskiy tupik
ОЗЕРКОВСКИЙ ТУПИК   7C3

P

Palace of Congresses   7A1

Palace of the Romanov Boyars   7B1

Palikha, ulitsa
ПАЛИХА, УЛИЦА   2E1

Panfilovskiy pereulok
ПАНФИЛОВСКИЙ ПЕРЕУЛОК   5C1

Pankratevskiy pereulok
ПАНКРАТЬЕВСКИЙ ПЕРЕУЛОК   3B3

Panteleevskaya ulitsa
ПАНТЕЛЕЕВСКАЯ УЛИЦА   3C1

Pashkov House   6F1

Patriarch's Palace   7A1

Patriarch's Pond   2D4

Patriarshiy prudy
ПАТРИАРШИЕ ПРУДЫ   2D4

Paveletskaya ploshchad
ПАВЕЛЕЦКАЯ ПЛОЩАДЬ   7C5

Pechatnikov pereulok
ПЕЧАТНИКОВ ПЕРЕУЛОК   3A3

Perlov Tea House   3D4

Pestovskiy pereulok
ПЕСТОВСКИЙ ПЕРЕУЛОК   8E2

Petropavlovskiy pereulok
ПЕТРОПАВЛОВСКИЙ ПЕРЕУЛОК   8D1

Petroverigskiy pereulok
ПЕТРОВЕРИГСКИЙ ПЕРЕУЛОК   3C5

Petrovka, ulitsa
ПЕТРОВКА, УЛИЦА   3A4

Petrovskie linii ulitsa
ПЕТРОВСКИЕ ЛИНИИ УЛИЦА   3A4

Petrovskiy bulvar
ПЕТРОВСКИЙ БУЛЬВАР   3A3

Petrovskiy pereulok
ПЕТРОВСКИЙ ПЕРЕУЛОК   2F4

Platovskaya ulitsa
ПЛАТОВСКАЯ УЛИЦА   5A2

Pleteshkovskiy pereulok
ПЛЕТЕШКОВСКИЙ ПЕРЕУЛОК   4F3

Plotnikov pereulok
ПЛОТНИКОВ ПЕРЕУЛОК   6D2

Plyushchikha, ulitsa
ПЛЮЩИХА, УЛИЦА   5C3

Podgorskaya naberezhnaya
ПОДГОРСКАЯ НАБЕРЕЖНАЯ   8D2

Podkolokolnyy pereulok
ПОДКОЛОКОЛЬНЫЙ ПЕРЕУЛОК   8D1

Podkopaevskiy pereulok
ПОДКОПАЕВСКИЙ ПЕРЕУЛОК   3C5, 8D1

Podsosenskiy pereulok
ПОДСОСЕНСКИЙ ПЕРЕУЛОК   4D5

Pogodinskaya ulitsa
ПОГОДИНСКАЯ УЛИЦА   5B4

Pogorelskiy pereulok
ПОГОРЕЛЬСКИЙ ПЕРЕУЛОК   7B4

Pokrovka, ulitsa
ПОКРОВКА, УЛИЦА   3C5

Pokrovskiy bulvar
ПОКРОВСКИЙ БУЛЬВАР   3C5

Poluyaroslavskaya naberezhnaya
ПОЛУЯРОСЛАВСКАЯ НАБЕРЕЖНАЯ   8E2

Polytechnical Museum   3B5

Pomerantsev pereulok
ПОМЕРАНЦЕВ ПЕРЕУЛОК   6D3

Posledniy pereulok
ПОСЛЕДНИЙ ПЕРЕУЛОК   3B3

Potapovskiy pereulok
ПОТАПОВСКИЙ ПЕРЕУЛОК   3C4

Povarskaya ulitsa
ПОВАРСКАЯ УЛИЦА   2D5

Pozharskiy pereulok
ПОЖАРСКИЙ ПЕРЕУЛОК   6E3

Pravdy, ulitsa
ПРАВДЫ, УЛИЦА   1C1

Prechistenka, ulitsa
ПРЕЧИСТЕНКА, УЛИЦА   6D3

Prechistenskaya naberezhnaya
ПРЕЧИСТЕНСКАЯ НАБЕРЕЖНАЯ   6E3

Prechistenskie vorota, ploshchad
ПРЕЧИСТЕНСКИЕ ВОРОТА, ПЛОЩАДЬ   6E2

Prechistenskiy pereulok
ПРЕЧИСТЕНСКИЙ ПЕРЕУЛОК   6D2

Presidium   7A1

Presnenskiy val, ulitsa
ПРЕСНЕНСКИЙ ВАЛ, УЛИЦА   1B3

Priyutskiy pereulok
ПРИЮТСКИЙ ПЕРЕУЛОК   2D1

Prosvirin pereulok
ПРОСВИРИН ПЕРЕУЛОК   3B3

Protochnyy pereulok
ПРОТОЧНЫЙ ПЕРЕУЛОК   5C1

Protopopovskiy pereulok
ПРОТОПОПОВСКИЙ ПЕРЕУЛОК   3B1

Pryamoy pereulok
ПРЯМОЙ ПЕРЕУЛОК   5C1

Pugovishnikov pereulok
ПУГОВИШНИКОВ ПЕРЕУЛОК   6D4

Pushechnaya ulitsa
ПУШЕЧНАЯ УЛИЦА   3A4

Pushkarev pereulok
ПУШКАРЕВ ПЕРЕУЛОК   3B3

Pushkin House-Museum   6D2

Pushkin Museum of Fine Arts   6F2

Pushkin Square   2F4

Pushkinskaya naberezhnaya
ПУШКИНСКАЯ НАБЕРЕЖНАЯ   6E5

Pushkinskaya ploshchad
ПУШКИНСКАЯ ПЛОЩАДЬ   2F4

Pyatnitskaya ulitsa
ПЯТНИЦКАЯ УЛИЦА   7B2

Pyzhevskiy pereulok
ПЫЖЕВСКИЙ ПЕРЕУЛОК   7B3

R

Radio, ulitsa
РАДИО, УЛИЦА   4F4

Raevskovo, ulitsa
РАЕВСКОГО УЛИЦА   5A2

Rastorguevskiy pereulok
РАСТОРГУЕВСКИЙ ПЕРЕУЛОК   1B4

Raushskaya naberezhnaya
РАУШСКАЯ НАБЕРЕЖНАЯ   7B2

Red Square   3A5, 7B1

Resurrection Gate   3A5, 7A1

Revolyutsii, ploshchad
РЕВОЛЮЦИИ, ПЛОЩАДЬ   3A5

Rochdelskaya ulitsa
РОЧДЕЛЬСКАЯ УЛИЦА   1D5

Romanov pereulok
РОМАНОВ ПЕРЕУЛОК   2F5

Rossolimo, ulitsa
РОССОЛИМО, УЛИЦА   5C4

Rostovskaya naberezhnaya
РОСТОВСКАЯ НАБЕРЕЖНАЯ   5B3

Rozhdestvenka, ulitsa
РОЖДЕСТВЕНКА, УЛИЦА   3A4

Rozhdestvenskiy bulvar
РОЖДЕСТВЕНСКИЙ БУЛЬВАР   3A3

Runovskiy pereulok
РУНОВСКИЙ ПЕРЕУЛОК   7C3

Rusakovskaya ulitsa
РУСАКОВСКАЯ УЛИЦА   4F1

Ruzheynyy pereulok
РУЖЕЙНЫЙ ПЕРЕУЛОК   5C2

Ryazanskiy proezd
РЯЗАНСКИЙ ПРОЕЗД   4D2

Rybnikov pereulok
РЫБНИКОВ ПЕРЕУЛОК   3B3

Rybnyy pereulok
РЫБНЫЙ ПЕРЕУЛОК   3B5, 7B1

S

Sadovaya-Chernogryazskaya ulitsa
САДОВАЯ-ЧЕРНОГРЯЗСКАЯ УЛИЦА   4D3

Sadovaya-Karetnaya ulitsa
САДОВАЯ-КАРЕТНАЯ УЛИЦА   2F2

Sadovaya-Kudrinskaya ulitsa
САДОВАЯ-КУДРИНСКАЯ УЛИЦА   2D4

Sadovaya-Samotechnaya, ulitsa
САДОВАЯ-САМОТЕЧНАЯ, УЛИЦА   3A2

Sadovaya-Spasskaya ulitsa
САДОВАЯ-СПАССКАЯ УЛИЦА   3C3

Sadovaya-Sukharevskaya ulitsa
САДОВАЯ-СУХАРЕВСКАЯ УЛИЦА — **3A2**

Sadovaya-Triumfalnaya ulitsa
САДОВАЯ-ТРИУМФАЛЬНАЯ УЛИЦА — **2E3**

Sadovnicheskaya naberezhnaya
САДОВНИЧЕСКАЯ НАБЕРЕЖНАЯ — **7B2**

Sadovnicheskaya ulitsa
САДОВНИЧЕСКАЯ УЛИДА — **7B2**

Sadovnicheskiy proezd
САДОВНИЧЕСКИЙ ПРОЕЗД — **7C3**

St Basil's Cathedral — **7B1**

Samarskaya ulitsa
САМАРСКАЯ УЛИЦА — **3A1**

Samarskiy pereulok
САМАРСКИЙ ПЕРЕУЛОК — **3A1**

Samokatnaya ulitsa
САМОКАТНАЯ УЛИЦА — **4F5**

Samotechnaya ploshchad
САМОТЕЧНАЯ ПЛОЩАДЬ — **3A2**

Samotechnaya ulitsa
САМОТЕЧНАЯ УЛИЦА — **3A1**

Sandunovsky Baths — **3A4**

Sandunovskiy pereulok
САНДУНОВСКИЙ ПЕРЕУЛОК — **3A4**

Saviour's Tower — **7B1**

Savvinskaya naberezhnaya
САВВИНСКАЯ НАБЕРЕЖНАЯ — **5A4**

Sechenovskiy pereulok
СЕЧЕНОВСКИЙ ПЕРЕУЛОК — **6E3**

Seleznevskaya ulitsa
СЕЛЕЗНЕВСКАЯ УЛИЦА — **2F1**

Seliverstov pereulok
СЕЛИВЕРСТОВ ПЕРЕУЛОК — **3B3**

Senate — **7A1**

Serafimovicha, ulitsa
СЕРАФИМОВИЧА, УЛИДА — **6F2, 7A2**

Serebryanicheskaya naberezhnaya
СЕРЕБРЯНИЧЕСКАЯ НАБЕРЕЖНАЯ — **8D2**

Serebryanicheskiy pereulok
СЕРЕБРЯНИЧЕСКИЙ ПЕРЕУЛОК — **8D2**

Sergeya Makeeva, ulitsa
СЕРГЕЯ МАКЕЕВА, УЛИЦА — **1A3**

Serpov pereulok
СЕРПОВ ПЕРЕУЛОК — **5C3**

Serpukhovskaya ploshchad
СЕРПУХОВСКАЯ ПЛОЩАДЬ — **7B5**

Shabolovka, ulitsa
ШАБОЛОВКА, УЛИЦА — **6F5**

Shalyapin House-Museum — **1C5**

Shchepkina, ulitsa
ЩЕПКИНА, УЛИДА — **3B2**

Shchetininskiy pereulok
ЩЕТИНИНСКИЙ ПЕРЕУЛОК — **7B4**

Shchusev Museum of Architecture — **6F1**

Shelaputinskiy pereulok
ШЕЛАПУТИНСКИЙ ПЕРЕУЛОК — **8E2**

Shlyuzovaya naberezhnaya
ШЛЮЗОВАЯ НАБЕРЕЖНАЯ — **8D4**

Shlyuzovoy most
ШЛЮЗОВОЙ МОСТ — **8D5**

Shmitovskiy proezd
ШМИТОВСКИЙ ПРОЕЗД — **1A5**

Shubinskiy pereulok
ШУБИНСКИЙ ПЕРЕУЛОК — **5C2**

Shvedskiy tupik
ШВЕДСКИЙ ТУПИК — **2E4**

Sivtsev Vrazhek, pereulok
СИВЦЕВ ВРАЖЕК, ПЕРЕУЛОК — **6D2**

Sivyakov pereulok
СИВЯКОВ ПЕРЕУЛОК — **8E2**

Skakovaya ulitsa
СКАКОВАЯ УЛИЦА — **1B1**

Skatertnyy pereulok
СКАТЕРНЫЙ ПЕРЕУЛОК — **2D5**

Skornyazhnyy pereulok
СКОРНЯЖНЫЙ ПЕРЕУЛОК — **3C2**

Skryabin House-Museum — **6D1**

Skver Devichevo Polya
СКВЕР ДЕВИЧЬЕГО ПОЛЯ — **5C3**

Slavyanskaya ploshchad
СЛАВЯНСКАЯ ПЛОЩАДЬ — **7C1**

Smolenskaya naberezhnaya
СМОЛЕНСКАЯ НАБЕРЕЖНАЯ — **5C1**

Smolenskaya ploshchad
СМОЛЕНСКАЯ ПЛОЩАДЬ — **5C1**

Smolenskaya ulitsa
СМОЛЕНСКАЯ УЛИЦА` — **5C2**

Smolenskaya-Sennaya ploshchad
СМОЛЕНСКАЯ-СЕННАЯ ПЛОЩАДЬ — **5C2**

Smolenskiy bulvar
СМОЛЕНСКИЙ БУЛЬВАР — **6D2**

Sofiyskaya naberezhnaya
СОФИЙСКАЯ НАБЕРЕЖНАЯ — **7A2**

Solyanka, ulitsa
СОЛЯНКА, УЛИЦА — **7C1**

Sosinskaya ulitsa
СОСИНСКАЯ УЛИЦА — **8F5**

Sovetskoy Armii, ulitsa
СОВЕТСКОЙ АРМИИ, УЛИЦА — **3A1**

Soymonovskiy prospekt
СОЙМОНОВСКИЙ ПРОСПЕКТ — **6F2**

Spartakovskaya ulitsa
СПАРТАКОВСКАЯ УЛИЦА — **4F3**

Spasopeskovskiy pereulok
СПАСОПЕСКОВСКИЙ ПЕРЕУЛОК — **6D1**

Spiridonevskiy pereulok
СПИРИДОНЬЕВСКИЙ ПЕРЕУЛОК — **2D4**

Spiridonovka, ulitsa
СПИРИДОНОВКА, УЛИЦА — **2D4**

Sredni Karetnyy pereulok
СРЕДНИЙ КАРЕТНЫЙ ПЕРЕУЛОК — **2F3**

Sredniy Ovchinnikovskiy pereulok
СРЕДНИЙ ОВЧИННИКОВСКИЙ ПЕРЕУЛОК — **7B2**

Sredniy Tishinskiy pereulok
СРЕДНИЙ ТИШИНСКИЙ ПЕРЕУЛОК — **1C3**

Sredniy Trekhgornyy pereulok
СРЕДНИЙ ТРЕХГОРНЫЙ ПЕРЕУЛОК — **1B5**

Sretenka, ulitsa
СРЕТЕНКА, УЛИЦА — **3B3**

Sretenskiy bulvar
СРЕТЕНСКИЙ БУЛЬВАР — **3B3**

Sretenskiy tupik
СРЕТЕНСКИЙ ТУПИК — **3B3**

Stanislavskiy House-Museum — **2E5**

Staraya Basmannaya ulitsa
СТАРАЯ БАСМАННАЯ УЛИЦА — **4E4**

Staraya ploshchad
СТАРАЯ ПЛОЩАДЬ — **3B5, 7B1**

Starokonyushennyy pereulok
СТАРОКОНЮШЕННЫЙ ПЕРЕУЛОК — **6E1**

Staromonetnyy pereulok
СТАРОМОНЕТНЫЙ ПЕРЕУЛОК — **7A3**

Staropimenovskiy pereulok
СТАРОПИМЕНОВСКИЙ ПЕРЕУЛОК — **2E3**

Starosadskiy pereulok
СТАРОСАДСКИЙ ПЕРЕУЛОК — **3C5, 7C1**

Staryy Tolmachevskiy pereulok
СТАРЫЙ ТОЛМАЧЕВСКИЙ ПЕРЕУЛОК — **7B3**

State Armoury — **6F1, 7A2**

Stoleshnikov pereulok
СТОЛЕШНИКОВ ПЕРЕУЛОК — **2F4**

Stolyarnyy pereulok
СТОЛЯРНЫЙ ПЕРЕУЛОК — **1B4**

Strastnoy bulvar
СТРАСТНОЙ БУЛЬВАР — **2F3**

Stremyannyy pereulok
СТРЕМЯННЫЙ ПЕРЕУЛОК — **7B5**

Sukharevskaya ploshchad
СУХАРЕВСКАЯ ПЛОЩАДЬ — **3B2**

Sushchevskaya ulitsa
СУЩЕВСКАЯ УЛИЦА — **2E1**

Sverchkov pereulok
СВЕРЧКОВ ПЕРЕУЛОК — **3C4**

Svobodnoy Rossii, ploshchad
СВОБОДНОЙ РОССИИ, ПЛОЩАДЬ — **1B5**

Syromyatnicheskaya naberezhnaya
СЫРОМЯТНИЧЕСКАЯ НАБЕРЕЖНАЯ — **4F5, 8F1**

Syromyatnicheskiy proezd
СЫРОМЯТНИЧЕСКИЙ ПРОЕЗД — **4F5, 8F1**

Sytinskiy pereulok
СЫТИНСКИЙ ПЕРЕУЛОК — **2E4**

Т

Taganskaya ulitsa
ТАГАНСКАЯ УЛИЦА — **8E3**

Tarasa Shevchenko, naberezhnaya
ТАРАСА ШЕВЧЕНКО, НАБЕРЕЖНАЯ — **5A1**

Tatarskaya ulitsa
ТАТАРСКАЯ УЛИЦА — **7C4**

Teatralnaya ploshchad
ТЕАТРАЛЬНАЯ ПЛОЩАДЬ — **3A5**

Teatralnyy proezd
ТЕАТРАЛЬНЫЙ ПРОЕЗД — **3A5**

Terem Palace — **7A2**

Teterinskiy pereulok
ТЕТЕРИНСКИЙ ПЕРЕУЛОК — **8D2**

Theatre Square — **3A5**

Timura Frunze, ulitsa
ТИМУРА ФРУНЗЕ, УЛИЦА — **6D3**

Tokmakov pereulok
ТОКМАКОВ ПЕРЕУЛОК — **4F3**

Tolstoy House-Museum **6D4**

Tovarishcheskiy pereulok
ТОВАРИЩЕСКИЙ ПЕРЕУЛОК **8E3**

Trekhgornyy val, ulitsa
ТРЕХГОРНЫЙ ВАЛ, УЛИЦА **1A5**

Trekhprudnyy pereulok
ТРЕХПРУДНЫЙ ПЕРЕУЛОК **2E4**

Tretyakov Gallery **7A3**

Trinity Tower **6F1, 7A1**

Triumfalnaya ploshchad
ТРИУМФАЛЬНАЯ ПЛОЩАДЬ **2E3**

Troitskaya ulitsa
ТРОИЦКАЯ УЛИЦА **3A2**

Tropinin Museum **7B4**

Trubnaya ulitsa
ТРУБНАЯ УЛИЦА **3A3**

Trubnikovskiy pereulok
ТРУБНИКОВСКИЙ ПЕРЕУЛОК **2D5**

TSDRA, sad
ЦДРА, САД **3A1**

Tsvetnoy bulvar
ЦВЕТНОЙ БУЛЬВАР **3A3**

Turchaninov pereulok
ТУРЧАНИНОВ ПЕРЕУЛОК **6E3**

Tverskaya ploshchad
ТВЕРСКАЯ ПЛОЩАДЬ **2F4**

Tverskaya ulitsa
ТВЕРСКАЯ УЛИЦА **2E3**

Tverskoy Zastavy, ploshchad
ТВЕРСКОЙ ЗАСТАВЫ, ПЛОЩАДЬ **2D2**

Tverskoy bulvar
ТВЕРСКОЙ БУЛЬВАР **2E4**

U

Uchebnyy pereulok
УЧЕБНЫЙ ПЕРЕУЛОК **5A5**

Ukrainskiy bulvar
УКРАИНСКИЙ БУЛЬВАР **5B1**

Ulanskiy pereulok
УЛАНСКИЙ ПЕРЕУЛОК **3C3**

Upper Monastery of St Peter **2F3, 3A3**

Usacheva, ulitsa
УСАЧЕВА, УЛИЦА **5B5**

Uspenskiy pereulok
УСПЕНСКИЙ ПЕРЕУЛОК **2F3**

Ustinskaya naberezhnaya
УСТЬИНСКАЯ НАБЕРЕЖНАЯ **7C2**

V

Vagankovskiy most
ВАГАНЬКОВСКИЙ МОСТ **1A2**

Valovaya, ulitsa
ВАЛОВАЯ УЛИЦА **7B5**

Varsonofevskiy pereulok
ВАРСОНОФЬЕВСКИЙ ПЕРЕУЛОК **3A4**

Varvarka, ulitsa
ВАРВАРКА, УЛИЦА **7B1**

Varvarskie vorota, ploshchad
ВАРВАРСКИЕ ВОРОТА, ПЛОЩАДЬ **7C1**

Vasilevskaya ulitsa
ВАСИЛЬЕВСКАЯ УЛИЦА **2D3**

Vasnetsov House-Museum **3B2**

Vasnetsova, pereulok
ВАСНЕЦОВА, ПЕРЕУЛОК **3B2**

Verkhniy Novospasskiy proezd
ВЕРХНИЙ НОВОСПАССКИЙ ПРОЕЗД **8E4**

Verkhnyaya Krasnoselskaya ulitsa
ВЕРХНЯЯ КРАСНОСЕЛЬСКАЯ УЛИЦА **4E1**

Verkhnyaya Radishchevskaya ulitsa
ВЕРХНЯЯ РАДИЩЕВСКАЯ УЛИДА **8D3**

Verkhnyaya Syromyatnicheskaya ulitsa
ВЕРХНЯЯ СЫРОМЯТНИЧЕСКАЯ УЛИЦА **4E5, 8E1**

Verkhnyaya Taganskaya ploshchad
ВЕРХНЯЯ ТАГАНСКАЯ ПЛОЩАДЬ **8E3**

Verkhnyaya ulitsa
ВЕРХНЯЯ УЛИЦА **1C2**

Vetoshnyy pereulok
ВЕТОШНЫЙ ПЕРЕУЛОК **3A5, 7B1**

Vishnyakovskiy pereulok
ВИШНЯКОВСКИЙ ПЕРЕУЛОК **7B4**

Volgogradskiy prospekt
ВОЛГОГРАДСКИЙ ПРОСПЕКТ **8F4**

Volkhonka, ulitsa
ВОЛХОНКА, УЛИЦА **6F2**

Volkov Pereulok
ВОЛКОВ ПЕРЕУЛОК **1C4**

Vorontsovo Pole, ulitsa
ВОРОНЦОВО ПОЛЕ, УЛИЦА **4D5, 8D1**

Vorontsovskaya ulitsa
ВОРОНЦОВСКАЯ УЛИЦА **8E3**

Vorontsovskiy pereulok
НОРОНЦОНСАЙЙ ПЕРЕУЛОК **8E4**

Vorotnikovskiy pereulok
ВОРОТНИКОВСКИЙ ПЕРЕУЛОК **2E3**

Vospitatelnyy pereulok
ВОСПИТАТЕЛЬНЫЙ ПЕРЕУЛОК **7C1**

Vozdvizhenka, ulitsa
ВОЗДНИЖЕНКА, УЛИЦА **6E1**

Voznesenskiy pereulok
ВОЗНЕСЕНСКИЯ ПЕРЕУЛОК **2E5**

Vsekhsvyatskiy pereulok
ВСЕХСВЯТСКИЙ ПЕРЕУЛОК **6F2**

Vsevolzhskiy pereulok
ВСЕВОЛЖСКИЙ ПЕРЕУЛОК **6E2**

Vspolnyy pereulok
ВСПОЛЬНЫЙ ПЕРЕУЛОК **2D4**

Vysokoyauzskiy most
ВЫСОКОЯУЗСКИЙ МОСТ **8E2**

W

White House **1C5**

Y

Yablonnyy pereulok
ЯБЛОННЫЙ ПЕРЕУЛОК **3C1**

Yakimanskaya naberezhnaya
ЯКИМАНСКАЯ НАБЕРЕЖНАЯ **6F3, 7A3**

Yakimanskiy pereulok
ЯКИМАНСКИЙ ПЕРЕУЛОК **6F4**

Yakovo-Apostolskiy pereulok
ЯКОВО-АПОСТОЛСКИЙ ПЕРЕУЛОК **4D5**

Yauzskaya ulitsa
ЯУЗСКАЯ УЛИЦА **8D2**

Yauzskie vorota, ploshchad
ЯУЗСКИЕ ВОРОТА, ПЛОЩАДЬ **8D2**

Yauzskiy bulvar
ЯУЗСКИЙ БУЛЬВАР **8D1**

Yazykovskiy pereulok
ЯЗЫКОВСКИЙ ПЕРЕУЛОК **6D4**

Yuliusa Fuchika, ulitsa
ЮЛИУСА ФУЧИКА, УЛИЦА **2D3**

Z

Zabelina ulitsa
ЗАБЕЛИНА УЛИЦА **3C5, 7C1**

Zamorenova, ulitsa
ЗАМОРЕНОВА, УЛИЦА **1B4**

Zatsepa, ulitsa
ЗАЦЕПА, УЛИЦА **7B5**

Zatsepskiy val, ulitsa
ЗАЦЕПСКИЙ, УЛИЦА **7C5**

Zemledelcheskiy pereulok
ЗЕМЛЕДЕЛЬЧЕСКИЙ ПЕРЕУЛОК **5C3**

Zemlyanoy val, ulitsa
ЗЕМЛЯНОЙ ВАЛ, УЛИЦА **4D4, 8E2**

Zemlyanskiy pereulok
ЗЕМЛЯНСКИЙ ПЕРЕУЛОК **8D2**

Zhitnaya, ulitsa
ЖИТНАЯ, УЛИЦА **7A5**

Zhivarev pereulok
ЖИВАРЕВ ПЕРЕУЛОК **3C2**

Zhukovskovo, ulitsa
ЖУКОВСКОВО, УЛИЦА **3C4**

Znamenka, ulitsa
ЗНАМЕНКА, УЛИЦА **6F1**

Zolotorozhskaya naberezhnaya
ЗОЛОТОРОЖСКАЯ НАБЕРЕЖНАЯ **4F5**

Zoologicheskaya ulitsa
ЗООЛОГИЧЕСКАЯ УЛИЦА **1C4**

Zoologicheskiy pereulok
ЗООЛОГИЧЕСКИЙ ПЕРЕУЛОК **1C4**

Zoopark
ЗООПАРК **1C4**

Zubovskaya ploshchad
ЗУБОВСКАЯ ПЛОЩАДЬ **6D3**

Zubovskiy bulvar
ЗУБОВСКИЙ БУЛЬВАР **6D3**

Zubovskiy prospekt
ЗУБОВСКИЙ ПРОСПЕКТ **6D3**

Zvenigorodskoe shosse
ЗВЕНИГОРОДСКОЕ ШОССЕ **1A4**

Zvonarskiy pereulok
ЗВОНАРСКИЙ ПЕРЕУЛОК **3A4**

General Index

Page numbers in **bold** type refer to main entries.

A

A Priori 203
Above the Eternal Peace (Levitan) 121
Abramov, Semen 63
Abramtsevo Estate-Museum 49, 144, **160**
   travel to 227
Adam, Adolphe 200
Addresses 207
Admission charges 206
Aeroflot 219
Aerotel 176
Ahasuerus, Haman and Esther (Rembrandt) 79, 80
Air travel **216**, 219
Airlines 219
Airports 216, 219
Akademiya 186
Aksakov, Sergey 160
Akvarel 174
Albion Pub 191
Alcohol
   What to Drink in Moscow **182–3**
Aleksandr Art Gallery 195
Aleksandrovskiy Convent (Suzdal) 166
Aleksey, Metropolitan 140
Aleksey II, Patriarch 105
Alexander I, Tsar 23
   Alexander Gardens 67
   Congress of Vienna 24
   Kolomenskoe 138
   Napoleonic Wars 24
   statue of 148
Alexander II, Tsar 23
   assassination of 26
   House of Unions 88
Alexander III, Tsar 26
Alexander Gardens 11, **67**, 148
Alexandra, Tsarina 26
Alexis, Tsar 19, 57
   Diamond Throne 65
   Izmaylovo Park 141
   Kolomenskoe 47, 138, 139
   Trinity Monastery of St Sergius 163, 165
Alexis, Tsarevich 26, 56, 57
Alfa-Bank 212
All-Russian Exhibition Centre **145**
Alternative Festival 32
Ambulances 210, 211
American Bar and Grill 191
American Embassy 209
American Express
   bank 212
   cash dispenser 212
   poste restante service 215
American House of Cinema 201
American Medical Center 211
Amvrosiy, Archbishop 136
Anastasia, Grand Duchess 26
Anastasia, Tsarina 18, 19
Andreev, Nikolay 88

Andrey Rublev Museum of Old Russian Art 140
Andropov, Yuriy 30, 31, 149
   grave of 107
Angel 226
Anna, Tsarina 22, 57
Annunciation (Botticelli) 78, 80
Antikvaz-Metropol 195
Antiques
   exporting 193
   shops **194**, 195
Apelsin 203
Apollo and the Muses (Titov) 91
Apollo in the Chariot of the Sun (Klodt) 90
The Appearance of Christ to the People (Ivanov) 11, 118, 120
April Fool's Day 32
Apted, Michael 129
Arbat (hotel) 174
Arbat Square **82**
Arbatskaya 41, **69–83**
   area map 69
   hotels 174
   Old Arbat 11, 70–71
   Pushkin Museum of Fine Arts **78–81**
   restaurants 184
Arbatskaya Lavitsa 195
Architecture **42–5**
   after the Revolution 45
   Baroque architecture 44
   Early-Russian architecture 44
   Historicism and Style Moderne 45
   Neo-Classical architecture 25, 44–5
   new patriotism 44
   Shchusev Museum of Architecture 49, 150
   Suzdal Museum of Wooden Architecture 166
Argunov, Fyodor 142, 143
Argunov, Pavel 142
Arkhangelskoe **158**
   travel to 227
Arlecchino Children's Club 199
Armenian food **190**, 191
Armoury *see* State Armoury
Arrarat Park Hyatt 174
Arsenal **67**
Arseneva, Yelizaveta 82
Art *see* Museums and galleries
Art cafés **202**, 203
Art Club Nostalgie 191
Art Garbage 203
Art Hotel 176
The Art of Icon Painting in Russia **61**
Art Nouveau 45
Arts and crafts shops **194**, 195
Arts Cinema 82, 201
Assist-24 (medical service) 211
Association of Travelling Art Exhibitions 120
Atrium 195
Austerlitz, Battle of (1805) 23, 24
Australian Embassy 209
Austrian Airlines 219
Autumn in Moscow 34
Avgur 221

Avis 226
Avocado 189

B

B2 203
Bagration, Prince Pyotr 158
Bakarev, Aleksandr 67
Bakhrushin, Aleksey 115, 125
Bakhrushin Theatre Museum 49, **125**
Balchug Kempinski 175
Ballet 200, 201
   Ballets Russes 125
   Bolshoy Ballet in the Soviet Era **91**
Balloons, hot air **220**
Bank notes 213
Banking **212–13**
Baptism of Russia (Vasnetsov) 17
Baranovskiy, Pyotr 105
Barbizon School 81
Bargaining etiquette 193
Barkhin, Grigoriy 45
Baroque architecture 44
Bars **190**, 191
Basil III, Grand Prince
   Convent of the Intercession (Suzdal) 166
   Kolomenskoe 138
   Novodevichiy Convent 130
Basil the Blessed, St 108
Basmanyy Market 195
Baths
   Sandunovskiy Baths **113**
Batu Khan 17
Bazaars **193**, 195
Bazhenov, Vasiliy
   Church of the Consolation of All Sorrows 116, 122
   Dolgov House 117
   Pashkov House 44, 75
   Tsaritsyno 137
Bed and Breakfast (company) 173
Beer 183
Belgrade (hotel) 177
Bell, Tsar 57
Belorusskaya 41
   Moscow's Best: Metro Stations 38
Belorusskiy station 219
Bely, Andrei
   Bely House-Museum 48, 70, **73**
   Line of Life 73
Bely House-Museum 48, **73**
   Street-by-Street map 70
Benoit, Nikolay 142
Berlin Wall 30
Béthencourt, General Augustin de 94
Biblio Globus 195
Blank, Karl 123, 142
Blini 180
"Bloody Sunday" (1905) 26
Blues music **202**, 203
Boats
   river cruises 11, **221**
Bogolyubskiy, Prince Andrey 161, 166
Bolshaya Nikitskaya Ulitsa **93**
Bolsheviks
   Russian Revolution 26–7, **28–9**

The Bolsheviks (Kustodiev) 26
Bolshoy Theatre 23, **90–91**, 149, 201
  Bolshoy Ballet in the Soviet Era **91**
  Street-by-Street map 87
Book shops **194**, 195
Border Troopers' Day 32
Borisov, Ivan 63
Borodino 49, **158**, 227
Borodino, Battle of (1812) 24, 129,
  155, 158
Borodino Panorama Museum 49,
  129
Borovikovskiy, Vladimir 120
Borovitskaya Tower 148
Borscht 180
Botanical Gardens 145
Botkin Hospital 211
Botticelli, Sandro 48
  Annunciation 78, 80
Boucher, François
  Hercules and Omphale 81
Bove, Osip
  Alexander Gardens 67
  Bolshoy Theatre 90
  Cathedral of the Trinity 137
  Church of the Consolation of All
    Sorrows 116, 122
  Manège 94
  Russian Academic Youth Theatre 88,
    199
  Theatre Square 45, 88
  Triumphal Arch 129
Boyars 20
Brandy 183
Breakfast 171, 172
Brenna, Vincenzo 127
Brest-Litovsk Treaty (1917) 29
Breughel, Pieter the Younger 80
Brezhnev, Leonid 30
  grave of 107
Brik, Lilya 111
Brik, Osip 111
British Airways 219
Bruce family 92
Bryullov, Karl 121
Bryusov Pereulok **92**
  Street by Street map 86
Budget accommodation 173
Budvar 188
Bugaev family 73
Bulgakov, Mikhail 200
  Bulgakov Flat-Museum **96–7**, 151
  The Master and Margarita 96, 150,
    151
  Moscow Arts Theatre 92
  Patriarch's Pond 96
Bulgakov Flat-Museum **96–7**, 151
Bungalo Bar 188
Bunker 203
Buran Shuttle 199
Buses 219, **225**
  from the airport 217
  suburban buses 227
Bush, George 30
Bykova, Natalia 117
Bykovo Airport 219
Byzantium 17, 18

C

Cabana 203
Café Ararat 185
Café Des Artistes 186
Café Margarita 191
Cafés **190–91**
Canadian Embassy 209
Canaletto 79, 81
  *Betrothal of the Venetian Doge
    to the Sea* 79
Capri 188
Carre Blanc 189
Cars
  driving in Moscow **226**
  driving outside Moscow 226
  hiring 226
  rescue services 226
  winter driving 226
Cash dispensers 212
Casinos **202**, 203
Cathedrals
  Cathedral of the Annunciation 53,
    55, **60**
  Cathedral of the Archangel 55, **60**
  Cathedral of the Assumption 10, 21,
    42, 44, 55, **58–9**
  Cathedral of the Assumption
    (Krutitskoe Mission) 140
  Cathedral of the Assumption (Trinity
    Monastery of St Sergius) 163, **164**
  Cathedral of the Assumption
    (Vladimir) 157, 167
  Cathedral of Christ the Redeemer 27,
    31, 44, 45, **74**, 148
  Cathedral of the Intercession
    (Izmaylovo Park) 141
  Cathedral of the Nativity (Suzdal)
    166
  Cathedral of St Dmitriy (Vladimir) 167
  Cathedral of the Saviour (Monastery
    of the Saviour and Andronicus) 140
  Cathedral of the Transfiguration
    (Pereslavl-Zalesskiy) 160
  Cathedral of the Trinity 137
  Cathedral of the Virgin of Smolensk
    (Novodevichiy Convent) 11, 130
  Kazan Cathedral 44, **105**, 148–9
  St Basil's Cathedral 10, 43, 44,
    108–9
  Trinity Cathedral (Trinity Monastery
    of St Sergius) 162, **164–5**
Catherine I, Tsarina 22
Catherine II the Great, Tsarina 22,
  23
  Church of St Catherine 123
  coronation dress 65
  Imperial Crown 64
  Izmaylovo Park 141
  Kolomenskoe 138
  Neo-Classical architecture 44
  Orlov Diamond 64
  State Armoury 64
  Tsaritsyno 49, 137
Catherine of Alexandria, St, 123
Caviar 180
  shops **194**, 195
  What to Buy in Moscow 196

Cemeteries
  Novodevichiy Cemetery **131**
Central Telegraph Office 89, 215
Ceramics
  Orangery (Kuskovo) 143
Cézanne, Paul 75
  Mont Ste-Victoire 75
Chagall, Marc 78, 81
Champagne Café 185
Chancellor, Richard 21, 102
Che 203
Chechen separatists 31
Cheka 26, 29, 112, 149
Chekhov, Anton
  Chekhov House-Museum 48, **96**
  grave of 11, 131
  Moscow Arts Theatre 86, 92, 200
  Slavyanskiy Bazaar restaurant 105
  Stanislavskiy and Chekhov **93**
Chekhov, Mikhail 96
Chekhov House-Museum 48, **96**
Chekhova, Mariya 96
Chekhovskaya 41
Cherkasskaya, Varvara 142
Cherkasskiy family 145
Cherkizovskiy Market 195
Chernenko, Konstantin 30, 31
Chernyy, Daniil 165, 167
Children 209
  entertainment 199
  in hotels 172
  in restaurants 179
  Russian Academic Youth Theatre 88,
    199
China Garden 189
Chistoprudnyy Bulvar **112**
Chistye Prudy 41
Christ in Majesty (unattrib) 164
Christmas 34, 35
Christmas Premier Festival 35
Churches (general)
  visiting churches 207
Churches (individual)
  Church of the Archangel Michael
    (Kuskovo) 142
  Church of the Ascension
    (Kolomenskoe) 138
  Church of the Assumption
    (Novodevichiy Convent) 130
  Church of the Conception of St Anna
    102
  Church of the Consolation of All
    Sorrows 116, **122**
  Church of the Deposition of the
    Robe 55, **62–3**
  Church of the Great Ascension 93
  Church of the Holy Fathers of the
    Seven Ecumenical Councils 137
  Church of the Icon of the Virgin of
    Bogolyubovo 97
  Church of the Intercession in Fili 44,
    128
  Church of the Little Ascension 93
  Church of the Metropolitan Peter
    97
  Church of the Nativity of the Virgin
    in Putinki 97
  Church of Our Lady of Kazan

Churches (individual) (cont.)
(Kolomenskoe) 139
Church of the Prophet Elijah
(Suzdal) 161
Church of the Resurrection in Kadashi
43, 44, 116, **122**
Church of St Barbara the Martyr 102
Church of St Catherine **123**
Church of St Clement 117, **122–3**
Church of St Fyodor Stratilit 113
Church of St George 102
Church of St George (Kolomenskoe)
138
Church of St John the Baptist 117
Church of St John the Baptist
(Kolomenskoe) 139
Church of St John the Warrior **136**
Church of St John of Zlatoust 113
Church of St Maxim the Blessed 101,
102
Church of SS Michael and Fyodor 117
Church of St Nicholas in Pyzhy **123**
Church of St Nicholas of the Weavers
135
Church of St Nicholas the Wonder-
Worker 110
Church of St Sergius (Trinity
Monastery of St Sergius) 162, **164**
Church of St Sophia 125
Church of St Vladimir 110
Church of the Saviour Not Made by
Human Hand (Abramtsevo) 160
Church of the Saviour on the Sands 72
Church of the Trinity in Nikitniki 101,
103
Church of the Twelve Apostles 56, 57
Church of the Virgin of Smolensk
(Trinity Monastery of St Sergius) 162
Gate Church of the Intercession
(Novodevichiy Convent) 130
Gate Church of St John the Baptist
(Trinity Monastery of St Sergius)
163
Gate Church of St Simeon the Stylite
137
Gate Church of the Transfiguration
(Novodevichiy Convent) 131
Menshikov's Tower **112–13**
Refectory Church of St Sergius 97
St Andrew's Anglican Church 93
SS Peter and Paul 110
see also Cathedrals; Convents;
Monasteries
Cinema see Film
Cinema Centre 201
Circus 199
Moscow State Circus 11, **198**
City Day 34
Civil War (1918–20) 27, 28
propaganda 29
Claudio, Antonio 136
Climate **32–5**
Clothes
in nightclubs and discos 202
in restaurants 179
visiting churches 207
Le Club 203
Coach travel 218, 219, 227
Coffee House 191
Coins 213

Cold War 27
Communications **214–15**
Communist Party
metro 40
October Revolution 28
outlawed 31
Stalinism 27
Composers' Union 92
Constantine Monomachus, Emperor
59, 65
Constructivism 44, 45, 111
Consulates 208, 209
Convents
Aleksandrovskiy Convent (Suzdal)
166
Convent of the Intercession (Suzdal)
166
Convent of the Nativity of the Virgin
113
Convent of SS Martha and Mary **124**
Novodevichiy Convent 44, **130–33**
Conversion table 209
Cosmonauts' Day 32
Country estates 49
Arkhangelskoe **158**
Izmaylovo Park **141**
Kolomenskoe 11, **138–9**
Kuskovo **142–3**
Ostankino Palace **144–5**
Yasnaya Polyana **167**
Courier services 215
Craft shops **194**, 195
Cranach, Lucas the Elder
Virgin and Child 80
Credit cards 207, 212
in hotels 172
in restaurants 179
in shops 192
Crime 31, 210
Crimean War (1853–6) 23
Crowne Plaza 177
Cruises, river 11, **221**
Cuban missile crisis (1962) 30
Cubism 121
Currency 213
currency exchange 212
legislation 208
Customs and excise 208
Cutty Sark 184
Cyprian, St 108
Cyril, St 17, 207
Cyrillic alphabet 207

D

Daniil, Prince 104, 136
Danilovskaya 176
Danilovskiy Market 195
Danilovskiy Monastery **136–7**
d'Anthès, Georges 73
Day of National Unity 34
Day of Russia 33, 34
Day trips 227
Decembrist Rebellion (1825) 23
Defenders of the Motherland Day 35
Demidov House
Street-by-Street map 116
Demon Seated (Vrubel) 118, 121
Dental care 211
Department stores **192–3**, 195
Detskiy Mir 149, 195

DHL Worldwide Express 215
Diaghilev, Sergey 125
Dialling codes 214
Diamonds
State Diamond Fund **64**
Dionysius
Cathedral of the Assumption 60
icons 61, 121
Scenes from the Life of Metropolitan
Peter 58
Disabled travellers 208
in hotels 173
in restaurants 179
Discos **202**, 203
Discovery 187
The Discreet Charm of the
Bourgeoisie 191
Dmitry, "False" 19, 106
Dmitry, Tsarevich 19
tomb of 55, 60
Doctors 211
Dolgorukiy, Prince Yuriy
builds first kremlin 17, 53
Pereslavl-Zalesskiy 160
statue of 86, 89
and Suzdal 166
and Vladimir 161, 166
Dolgorukov family 74
Dolgov family 122
Dolgov House
Street-by-Street map 117
Dom Farfora 195
Dom Inostrannoi Knigi 195
Domodedovo Airport 219
Donskoy, Prince Dmitriy 21
Battle of Kulikovo 18, 161, 165
coronation 167
Icon of the Donskoy Virgin 136
Donskoy Monastery **136**
Dorian Gray 187
Dostoevsky, Fyodor 97
statue of 150
Doug and Marty's Boar House 203
Drinks
in restaurants 178–9
What to Drink in Moscow **182–3**
Duma 26
Duncan, Isadora 74, 93, 150
Durdin 191
Dushkin, Aleksey 38, 40
Duty-free shops 192
Dynamo Central House of Sports 199
Dzerzhinskiy, Feliks 112
statue of 112, 135, 149

E

E-mail services 215
Easter Sunday 32, 34
Eastways Travel Service 219
Eisenstein, Sergey 112
Electrical appliances 209
Elizabeth, Tsarina 22–3, 110
Elizabeth I, Queen of England 102
Elizabeth II, Queen of England 102
Elki-Palki 191
Emancipation of the Serfs (1861) 23
Embassies 208, 209
Emergency Service Station 226
Emergency services 211
Empire style 25, 45

Engels, Friedrich 67
Entertainment **198–203**
  ballet and opera **200**, 201
  booking tickets 198
  casinos **202**, 203
  children's entertainment 199
  classical music **200**, 201
  film 201
  jazz, blues and Latin music **202**, 203
  Moscow State Circus 11, **198**
  nightclubs and discos **202**, 203
  rock venues **202**, 203
  theatre **200**, 201
Ermak 189
Ethnic restaurants **190**, 191
Etiquette 207
  bargaining 193
  in restaurants 179
Europcar 226
European Medical Centre 211
"Ex-Soviet" hotels 170
Excursions **155–67**
  guided tours 206
  The History of the Golden Ring **161**
  map 156–7
  travel **227**
  Trinity Monastery of St Sergius **162–5**

F

Fabergé 64
Fabrique 203
Faceted Palace **62**
  Street-by-Street map 55
"False Dmitry" 19, 106
Families, staying with 173
Fashion shops **194**, 195
Fast food **190**, 191
Fax services 215
February Revolution (1917) 28
Federal Express 215
Feodosiur 60
Festivals **32–5**
Filaret, Patriarch Fyodor 19, 57, 103
Film 201
  Moscow International Film Festival 33
  Russian Cinema Day 33
Fioravanti, Aristotele
  Cathedral of the Assumption 42, 58, 164, 167
Fire service 211
5-Spice 184
Flea market
  Izmaylovo Park 141
Fokine, Michel 125
Food and drink
  health precautions 211
  light meals and snacks **190–91**
  What to Drink in Moscow **182–3**
  What to Eat in Moscow **180–81**
  see also Restaurants
Foreign Book Store 195
Foreign Ministry 45, 69
  Moscow's Best: Architecture 42
  Street-by-Street map 70
Freeman, Richard 93
Freidenberg, Boris 88, 113
Friazin, Marco Bon 57
Friedland, Battle of (1807) 23
Frolov, Viktor 41

Front Gate Museum (Kolomenskoe) 138
Futurism 111, 121
Fyodor, Tsar 19, 130
Fyodorov, Ivan 105

G

Gagarin, Yuriy 30
  grave of 10, 107
  Space Museum 145
Galleries see Museums and galleries
Gallery Aktyor 195
Gallery of European and American Art of the 19th–20th Centuries 48, 75
Galloway, Christopher 66
Gartman, Viktor 160
Gate Church of the Intercession (Novodevichiy Convent) 130
Gate Church of St Simeon the Stylite 137
Gate Church of the Transfiguration (Novodevichiy Convent) 131
Gauguin, Paul 75
Gelfreikh, Vladimir 41, 45
Genatsvale 191
Genatsvale VIP 189
George, St 17
Georgian food **190**, 191
Gilardi, Domenico 94
Gippius, Karl 113
Girl in Ukrainian Dress (Tropinin) 124
Girl with Peaches (Serov) 47, 121, 160
Glasnost (openness) 30
Glinska, Elena 110
Gnesin Music Academy Opera Studio 201
Godunov, Boris 19
  Donskoy Monastery 136
  Ivan the Great Bell Tower 57
  State Armoury 64
  tomb of 163
Godunov (restaurant) 186
Godzillas 175, 177
Gogol, Nikolai 160
  grave of 131
Gogol (rock venue) 203
Golden Apple 176
Golden Ring **161**
Goldfish (Matisse) 79, 81
Golenishchev, Vladimir 48, 80
Golitsyn, Prince Nikolay 136, 158
Golitsyn family 158
Golitsyn Gardens 129
Golovin, Aleksandr 170
Goncharova, Natalya (painter) 121
Goncharova, Natalya (Pushkin's wife) 25, 73, 93
Gorbachev, Mikhail 31
  coup against 112, 128
  outlaws Communist Party 31
  perestroika and glasnost 30
Gorbushka 195
Goritskiy Monastery of the Assumption (Pereslavl-Zalesskiy) 160
Gorizont 201
Gorky, Maxim 75
  Gorky Art Theatre 150
  Gorky House-Museum 42, 45, **95**
  Gorky Park 129
  grave of 107

Gorky, Maxim (cont.)
  Moscow Arts Theatre 92
  Shalyapin House-Museum 83
  Tolstoy House-Museum 134
  Tverskaya Ulitsa 89
Gorky Art Theatre 150
Gorky House-Museum 45, **95**
  Moscow's Best: Architecture 42
Gorky Park 11, **129**
  Ice Sculpture Festival 35
Gorodetskiy, Prokhor 60
Graham Ring (hotel) 177
Grande Armée 24
Graveyard of Fallen Monuments 135
Great Kremlin Palace 45, **63**
  Street-by-Street map 54
Great Northern War (1700–21) 22
Grigorev, Afanasiy 45, 74
Grigorev, Dmitriy 164
Gudunova, Irina 130
Guerne, Charles de 158
Guided tours 206, 209
GUM 45, **107**, 195
Gypsies 210
Gypsy Theatre 201

H

Health care 211
Helicon Opera 201
Hercules and Omphale (Boucher) 81
Hermogen, Patriarch 58
Hero Cities of the Soviet Union, monument to 148
Hertz 226
Herzen, Aleksandr 23
  Herzen House Museum 71
  statue of 94
Herzen House-Museum
  Street-by-Street map 71
Hilton-Leningradskaya 175
Hiring cars 226
Historical Museum 45, 99, 106
  Historicism, architecture 45
History **17–31**
History of Moscow Museum 49, **111**
History museums 49
Hitler, Adolf 27
Hogg Robinson Business Travel 219
Holiday Inn Lesnaya 176
Holiday Inn Vinogradovo 176
Holidays, public 34
Hooch, Pieter de 80
Hospitals 211
Hostel Asia 173
Hostel Snail 173
Hostels 173
Hot air balloons **220**
Hotel Metropol 45, **88**
  Street-by-Street map 87
Hotel National **89**
  Street-by-Street map 86
Hotels **170–77**
  budget accommodation 173
  children in 172
  disabled travellers 173
  facilities 171
  location 171
  payment 172
  reservations 171
  security 173

Hotels (cont.)
  types of hotel 170
House-museums 48–9
House of Friendship 45, **95**, 150
House of Unions 45, **88–9**
  Street-by-Street map 87
Hungarian uprising (1956) 30

I

Ice Sculpture Festival in Gorky Park 35
Iconostasis 61
Icons **61**
  Tretyakov Gallery 121
Ikra 203
Illuzion 201
Immigration 208
Impressionists 75
Independent Postal Service 215
Inoculations 211
Insect repellents 211
Insurance
  medical 211
  travel 210
Interchange 173
International Festival of the Orthodox
  Church 35
International Music Assemblies Festival
  33
International Women's Day 32, 34
Internet cafés 215
Irbis 175
Irish Embassy 209
Istomin, Nazariy 63
ITAR-TASS news agency 93, 150
Ivan (brother of Peter the Great) 22
Ivan the Great Bell Tower 10, 37, **57**,
  112
  Street-by-Street map 55
Ivan I "Kalita", Grand Prince 18
  Cathedral of the Assumption 21
  Kolomenskoe 138
Ivan III the Great, Grand Prince 18,
  53
  Cathedral of the Annunciation 60
  Cathedral of the Archangel 60
  Cathedral of the Assumption 58
  Convent of the Nativity of the Virgin
  113
  Faceted Palace 62
  Red Square 106
  Vladimir 167
Ivan IV the Terrible, Tsar 18–19, 21,
  102
  Cathedral of the Annunciation 60
  Cathedral of the Assumption (Trinity
  Monastery of St Sergius) 163
  Church of the Holy Fathers of the
  Seven Ecumenical Councils 137
  Ivanovskaya Hill 110
  Kolomenskoe 138, 139
  Monomakh Throne 59
  Old English Court 101
  St Basil's Cathedral 10, 43, 108
  Trinity Monastery of St Sergius 164,
  165
Ivan the Terrible and his Son on 16
November, 1581 (Repin) 120
Ivan V, Tsar 164
Ivanov, Aleksandr
  The Appearance of Christ to the

Ivanov, Aleksandr (cont.)
  People 11, 118, 120
  Hotel National 86, 89
  watercolours 121
Ivanov, Viktor 28
Ivanovskaya Hill **110**
Ivantsarevich 195
Izmailovo Delta 175
Izmaylovo Market 195
Izmaylovo Park 44, **141**
Izola 189
Izvestiya 45, 97

J

Jackson, Michael 88
Jagannat 187, 191
James I, King of England 64
Jazz **202**, 203
Jazz Town Casino 203
Jewellery
  Tretyakov Gallery 121
Jordaens, Jacob 79

K

Kachalov, Vasiliy 92
Kaganovich, Lazar 40
Kamenka river 166
Kaminskiy, Aleksandr
  Church of St Sophia 125
  Stock Exchange 100, 104
Kandinsky, Vasily 75
Karin, Semen 102
Karma Bar 203
Katerina (hotel) 177
Kavkazskaya Plenitsa 188
Kavos, Albert 87, 90, 91
Kazakov, Matvey 44–5
  city hall 89
  Golitsyn Gardens 129
  House of Unions 87, 88
  Moscow Old University 94
  Senate 66
  Tsaritsyno 137
Kazakov, Rodion 102
Kazan 19
Kazan Cathedral 44, **105**, 148–9
Kazanskiy station 144, 219
Kazy Girei, Khan 136
Kebur Palace 177
Kekushev, Lev 88
Kerbel, Leonid 88
Kerenskiy, Aleksandr 29
KGB 112, 149
Khachaturian, Aram 91
Khanzhonkov, Aleksandr 82
Khodzha Nasreddin v Khive 186,
  191
Khrushchev, Nikita
  denounces Stalin 30
  grave of 11, 131
  Manège 94
  metro system 40
  Museum of Modern History 97
  Palace of Congresses 56
Kiev
  Golden Ring 161
  history 17
  icons 61
Kievskaya 41
  Moscow's Best: Metro Stations 38

Kievskiy station 219
Kinostar De Lux 201
Kiprenskiy, Orest 120, 125
Kirov, Sergey 27
Kish Mish 191
Kissel 181
Kitaiskiy Lyotchik Djao Da 191, 203
Kitay Gorod *see* Red Square and Kitay
  Gorod
Klein, Roman
  Perlov Tea House 113
  Pushkin Museum of Fine Arts 78
  Sovremennik Theatre 112
KLM 219
Klodt, Pyotr
  Apollo in the Chariot of the Sun 90
Klykov, Vyacheslav 106
Knipper-Chekhova, Olga 96
Kologrivov, Yuriy 143
Kolomenskoe 11, 49, **138–9**
  Moscow's Best: Museums 47
  travel to 227
Kompot 183
Komsomol 40, 144
Komsomolskaya 40–41, 144
  Moscow's Best: Metro Stations 39
Komsomolskaya Ploshchad **144**
Korchma Taras Bulba 191
Korean War (1950–54) 30
Korin, Pavel 41
Korolkov, Aleksey 56
Korovin, Konstantin 83, 121
Korston 176
Kosmos 175
Kozlovskiy, Nikolay 113
Kramskoy, Ivan 118
  Portrait of Pavel Tretyakov 120
Kremlin 10, **53–67**
  area map 53
  Cathedral of the Assumption 10,
  58–9
  history 20
  A One-hour Stroll through Central
  Moscow 148
  State Armoury 10, **64–5**
  Street-by-Street map 54–5
  towers **66**
Krizis Zhanra 203
Kropotkin, Prince Pyotr 38, 74
Kropotkinskaya 40
  Moscow's Best: Metro Stations 38
Krushchev family 74
Krutitskoe Mission 44, **140**
Krylov, Ivan
  statue of 96
Kulebiaka 181
Kulikovo, Battle of (1380) 18, 161,
  165
Kult 191, 203
Kumanin family 122
Kursk, Battle of (1943) 148
Kurskiy station 219
Kuskovo 49, **142–3**
  Moscow's Best: Museums 47
  travel to 227
Kustodiev, Boris
  The Bolsheviks 26
Kutuzov, Field Marshal Mikhail
  Battle of Borodino 24, 155, 158
  Novokuznetskaya metro station 41

Kvas 180, 183

L

Labour Day 32, 34
Lacquered artifacts 197
Laika 30
Language 207
Lanseray, Yevgeniy 40
Latin music **202**, 203
Lenin 97
  Civil War 27
  embalming **107**
  and film industry 201
  funeral 89
  Hotel National 89
  Lenin Mausoleum 10, 47, 49, 82, 106, **107**
  Palace of Soviets 75
  Russian Revolution 28
  Senate 67
  statue of 145
  Tolstoy House-Museum 134
  What is to be Done? 26
Lenin Mausoleum 10, 49, 82, 106, **107**
  Moscow's Best: Museums 47
Leningrad *see* St Petersburg
Leningradskiy station 144, 219
Lenkom Theatre 201
Lermontov, Mikhail
  The Demon 118
  Lermontov House-Museum 49, **82–3**
  portrait of 82
Lermontov House-Museum 48, 49, **82 3**
Levitan, Isaak 121
  Above the Eternal Peace 121
Levitskiy, Dmitriy 123, 125
  Portrait of Ursula Mnichek 120
Libraries
  Russian State Library 75, 150
Lilina, Maria 93
Line of Life (Bely) 73
Lomonosov, Mikhail
  Moscow University 22, 23, 94
  Slavic Greek-Latin Academy 105
  statue of 94
Lopukhin family 74
Lopukhin Palace 131
Lopukhina, Yevdokiya 131
Lubyanka Square **112**, 149
Luxury hotels 170
Luzhkov, Yuriy
  Cathedral of Christ the Redeemer 74
  hotels 170
  Kazan Cathedral 105
Luzhniki Stadium 199, 203
Lvov, Prince 29

M

Mafiya (mafia) 31, 210
Magazines 215
Maharaja 186
Main Post Office 215
Makarov, Terentiy 141
Maki Café 185, 191
Malenkiy Genii 193
Malevich, Kazimir 135
  Supremus No. 56 29
Maliy, Petrok 57
Malyy Theatre 88, 201
  Street-by-Street map 87

Mamontov, Andrey 160
Mamontov, Savva 121, 124
  Abramtsevo Estate-Museum 144, 160
  Operetta Theatre 88
Mamontova, Vera 160
Manège **94**, 150
Manizer, Matvey 40
Maps
  Arbatskaya 69
  Around Pyatnitskaya Ulitsa 116–17
  Around Theatre Square 86–7
  bus and metro links into the city centre 217
  Central Moscow 14–15
  Further Afield 127
  Golden Ring 161
  Kitay Gorod 100–101
  Kremlin 53, 54–5
  Metro 224
  Moscow and environs 13
  Moscow Region 156–7
  Moscow's Best: Architecture 42–3
  Moscow's Best: Metro Stations 38–9
  Moscow's Best: Museums 46–7
  A 90-minute Literary Walk 150–51
  Old Arbat 70–71
  A One-hour Stroll through Central Moscow 148–9
  railway stations 218
  Red Square 106
  Red Square and Kitay Gorod 99
  river cruise route 221
  Russian Federation 12–13
  Russian Revolution 28
  Tverskaya 85
  Zamoskvoreche 115
Mari Vanna 184
Maria, Grand Duchess 26
Maria (daughter of Tsar Alexis) 130
Market (restaurant) 188
Markets **193**, 195
Marriott Grand Hotel 174
Martini, Simone 80
Martos, Ivan
  Minin and Pozharskiy 108
Marx, Karl 49, 97
  Alexander Gardens 67
  statue of 88, 149
Masha Tsigal 194
Maslenitsa 32
Mateev, Kuzma 122–3
Matisse, Henri 75
Maxim, St 102
Mayak 185
Mayakovskaya 40, 41
  Moscow's Best: Metro Stations 38
Mayakovsky, Vladimir 92, **111**
  Mayakovskaya metro station 38
  Mayakovsky Museum 47, 49, **111**, 149
  Mayakovsky Theatre 93
  statue of 151
Mayakovsky Museum 49, **111**, 149
  Moscow's Best: Museums 47
Mayakovsky Theatre 93
Mayat, Vladimir 104
Mazepa, Ivan 110
Mazyrin, Vladimir 45, 95
Medical treatment 211
Medieval Moscow 18–19, **20–21**
Mega 195

Mekhana Bansko 184
Melnikov, Konstantin 45
  Melnikov House 11, 71, **72**
Melnikov, Viktor 72
Melnikov House 11, 45, **72**
  Street-by-Street map 71
Menshikov, Prince Aleksandr 112
Menshikov, Prince Sergey 93
Menshikov family 93
Menshikov's Tower **112–13**
Menus 178
Le Meridien Country Club 176
Methodius, St 17
Metro **38–41**, **222–4**
  map 217, 224
  Moscow Metro Museum 41
  Moscow's Best: Metro Stations **38–9**
  tickets and travel cards 223
Metropol 174
Metsu, Gabriel 80
Meyerhold, Vsevolod
  Bakhrushin Theatre Museum 125
  Bryusov Pereulok 86, 92
  Mayakovsky Theatre 93
Mikhail Romanov, Tsar 19
  Palace of the Romanov Boyars 103
  Terem Palace 63
Mikhaylov, Andrey 90
The Millstone of Serfdom (unattrib) 25
Miloslavskiy family 22
Minin, Kuzma 19
  expels "False Dmitry" 106
  Novokuznetskaya metro station 41
  statue of 108
Minin and Pozharskiy (Martos) 108
Minkus, Mikhail 45
Miracle City 199
Mironov, Aleksey 142, 144
Mironovskiy, Ivan 67
Mirza, Shah of Iran 64
Mnichek, Ursula
  portrait of 120
Monasteries
  Danilovskiy Monastery **136–7**
  Donskoy Monastery **136**
  Goritskiy Monastery of the Assumption (Pereslavl Zalesskiy) 160
  Monastery of the Epiphany 100, **104**
  Monastery of St Euthymius (Suzdal) 166
  Monastery of the Saviour and Andronicus 44, **140**
  Monastery of the Sign 102
  Trinity Monastery of St Sergius 155, 156, **162–5**
  Upper Monastery of St Peter **97**
Money **212–13**
Mongols
  Battle of Kulikovo 18, 161, 165
  invasion 17–18
Monighetti, Ippolit 43, 110
Monomakh, Prince Vladimir 161, 166
Monomakh Throne 59
Mont Ste-Victoire (Cézanne) 75
Moo Moo 191
The Morning of the Execution of the Streltsy (Surikov) 119, 120
Morozov, Aleksey 143

Morozov, Arseny 95
Morozov, Savva 96
Morozov Mansion **96**, 150
Moscow Annual Airshow 33
Moscow Arts Theatre **92**, 93, 105, 201
  Street-by-Street map 86
Moscow Bed and Breakfast 173
Moscow Bus/Coach Station 219
Moscow Conservatory 93, **94**, 201
Moscow Forum 32
Moscow House of Books 195
Moscow International Film Festival 33
Moscow Metro Museum 41
Moscow Old University 45, **94**
  history 22, 23, 25
  Moscow's Best: Architecture 42
Moscow Puppet Theatre 11, 199
Moscow River Line 221
Moscow School icons 61, 121
Moscow State Circus **198**
Moscow State University (MGU) 129
Moscow Taxi 221
Moscow Zoo 199
Moskovsky 186
Moskva river
  cruises on 11, **221**
  A One-hour Stroll through Central
    Moscow 148
Moskva Trade House 195
Moskvin, Ivan 92
Mosquitoes 211
Mossoviet Theatre 201
Mukhina, Vera 94, 145
Murillo, Bartholomé Esteban 80
Muscat 188
Museums and galleries (general) **46–9**
  admission charges 206
  country estates 49
  history museums 49
  house-museums 48–9
  Moscow's Best: Museums **46–7**
  opening hours 207
  painting and decorative arts 48
  shops **193**, 195
  specialist museums 49
Museums and galleries (individual)
  Abramtsevo Estate-Museum 49,
    160
  All-Russian Exhibition Centre **145**
  Andrey Rublev Museum of Old
    Russian Art 140
  Arkhangelskoe 158
  Bakhrushin Theatre Museum 49,
    125
  Bely House-Museum 48, 70, **73**
  Borodino 49, 158
  Borodino Panorama Museum 49,
    129
  Bulgakov Flat-Museum **96–7**, 151
  Chekhov House-Museum 48, **96**
  Front Gate Museum (Kolomenskoe)
    138
  Gallery of 19th- and 20th-Century
    European and American Art 75
  Gorky House-Museum 42, 45, **95**
  Herzen House-Museum 71
  Historical Museum 45, 99, 106
  History of Moscow Museum 49, **111**
  Kolomenskoe **138–9**
  Lenin Mausoleum 10, 47, 49, 82,

Museums and galleries (cont.)
  106, **107**
  Lermontov House-Museum 48, 49,
    82–3
  Mayakovsky Museum 47, 49, **111**,
    149
  Moscow Metro Museum 41
  Museum of Arts and Crafts (Suzdal)
    166
  Museum of Eastern Peoples 150
  Museum of the Great Patriotic War
    49, 129
  Museum of Modern History 49, **97**,
    151, 195
  Museum of Private Collections 48, **75**
  Museum of the Revolution see
    Museum of Modern History
  Museum of 17th-Century Life and
    Applied Art 55, 56–7
  New Tretyakov Gallery 48, **135**
  Orangery (Kuskovo) 143
  Palace of the Romanov Boyars 47,
    49, **102–3**
  Polytechnical Museum 43, 45, 49, **110**
  Pushkin House-Museum 11, 48, 70,
    73
  Pushkin Literary Museum 74
  Pushkin Museum of Fine Arts 46, 48,
    78–81, 195
  Rumyantsev Museum 75
  Shalyapin House-Museum 46, 48, **83**
  Shchusev Museum of Architecture
    49, 150
  Skryabin House-Museum 48, 71, **72**
  Space Museum 145
  Stanislavskiy House-Museum 48, **93**
  State Armoury 10, 46, 48, 54, **64–5**
  Suzdal Museum 157, 166
  Suzdal Museum of Wooden
    Architecture 166
  Tchaikovsky House-Museum 49, **159**
  Tolstoy House-Museum 46, 48, **134**
  Tolstoy Literary Museum 74
  Tretyakov Gallery 10–11, 47, 48, 116,
    118–21, 195
  Tropinin Museum 48, **124–5**
  Tsaritsyno 137
  Vasnetsov House-Museum 49, **144**
  Yasnaya Polyana 167
Mushroom gathering 34
Music
  ballet and opera 200, 201
  Christmas in Moscow 35
  Christmas Premier Festival 35
  classical music 200, 201
  International Music Assemblies
    Festival 33
  jazz, blues and Latin **202**, 203
  Moscow Conservatory 93, **94**
  Punk Festival 34
  rock venues **202**, 203
  Russian Winter (festival) 35
  Shalyapin House-Museum **83**
  shops **194**, 195
  Skryabin House-Museum **72**
  Summer Music Festival 33
  Svyatoslav Richter December Nights
    35
  Talents of Russia 34
  Tchaikovsky **159**

Music (cont.)
  Tchaikovsky House-Museum **159**
  Tchaikovsky International
    Competition 33
  Mussorgsky, Modest 125, 200
  MXAT Gorky Art Theatre 150

N

Napoleon I, Emperor
  Arsenal 67
  Borodino 49, 158
  Cathedral of Christ the Redeemer 74
  invasion of Russia 23, 24
  in the Kremlin 56
  Novodevichiy Convent 130
  occupation of Moscow 45
  retreat from Moscow 158
  Trinity Tower 54
Napoleonic Wars 23, 24, 129
Naryshkin, Prince Lev 128
Naryshkin family 22, 44, 97
Naryshkina, Natalya 166
Nataliya Sats Children's Musical
  Theatre 199
National (hotel) 174
National Car Rental 226
Natura Viva 188
Navy Day 33
Nazi-Soviet Pact (1939) 27
Neizvestniy, Ernst 94
Nemirovich-Danchenko, Vladimir 92,
  105
Neo-Classical architecture 25, 44–5
NEP (New Economic Policy) 27
Nesterov, Mikhail 124
Netland 215
Nevrev, Nikolay 160
Nevskiy, Prince Aleksandr 17, 167
New Academic Year 34
New Circus 198, 199
"New Russians" 31
New Tretyakov Gallery 48, **135**
New Year 34, 35
New York Casino 203
New Zealand Embassy 209
Newspapers 215
Nicholas I, Tsar 23
  Great Kremlin Palace 63
  Izmaylovo Park 141
  and Pushkin 25
  Shah Diamond 64
  State Armoury 46, 64
Nicholas II, Tsar
  assassination 27, 28, 124
  Faceted Palace 62
  Russian Revolution 26, 28, 29
  war with Japan 26
Nicholas of Zaraysk, St 140
Nicholas Railway 23
Nightclubs **202**, 203
Nightlife **202–3**
Nijinsky, Vaslaw
  ballet shoes 48, 49, 125
Nike Monument 129
Nikitnikov, Grigoriy 101, 103
Nikolskaya Ulitsa **104–5**
  Street-by-Street map 100
Nikon, Patriarch **57**, 122
  church design 44
  Patriarch's Palace 55, 56

Nikon, Patriarch (cont.)
  split with Old Believers 19, 57
Noev Kovcheg 187
Nostalgie 187
Novaya Opera 201
Novgorod
  Golden Ring 161
  history 17, 19
  icons 61, 161
Novodevichiy Cemetery 11, **131**
Novodevichiy Convent 11, 44,
  130–33
  travel to 227
Novokuznetskaya 41
  Moscow's Best: Metro Stations 39
  Street-by-Street map 117
Novotel 176
Novyy, Aleviz
  Cathedral of the Archangel 60
  Church of St Vladimir 110
  Upper Monastery of St Peter 97

O

Oblomov 187
Obraztsov, Sergey 200
Obraztsov Puppet Theatre 199
October Revolution (1917) 28
Ogarev, Nikolay
  statue of 94
Ogurtsov, Bazhen 63, 66
Okhotnyy Ryad 195
Oktyabp 201
Old Arbat 11
  Street-by-Street map 70–71
Old Believers 19, 57
Old Circus 11, 198, 199
Old English Court 44, **102**
  Moscow's Best: Architecture 43
  Street-by-Street map 101
Old Merchants' Chambers
  Street-by-Street map 100
Oleg, Varangian chief 17
Olga, Grand Duchess 26
Olympic Sports Complex 199
Olympiyskiy Stadium 203
One-day trips 227
Opekushin, Alexander 97
Opening hours 207
  nightclubs and discos 202
  restaurants 179
  shops 192
Opera 200, 201
Operetta Theatre 88, 201
Oprichniki 18
Orangery (Kuskovo) 143
Order of the Sisters of Charity 124
Orlov, Count Grigoriy 23, 64
Orlov family 93
Orthodox Church see Russian
  Orthodox Church
Ostankino Palace 49, 127, **144–5**
Ostrovskiy, Aleksandr 88
  statue of 87, 88
OVIR 209

P

Painting
  The Art of Icon Painting in Russia **61**
  see also Museums and galleries
Paisein, Ivan and Boris 58

Palace (hotel) 176
Palace of Congresses 56
Palace of the Romanov Boyars 44, 49,
  102–3
  Moscow's Best: Museums 47
  Street-by-Street map 101
Palace of Soviets **75**
Palaces
  Faceted Palace 55, **62**
  Great Kremlin Palace 45, 54, **63**
  Kuskovo 49
  Lopukhin Palace 131
  Ostankino Palace 49, 127, **144–5**
  Palace of the Romanov Boyars 44,
    47, 49, 101, **102–3**
  Patriarch's Palace 55, **56–7**
  State Kremlin Palace 54, **56**
  Terem Palace 54, **63**
  Trinity Monastery of St Sergius 165
  Tsaritsyno 49, **137**
  Wooden Palace (Kuskovo) 142
  see also Country estates
Papa Johns 203
Paper Moon 186
Park Kultury 40, 41
  Moscow's Best: Metro Stations 38
Park Pobedy 41
Parking 226
Parks and gardens
  Alexander Gardens 11, **67**, 148
  Arkhangelskoe 158
  Botanical Gardens 145
  Gorky Park 11, **129**
  Izmaylovo Park **141**
  Kolomenskoe 138
  Kuskovo 142
  Tsaritsyno 137
  Victory Park **128–9**
Pashkov, Captain Pyotr 75
Pashkov House 44, **82**
  Moscow's Best: Architecture 42
Passports 208
Pasta **190**, 191
Pastries and sweets **190**, 191
Il Patio 191
Patriarch's Palace **56–7**
  Street-by-Street map 55
Patriarch's Pond **96**, 151
Patriarshiy Dom Tours 209
Paul I, Tsar 23
Paveletskiy station 219
Peace Travel Services 209
Peking (hotel) 174
Pelmeni 181
"People's Will" group 26
Pereslavl-Zalesskiy **160**, 227
Perestroika (restructuring) 30
Perlov Tea House **113**
Perov, Vasiliy 120
Personal safety **210–11**
Perugino, Pietro 80
Peter, Metropolitan 21
Peter I the Great, Tsar **22**, 131
  Arsenal 67
  Church of the Intercession in Fili 128
  Church of St John the Warrior 136
  Faceted Palace 62
  Izmaylovo Park 141
  Kolomenskoe 11, 138, 139
  Mazepa betrays 110

Peter I the Great, Tsar (cont.)
  and Menshikov 112
  Novodevichiy Convent 130
  Pereslavl-Zalesskiy 160
  Peter the Great's Birthday 33
  Polytechnical Museum 110
  statue of 135
  Streltsy Rebellion 22, 123
  Trinity Monastery of St Sergius 162–5
  Upper Monastery of St Peter 97
Peter II, Tsar 22
  tomb of 60
Peter III, Tsar 22, 23
Petrol 226
Petrov-Vodkin, Kuzma 121
Petrovskiy Passage 195
  Street-by-Street map 87
Pharmacies 211
Phonecards 214
Photography 209
Picasso, Pablo 75
  Young Acrobat on a Ball 48
Pickpockets 173, 210
Pizzas **190**, 191
Pletnev, Pyotr 73
Ploshchad Revolyutsii 40
  Moscow's Best: Metro Stations 39
Polenov, Vasiliy
  Abramtsevo Estate-Museum 160
  A Moscow Courtyard 72, 120
  Operetta Theatre 88
Police **210**, 211
  traffic police 226
Politburo 30
Polo Club 185
Poltava, Battle of (1709) 22
Polubes, Stepan 141
Polytechnical Museum 45, 49, **110**
  Moscow's Best: Architecture 43
Pomerantsev, Aleksandr 45, 107
Popov factory 25
Portofino 187
Portrait of Arseny Tropinin, the Artist's
  Son (Tropinin) 118, 120
Portrait of Pavel Tretyakov (Kramskoy)
  120
Portrait of Ursula Mnichek (Levitskiy)
  120
Posokhin, Mikhail 56
Pospeev, Sidor 58, 63
Postal services 215
Poussin, Nicolas 81
Pozdeev, Nikolay 136
Pozharskiy, Prince Dmitry 19
  expels "False Dmitry" 106
  Icon of the Kazan Virgin 105
  Novokuznetskaya metro station 41
  statue of 108
Praga 184
"Prague Spring" 30
Prakash Guest House 173
Pravda 26, 151
President (hotel) 177
Presidential Administration **66**
Primitivism 121
Prokofiev, Sergey 92
  grave of 131
Propaganda (bar) 191, 203
Proton 177
Public holidays 34

Public toilets 209
Pubs **190**, 191
Pugachev Rebellion (1773–4) 22
Punk Festival 34
Puppet theatres 11, 199
Pushkin, Alexander 25, **73**, 89, 159
  death of 73, 83
  marriage 93
  portrait of 120
  Pushkin House-Museum 11, 48, 70,
  73
  Spasopeskovskiy Pereulok 72
  statues of 70, 97, 150
Pushkin (restaurant) 186
Pushkin House-Museum 11, 48, **73**
  Street-by-Street map 70
Pushkin Literary Museum 74
Pushkin Museum of Fine Arts 48, **78–81**
  art of ancient civilizations 80
  European art 80–81
  floorplan 78–9
  Moscow's Best: Museums 46
  shop 195
  Visitors' Checklist 79
Pushkin Square **97**, 150
Pushkin Theatre 150
Putin, Vladimir 31, 200
Pyatnitskaya Ulitsa
  Street-by-Street map **116–17**

Q

Quarenghi, Giacomo 102

R

Rabinovich, Sergey 41
Rachmaninov, Sergei 134
  Moscow Conservatory 94
  Operetta Theatre 88
  Skryabin House-Museum 72
Radio 215
Radisson 177
  cash dispenser 212
Railways *see* Trains
Rainfall 34
Rapsodia 195
Rasputin, Grigoriy 26
Razumovskiy, Count Aleksey 110
The Real McCoy 191
Realist art 120
Red Army 27, 28, 40
1 Red Square (restaurant) 186
Red Square and Kitay Gorod **99–113**
  area map 99
  hotels 174–5
  Red Square 10, **106**, 148
  restaurants 186–7
  St Basil's Cathedral **108–9**
  Street-by-Street map 100–101
Reed, John
  grave of 107
Registration 208
Religious Procession in Kursk Province
  (Repin) 119, 120
Rembrandt 48, 80
  Abasuerus, Haman and Esther 79, 80
Renaissance (hotel) 176
Renoir, Pierre Auguste 75
Repin, Ilya 75
  Abramtsevo Estate-Museum 160
  drawings 121

Repin, Ilya (cont.)
  *Ivan the Terrible and his Son on 16
  November, 1581* 120
  portrait of Tolstoy's daughter
  134
  *Religious Procession in Kursk
  Province* 119, 120
  Tretyakov Gallery 120
Repin, Vera 160
Republics' Tree 150
Rerberg, Ilya 89
Rescue services 226
Restaurants **178–91**
  disabled travellers 179
  etiquette 179
  in hotels 171
  opening times 179
  payment and tipping 179
  reading the menu 178
  reservations 179
  smoking in 179
  types of cuisine 178
  vegetarian meals 179
  What to Drink in Moscow 178–9,
  182–3
  What to Eat in Moscow **180–81**
  where to eat 178
  see also Food and drink
Resurrection Gate **105**, 147, 148
Revolution (1905) 26
Revolution (1917) 26–7, **28–9**
  Museum of Modern History 97
Richter, Svyatoslav 35
Rimsky-Korsakov, Nikolai 200
Ritz-Carlton 174
River cruises 11, **221**
Rizhskiy station 219
Roadhouse 203
Roberto 185
Rock music **202**, 203
Rodchenko, Aleksandr 75, 111, 135
Rodin, Auguste 75
Rokoko 195
Rokotov, Fyodor 120
Romanov, Nikita 47, 101, 102
Romanov dynasty 19
  Alexander Gardens 67
  assassination of Nicholas II 27, 28
The Rooks Have Come (Savrasov) 118,
  120
Ropet, Ivan 160
Rossiya 201
Rostand, Edmond 88
Rosticks 191
Rostov
  Golden Ring 161
  history 17
Roubaud, Franz 129
Rozhin, Igor 41
Rubens, Peter Paul 48, 79, 80, 81
  Bacchanalia 79
Rubinstein, Anton 94
Rubinstein, Nikolay 94
Rublev, Andrey
  Andrey Rublev Museum of Old
  Russian Art 140
  Andronikov Monastery 20
  Cathedral of the Annunciation
  60
  Cathedral of the Assumption

Rublev, Andrey (cont.)
  (Vladimir) 167
  icons 61
  Monastery of the Saviour and
  Andronicus 140
  The Trinity 10–11, 119, 121, 165
  Trinity Cathedral (Trinity Monastery
  of St Sergius) 162, 165
Rudnev, Lev 129
Ruffo, Marco
  Faceted Palace 55, 62
Rumyantsev Museum 75
Rurik, Varangian chief 17
Rus' (restaurant) 184
Russia Direct Ltd 219
Russian Academic Youth Theatre 88, 199
Russian cafés **190**, 191
Russian Cinema Day 33
Russian Federation, map 12–13
Russian National Group 219
Russian Orthodox Church **137**
  The Art of Icon Painting in Russia **61**
  Cathedral of the Assumption **58–9**
  Christmas 34, 35
  Easter Sunday 32
  history 17
  International Festival of the
  Orthodox Church 35
  Krutitskoe Mission **140**
  Patriarch's Palace **56–7**
  Patriarch's Pond 96
  renewed importance 31
  restoration of churches 44
  Trinity Monastery of St Sergius 162
  visiting churches 207
  see also Cathedrals; Churches;
  Convents; Monasteries
Russian-Revival architecture 43, 45
Russian State Library 75, 150
Russian Winter (festival) 35
Russkaya Galeria 195
Russkaya Vyshivka 195
Russkiy Uzory 195
Russkoe Bistro 191
Russo-Japanese War (1904–5) 26
Russo-Turkish Wars 23
Ruysdael, Jacob van 80
Ryabushinskiy, Stepan 45, 95

S

The Sacred Supper (unattrib) 155
Safety 210
Sally O'Brien's 190
St Andrew's Anglican Church 93
St Basil's Cathedral 10, 44, **108–9**
  Moscow's Best: Architecture 43
St Patrick's Day 32
SS Peter and Paul 110
St Petersburg
  February Revolution (1917) 26
  history 22
  1905 Revolution 26
  siege of Leningrad (1941–4) 27
  travelling to Moscow from 219
Sakharov, Andrey 30
Salamonskiy, Albert 198
Salon of the Moscow Cultural Fund 195
Samotsvety 195
Samovars 183
San Marco 184

Sandunov, Sila 113
Sandunovskiy Baths **113**
SAS 219
Savelouskiy Station 219
Saviour's Tower **66**
Savoy 175
Savrasov, Aleksey
    The Rooks Have Come 118, 120
Sberbank 212
Scandinavia (restaurant) 186
Scenes from the Life of Metropolitan Peter (Dionysius) 58
Sculpture
    Graveyard of Fallen Monuments 135
    see also Museums and galleries
Sea Time 187
Security 210
    in hotels 173
Sedmoi Kontinent 195
Selekhov, Ivan 102
Semenov, Ivan 56
Senate 45, **66–7**
Serebryaniy Ryad 195
Sergei, Grand Prince 124
Sergei (restaurant) 185
Sergiev Posad
    Golden Ring 161
Sergius of Radonezh, St **165**
    Battle of Kulikovo 161
    tomb of 164–5
    Trinity Monastery of St Sergius 18, 162, 164
Serov, Valentin
    Abramtsevo Estate-Museum 160
    drawings 121
    Girl with Peaches 47, 121, 160
Serpukhovskiy, Princess Maria 113
Shalyapin, Fyodor
    Bakhrushin Theatre Museum 125
    grave of 131
    Operetta Theatre 88
    Shalyapin House-Museum 46, 48, **83**
    Tolstoy House-Museum 134
Shalyapin House-Museum 48, **83**
    Moscow's Best: Museums 46
Shangri-La 203
Shaw, George Bernard 88
Shchusev, Aleksey
    Convent of SS Martha and Mary 124
    Kazanskiy station 144
    Komsomolskaya metro station 40–41
    Lenin Mausoleum 47, 106, 107
    Lubyanka 112
    Shchusev Museum of Architecture 49
    Tverskaya ulitsa apartments 45
Shchusev Museum of Architecture 49
Shekhtel, Fyodor
    Arts Cinema 82
    Gorky House-Museum 42, 45, 95
    Morozov Mansion 96
    Moscow Arts Theatre 92
    Sophia Embankment mansion 125
    Yaroslavskiy station 144
Sheremetev, Count Nikolay 144–5
Sheremetev, Count Pyotr 142
Sheremetev family
    Kuskovo 47, 49, 142
    Ostankino Palace 49, 144
Sheremetevo 1 Airport 219
Sheremetevo 2 Airport 219

Sherston 173, 175
Sherwood, Vladimir 106
Shesh Besh 191
Shinok 189
Shishkin, Ivan 75
Shokoladnitsa 191
Shopping **192–7**
    antiques **194**, 195
    arts and crafts **194**, 195
    bargaining etiquette 193
    bazaars and markets **193**, 195
    books and music **194**, 195
    buying antiques 193
    department stores **192–3**, 195
    fashion and accessories **194**, 195
    GUM 45, **107**
    how to pay 192
    museum shops **193**, 195
    opening hours 192
    vodka and caviar **194**, 195
    What to Buy in Moscow **196–7**
Shostakovich, Dmitriy 92, 94
    grave of 131
Shuiskiy, Vasiliy 19
Simple Pleasures 188
Sixteen Tons 203
Skazka Vostoka 188
Skomoroshenko, Pavel 104
Skryabin, Aleksandr
    grave of 131
    Moscow Conservatory 94
    Skryabin House-Museum 48, 71, **72**
Skryabin House-Museum 48, **72**
    Street-by-Street map 71
Sky Lounge 189
Slava 203
Slavs 17
Smoking 207
    in restaurants 179
Snow 34
Snyders, Frans 80
Social-Democratic Workers' Party 26
Socialist Realism 27, 40, 135
Solario, Pietro
    Faceted Palace 55, 62
    Saviour's Tower 66
Solianka 180
Somov, Konstantin 75
Sophia, Regent
    Donskoy Monastery 136
    Novodevichiy Convent 130, 131
Sophia Embankment **125**
South African Embassy 209
Souvenirs
    What to Buy in Moscow **196–7**
Sovetskiy 175
Soviet Union, dissolution of 31, 149
Sovremennik Theatre 112
Space Museum 145
Space Obelisk 145
Space travel 30
Sparrow Hills **129**
Spaso House
    Street-by-Street map 70
Spasopeskovskiy Pereulok **72**
    Street-by-Street map 71
Sports, spectator 199
Spring in Moscow 32
Sputnik (hotel) 176
Sputnik 1 30

Sputnik 2 30
Stalin, Joseph 27, 31
    architecture 45
    and Bulgakov 96
    Cathedral of Christ the Redeemer 74, 148
    collectivization policy 41
    death of 30
    exiles Trotsky 27, 29
    Faceted Palace 62
    funeral 89
    Gorky House-Museum 95
    grave of 10, 107
    hotels 170
    Khrushchev denounces 30
    Lubyanka 112
    and Mayakovsky 111, 151
    metro system 222
    Moscow State University (MGU) 129
    Palace of Soviets **75**
    purges 94
    reconstruction of Moscow 82, 89, 147
    Senate 67
    Socialist-Realist art 135
    World War II 41
Stalinist-Gothic architecture 45
Stanislavskiy, Konstantin
    Bakhrushin Theatre Museum 125
    Moscow Arts Theatre 92, 105
    Stanislavskiy and Chekhov **93**
    Stanislavskiy House-Museum 48, **93**
    Stanislavskiy and Nemirovich-Danchenko Musical Theatre 201
    Stanislavskiy House-Museum 48, **93**
STAR Travel 209
Starlight Diner 191
Startsev, Osip 140
Stasov, Vladimir 134
State Armoury 10, 45, 48, **64–5**
    Moscow's Best: Museums 46
    Street-by-Street map 54
State Diamond Fund 64
State Kremlin Palace **56**
    ballet and opera 201
    Street-by-Street map 54
Stations
    Moscow's Best: Metro Stations **38–9**
    railway stations 218, 219
Steen, Jan 80
Stenberg, Georgiy 135
Stenberg, Vladimir 135
Stock Exchange 100
Strategic Arms Limitation Talks (SALT) 30
Stravinsky, Igor 72
Streltsy Guard
    Church of St Nicholas in Pyzhy 123
    The Morning of the Execution of the Streltsy (Surikov) 119, 120
    Streltsy Rebellion (1682) 22, 123
Stretenskaya 175
Student travellers 208, 209
Style Moderne 45
Suliko 187
Summer in Moscow 33
Summer Music Festival 33
Sunshine 33
Superstitions 207
Supremus No. 56 (Malevich) 29

Surikov, Vasiliy
  The Morning of the Execution of the Streltsy 119, 120
Sushi **190**, 191
Suzdal **166**
  Golden Ring 161
  history 17
  icons 61
  travel to 227
Suzdal Museum (Suzdal) 157, 166
Suzdal Museum of Wooden Architecture (Suzdal) 166
Svyatoslav Richter December Nights 35
Swissotel Krasnye Holmy 177

T

Taganka Theatre 201
Talents of Russia 34
Tamanskiy, Ivan 67
Tandoor 185
Tarakanova, Avgusta 110
Taranov, Ivan 117
Il Tartufo 185
Tatiana, Grand Duchess 26
Tatiana (hotel) 177
Tatlin, Vladimir 121
Tatyana's Day 35
Taxes
  hotel 172
  VAT 192
Taxis 217, **220–21**
Tchaikovsky, Modest 159
Tchaikovsky, Pyotr **159**
  ballet and opera 200
  Mazepa 110
  Moscow Conservatory 94
  statue of 94
  Tchaikovsky House-Museum 49, **159**
Tchaikovsky Concert Hall 151, 201
Tchaikovsky House-Museum 49, **159**
  travel to 227
Tchaikovsky International Competition 33
Tea 183
Teatralnaya 41
  Moscow's Best: Metro Stations 39
Teatro (restaurant) 185
Telegrams 215
Telephones **214**, 215
  in hotels 172
Television 215
Temperatures 35
Terem Palace **63**
  Street-by-Street map 54
Tesoro 185
Teutonic Knights 17
"The Thaw" 30
Theatre 200, 201
  Bakhrushin Theatre Museum 49, **125**
  Bolshoy Theatre 23, 87, **90–91**, 149
  Malyy Theatre 87, 88
  Mayakovsky Theatre 93
  Moscow Arts Theatre 86, **92**, 93
  MXAT Gorky Art Theatre 150
  Operetta Theatre 88
  Ostankino Palace 145
  Pushkin Theatre 150
  Russian Academic Youth Theatre 88, 199
  Sovremennik Theatre 112

Theatre Square 45, **88**
  Street-by-Street map 86–7
Theft 210
  in hotels 173
Theophanes the Greek
  Cathedral of the Annunciation 60
  icons 61
  The Transfiguration 121
35MM 201
Tibet Kitchen 185
Tickets
  for concerts, ballets and the theatre 198
  metro 223
  trams, trolleybuses and buses 225
Ticks 211
Tikhon, Patriarch 136
Tilsit, Treaty of (1807) 23, 24
Time Online 215
Time of Troubles 19
  Trinity Monastery of St Sergius 162
Time zones 209
Timiryazev, Kliment
  statue of 150
Timofeev, Ivan 129
Tinkoff 191
Tipping 207
  in restaurants 179
Titov, Pyotr
  Apollo and the Muses 91
TNT Express Worldwide 215
Toasts 207
Tochka 203
Tofu 188
Toilets, public 209
Tolstoy, Leo 96, **134**
  Church of St Nicholas of the Weavers 135
  Tolstoy House-Museum 46, 48, **134**
  Tolstoy Literary Museum 74
  War and Peace 23, 158
  Yasnaya Polyana **167**
Tolstoy, Sofya Andreevna 134
Tolstoy House-Museum 48, **134**
  Moscow's Best: Museums 46
Tolstoy Literary Museum 74
Tomb of the Unknown Soldier 67, 148
Tomskiy, Nikolay 41
Ton, Konstantin
  Cathedral of Christ the Redeemer 74
  Great Kremlin Palace 45, 63
  Izmaylovo Park 141
  Leningradskiy station 144
  State Armoury 45, 54, 64
Tourist (hotel) 175
Tourist information 198, 206, 209
Towers, Kremlin **66**
Trains **218–19**
  Nicholas Railway 23
  stations 144, 218, 219
  suburban trains 227
  travelling to Moscow from St Petersburg 219
Traktir Khlestakov 189
Trams **225**
Trans-Siberian Railway 144
Transaero 219
The Transfiguration (Theophanes the Greek) 121
Transylvania 195

Travel **216–27**
  air **216**, 219
  Arbatskaya 69
  buses 217, 219, **225**
  cars 226
  children 209
  coach 218, 219, 227
  excursions from Moscow **227**
  hot air balloons **220**
  insurance 210
  Kremlin 53
  metro 217, **222–4**
  Moscow Region 157
  Moscow's Best: Metro Stations **38–9**
  Red Square and Kitay Gorod 99
  river cruises 11, **221**
  taxis 217, **220–21**
  trains **218–19**
  trams **225**
  trolleybuses **225**
  Tverskaya 85
  walking in Moscow **220**
  Zamoskvoreche 115
Travel agencies 219
Travellers' cheques 213
  in hotels 172
  safety 210
Travellers' Guest House 173
Tretyakov, Pavel 115, **120**
  portrait of 120
  statue of 116
  Tretyakov Gallery 118–21
Tretyakov, Sergey 118
Tretyakov Gallery 10–11, 48, **118–21**
  drawings and watercolours 121
  floorplan 118–19
  icons and jewellery 121
  Moscow's Best: Museums 47
  shop 195
  Street-by-Street map 116
  Visitors' Checklist 119
Trezzini, Pietro Antonio 123
The Trinity (Rublev) 10–11, 119, 121, 165
Trinity Monastery of St Sergius 155, **162–5**
  Cathedral of the Assumption 164
  Church of the Holy Spirit 156
  Church of St Sergius and Refectory 164
  palaces and museums 165
  Sergius of Radonezh **165**
  towers and gate churches 165
  travel to 227
  Trinity Cathedral 164–5
Trinity Sunday 33
Trinity Tower **56**, 148
  Street-by-Street map 54
Trolleybuses **225**
Tropinin, Vasiliy **124**
  Girl in Ukrainian Dress 124
  Portrait of Arseny Tropinin, the Artist's Son 118, 120
  Tropinin Museum 48, **124–5**
Tropinin Museum 48, **124–5**
Trotsky, Leon 27, 29
Tsar Bell 37, 57
Tsar Cannon
  Street-by-Street map 55
Tsaritsyno 49, **137**
Tsereteli, Zurab 129, 135
TsUM 195

Turchaninov, Sergey 122
Turgenev, Ivan 97, 160
Tverskaya **85–97**
  area map 85
  Around Theatre Square 86–7
  Bolshoy Theatre **90–91**
  hotels 174
  restaurants 184–6
Tverskaya Ulitsa 10, **89**
  Street-by-Street map 86
Two-day trips 227
Tyurin, Evgraf 67
Tzimmes 189

U

U Pirosmani 189
Udarnik 201
Udarnik Casino 203
Ulitsa Arbat
  Street-by-Street map 70
Ulitsa Ilinka **104**
  Street-by-Street map 100
Ulitsa Prechistenka 45, **74**
Ulitsa Varvarka **102**
  Street-by-Street map 101
Uncle Guillys 186
Uncle Vanya 187
Underground railway see Metro
United Kingdom Embassy 209
Universities
  Moscow Old University 22, 23, 25,
    42, 45, **94**
  Moscow State University (MGU) 129
Upper Monastery of St Peter **97**
US Dental Care 211
US Embassy 209
US Independence Day 33
Ushakov, Simon 101
  Cathedral of the Archangel 60
  Church of the Trinity in Nikitniki 103
  house on Ipatevskiy pereulok 103
  Patriarch's Palace 57
  Trinity Cathedral (Trinity Monastery
    of St Sergius) 165
Uzbek food **190**, 191

V

Vaccinations 211
Vakhtangov, Yevgeniy 71
Vakhtangova Theatre
  Street-by-Street map 71
Valentine's Day 35
Van Dyck, Anthony 80
Van Gogh, Vincent 75
Van Goyen, Jan 80
Vanil 189
Varangians 17, 19
Vasilevsky 123
Vasnetsov, Apollinariy 144
Vasnetsov, Viktor
  Abramtsevo Estate-Museum 160
  Baptism of Russia 17
  Tretyakov Gallery 118, 119
  Vasnetsov House-Museum 49, **144**
  The Walled City 20–21
Vasnetsov House-Museum 49, **144**
VAT 192
VDNKh 145
Vegetarian meals 179
Vereschagin, Vasiliy 121

Victory Day 32, 34
Victory Park **128–9**
Vienna, Congress of (1815) 24
Vikings 17
Villa (restaurant) 187
Virgin and Child (Cranach) 80
Visa Express 209
Visa House 209
Visas 208, 209, 216
Vishnevskiy, Feliks 124
Vitali, Ivan 129
Vladimir **166–7**
  Golden Ring 161
  history 17
  icons 61
  travel to 227
Vladimir I, Grand Prince of Kiev
  Crown of Monomakh 65
  Monomakh Throne 59
  Russian Orthodox Church 17, 137
Vneshtorgbank 212
Vnukovo Airport 219
Vodka
  in restaurants 178
  shops **194**, 195
  What to Buy in Moscow 196
  What to Drink in Moscow 182
Vodootvodnyy canal 115
  Street-by-Street map 116
Volkonskaya, Princess Zinaida 89
Voltaire 23
Vostochnaya Komnata 184
Vrubel, Mikhail
  Abramtsevo Estate-Museum 156, 160
  Demon Seated 118, 121
  Hotel Metropol 88
  Morozov Mansion 96
Vsevolod III, Prince 167
VVTs see All-Russian Exhibition Centre

W

Walcot, William 45, 87, 88
Walking in Moscow **220**
Walks **147–51**
  A 90-minute Literary Walk **150–51**
  A One-hour Stroll through Central
    Moscow **148–9**
  The Walled City (Vasnetsov) 20–21
Wanderers 48, 120–21, 135
Warsaw Pact 30
Water, health precautions 211
Weather **32–5**
"wedding cake" architecture 45
Wheelchair access see Disabled
  travellers
White House **128**
White Russians 27
Wine 183
Winter driving 226
Winter in Moscow 35
Women, safety 210
Wooden Palace (Kuskovo) 142
Woodstock-Mkhat 203
World War I 26–7, 28
World War II 27, 67, 148
  metro system 41
  Museum of the Great Patriotic War
    49, 129
  Siege of Leningrad (1941–4) 27
  Victory Park 128

Writers
  A 90-minute Literary Walk 150–51

X

XIII 203

Y

Yagoda, Genrikh 95
Yakitoria 191
Yakovlev, Postnik 108
Yapona Mama 188, 191
Yaroslavl
  Golden Ring 161
  icons 164
Yaroslavskiy station 144, 219
Yasnaya Polyana **167**
  travel to 227
Yegotov, Ivan 113
Yekaterinburg 27, 28
Yeliseev, Grigoriy 89
Yeliseev's Food Hall 85, 89, 195
Yelizaveta Fyodorovna, Grand
  Duchess 124
Yeltsin, Boris 30, 31
  Kazan Cathedral 105
  Russian Orthodox Church 137
  White House 128
Yermolov, General Aleksey 74
Yesenin, Sergey 74
  statue of 150, 151
Young Acrobat on a Ball (Picasso)
  48
Young Pioneers 95
Yunost 177
Yusupov, Prince Nikolay 158
Yusupov family 158

Z

Zakuski 182
Zalesskiy, Vasiliy 125
Zamoskvoreche **115–25**
  area map 115
  Around Pyatnitskaya Ulitsa **116–17**
  hotels 173
  restaurants 186–7
  Tretyakov Gallery **118–21**
Zarudniy, Ivan 112, 136
Zarya 173
Zen Coffee 191
Zhemchugova-Kovaleva, Praskovia
  144–5
Zhizn Zamechatelnikh Lyudey 203
Zhukov, Marshal Georgiy
  statue of 106, 148, 149
Zilberstein, Ilya 75
Zolotarev, Karp 128
Zoo (Moscow Zoo) 199

Acknowledgments

Dorling Kindersley would like to thank the following people whose contributions and assistance have made the preparation of this book possible.

Main Contributor

Chistopher Rice holds a PhD in Russian history from the University of Birmingham. He and his wife Melanie, also a writer, first visited Russia in 1978 and have been returning regularly ever since. They have written numerous travel guides to the city, and to a variety of other destinations including Prague, Berlin, and Istanbul, as well as the *Eyewitness Travel Guide to St. Petersburg.*

Additional Contributors

Rose Baring studied Russian from the age of 12. She has an MA in Modern History and divided her time between London, Moscow and St. Petersburg for much of the early 1990s. She has written guides to St. Petersburg, Moscow, and other destinations, including the *Eyewitness Travel Guide to Istanbul.*

Marina Boughton has a BA in Film Studies from the University of Central London. She also studied in Russia and has worked there for a number of years. She is now a correspondent for BBC Radio in Moscow.

Sergey Konstantinovich Romanuik is a graduate of the Moscow State University. Specializing in Economic Geography and the history and cultural life of Moscow, he has written around 200 articles and books about the city.

Senior Editor Anna Streiffert
Managing Editors Fay Franklin, Georgina Matthews
Managing Art Editor Annette Jacobs
Senior Managing Editor Vivien Crump
Deputy Art Director Gillian Allan

Special Assistance

Dorling Kindersley would like to thank Ian Wizniewski (food and drink author), Frank Althaus (hotels), Radhika Jones (restaurants), Natasha Linkova (researcher in Moscow), Maria Fetisova (photo permissions), Elena Mirskaya (DK Moscow), Oleksiy Nesnov (language consultant), Victoria Rachevskaya (language consultant), and Sylvain Borsi of Nikita's restaurant, London (food preparation for *What to Eat in Moscow*).

Proofreader

Stewart J Wild.

Production

Jo Blackmore, David Proffit.

Design and Editorial Assistance

Brigitte Arora, Liz Atherton, Claire Baranowski, Marc Bennetts, Sonal Bhatt, Laurence Broers, Dawn Davies-Cooke, Claire Folkard, Rhiannon Furbear, Freddy Hamilton, Leanne Hogbin, Nicola Malone, Sarah Martin, Sam Merrell, Adam Moore, Ellen Root, Luke Rozkowski, Pamela Shiels, Ingrid Vienings, Dora Whitaker, Veronica Wood.

Additional Illustrations

Paul Weston, Joy Fitzsimmonds.

Additional Photography

Andy Crawford, Erich Crichton, Neil Fletcher, Steve Gorton, Ian O'Leary, Gary Ombler, Clive Streeter.

Relaunch

Senior Editor Kathryn Lane; *Contributors* Marc Bennetts, Paul Friar; *Fact Checkers* Marc Bennetts, Tatiana Nevinskaya; *Editor* Matthew Tanner; *Editorial Assistants* Alexandra Farrell, Pollyanna Poulter; *Indexer* Hilary Bird; *Designer* Maite Lantaron; *DTP Designer* Jill Stevens.

Photography Permissions

Dorling Kindersley would like to thank all those who gave permission to photograph at the various cathedrals, churches, museums, restaurants, hotels, shops, galleries and transport services and other sights too numerous to thank individually.

Picture Credits

t = top; tl = top left; tlc = top left centre; tc = top centre; trc = top right centre; tr = top right; cla = centre left above; ca = centre above; cra = centre right above; cl = centre left; c = centre; cr = centre right; clb = centre left below; cb = centre below; crb = centre right below; bl = bottom left; b = bottom; bc = bottom centre; bcl = bottom centre left; br = bottom right; d = detail

Works of art have been reproduced with the permission of the following copyright holders:

Young Acrobat on a Ball, Pablo Picasso © Succession Picasso/DACS 2006 48c.

The publisher would like to thank the following individuals, companies and picture libraries for their kind permission to reproduce their photographs: AISA, BARCELONA: 21b, 22clb, 51 (insert), 46t, 58t, 59tl, 61cr, 64b; AKG, LONDON: 17cl, 18c, 27cl, 28br, 28–29c, 29ca, 55br, 107b, 118br, 120tr, 121b, 161cra/bl; Erich Lessing 26t, 28bl, 161clb; ALAMY IMAGES: Cullinganphoto 147tc, 147cr; Bernie Epstein 150cl; Jon Arnold Images 11tl; Robert Harding Picture Library Ltd/Sylvain Grandadam 180cl, 181tl; ARTEPHOT, PARIS: 16, 118bl; AVANT-GARDE PUBLISHING HOUSE: Victor Korniushin 4b, 204–205.

BALTIKA BREWERIES: 183c; KATHLEEN BERTON MURRELL: 42cb, 62b; BOLSHOY THEATRE: 90t/b, 91tl/tr; THE BRIDGEMAN ART LIBRARY, LONDON/ NEW YORK: The Hermitage, St. Petersburg 25tl; Kremlin Museums 64c; Mark Gallery 165t; Novosti 21 crb, 25 crb; Private Collection 23c, 29tr; Pushkin Museum, Moscow 79tl, 81tr; Richardson and Kailas Icons, London 161t; Tretyakov Gallery 22t, 47bl, 118cl, 119tl, 120br, 121tl.

CAMERA PRESS: Richard Ellis 76–77 and 220br; DEMETRIO CARRASCO: 117tc; JEAN-LOUP CHARMET: 18t; CATHERINE COOKE: /1bl; CORBIS UK: Dean Conger 34cl, 198cl; Rob Howard 181c; Library of Congress 28cl; Steve Raymer 31crb.

David King Collection: 27t, 29tl, 30t, 40c, 75br, 111br. *Et Archive*: 24–25c.

FRANK SPOONER PICTURES: Georges Merillon/ Gamma 31t; JOHN FREEMAN: 37tl, 54cl, 55bl, 58cl, 60b, 62t, 63t/b, 96cl.

GETTY IMAGES: Panoramic Images 10bl; GIRAUDON: 24bl; Bildarchiv Preussischer Kulturbesitz 25b; Bridgeman 119cr; Lauros 61t; GOLDEN APPLE BOUTIQUE HOTEL: 172bl.

MICHAEL HOLFORD: 17t, 20b, 22c; HULTON-GETTY: 169 (insert), 182tr.

JAMES DAVIS TRAVEL PHOTOGRAPHY: 57t, 60t.; JON ARNOLD IMAGES: Demetrio Carrasco 11br.

KEA PUBLISHING SERVICES: Francesco Venturi 47tl. MARY EVANS PICTURE LIBRARY: 9 (insert), 21t, 22b, 24br, 29cb, 134t, 205 (insert); JOHN MASSEY STEWART: 19cr, 57cl, 153 (insert).

NETWORK PHOTOGRAPHERS: H-J Burkhard /Bilderberg 32cl; A Reiser/Bilderberg 72br; Nikolai Ignatiev 31crb; NOVOSTI (LONDON): 19t, 20cla, 26cl, 27cr, 30cl, 32cr/bl, 34b, 35c, 56c/b, 61cl, 93t, 112c, 124bl.

ORONOZ, MADRID: 23t. PLODIMEX AUSSENHANDELS GMBH, HAMBURG: 182cr/bl.

RAYMOND MANDER & JOE MITCHENSON THEATRE COLLECTION: 91b; REX FEATURES: SIPA 2–3, 30cr; ROBERT HARDING PICTURE LIBRARY: 63l; ELLEN ROONEY: 33b, 35b, 56t, 148bl.

ST CATHERINE THE GREAT MARTYR ORTHODOX CHURCH: Dean Archimandrite Zacchaeus 123crb; PHOTO SCALA, FLORENCE: Pushkin Museum *Bacchanal* Peter Paul Rubens (1577–1640) 79crb. GREGOR M SCHMID: 59cr, 65c/b; SCIENCE PHOTO LIBRARY: SNES, 1995 Distribution Spot Image 11c; VLADIMIR SIDOROPOLEV (WWW.PHOTOGRAPHERSDIRECT.COM): 10cr, 147bl, 150tr; SINY MOST: N Alexeiev 20clb, 37cl, 48b, 55cr, 65t; V Tetebenine 24tl, 161b; JON SMITH: 146, 148cl, 149tc, 149cr, 149bc, 150br, 151tr, 151crb; SOCIETY FOR COOPERATION IN RUSSIAN AND SOVIET STUDIES: 18b, 64t; Novosti 191c; STA TRAVEL: 208br; STOCKMARKET: 57br.

TONY STONE IMAGES: Demetrio Carrasco 67t; TRIP: N & J Wiseman 160b.

VISUAL ARTS LIBRARY: 25cra, 61c, 73t, 81c, 120tl.

YAKITORIA RESTAURANT: 178cl.

Jacket FRONT – CORBIS: Zefa/Herbert Spichtinger main; DK IMAGES: Sergei Pasao clb. BACK – DK IMAGES: Demetrio Carrasco tl, cla, clb, bl. SPINE – CORBIS: Zefa/Herbert Spichtinger t; DK IMAGES: Andy Crawford.

All other images © Dorling Kindersley. For further information see:
www.dkimages.com

SPECIAL EDITIONS OF DK TRAVEL GUIDES

DK Travel Guides can be purchased in bulk quantities at discounted prices for use in promotions or as premiums.
We are also able to offer special editions and personalized jackets, corporate imprints, and excerpts from all of our books, tailored specifically to meet your own needs.

To find out more, please contact:
(in the United States) **SpecialSales@dk.com**
(in the UK) **TravelSpecialSales@uk.dk.com**
(in Canada) DK Special Sales at **general@tourmaline.ca**
(in Australia)
business.development@pearson.com.au

Phrase Book

In this guide the Russian language has been transliterated into Roman script following a consistent system used by the US Board on Geographic Names. All street and place names, and the names of most people, are transliterated according to this system. For some names, where a well-known English form exists, this has been used – hence, Leo (not Lev) Tolstoy.

In particular, the names of Russian rulers, such as Peter the Great, are given in their anglicized forms. Throughout the book, transliterated names can be taken as an accurate guide to pronunciation. The Phrase Book also gives a phonetic guide to the pronunciation of words and phrases used in everyday situations, such as when eating out or shopping.

GUIDELINES FOR PRONUNCIATION

The Cyrillic alphabet has 33 letters, of which only five (а, к, м, о, т) correspond exactly to their counterparts in English. Russian has two pronunciations (hard and soft) of each of its vowels, and several consonants without an equivalent.
The right-hand column of the alphabet, below, demonstrates how Cyrillic letters are pronounced by comparing them to sounds in English words. However, some letters vary in how they are pronounced according to their position in a word. Important exceptions are also noted below.
On the following pages, the English is given in the left-hand column, with the Russian and its transliteration in the middle column. The right-hand column provides a literal system of pronunciation and indicates the stressed syllable in bold. The exception is in the *Menu Decoder* section, where the Russian is given in the left-hand column and the English translation in the right-hand column, for ease of use. Because of the existence of genders in Russian, in a few cases both masculine and feminine forms of a phrase are given.

The Cyrillic Alphabet

А а	a	al**i**mony
Б б	b	**b**ed
В в	v	**v**et
Г г	g	**g**et (see note 1)
Д д	d	**d**ebt
Е е	e	**y**et (see note 2)
Ё ё	e	**yo**nder
Ж ж	zh	lei**s**ure (but a little harder)
З з	z	**z**ither
И и	i	s**ee**
Й й	y	**b**oy (see note 3)
К к	k	**k**ing
Л л	l	l**oo**t
М м	m	**m**atch
Н н	n	**n**ever
О о	o	r**o**b (see note 4)
П п	p	**p**ea
Р р	r	**r**at (rolling, as in Italian)
С с	s	**s**top
Т т	t	**t**offee
У у	u	b**oo**t
Ф ф	f	**f**ellow
Х х	kh	**kh** (like loch)
Ц ц	ts	le**ts**
Ч ч	ch	**ch**air
Ш ш	sh	**sh**ove
Щ щ	shch	fre**sh sh**eet (as above but with a slight roll)
ъ		hard sign (no sound, but see note 5)
Ы ы	y	l**i**d
ь		soft sign (no sound, but see note 5)
Э э	e	**e**gg
Ю ю	yu	**you**th
Я я	ya	**ya**k

Notes

1) Г   Pronounced as *v* in endings -ого and -его.
2) Е   Always pronounced *ye* at the beginning of a word, but in the middle of a word sometimes less distinctly (more like *e*).
3) Й   This letter has no distinct sound of its own. It usually lengthens the preceeding vowel.
4) О   When not stressed it is pronounced like *a* in **a**cross.
5) ъ, ь   The hard sign (ъ) is rare and indicates a very brief pause before the next letter. The soft sign (ь, marked in the pronunciation guide as ') softens the preceeding consonant and adds a slight *y* sound: for instance, *n'* would sound like *ny* in '**ca**nyon'.

In an Emergency

Help!	Помогите! *Pomogite!*	pamag**ee**tye!
Stop!	Стоп! *Stop!*	Stop!
Leave me alone!	Оставьте меня в покое! *Ostavte menya v pokoe!*	astavt'ye myen**ya** v pak**o**ye!
Call a doctor!	Позовите врача! *Pozovite vracha!*	pazav**ee**tye vrach**a**!
Call an ambulance!	Вызовите скорую помощь! *Vyzovite skoruyu pomoshch!*	vizav**ee**tye skoru-yu p**o**mash'!
Fire!	Пожар! *Pozbar!*	pazh**a**r!
Call the fire brigade!	Вызовите пожарных! *Vyzovite pozharnykh!*	vizav**ee**tye pazh**a**rnikh!
Police!	Милиция! *Militsiya!*	meel**ee**tseeya!
Where is the nearest...	Где ближайший... *Gde blizhayshiy...*	gdye bleezh**ay**sheey...
...telephone?	...телефон? *...telefon?*	...tyelyef**o**n?
...hospital?	...больница? *...bolnitsa?*	...bal'n**ee**tsa?
...police station?	...отделение милиции? *...otdelenie militsii?*	...atdyel**ye**nye meel**ee**tsee-ee?

Communication Essentials

Yes	Да *Da*	da
No	Нет *Net*	nyet
Please	Пожалуйста *Pozhaluysta*	pazh**a**lsta
Thank you	Спасибо *Spasibo*	spas**ee**ba
You are welcome	Пожалуйста *Pozhaluysta*	pazh**a**lsta
Excuse me	Извините *Izvinite*	eezveen**ee**t-ye
Hello	Здравствуйте *Zdravstvuyte*	zdrastv**oo**yt-ye
Goodbye	До свидания *Do svidaniya*	da sveed**a**nya
Good morning	Доброе утро *Dobroe utro*	d**o**bra-ye **oo**tra
Good afternoon/day	Добрый день *Dobryy den*	d**o**bree dyen'
Good evening	Добрый вечер *Dobryy vecher*	d**o**bree v**ye**chyer
Good night	Спокойной ночи *Spokoynoy nochi*	spak**o**ynay n**o**chee
Morning	утро *utro*	**oo**tra
Afternoon	день *den*	dyen'
Evening	вечер *vecher*	v**ye**chyer
Yesterday	вчера *vchera*	fchyer**a**
Today	сегодня *sevodnya*	syev**o**dnya
Tomorrow	завтра *zavtra*	z**a**ftra
Here	здесь *zdes*	zdyes'
There	там *tam*	tam

What?	Что?	shto?
	Chto?	
Where?	Где?	gdye?
	Gde?	
Why?	Почему?	pachyemoo?
	Pochemu?	
When?	Когда?	kagda?
	Kogda?	
Now	сейчас	seychas
	seychas	
Later	позже	pozhe
	pozzhe	
Can I...?	можно?	mozhna...?
	mozhno?	
It is possible/allowed	можно	mozhna
	mozhno	
It is not possible/allowed	нельзя	nyelzya
	nelzya	

Useful Phrases

How are you?	Как дела?	kak dyela?
	Kak dela?	
Very well, thank you	Хорошо, спасибо	kharasho, spaseeba
	Khorosho, spasibo	
Pleased to meet you	Очень приятно	ochen' pree-yatna
	Ochen priyatno	
How do I get to...?	Как добраться до...?	kak dabrat'sya da...?
	Kak dobratsya do...?	
Would you tell me when we get to...?	Скажите, пожалуйста, когда мы приедем в...?	skazheet-ye, pazhalsta, kagda mi pree yedyem v...?
	Skazhite, pozhaluysta, kogda my priedem v...?	
Is it very far?	Это далеко?	eta dalyeko?
	Eto daleko?	
Do you speak English?	Вы говорите по-английски?	vi gavareet-ye po-angleeskee?
	Vy govorite po-angliyski?	
I don't understand	Я не понимаю	ya nye paneema-yoo
	Ya ne ponimayu	
Could you speak more slowly?	Говорите медленнее	gavareet-ye myedlyenye-ye
	Govorite medlennee	
Could you say it again please?	Повторите, пожалуйста	paftareet-ye, pazhalsta
	Povtorite, pozhaluysta	
I am lost	Я заблудился (заблудилась)	ya zabloodeelsya (zabloodeelas')
	Ya zabludilsya (zabludilas)	
How do you say... in Russian?	Как по-русски...?	kak pa-rooskee...?

Useful Words

big	большой	bal'shoy
	bolshoy	
small	маленький	malyen'kee
	malenkiy	
hot (water, food)	горячий	garyachee
	goryachiy	
hot (weather)	жарко	zharka
	zharko	
cold	холодный	khalodnee
	kholodnyy	
good	хорошо	kharasho
	khorosho	
bad	плохо	plokha
	plokho	
okay/fine	нормально	narmal'na
	normalno	
near	близко	bleezka
	blizko	
far	далеко	dalyeko
	daleko	
up	наверху	navyerkhoo
	naverkhu	

down	внизу	fneezoo
	vnizu	
early	рано	rana
	rano	
late	поздно	pozdna
	pozdno	
vacant (unoccupied)	свободно	svabodna
	svobodno	
free (no charge)	бесплатно	byesplatna
	besplatno	
cashier/ticket office	касса	kasa
	kassa	
avenue	проспект	praspyekt
	prospekt	
bridge	мост	most
	most	
embankment	набережная	nabyeryezhnaya
	naberezhnaya	
highway/motorway	шоссе	shasse
	shosse	
lane/passage	переулок	pyeryeoolak
	pereulok	
square	площадь	ploshat'
	ploshchad	
street	улица	ooleetsa
	ulitsa	
flat/apartment	квартира	kvarteera
	kvartira	
floor	этаж	etash
	etazh	
house/block	дом	dom
	dom	
entrance	вход	fkhot
	vkhod	
exit	выход	vikhot
	vykhod	
river	река	ryeka
	reka	
summer country house	дача	dacha
	dacha	
swimming pool	бассейн	basyeyn
	basseyn	
town	город	gorat
	gorod	
toilet	туалет	tooalyet
	tualet	

Making a Telephone Call

Can I call abroad from here?	Можно отсюда позвонить за границу?	mozhna atsyooda pazvaneet' za graneetsoo?
	Mozhno ostyuda pozvonit za granitsu?	
I would like to speak to...	Позовите, пожалуйста...	pazaveet-ye, pazhalsta...
	Pozovite, pozhaluysta	
Could you leave him/her a message?	Вы можете передать ему/ей pyeryedat' yemoo/yay?	vi mozhet-ye
	Vy mozhete peredat emu/ey	
My number is...	Мой номер...	moy nomyer...
	Moy nomer...	
I'll ring back later	Я позвоню позже	ya pazvanyoo pozhe
	Ya pozvonyu pozzhe	

Sightseeing

castle	замок	zamak
	zamok	
cathedral	собор	sabor
	sobor	
church	церковь	tserkaf
	tserkov	
circus	цирк	tseerk
	tsirk	
closed for cleaning "cleaning day"	санитарный день	saneetarnee dyen'
	sanitarnyy den	
undergoing restoration	ремонт	remont
	remont	
exhibition	выставка	vistafka
	vystavka	
fortress	крепость	kryepost'
	krepost	
gallery	галерея	galeryeya
	galereya	

English	Russian	Transliteration
garden	сад	sad
	sad	
island	остров	ostraf
	ostrov	
kremlin/fortified stronghold	Кремль	kryeml'
	kreml	
library	библиотека	beeblee-atyeka
	biblioteka	
monument	памятник	pamyatneek
	pamyatnik	
mosque	мечеть	myechyet'
	mechet	
museum	музей	moozyey
	muzey	
palace	дворец	dvaryets
	dvorets	
park	парк	park
	park	
parliament	дума	dooma
	duma	
synagogue	синагога	seenagoga
	sinagoga	
tourist information	пункт информации для туристов	poonkt eenfarmatsee-ee dlya tooreestaf
	punkt informatsii dlya turistov	
zoo	зоопарк	zapark
	zoopark	

Shopping

open	открыто	atkrita
	otkryto	
closed	закрыто	zakrita
	zakryto	
How much does this cost?	Сколько это стоит?	skol'ka eta stoeet?
	Skolko eto stoit?	
I would like to buy…	Я хотел (хотела) бы купить…	ya khatyel (khatyela) bi koopeet'…
	Ya khotel (khotela) by kupit…	
Do you have…?	У вас есть…?	oo vas yest'…?
	U vas yest…?	
Do you take credit cards?	Кредитные карточки вы принимаете?	kryedeetnye kartachkee vy preeneemayetye?
	Kreditnye kartochki vy prinimaete?	
What time do you open/close?	Во сколько вы открываетесь/закрываетесь?	Va skol'ka vy atkrivayetyes'/zakrivayetyes?
	Vo skolko vy otkryvaetes/zakryvaetes?	
This one	этот	etat
	etot	
expensive	дорого	doraga
	dorogo	
cheap	дёшево	dyoshyeva
	desbevo	
size	размер	razmyer
	razmer	
white	белый	byelee
	belyy	
black	чёрный	chyornee
	chernyy	
red	красный	krasnee
	krasnyy	
yellow	жёлтый	zholtee
	zheltyy	
green	зелёный	zyelyonee
	zelenyy	
dark blue	синий	seenee
	sinty	
light blue	голубой	galooboy
	goluboy	
brown	коричневый	kareechnyevee
	korichnevy	

Types of Shop

English	Russian	Transliteration
bakery	булочная	boolachna-ya
	bulochnaya	
bookshop	книжный магазин	kneezhnee magazeen
	knizhnyy magazin	
butcher	мясной магазин	myasnoy magazeen
	myasnoy magazin	

English	Russian	Transliteration
camera shop	фото-товары	foto-tavari
	foto-tovary	
chemist	аптека	aptyeka
	apteka	
delicatessen	гастроном	gastranom
	gastronom	
department store	универмаг	ooneevyermag
	univermag	
florist	цветы	tsvyeti
	tsvety	
grocer	бакалея	bakalye-ya
	bakaleya	
hairdresser	парикмахерская	pareekmakhyerskaya
	parikmakherskaya	
market	рынок	rinak
	rynok	
newspaper stand	газетный киоск	gazyetnee kee-osk
	gazetniy kiosk	
post office	почта	pochta
	pochta	
record shop	грампластинки	gramplasteenkee
	gramplastinki	
shoe shop	обувь	oboof
	obuv	
travel agent	бюро путешествий	byooro pootyeshestvee
	byuro puteshestviy	
bank	банк	bank
	bank	

Staying in a Hotel

English	Russian	Transliteration
Do you have a vacant room?	У вас есть свободный номер?	oo vas yest' svabodnee nomyer?
	U vas yest svobodnyy nomyer?	
double room with double bed	номер с двуспальной кроватью	nomyer s dvoospal'noy kravat'-yoo
	nomer s dvuspalnoy krovatyu	
twin room	двухместный номер	dvookhmyestnee nomyer
	dvukhmestnyy nomer	
single room	одноместный номер	adnamyestnee nomyer
	odnomestnyy nomer	
bath	ванная	vana-ya
	vannaya	
shower	душ	doosh
	dush	
porter	носильщик	naseel'sheek
	nosilshchik	
key	ключ	klyooch

Eating Out

English	Russian	Transliteration
A table for two, please	Стол на двоих, пожалуйста	stol na dva-eekh, pazhalsta
I would like to book a table	Я хочу заказать стол	ya khachoo zakazat' stol
	Ya khochu zakazat stol	
The bill, please	Счёт, пожалуйста	shyot, pazhalsta
	Schet, pozhaluysta	
I am a vegetarian	Я вегетерианец (вегетерианка)	ya vyegyetareeanyets (vyegetareeanka)
	Ya vegeterianets (vegeterianka)	
breakfast	завтрак	zaftrak
	zavtrak	
lunch	обед	abyet
	obed	
dinner	ужин	oozheen
	uzhin	
waiter!	официант!	afeetsee-ant!
	ofitsiant!	
waitress!	официантка!	afeetsee-antka!
	ofitsiantka!	
dish of the day	фирменное блюдо	feermenoye blyooda
	firmennoe blyudo	
appetizers/starters	закуски	zakooskee

main course	zakuski / второе блюдо	ftaroye blyooda
meat and poultry dishes	vtoroe blyudo / мясные блюда	myasniye blyooda
fish and seafood dishes	myasnye blyuda / рыбные блюда	ribniye blyooda
vegetable dishes	rybnye blyuda / овощные блюда	avashshniye blyooda
dessert	ovoshchnye blyuda / десерт	dyesyert
drinks	desert / напитки	napeetkee
vegetables	napitki / овощи	ovashshee
bread	ovoshchi / хлеб	khlyeb
wine list	khleb / карта вин	karta veen
rare (steak)	karta vin / недожаренный	nyedazharenee
well done (steak)	nedozharennyy / прожаренный	prozharenee
glass	prozharennyy / стакан	stakan
bottle	stakan / бутылка	bootilka
knife	butylka / нож	nosh
fork	nozh / вилка	veelka
spoon	vilka / ложка	loshka
plate	lozhka / тарелка	taryelka
napkin	tarelka / салфетка	salfyetka
salt	salfetka / соль	sol
pepper	sol / перец	pyeryets
butter/oil	perets / масло	masla
sugar	maslo / сахар	sakhar

Menu Decoder

абрикос *abrikos*	abreekos	apricot
апельсин *apelsin*	apyel'seen	orange
апельсиновый сок *apelsinovyy sok*	apyel'seenavee sok	orange juice
арбуз *arbuz*	arbooz	water melon
белое вино *beloe vino*	byelaye veeno	white wine
бифштекс *bifshteks*	beefshtyeks	steak
блины *bliny*	bleeni	pancakes
борщ *borshch*	borshsh	borsch (beetroot soup)
варенье *varene*	varyen'ye	Russian syrup-jam
варёный *varenyy*	varyonee	boiled
ветчина *vetchina*	vyetcheena	ham
вода *voda*	vada	water
говядина *govyadina*	gavyadeena	beef
грибы *griby*	greebi	mushrooms
груша *grusha*	groosha	pear
гусь *gus*	goos	goose
джем *dzhem*	dzhem	jam
жареный *zharenyy*	zharyenee	roasted/grilled/fried
икра *ikra*	eekra	black caviar
икра красная/кета *ikra krasna-ya/keta*	eekra krasna-ya/kyeta	red caviar

капуста *kapusta*	kapoosta	cabbage
картофель *kartofel*	kartofyel'	potato
квас *kvas*	kvas	kvas (sweet, mildly alcoholic drink)
клубника *klubnika*	kloobneeka	strawberries
колбаса *kolbasa*	kalbasa	salami sausage
кофе *kofe*	kofye	coffee
красное вино *krasnoe vino*	krasnoye veeno	red wine
креветки *krevetki*	kryevyetkee	prawns
курица *kuritsa*	kooreetsa	chicken
лук *luk*	look	onion
малина *malina*	maleena	raspberries
минеральная вода *mineralnaya voda*	mineral'naya vada	mineral water
мороженое *morozhenoe*	marozhena-ye	ice-cream
мясо *myaso*	myasa	meat
огурец *ogurets*	agooryets	cucumber
осетрина *osetrina*	asyetreena	sturgeon
пельмени *pelmeni*	pyel'myenee	meat or fish dumplings
персик *persik*	pyerseek	peach
печенье *pechene*	pyechyen'ye	biscuit
печёнка *pechenka*	pyechyonka	liver
печёный *pechenyy*	pyechyonee	baked
пиво *pivo*	peeva	beer
пирог *pirog*	peerok	pie
пирожки *pirozhki*	peerashkee	small parcels with savoury fillings
помидор *pomidor*	pameedor	tomato
продукты моря *produkty morya*	pradookti morya	seafood
рыба *ryba*	riba	fish
салат *salat*	salat	salad
свинина *svinina*	sveeneena	pork
сельдь *seld*	sye'ld'	herring
сосиски *sosiski*	saseeskee	sausages
сыр *syr*	sir	cheese
сырой *syroy*	siroy	raw
утка *utka*	ootka	duck
фасоль *fasol*	fasol'	beans
форель *forel*	faryel'	trout
чай *chay*	chai	tea
чеснок *chesnok*	chyesnok	garlic
шашлык *shashlyk*	shashlik	kebab
яйцо *yaytso*	yaytso	egg
слива *sliva*	sleeva	plum
фрукты *frukty*	frookti	fruit
яблоко *yabloko*	yablaka	apple

Transport

north	север *sever*	**sy**ever
south	юг *yug*	yook
east	восток *vostok*	vast**ok**
west	запад *zapad*	**za**pat
airport	аэропорт *aeroport*	aerap**ort**
aeroplane	самолёт *samolet*	samal**yot**
traffic police	ГАИ *GAI*	Ga-ee
bus	автобус *avtobus*	aft**o**boos
bus station	автобусная станция *avtobusnaya stantsiya*	aft**o**boosna-ya stantsee-ya
bus stop	остановка автобса *ostanovka avtobusa*	astan**o**fka aft**o**boosa
car	машина *mashina*	mash**ee**na
flight	рейс *reys*	ryeys
metro (station)	(станция) метро *(stantsiya) metro*	(stantsee-ya) myetr**o**
no entry	нет входа *net vkhoda*	nyet fkh**o**da
no exit	нет выхода *net vykhoda*	nyet v**i**khada
parking	автостоянка *avtostoyanka*	aftost**o**yanka
petrol	бензин *benzin*	byenz**een**
railway	железная дорога *zheleznaya doroga*	zhel**ye**zna-ya dar**o**ga
railway station	вокзал *vokzal*	vagz**al**
return ticket	обратный билет *obratniy bilet*	obratnee beel**yet**
seat	место *mesto*	my**es**ta
suburban train	пригородный поезд *prigorodniy poezd*	pre**e**garadnee po-yezd
straight on	прямо *pryamo*	pr**ya**ma
taxi	такси *taksi*	taks**ee**
ticket	билет *bilet*	beel**yet**
token (for a single metro journey)	жетон *zheton*	zhet**on**
to the left	налево *nalevo*	nal**ye**va
to the right	направо *napravo*	napr**a**va
train	поезд *poezd*	po-yezd
tram	трамвай *tramvay*	tramv**ay**
trolleybus	троллейбус *trolleybus*	tral**ye**yboos

Numbers

1	один/одна/одно *odin/odna/odno*	ad**een**/adn**a**/adn**o**
2	два/две *dva/dve*	dva/dvye
3	три *tri*	tree
4	четыре *chetyre*	chyet**ir**-ye
5	пять *pyat*	pyat'
6	шесть *shest*	shest'
7	семь *sem*	syem'
8	восемь *vosem*	**vo**syem'
9	девять *devyat*	d**ye**vyat'
10	десять *desyat*	d**ye**syat'

11	одиннадцать *odinnadtsat*	ad**ee**natsat'
12	двенадцать *dvenadtsat*	dvyen**a**tsat'
13	тринадцать *trinadtsat*	treen**a**tsat'
14	четырнадцать *chetyrnadtsat*	chyet**ir**natsat'
15	пятнадцать *pyatnadtsat*	pyatn**a**tsat'
16	шестнадцать *shestnadtsat*	shestn**a**tsat'
17	семнадцать *semnadtsat*	syemn**a**tsat'
18	восемнадцать *vosemnadtsat*	vasyemn**a**tsat'
19	девятнадцать *devyatnadtsat*	dyevyatn**a**tsat'
20	двадцать *dvadtsat*	dv**a**tsat'
21	двадцать один *dvadtsat odin*	dv**a**tsat' ad**een**
22	двадцать два *dvadtsat dva*	dv**a**tsat' dva
23	двадцать три *dvadtsat tri*	dv**a**tsat' tree
24	двадцать четыре *dvadtsat chetyre*	dv**a**tsat' chyet**ir**-ye
25	двадцать пять *dvadtsat pyat*	dv**a**tsat' pyat'
30	тридцать *tridtsat*	tr**ee**tsat'
40	сорок *sorok*	s**o**rak
50	пятьдесят *pyatdesyat*	pyadyes**yat**'
60	шестьдесят *shestdesyat*	shes' dyes**yat**
70	семьдесят *semdesyat*	s**yem**'dyesyat
80	восемьдесят *vosemdesyat*	v**o**syem'dyesyat
90	девяносто *devyanosto*	dyevyan**o**sta
100	сто *sto*	sto
200	двести *dvesti*	dv**ye**stee
300	триста *trista*	treest**a**
400	четыреста *chetyresta*	chyet**ir**yesta
500	пятьсот *pyatsot*	pyat's**ot**
1,000	тысяча *tysyacha*	t**i**syacha
2,000	две тысяч *dve tysyach*	dvye t**i**syach
5,000	пять тысяч *pyat tysyach*	pyat' t**i**syach
1,000,000	миллион *million*	meelee-**on**

Time, Days and Dates

one minute	одна минута *odna minuta*	adn**a** meen**oo**ta
one hour	час *chas*	chas
half an hour	полчаса *polchasa*	polchas**a**
day	день *den*	dyen'
week	неделя *nedelya*	nyed**yel**-ya
Monday	понедельник *ponedelnik*	panyed**yel**'neek
Tuesday	вторник *vtornik*	ft**o**rneek
Wednesday	среда *sreda*	sry**ed**a
Thursday	четверг *chetverg*	chyetv**yer**k
Friday	пятница *pyatnitsa*	p**ya**tneetsa
Saturday	суббота *subbota*	soob**o**ta
Sunday	воскресенье *voskresene*	vaskryesy**en**'ye